The stature of Dickens

Charles Dickens at 27. From a drawing by D. Maclise, engraved by R. Graves

The stature of DICKENS

A centenary bibliography

compiled by

Joseph Gold

Published for University of Manitoba Press by
University of Toronto Press

© University of Toronto Press 1971
Toronto and Buffalo
Printed in Canada by
University of Toronto Press
ISBN 0 – 8020 – 3265 – 6
Microfiche ISBN 0 – 8020 – 0014 – 2
LC 70 – 151368

Published with financial support of the
Alumni Association of the University of Manitoba

To Sandra, and indeed, to all librarians

Doctor Blimber's Young Gentlemen as they appeared when enjoying themselves.
Dombey and Son, drawn by Phiz

Contents

Acknowledgements

This project could not have been undertaken without the financial assistance of the Canada Council and the University of Manitoba. The University of Manitoba could not, in turn, have proceeded without substantial financial aid from the Alumni Association of that institution, and to them I am indebted for making the whole project a publishable reality.

The actual labour reflected by these listings would have been impossible without the hard work of many people. Hundreds of hours of research time were cheerfully given by Ronald Bonham, Ian Kay, and Terry Fitzgerald, my research assistants, and by Sandra Gold, my wife, who spent the best part of two years in the library and at the typewriter. Lauriat Lane Jr gave me the benefit of his wise and good-natured counsel at every stage and to him I am deeply grateful. If this book has merit, much of the credit belongs to him. Many others made important contributions, both of actual lists of items and of equally valuable suggestions. For their ready co-operation I would like to thank Douglas Bush; Donald H. Ericksen; K. J. Fielding; Ada Nisbet; Robert L. Patten; Robert Partlow Jr; J. C. Reid, Heinz Reinhold, who provided the German listing; Edgar Rosenberg, whose graduate students, a few years ago, compiled under his direction an impressive Dickens bibliography; Michael Steig, Harry Stone, and Deborah Thomas of the University of Rochester, NY.

In addition to acting as an advisory editor, Sylvère Monod provided the list of French books and Donald Fanger, with the kind assistance of S. V. Belov of Leningrad, provided the Slavic items. To these men and to George Ford whose editorial support was a continuous source of encouragement, I am greatly indebted. In the course of this work I was entirely dependent on the following institutions and their staffs: The British Museum Library, The Collingdale Newspaper Library, The New York Public Library, The Pierpont Morgan Library, The Royal Library of Denmark, Universtetets Filologiske Laboratorium of the University of Copenhagen, The Elizabeth Dafoe Library of the University of Manitoba, and the library of the Victoria and Albert Museum.

The University of Manitoba Press – and particularly Gordon Leckie – and the editors of the University of Toronto Press have given me advice, help, and encouragement that have eased my way considerably. To all of the above, to all former bibliographers in this field, and to Dickens scholars everywhere I humbly offer my thanks.

JG

The Last Cabdriver.
Sketches by Boz, drawn by George Cruikshank

Preface A description of this book

Discussing Dickens bibliographical work in 1947, Philo Calhoun and Howell J. Heaney noted that "the field is limitless, and far beyond the scope of published lists and indexes."[1] Naturally the situation has become more rather than less complicated in the twenty or so years since then. There are hundreds, probably thousands of items that relate peripherally to Dickens and related matters – every place, every person, every association of the man and his work has been noted, explored, mentioned and pursued. Hundreds of items including many books are out of print and rare and old. It would take at least one lifetime to look at most or all of this material. To even attempt to collect all such titles would be, in my opinion, the most fruitless kind of academic exercise. It would seriously detract from, distort, make difficult to use, that part of a bibliography of more immediate and practical use to active scholars and critics. This list would become "a scholar's stunt rather than a useful students' hand-book."[2] It would be "more and more a census of paper spoiled by being printed on ... a ghastly company of corpses buried by time and dug up for the greater glory of the compiler and the greater confusion of the researcher."[3] Rather than create such a morgue I have attempted to assemble the critical and biographical writings of the last one hundred years. While there will be found many items pre-dating the year of Dickens' death, the heaviest concentration of listings occurs between 1870 and 1968. Exigencies of publication schedule necessitated making the end of 1968 the official cut-off date, but I have attempted to extend listings into 1969 as far as possible. Users should consult the 1969 and 1970 *MLA International Bibliographies* to bring the list more fully up to date.

This is not, therefore, a definitive listing. We have as a matter of editorial policy omitted the vast majority of peripheral, occasional, and ephemeral items. For instance: most of the topographical tours and guides to places mentioned in the novels; the toasts, memorials, poems, and brief notes; most of the biographies of the lives of Dickens' friends and relatives; almost all of the anthologies of extractions from Dickens' works; collections of quotations, and all the adaptations, songs, plays, fantasies and apocrypha that have accumulated over the years. We have also left out records of sales and exhibitions, of which there

1 Philo Calhoun and Howell J. Heaney, "Dickensiana in the Rough," *Papers of the Bibliographical Society of America*, 40 (1947):302.
2 *Ibid.*
3 *Ibid.*

are many, except where they seem especially useful to critics. The result is, I
hope, a presentation of what is of lasting, scholarly value or interest. For those
who wish to locate the kind of material mentioned above, the pages of *The
Dickensian* will be of continuing fascination. This periodical deserves special
mention, for I have necessarily drawn heavily from it, yet I should dispel any
impression that this is in any way a comprehensive index to its contents.

My book consists, then, of four sections of scholarly items, preceded by an
introductory list of sources and aids to the bibliographer and scholar. I have
included a Dickens Chronology in lieu of the canon, and an index to authors
and editors. Section I lists books, essays, and articles primarily on Dickens and
includes selected reviews of some significant recent works of criticism. Section
II lists books, essays, selected early reviews and articles on single novels and on
A Christmas Carol and includes a section on Dickens' Letters. Section III lists
Doctoral Dissertations. *Dissertation Abstracts* is given as the source except
where not available (as at Harvard), and there the listing is by university and
date. Section IV lists books either making significant mention of Dickens or
which seem important to the background study of some aspect of Dickens'
work.

Foreign books for those countries where Dickens interest and scholarly production seems obviously greatest are included. A complete foreign listing
would require a separate bibliography.

The listing is chronological following the usual form. Where a composite date
occurs (e.g. 1912-14) the item appears at the end of the listing for the first of
the two dates. Where a journal uses two months to describe an issue (e.g. June-
July) the listing is under the first month.

I have tried to use the *Style Sheet* for the *MLA International Bibliography*
by Harrison T. Messerole, but I have introduced certain modifications for the
special purposes of this work. I have omitted giving pages for reprints and for
introductions since the item is readily identifiable and I have not given as separate entries periodical excerpts from books devoted entirely to Dickens since
we list the book itself. Where no author could be found I have placed the entry
under its title. Wherever possible I have attempted to clarify by a brief note
titles that might be obscure. Every effort has been made to list significant reprints.

Every bibliographer knows the problems of dependence on former bibliographies, and he quickly discovers in such work that hundreds of items are listed
inaccurately and that bibliographic inaccuracies tend to recur. Moreover, form
varies from one list to another with different information omitted in different
cases. As a result, where one attempts to be complete in providing information
for a given item the task is greatly complicated. It would be too much to hope
that this bibliography is entirely free from those errors that characteristically
afflict such lists. Ghost items constitute a special problem, reappearing as they
do from list to list. I have, wherever possible, tried to return to the original appearance of an item to verify a doubtful or confusing listing. In those cases

where no trace of an item mentioned in an earlier bibliography could be found,
I have omitted the entry rather than consolidate a misleading reference.

Whatever shortcomings are found in this work are wholly mine. I have tried,
over the past five years, to compile an accurate, useful and usable listing of
Dickens scholarship as an aid to scholars, students and Dickensians everywhere.
It is in its use by these people, above all, that it will be tested.

JG

From *Sketches by Boz*, drawn by George Cruikshank

A Dickens chronology

1809
John Dickens, clerk in Navy Pay Office, employed in Portsmouth Dockyard, marries Elizabeth Barrow

1810
Fanny, their first child, born

1812 February 7
CHARLES DICKENS born at 1 Mile End Terrance, Landport, in Portsea
(baptismal names: CHARLES JOHN HUFFHAM)
Family moves to Hawke St, Portsmouth

1813
Alfred, third child, born. Died an infant

1814
Father summoned to Somerset House in London. Family lodges at
10 Norfolk St

1816
Letitia, fourth child, born

1819
Harriet, fifth child, born

1820
Frederick, sixth child, born

1817-22
Residence at Chatham. Father transferred here also. Family lives at
2 Ordnance Terrace in Chatham. It is due to John Dickens' increase in
salary that the family moves here

1821-22
Family moves to smaller house in St Mary's Place, called "The Brook"
Charles Dickens goes to Baptist School of Mr Giles

1822
Father recalled to Somerset House
Family moves to 16 Bayham St, Camden Town

1823

Move to 4 Gower St North. Mrs Dickens tries to establish a school for
young ladies. A plate inscribed "Mrs Dickens's Establishment" was fastened
to the door

1824 February

Father arrested for debt and imprisoned at Marshalsea. The family (except
for Charles and Fanny) join him
Charles Dickens put to work at Warren's Blacking Factory, Hungerford
Market. Lodgings taken for him in Little College St, from which he moves
to a back attic in Lant St, in order to be nearer his parents

   May

John Dickens released on inheriting a legacy which enabled him to discharge
his debts
Family lives in Johnson St, Somers Town. Charles Dickens resumes his
education now at Wellington House Academy, Hampstead Road

1825

Father leaves Navy Pay Office
John Dickens' older brother, William, dies, bequeathing £1000 to be
divided at his widow's death among his brother's children

1827 March

Charles Dickens leaves school and finds employment with Charles Molloy,
solicitor, Symond's Inn

   May

Charles Dickens leaves Molloy and engages himself to Ellis and Blackmore,
solicitors, 1 Raymond Buildings, Gray's Inn
Family again in financial straits and moves to lodgings in the Polygon,
Camden Town

1828

Charles Dickens leaves Ellis and Blackmore and learns shorthand with a
view to becoming a reporter
Father works on *The Mirror of Parliament*
Charles Dickens becomes reporter at Doctor's Commons

1830

Charles Dickens sets up as a shorthand-writer in a one-room office at
5 Bell Yard, Carter Lane

   February 8

Acquires a reader's ticket at the British Museum
Meets the Beadnells, and falls in love with Maria, the youngest daughter

1831
Charles Dickens' name appears in the Law List as a "shorthand writer"
Maria sent to Paris in order to end the attachment to Charles

1832 February
Charles Dickens tries to get an engagement on the stage, address now
70 Margaret St, Cavendish Sq
Obtains post on the staff of *The True Sun.* Enters the Reporters' Gallery of
the House of Commons

July
Address, 13 Fitzroy St
Charles Dickens working exclusively for *The Mirror of Parliament*

1833 January
Family moves to 18 Bentinck St

December
First story published, "A Dinner at Poplar Walk," in *Monthly Magazine*
(cf. "Mr Minns and His Cousin" in SKETCHES BY BOZ)

1834
Dickens joins the staff of the *Morning Chronicle,* a paper liberal in its
politics. Works with Thomas Beard, shorthand writer. This man becomes
his closest friend in the Gallery

1833-35
Nine pieces appear in *Monthly Magazine.* The latter ones are signed "BOZ"

1835
Dickens and his brother, Frederick, move to Furnival's Inn

May
He becomes engaged to Catherine, daughter of George Hogarth, editor of
The Evening Chronicle.
Places his first book, SKETCHES BY BOZ, with Macrone for publication

1836 February
SKETCHES BY BOZ published in 2 volumes, by John Macrone

March
First instalment of PICKWICK PAPERS published. 400 copies printed.
Before its conclusion, circulation up to 40,000. Published by Chapman
and Hall

April 2
Marries Catherine Hogarth at St Luke's Church, Chelsea. Honeymoon at
Chalk
Leaves the Commons Gallery
Seymour, artist of PICKWICK, kills himself, before the 2nd instalment
appears. Hablôt Knight Browne ("Phiz") engaged as illustrator

December
SKETCHES BY BOZ, 2nd series – preface dated December 17, 1836,
published by Macrone. The first complete edition (containing both series)
was issued by Chapman and Hall in monthly parts from 1837 to 1839

1837 February
First instalment of OLIVER TWIST published in *Bentley's Miscellany*
Mary Hogarth, Catherine's sister and close friend to Charles Dickens, dies
suddenly
Move to 48 Doughty St
Visits Belgium with wife and "Phiz"
Charles Culliford Boz, first child, born (1837-96)

November
Concludes the serial of PICKWICK PAPERS. PICKWICK PAPERS published
in one volume.

December
"The Village Coquette": operetta, published by Bentley. "The Strange
Gentleman": farce, brought out by Chapman and Hall at the same time
(December)
Copyright of SKETCHES BY BOZ bought back from Macrone for £2000

1837-39
"Mudfog Papers" in *Bentley's Miscellany*

1838 April
First instalment of NICHOLAS NICKLEBY, Chapman and Hall
Dickens "edits" the memoirs of Grimaldi in 2 volumes, London: Richard
Bentley
Mary, second child, born (1838-96)

November
OLIVER TWIST published in 3 volumes, R. Bentley

1839 April
Last instalment of OLIVER TWIST

October
Last instalment of NICHOLAS NICKLEBY. NICHOLAS NICKLEBY
published, London: Chapman and Hall
Kate Macready, third child, born (1839-1929)
Dickens buys house a mile out of Exeter at Alphington for his parents

December
Dickens moves to Devonshire Terrace

1840 April
First number of *Master Humphrey's Clock.* In its fourth number,
OLD CURIOSITY SHOP begins.

1841 February
First instalment of BARNABY RUDGE
Master Humphrey's Clock in 3 volumes. Included OLD CURIOSITY SHOP
and BARNABY RUDGE
Walter Landor, fourth child, born (1841-63)

1842 January 4
Leaves for America

June 7
Sails from NY to England

October
AMERICAN NOTES published, 2 volumes, London: Chapman and Hall

1843 January
First instalment of MARTIN CHUZZLEWIT

Christmas
CHRISTMAS CAROL, London: Chapman and Hall

1844 February
Quarrel with Chapman and Hall

July
Last instalment of MARTIN CHUZZLEWIT. Published in 1 volume,
London: Chapman and Hall

November
THE CHIMES completed. London: Chapman and Hall. (Christmas Book,
1844, although publishing date given is 1845)

1844-45
Dickens lives in Italy (visits England briefly)
Francis Jeffrey, fifth child, born (1844-86)

1845 January 21–February 9
Editor of *The Daily News*

January
The first instalment of a series of seven letters under the general title
"Travelling Sketches – Written on the Road." In May 1846, they were
collected and reprinted under the title PICTURES FROM ITALY with
five additional chapters. Published for the author by Bradbury and Evans

October
First instalment of DOMBEY AND SON

Christmas
CRICKET ON THE HEARTH

1846-47 June–February
Stays at Lausanne, then Paris

1846 Christmas
      THE BATTLE OF LIFE
1847
      Sydney Smith Haldimand, seventh child, born (1847-72)

1848 April
      Last instalment of DOMBEY AND SON. Published in 1 volume, Bradbury
      and Evans

      Christmas
      THE HAUNTED MAN published by Bradbury and Evans

1849 February
      At Brighton

      May
      First instalment of DAVID COPPERFIELD
      Henry Fielding, eighth child, born (1849-1938)
      Takes house at Bonchurch, Isle of Wight, for the summer for wife and
      family
      THE LIFE OF OUR LORD written for his children. Not published until
      1934

1850 March
      First number of *Household Words*

      July
      In Paris with Maclise
      Dora Annie, ninth child, born (1850-51)

      November
      Last instalment of DAVID COPPERFIELD. Published in 1 volume,
      Bradbury and Evans

1851 February
      In Paris

      March 31
      John Dickens dies

      November
      Moves to Tavistock House

      January 1851–September 1853
      A CHILD'S HISTORY OF ENGLAND serialized in *Household Words*.
      Published in 3 volumes, Bradbury and Evans in 1852

1852 March
      First instalment of BLEAK HOUSE
      Edward Bulwer Lytton, tenth child, born (1852-1902)

1853
Tour of Italy and Switzerland with wife and family
> September
Last instalment of BLEAK HOUSE. Published in 1 volume, Bradbury and
Evans

1853-56
Summer holidays in Boulogne

1853 October–December
In Switzerland with wife and family

1854 April
First instalment of HARD TIMES published in *Household Words*
> August
Last instalment of HARD TIMES. HARD TIMES FOR THESE TIMES
published in 1 volume, Bradbury and Evans, 1854

1855 December
First instalment of LITTLE DORRIT
Travels in Paris with Wilkie Collins
Dickens meets Mrs Winter (Maria Beadnell)

1855-56
Winter. Dickens lives in Paris

1856 March 14
Buys Gad's Hill Place

1857 January 6
First of the performances of "The Frozen Deep" by Collins, prologue by
Dickens, who also plays the part of Wardour, the rejected lover
Ellen Lawless Ternan hired for a role in "The Frozen Deep" along with
her mother, Mrs Ternan and her sister, Maria
> June
Last instalment of LITTLE DORRIT. Published in 1 volume, London:
Bradbury and Evans, the same month
In the Lake District with Wilkie Collins

1858
First series of public readings. This series begins with readings at St Martin's
Hall, London (April–July). This is followed by provincial readings
(August 2–November 13)
> May
Separation from wife

1859
Dickens breaks with *Punch,* severs his connection with Bradbury and Evans, returns to Chapman and Hall. First number of *All The Year Round*

May
Last number of *Household Words* ("A Last Household Word")

April–November
A TALE OF TWO CITIES in *All The Year Round.* Published in 1 volume, December 1859

October
125 readings ended

1860
Move from Tavistock House to Gad's Hill Place

January
First instalment of THE UNCOMMERCIAL TRAVELLER

July 17
Kate, his daughter, weds Charles Allston Collins

August
Last instalment of THE UNCOMMERCIAL TRAVELLER

December
THE UNCOMMERCIAL TRAVELLER published

December
First instalment of GREAT EXPECTATIONS in *All The Year Round*

1861 August
Last instalment of GREAT EXPECTATIONS. Published in 3 volumes, London: Chapman and Hall; later published in 1 volume, that same year

October 28
Second series of readings starts in Norwich

November
Charles, his son, weds Bessie Evans

1862 January
Second series of provincial readings ends
Dickens a grandfather

October and November
In Paris

1864 May
First instalment of OUR MUTUAL FRIEND

February–June
Living in Hyde Park area

1865 November
   Last instalment of OUR MUTUAL FRIEND. Published in 2 volumes
   Dickens with Ellen Ternan on train after visit to Paris. The train is derailed.
   Dickens' private life is forced into the public limelight again

1864-67
   Third series of readings

1867
   Second trip to America

1868 May
   Returns home from America

       October
   Fourth series of readings. Farewell tour begins October 6
   THE UNCOMMERCIAL TRAVELLER, with eleven new papers from
   All The Year Round

1869
   End of readings. Dickens in poor health. Breaks down at Preston

1870 March 15
   Last reading

       April
   First instalment of EDWIN DROOD

       June 9
   Charles Dickens dies at Gad's Hill

       June 14
   Charles Dickens is buried at Westminster Abbey amid national mourning

1870 September
   Last instalment of EDWIN DROOD (unfinished). Published in 1 volume,
   London: Chapman and Hall, 1870

From *David Copperfield,* drawn by Phiz

Introduction
General and special bibliographic aids

ALTICK, RICHARD D. and W. R. MATHEWS. *Guide to Doctoral Dissertations in Victorian Literature, 1886-1958.* Urbana: Univ. of Illinois Press, 1960.

ASLIB. *Index to Theses Accepted for Higher Degrees in the Universities of Great Britain and Ireland.* London: ASLIB, 1950/51–.

BAY, JENS C. *The Pickwick Papers. Some Bibliographical Remarks.* Chicago: Caxton Club, 1938.

BELL, INGLIS F. and DONALD BAIRD, comps. *The English Novel 1578-1956: A Checklist of Twentieth-Century Criticisms.* Denver: Alan Swallow, 1958.

BRITISH MUSEUM. *Dickens. An Excerpt from The General Catalogue of Printed Books* [in the British Museum]. London: British Museum, 1960.

CALHOUN, PHILO and HOWELL J. HEANEY. "Dickens' *Christmas Carol* after a Hundred Years: A Study in Bibliographical Evidence." *Papers of the Bibliographical Society of America* 39 (4th quarter 1945):271-317.

CALHOUN, PHILO and HOWELL J. HEANEY. "Dickensiana in the Rough." *Papers of the Bibliographical Society of America* 41 (4th quarter, 1947): 293-320.

Cambridge Bibliography of English Literature, ed. F. W. Bateson. Cambridge, Eng.: The University Press, 1940, and supplement, 1957.

CARR, LUCILE [Mary Callista]. *A Catalogue of the Dickens Collection at the University of Texas.* Austin: Univ. of Texas Press, 1951. 2nd edition revised and enlarged as *A Catalogue of the Vanderpoel Dickens Collection at the University of Texas.* Austin: Univ. of Texas Press, 1968.

CAVANAUGH, CORTES W. *Charles Dickens: His Life as Traced by his Works.* Early American editions of the works of Charles Dickens by Herman Leroy Edgar and R. W. G. Vail. New York: New York Public Library, 1929. [Reprinted from *Bulletin of New York Public Library,* May 1929.]

CHAPMAN and HALL LTD. *The Works of Dickens and Thomas Carlyle.* With full particulars of each edition and biographical introductions. London: Chapman and Hall, 1900.

CLARK, J. SCOTT. "Bibliography on Dickens's Style." *A Study of English Prose Writers: a Laboratory Method,* 610-12. New York, Scribners: 1898.

COLLINS, PHILIP A. W. "Bibliography." *Dickens and Crime,* 357-62. Second edition. (Cambridge Studies in Criminology 17.) London: Macmillan, 1964.

COLLINS, PHILIP A. W. "Bibliography." *Dickens and Education,* 248-51. London: Macmillan, 1964. [Reprinted with alterations and new preface.]

COLLINS, PHILIP A. W. "Charles Dickens 1812-70." *The New Cambridge Bibliography of English Literature,* ed. George Watson, III:779-850. Cambridge, Eng.: Cambridge Univ. Press, 1969.

COLLINS, PHILIP A. W. *Dickens's Periodicals: Articles on Education.* An annotated bibliography. (Vaughan College Papers 3.) Leicester, Eng.: Univ. of Leicester, 1957.

COOK, JAMES. *Bibliography of the Writings of Charles Dickens.* London: F. Kerslake; Paisley: J. and J. Cook, 1879.

Cumulated Magazine Subject Index, 1907-1949. Boston: G. K. Hall, 1964. 2 vols.

DEXTER, JOHN F. *Dickens Memento.* Introd. Francis Phillimore. London: Field and Tuer, The Leadenhall Press, 1884. [Includes reprint of *Catalogue of Dickens Sale* with purchasers' names and prices realized, of pictures, drawings, and objects of art of Charles Dickens, disposed at Christie, Manson and Woods in 1870, and "Hints to Dickens Collectors," by John F. Dexter.]

DIBELIUS, WILHELM. "Versuch einer Dickensbibliographie." *Charles Dickens,* 479-504. Leipzig and Berlin: Teubner, 1916.

Dickens Studies: A Journal of Modern Research and Criticism, ed. Noel C. Peyrouton. Boston: Emerson College. Vol. 1, 1965-69.

The Dickensian. London: Chapman and Hall. Vol. 1, 1905-.

Dissertation Abstracts. Ann Arbor, Mich.: University Microfilms, 1955-.

Doctoral Dissertations Accepted by American Universities, 1933/34-1954/55. New York: H. W. Wilson, 1934-56. [Continued by *American Doctoral Dissertations. Index.* Ann Arbor, Mich.: University Microfilms, 1957-.]

DUTU, ALEXANDRU and SORIN ALEXANDRESCU. *Dickens in Rumania; A Bibliography for the 150th Anniversary.* Bucharest: National Commission of the Rumanian People's Republic for UNESCO and "Secolul 20," 1962.

ECKEL, JOHN C. *The First Editions of the Writings of Charles Dickens and Their Values: A Bibliography.* London: Chapman and Hall, 1913.

ELKINS, WILLIAM M. *The Life and Works of Charles Dickens: An Exhibition from the Collection of W. M. Elkins, Esq. of Philadelphia, held at the Free Library, June-July, 1946.* Philadelphia: Free Library, 1946. [Catalogue.]

FAWCETT, FRANK D. "Plays and Adaptations of the Works of Charles Dickens for Stage, Screen and Television." Appendix A of *Dickens the Dramatist.* London: Allen, 1952.

FIELDING, KENNETH J. "Dickens: A Guide to Research Materials." *Victorian Newsletter* 14 (Fall 1958):22-23.

FORD, GEORGE H. "Bibliography, Pt. 2: Studies of Dickens' Reputation." *Dickens and his Readers,* 304-5. New York: Norton, 1965.

FORD, GEORGE H. and LAURIAT LANE, Jr. "Bibliography." *The Dickens Critics*, 387-410. Ithaca, NY: Cornell Univ. Press, 1961.

FRIDLENDER, JU. V. *Čarl'z Dikkens: Ukazatel' Važnejšej Literatury na Russkom Jazyke, 1838-1945*. Leningrad: Leningradskaja Publičnaja Biblioteka, 1946. [*Charles Dickens: An Index of the Most Important Literature in Russian, 1843-1945*.]

FRIDLENDER, JU. V., and I. M. KATARSKIJ. *Čarl'z Dikkens: Bibliografija Russkix Perevodov i Kritičeskoj Literatury na Russkom Jazyke, 1838-1960*. Moscow: Izdatel'stvo Vsesojuznoj Knižnoj Palaty, 1962. [*Charles Dickens: A Bibliography of Russian Translations and Critical Literature in Russian, 1838-1960*.]

GORDAN, JOHN D., ed. *Reading for Profit: The Other Career of Charles Dickens*. An Exhibition from the Berg Collection. New York: New York Public Library, 1958. Also published in the *Bulletin of the New York Public Library* 62 (Sept. 1958):425-42; (Oct. 1958):515-22.

GROLIER CLUB. *The Catalogue of an Exhibition of the Works of Charles Dickens, January 23rd to March 8th*. New York: Grolier Club, 1913.

GUMMER, ELLIS N. *Dickens' Works in Germany, 1837-1937*. Oxford: Clarendon Press, 1939.

HATTON, THOMAS and ARTHUR H. CLEAVER. *A Bibliography of the Periodical Works of Charles Dickens*. London: Chapman and Hall, 1933.

International Index. New York: H. W. Wilson, 1916–. [Continued by *Social Sciences and Humanities Index*, June 1965–.]

JOHNSON, CHARLES P. *Hints to the Collectors of the Original Editions of the Works of Charles Dickens*. London: Redway, 1885.

JOHNSON, EDGAR. "Bibliography." *Charles Dickens: His Tragedy and Triumph*, II, xcix-cxv. Boston: Little, Brown, 1952.

KITTON, FREDERIC G. *Dickensiana; a Bibliography of the Literature Relating to Charles Dickens and his Writings*. London: Redway, 1886.

KITTON, FREDERIC G. *The Minor Writings of Charles Dickens*. A bibliography and sketch. London: E. Stock, 1900.

McNAMEE, LAWRENCE F. *Dissertations in English and American Literature*. Theses accepted by American, British, and German universities, 1865-1964. New York: Bowker, 1968.

MILLER, WILLIAM, comp. *The Dickens Student and Collector; a List of Writings Relating to Charles Dickens and His World, 1836-1945*. Cambridge, Mass.: Harvard Univ. Press, 1946.

MILLER, WILLIAM and STRANGE, E. H. *A Centenary Bibliography of The Pickwick Papers*. London: Argonaut; Toronto: S. J. R. Saunders, 1936.

MODERN HUMANITIES RESEARCH ASSOCIATION. *Annual Bibliography of English Language and Literature*. Cambridge, Eng.: Bowes and Bowes, 1921-.

MODERN LANGUAGE ASSOCIATION OF AMERICA. *MLA International Bibliography,* 1921-. New York: Kraus Reprint Corp., 1964. New York: New York Univ. Press, 1964-.

MOULTON, CHARLES W. *The Library of Literary Criticism,* vol. 6. Buffalo, NY: 1902-4.

"A New Dickens Bibliography." *Dickensian* 39 (Mar. 1943):99-101; (June 1943):149-53; (Sept. 1943):173-75; 40 (Dec. 1943):36-38; (Mar. 1944) 76-78; (June 1944):143-45. [Guide to the collection of first editions of Dickens.]

Nineteenth Century Fiction. Berkeley: Univ. of California Press, 1945-.

Nineteenth Century Readers' Guide to Periodical Literature, 1890-99, with Supplement, 1900-22. 2 vols. New York: H. W. Wilson, 1944.

NISBET, ADA B. "Charles Dickens." *Victorian Fiction: A Guide to Research,* ed. Lionel Stevenson, 44-153. Cambridge, Mass.: Harvard Univ. Press, 1964.

NONESUCH PRESS, LONDON. *Retrospectus and Prospectus: The Nonesuch Dickens.* Bloomsbury, London: Nonesuch, 1937.

PIERCE, DOROTHY, comp. "Special Bibliography; The Stage Versions of Dickens's Novels, Including Those Plays Listed by S. J. Adair Fitzgerald in his Work *Dickens and the Drama,* London, 1910." *Bulletin of Bibliography and Dramatic Index* 16 (Sept.-Dec. 1936):10; (Jan.-Apr. 1937):30-32; (May-Aug. 1937):52-54.

Poole's Index to Periodical Literature, 1802-81. 2 vols. Boston: Houghton Mifflin, 1891.

Readers' Guide to Periodical Literature, 1900-. New York: H. W. Wilson, 1905-.

ROSENBACH, A. S. W., ed. *A Catalogue of the Writings of Charles Dickens in the Library of Harry Elkins Widener.* Philadelphia: privately printed, 1917. [With texts of many letters and publisher's agreements; collection now at Harvard.]

SARGENT, GEORGE H. "Dickensiana in America." *Bookman's Journal* NS 5 (Apr. 1922):23-24.

SAWYER, CHARLES J. *A Dickens Library; Exhibition Catalogue of the Sawyer Collection.* Letchworth, Eng.: Garden City Press, 1936.

SHORTER, CLEMENT. *Victorian Literature: Sixty Years of Books and Bookmen.* New York: Dodd, Mead, 1897.

SLACK, ROBERT C. *Bibliographies of Studies in Victorian Literature for the Ten Years 1955-1964.* Urbana: Univ. of Illinois Press, 1967.

SLATER, MICHAEL. "The Year's Work in Dickens Studies." *Dickensian* 1968-.

SPENCER, WALTER T. "Dickensiana." *Forty Years in My Bookshop,* 89-152 London: Constable, 1923.

STONEHOUSE, JOHN H. *Catalogue of the Libraries of Charles Dickens and William Thackeray*. London: Piccadilly Fountain Press, 1935.

STONEHOUSE, JOHN H. "A First Bibliography of the Reading Editions of Charles Dickens' Works." *Sikes and Nancy. A Reading by Charles Dickens*, 49-57. London: H. Sotheran, 1921.

Subject Index to Periodicals, 1926-1928. 3 vols. London: Library Association, 1928-30.

SUZANNET, ALAIN de. *Catalogue d'un Choix de Livres Imprimés et Manuscrits Provenant de ma Bibliothèque de Biarritz. I. Oeuvres de Charles Dickens*. Privately printed, 1925.

SUZANNET, ALAIN de. *Catalogue des Manuscrits, Livres Imprimés et Lettres Autographes Composant la Bibliothèque de la Petite Chardière. Oeuvres de Charles Dickens*. 3 vols. Lausanne: Imprimeries Réunies, n.d. [First vol. lists mss., second and third list autograph letters, 1832-48, and 1849-70 respectively.]

TEMPLEMAN, WILLIAM D., ed. *Bibliographies of Studies in Victorian Literature for the Thirteen Years 1932-1944*. Urbana: Univ. of Illinois Press, 1945.

US LIBRARY OF CONGRESS. CATALOG DIVISION. *Books: Subjects*, 1950-. Ann Arbor, Mich.: J. W. Edwards, 1955-64. Washington, DC: Library of Congress, 1965-.

US LIBRARY OF CONGRESS. CATALOG DIVISION. *A List of American Doctoral Dissertations Printed in [1912]-1938*. 27 vols. Washington, DC: US Government Printing Office, 1913-39.

VANN, J. DON. "Dickens Criticism, 1963-67." *Studies in the Novel* 1 (Summer 1969):255-78.

VICTORIA AND ALBERT MUSEUM, LONDON. *A Catalogue of the Printed Books Bequeathed by John Forster*. London: The Museum, 1888.

Victorian Newsletter. Modern Language Association. English X Group, 1, Apr. 1952-. New York University, 8, Autumn 1955-.

Victorian Studies. Bloomington: Indiana University, vol. 1, 1957-.

The Wellesley Index to Victorian Periodicals, 1824-1900. Vol. 1., ed. Walter E. Houghton. Toronto: Univ. of Toronto Press; London: Routledge and K. Paul, 1966.

WRIGHT, AUSTIN, ed. *Bibliographies of Studies in Victorian Literature for the Ten Years 1945-1954*. Urbana: Univ. of Illinois Press, 1956.

The Year's Work in English Studies. London: Murray, 1919-.

Zeitschrift für Anglistik und Amerikanistik. Berlin: Deutscher Verlag der Wissenschaften, 1953-.

The Bibliography

Books, essays, and articles
primarily on Dickens:
including selected reviews
of recent criticism

The "breaking up" at Dotheboys Hall. *Nicholas Nickleby*, drawn by Phiz

1 "Dickens in 1837." *Dickensian* 1 (Jan. 1905):9-13. [Reprinted from *National Magazine* and *Monthly Critic*, Dec. 1837.]

2 "Charles Dickens and his Works." *Fraser's Magazine* 21 (Apr. 1840): 381-400.

3 "*Master Humphrey's Clock.*" *Athenaeum* (Nov. 7, 1840):887-88.

4 POE, EDGAR ALLEN. *English Notes: a Rare and Unknown Work, Being a Reply to Charles Dickens's American Notes.* With critical comments by Joseph Jackson and George H. Sargent. New York: L. M. Thompson, 1920. [Originally published in Boston in 1842 under pseud. "Quarles Quickens."]

5 WARREN, SAMUEL (Q. Q. Q., pseud.). "Dickens' *American Notes for General Circulation.*" *Blackwood's Edinburgh Magazine* 52 (Dec. 1842):783-801.

6 SPEDDING, JAMES. "Dickens's *American Notes.*" *Edinburgh Review* 77 (Jan. 1843):497-522. Reprinted in *Reviews and Discussions: Literary, Political and Historical.* London: K. Paul, 1879.

7 "*The Chimes.*" *Edinburgh Review* 81 (Jan. 1845):181-89.

8 PICHOT, AMÉDÉE. "Introduction." *Les Contes de Charles Dickens.* 6 vols. Paris: Amyot, 1847-53.

9 "*Master Humphrey's Clock.*" *Polytechnic Review* 1 (Jan. 3, 1848): 315-18.

10 "Dickens and Thackeray." *English Review* 10 (Dec. 1848):266-75.

11 WHIPPLE, EDWIN P. "Novels and Novelists: Charles Dickens." *North American Review* 69 (Oct. 1849):383-406. Reprinted in *Literature and Life.* London: J. Chapman, 1851.

12 HEAVISIDES, EDWARD M. "Charles Dickens." *The Poetical and Prose Remains of E. M. Heavisides,* 1-27. London: Longman, Broun, 1850.

13 SCHMIDT, JULIAN. *Boz (Dickens), eine Charakteristik.* Leipzig: Carl B. Lorck, 1852.

14 SHELTON, F. W. "On the Genius of Dickens." *The Knickerbocker* 39 (May 1852):421-31.

15 "The Genius and Characteristics of Charles Dickens." *Workingman's Friend and Family Instructor* 2 (Aug. 14, 1852):326-28.

16 "Charles Dickens." *National Magazine* 1 (1854):83-85.

17 MARTINEAU, HARRIET. "Misstatements in *Household Words.*" *The Factory Controversy,* 35-47. London: National Association of Factory Occupiers, 1855.

18 STEPHEN, JAMES FITZJAMES. "The Relation of Novels to Life." *Cambridge Essays, Contributed by Members of the University,* 1:148-92. London: J. N. Parker, 1855.

19 TALBOT, G. F. "The Genius of Charles Dickens." *Putnam's Monthly Magazine* 5 (Mar. 1855):263-72.

20 OLIPHANT, MARGARET [?]. "Charles Dickens." *Blackwood's Edinburgh Magazine* 77 (Apr. 1855):451-66.

21 VAN SANTVOORD, CORNELIUS. "Charles Dickens and his Philosophy." *Discourses on Special Occasions and Miscellaneous Papers,* 333-59. New York: Dodd, 1856.

22 BAYNE, PETER. "The Modern Novel, – Dickens – Bulwer – Thackeray." *Essays in Biography and Criticism,* 363-92. Boston: Gould and Lincoln, 1857.

23 STEPHEN, JAMES FITZJAMES. "Mr Dickens as a Politician." *Saturday Review* 3 (Jan. 1857):8-9.

24 HAMLEY, E. B. "Remonstrance with Dickens." *Blackwood's Edinburgh Magazine* 81 (Apr. 1857):490-503.

25 STEPHEN, JAMES FITZJAMES. "The License of Modern Novelists." *Edinburgh Review* 106 (July 1857):124-56.

26 TAINE, HIPPOLYTE. *Essais de Critique et d'Histoire.* Paris: Hachette, 1858.

27 STEPHEN, JAMES FITZJAMES. "Mr Dickens." *Saturday Review* 5 (May 1858):474-75. Reprinted in *Notorious Literary Attacks,* ed. Albert Mordell. New York: Boni and Liveright, 1926.

28 BAGEHOT, WALTER. "Charles Dickens." *National Review* 7 (Oct. 1858):458-86; *Littell's Living Age* 59 (Nov. 1858):643-59. Reprinted in *Literary Studies,* vol. 2. London: Longmans, 1879; and in *Literary Essays,* vol. 2, ed. Norman St. John-Stevas. Cambridge, Mass.: Harvard Univ. Press, 1965.

29 "Charles Dickens and His Reviewers." *Welcome Guest* 1 (1860):375-7

30 WALKER, FRANK A. "Dickens – How Far a Literary Exemplar?" *University Quarterly* 1 (Jan. 1860):91-101.

31 DENNISON, H. "Work of Charles Dickens." *National Quarterly Review* 1 (June 1860):91-113.

32 "Mr Dickens's Last Novel." *The Dublin University Magazine* 58 (Dec. 1861):685-93.

33 CLARK, LEWIS G. "Letters from Charles Dickens to L. Gaylord Clark." *Harper's Magazine* 25 (Aug. 1862):376-80.

34 TAINE, HIPPOLYTE. "The Novel: Dickens." *History of English Literature,* IV:115-64, trans. H. Van Laun. New York: Ungar, 1965. [Translation of *Histoire de la Littérature Anglaise.* Paris: Hachette, 1863-64.]

35 FITZGERALD, PERCY H. "Two English Essayists: Charles Lamb and Charles Dickens." *Afternoon Lectures on Literature and Art.*

Delivered in the Theatre of the Museum of Industry, S. Stephen's
Green, Dublin, in April and May, 1864. Second series, 85-100. London:
Bell and Daldy, 1864.

36 "Modern Novelists. Charles Dickens." *Westminster Review* 82
   (Oct. 1864):414-41.

37 LINNIČENKO, A. I. *Obzor Poetičeskoj Dejatel'nosti Anglijskogo
   Romanista Čarl'za Dikkensa.* Kiev, 1866. [*A Survey of the Poetic
   Activity of the English Novelist, Charles Dickens.*]

38 WHIPPLE, EDWIN P. "The Genius of Dickens." *Atlantic Monthly* 19
   (May 1867):546-54; *Ladies Treasury* (July 1867):305-10. Reprinted
   in *Success and its Conditions.* Boston: J. R. Osgood, 1871.

39 FIELD, KATE. *Pen Photographs of Charles Dickens' Readings.*
   Boston: Loring, 1868. New and enlarged edition. Boston: J. Osgood,
   1871.

40 STOTT, GEORGE. "Charles Dickens." *Contemporary Review* 10
   (Feb. 1869):203-25.

41 "Mr Dickens's Moral Services to Literature." *Spectator* 42
   (Apr. 17, 1869):474-75.

42 FRISWELL, J. HAIN. "Mr Charles Dickens." *Modern Men of Letters
   Honestly Criticized,* 1-45. London: Hodder and Stoughton, 1870.

43 FULTON, JUSTIN D. *Whither Bound? A Sermon Occasioned by the
   Canonization of Charles Dickens.* Boston: J. W. Olmstead, 1870.

44 HAM, JAMES P. (The Elder). *Parables of Fiction.* London: Trübner,
   1870. [A memorial discourse on Dickens.]

45 HUME, A. B. *A Christmas Memorial of the Greatest of Christmas
   Writers, Charles Dickens.* London: Pitman, 1870.

46 MACKENZIE, ROBERT S. *Life of Charles Dickens.* With personal
   recollections, etc. Philadelphia: T. B. Peterson, 1870.

47 PERKINS, FREDERIC B. *Charles Dickens: A Sketch of His Life and
   Works.* London: Putnam, 1870.

48 SALA, GEORGE A. *Charles Dickens.* London: Routledge, 1870.

49 SHEPHERD, RICHARD H., ed. *Speeches, Literary and Social.* By
   Charles Dickens. Now first collected with chapters on "Charles
   Dickens as a letter writer, poet and public reader." London: J. C.
   Hotten, 1870. New edition: *The Speeches of Charles Dickens.* Lon-
   don: Chatto and Windus, 1884. New edition with introduction by
   Bernard Darwin. London: Michael Joseph, 1937.

50 STANLEY, ARTHUR P. *Sermon in Westminster Abbey, June 19,
   1870.* Being the Sunday Following the Funeral of Charles Dickens.
   London: Macmillan, 1870. Reprinted in *Sermons on Special
   Occasions, Preached in Westminster Abbey.* London: J. Murray, 1882.

51 TAYLOR, T. *Charles Dickens: The Story of his Life.* London: J. C. Hotten; New York: Harper, 1870.

52 HUTTON, RICHARD H. "The Genius of Dickens." *Spectator* 43 (June 1870):749-51. Reprinted in *Brief Literary Criticisms.* London: Macmillan, 1906.

53 CHORLEY, HENRY F. "Mr Charles Dickens." *Athenaeum* (June 18, 1870):804-5.

54 "The Late Charles Dickens." *Illustrated London News* 56 (June 18, 1870):639.

55 AUSTIN, ALFRED. "Charles Dickens." *Temple Bar* 29 (July 1870): 554-62.

56 "Charles Dickens." *Fraser's Magazine* 82 (July 1870):130-34.

57 JERROLD, BLANCHARD. "Charles Dickens: In Memoriam." *Gentleman's Magazine* 5 (July 1870):228-41. Reprinted in *New Eclectic Magazine* 7 (Sept. 1870):332-42. Reprinted with other material as "A Day With Dickens," in *The Best of All Good Company.* London: Useful Knowledge, 1871.

58 TROLLOPE, ANTHONY. "Charles Dickens." *St. Paul's Magazine* 6 (July 1870):370-75. Reprinted in *Dickensian* 6 (June 1910):145-49.

59 "The Positive Qualities of Dickens." *Dickensian* 3 (June 1907): 145-48. [Translated from *Illustrierte Zeitung* July 9, 1870.]

60 FIELDS, JAMES T. "Some Memoirs of Dickens." *Atlantic Monthly* 26 (Aug. 1870):235. Revised and enlarged in *Yesterdays with Authors* Boston: Osgood, 1872. Reprinted as *In and Out of Doors with Dicken* Boston: Osgood, 1876.

61 WHITE, RICHARD G. "The Styles of Disraeli and Dickens." *Galaxy* 10 (Aug. 1870):253-63.

62 PUTNAM, GEORGE W. "Four Months with Charles Dickens: During his First Visit to America (1842)." *Atlantic Monthly* 26 (Oct. 1870): 476-82; (Nov. 1870):591-99.

63 ANDERSEN, HANS CHRISTIAN. "A Visit at Dickens's House." *Pictures of Travel,* 267-93. New York: Hurd and Houghton, 1871.

64 HANAFORD, PHEBE A. (COFFIN). *The Life and Writings of Charles Dickens: A Woman's Memorial Volume.* Boston: B. B. Russell, 1871.

65 JERROLD, BLANCHARD. *The Best of All Good Company.* London: Useful Knowledge, 1871.

66 MACRAE, DAVID. "Carlyle and Dickens." *Home and Abroad: Sketches and Gleanings,* 122-28. Glasgow: John S. Marr, 1871.

67 AINGER, A. "Mr Dickens's Amateur Theatricals." *Macmillan's Magazine* 23 (Jan. 1871):206. Reprinted in *Eclectic Magazine* 76 (1871): 322; *Every Saturday* 10 (1871):70; *Lectures and Essays,* vol. 2. London: Macmillan, 1905.

68 "Charles Dickens." *London Quarterly Review* 35 (Jan. 1871):265-86.

69 ANDERSEN, HANS CHRISTIAN. "A Visit to Charles Dickens." *Eclectic Magazine* 76 (Feb. 1871):183+.

70 "Two English Novelists: Dickens and Thackeray." *Dublin Review* 68 (Apr. 1871):315-50.

71 CHRISTIAN, ELEANOR E. "Recollections of Charles Dickens." *Englishwoman's Domestic Magazine* 10 (June 1871):336. Reprinted as *Recollections of Charles Dickens.* London: Temple Bar, 1888.

72 OLIPHANT, MARGARET. "Charles Dickens." *Blackwood's Edinburgh Magazine* 109 (June 1871):673-95.

73 GRANT, JAMES. "The Daily News." *The Newspaper Press,* II:79-89. London: Tinsley, 1871-72.

74 BEHN-ESCHENBURG, HANS. *Charles Dickens.* Basel: B. Schwabe, 1872.

75 KENT, CHARLES. *Charles Dickens as a Reader.* London: Chapman and Hall, 1872.

76 PIERCE, GILBERT A. *The Dickens Dictionary: a Key to the Characters and Principal Incidents in the Tales of Charles Dickens.* London: Chapman and Hall, 1872. Reprinted, with additions by William A. Wheeler, 1914.

77 BUCHANAN, ROBERT W. "The 'Good Genie' of Fiction (Charles Dickens)." *St. Paul's Magazine* 10 (Feb. 1872):130-48. Reprinted in *Master-Spirits.* London: H. S. King, 1873; *A Poet's Sketchbook: Selections from the Prose Writings of Robert Buchanan.* London: Chatto and Windus, 1883.

78 LEWES, G. H. "Dickens in Relation to Criticism." *Fortnightly Review* 17 (Feb. 1872):141-54. Reprinted in *Eclectic Magazine* 78 (Apr. 1872):445-53; *Every Saturday* 12 (1872):246-51; *The Dickens Critics,* ed. G. H. Ford and Lauriat Lane, Jr., 1961 q.v.

79 FORSTER, JOHN. *The Life of Charles Dickens.* 3 vols. London: Chapman and Hall, 1872-74. Edited and annotated with introduction by J. W. T. Ley. London: Palmer; New York: Doubleday, Doran, 1928. New edition, with notes and index by A. J. Hoppé. London: Dent, 1966.

80 DUYCKINCK, EVERT A. "Charles Dickens." *Portrait Gallery of Eminent Men and Women of Europe and America,* II:383-98. New York: Johnson, Wilson, 1873.

81 PEACOCK, WILLIAM F. "Charles Dickens's Nomenclature." *Belgravia* 20 (Apr. 1873):267-76; (May 1873):393-402.

82 HOLLINGSHEAD, JOHN. "Mr Dickens and His Critics." *Miscellanies,* III. London: 1874.

83 IRVING, WALTER. *Charles Dickens: An Essay.* London: Simpkin, Marshall; Edinburgh: Maclachlan and Stewart, 1874.

84 STODDARD, R. H., ed. *Anecdote Biographies of Thackeray and Dickens.* New York: Scribners, 1874.

85 HUTTON, RICHARD H. "The Dispute About the Genius of Dickens." *Spectator* 32 (Feb. 7, 1874):169-70. Reprinted as "The Genius of Dickens," in *Criticism on Contemporary Thought and Thinkers.* London: Macmillan, 1894.

86 DAVEY, SAMUEL J. "Charles Dickens." *Darwin, Carlyle and Dickens With Other Essays,* 121-56. London: James Clark, 1876.

87 HORNE, RICHARD H. "John Forster: His Early Life and Friendships." *Temple Bar* 46 (Apr. 1876):491.

88 "Charles Dickens' Verse." *Spectator* 25 (Dec. 1877):1651-53. Reprinted in *Littell's Living Age* 139 (Jan. 26, 1878):252-54.

89 CAREY, WALTER. "Hook, Thackeray, and Dickens." *Galaxy* 25 (Jan. 1878):31-43.

90 CANNING, ALBERT S. *Philosophy of Charles Dickens.* London: Smith, Elder, 1880.

91 JONES, CHARLES H. *A Short Life of Charles Dickens.* With Selections from His Letters. New York: Appleton, 1880.

92 LANGTON, ROBERT. *Dickens and Rochester.* London: Chapman and Hall, 1880. Partly reprinted in *The Childhood and Youth of Dickens.* Manchester: the Author, 1883.

93 WATT, JAMES C. "Dickens." *Great Novelists: Scott, Thackeray, Dickens, Lytton,* 163-218. Edinburgh: Macniver and Wallace, 1880.

94 WEIZMANN, LOUIS. *Dickens und Daudet in deutscher Uebersetzung.* Berlin: H. S. Hermann, 1880.

95 RANDS, WILLIAM B. (Matthew Browne, pseud.). "From Faust to Mr Pickwick." *Contemporary Review* 38 (July 1880):162-76.

96 KIRPIČNIKOV, A. I. *Dikkens Kak Pedagog.* Xar'kov: Izd. V. A. Syxra, 1881. [*Dickens as Pedagogue.*]

97 TOPP, ST. JOHN. "Dickens." *Melbourne Review* 6 (July 1881): 265-82.

98 FITZGERALD, PERCY H. "Charles Dickens as an Editor." *Recreations of a Literary Man, or Does Writing Pay?* I:48-96. London: Chatto and Windus, 1882.

99 FITZGERALD, PERCY H. "Dickens at Home." *Recreations of a Literary Man, or Does Writing Pay?* I:97-171. London: Chatto and Windus, 1882.

100 SHEPHERD, RICHARD H. "Introductory Monograph." *The Plays and Poems of Charles Dickens. With a Few Miscellanies in Prose.* London: W. H. Allen, 1882.

101 WARD, ADOLPHUS W. *Charles Dickens.* (English Men of Letters.)
London: Macmillan, 1882.

102 MORRIS, MOWBRAY. "Charles Dickens." *Fortnightly Review* 38
(Dec. 1882):762-79. Reprinted in *Living Age* 155 (Dec. 1882):
793-803; *Eclectic Magazine* 100 (Feb. 1883):182-94; *Manhattan* 1
(Apr. 1883):296-306.

103 LANGTON, ROBERT. *The Childhood and Youth of Charles Dickens.*
Manchester: the Author, 1883. Reprinted with additional material.
London: Hutchinson, 1891. Enlarged revision, 1917. [With retro-
spective notes and elucidations from his books and letters.]

104 RIMMER, ALFRED. *About England with Dickens.* London: Chatto
and Windus, 1883.

105 MATTHEWS, CORNELIUS. "Charles Dickens His Own Trumpeter."
Manhattan 1 (Apr. 1883):274-79.

106 COOK, D. "Dickens as a Dramatic Critic." *Longman's Magazine* 2
(May 1883):29.

107 KENT, CHARLES. *The Humour and Pathos of Charles Dickens.*
London: Chapman and Hall, 1884.

108 PHILLIMORE, FRANCIS. "Introduction." *Dickens Memento.* London: Field and Tuer; New York: Scribner and Welford, 1884.
[Catalogue of Dickens' possessions auctioned on July 9, 1870.]

109 THOMSON, DAVID C. *Life and Labours of Hablôt Knight Browne,*
"Phiz." London: Chapman and Hall, 1884.

110 DICKENS, MARY. *Charles Dickens by His Eldest Daughter.* London:
Cassell, 1885. Published as *My Father as I Recall Him.* London:
Roxburghe Press, 1897.

111 DOLBY, GEORGE. *Charles Dickens as I Knew Him.* The Story of the
Reading Tours in Great Britain. London: T. Fisher Unwin, 1885.

112 MASON, EDWARD T. "Dickens, 1812-1870." *Personal Traits of*
British Authors, 171-232. New York: Scribners, 1885.

113 DICKENS, MARY. "Charles Dickens at Home." *Cornhill Magazine*
N.S. 4 (Jan. 1885):32-51.

114 PROCTOR, RICHARD A. "Dickens and Thackeray." *Knowledge* 7
(June 1885):493-537.

115 LANG, ANDREW. "Charles Dickens." *Letters to Dead Authors,*
10-21. London: Longmans, Green, 1886.

116 HUNT, THEODORE W. "The Prose Style of Charles Dickens." *Rep-*
resentative English Prose and Prose Writers, 444-78. New York: A. C.
Armstrong, 1887.

117 MARZIALS, FRANK T. *Life of Charles Dickens.* London: W. Scott,
1887.

118 MORLEY, HENRY. "Introduction." *The Cricket on the Hearth*. Wit. selections from *Sketches by Boz*. London: Cassell, 1887.

119 WHIPPLE, EDWIN P. "In Dickens-Land." *Scribner's Magazine* 2 (July-Dec. 1887):743-52.

120 LANG, ANDREW. "Dickens." *Good Words* 29 (1888):233-37. Reprinted in *Essays in Little*. New York: Scribners, 1891.

121 MORLEY, HENRY. "Introduction." *The Battle of Life*. London: Cassell, 1888.

122 PEMBERTON, THOMAS E. *Charles Dickens and the Stage*. London: Redway, 1888. [A record of his connection with the drama as playwright, actor, and critic.]

123 HENNEQUIN, EMILE. *Etudes de Critique Scientifique. Ecrivains Francisés. Dickens, Heine, Tourguenieff, Poe, Dostoëvski, Tolstoï*. Paris: Perrin, 1889.

124 PONTAVICE DE HEUSSEY, ROBERT Y. M. du. *Un Maitre du Roman Contemporain. L'Inimitable Boz. Étude Historique et Anecdotique sur la Vie et l'Oeuvre de Charles Dickens*. Paris: Maison Quantin, 1889.

125 DICKENS, CHARLES Jr. "Dickens as an Editor." *English Illustrated Magazine* 6 (Aug. 1889):822.

126 "Wilkie Collins About Charles Dickens." *Pall Mall Gazette* (Jan. 20, 1890):3. [The marginalia in Collins' copy of Forster's *Life* sold on the above date.]

127 KITTON, FREDERIC G. *Charles Dickens by Pen and Pencil*. 3 vols. London: F. T. Sabin, 1890-92.

128 PLEŠČEEV, N. N. *Žizn' Dikkensa*. St. Petersburg: I. N. Skoroxodov, 1891. [*A Life of Dickens*.]

129 KITTON, FREDERIC G. "Dickens and 'Punch'." *English Illustrated Magazine* 8 (Aug. 1891):799.

130 "Dickens and Daudet." *Cornhill Magazine* N.S. 17 (Oct. 1891):400-

131 ANNENSKAJA, A. N. Č. *Dikkens; Ego Žizn' i Literaturnaja Dejatel'nost'*. St. Petersburg: Tip. Ju. N. Erlix, 1892. [*Charles Dickens; His Life and Literary Activity*.]

132 AXON, WILLIAM E. A. *Charles Dickens and Shorthand*. Manchester John Heywood, 1892. [Dickens as a reporter.]

133 OLIPHANT, MARGARET. "Of Charles Dickens." *The Victorian Age in English Literature*, 247-61. New York: Dodd, Mead, 1892.

134 KITTON, FREDERIC G. *"Master Humphrey's Clock." Library Review* 1 (Oct. 1892):494-500. [Review article of *Works*, edited by Charles Dickens the Younger.]

135 MALLOCK, W. H. "Are Scott, Dickens, and Thackeray Obsolete?" *Forum* 14 (Dec. 1892):503-13.

136 DICKENS, CHARLES Jr. "Introductions." *The Works of Charles Dickens.* 21 vols. London: Macmillan, 1892-1925.

137 DICKENS, CHARLES Jr. "Disappearing Dickensland." *North American Review* 156 (June 1893):670-84.

138 LATIMER, E. W. "A Girl's Recollection of Dickens." *Lippincott's Magazine* 52 (Sept. 1893):338.

139 ARCHER, THOMAS. *Dickens: A Gossip About his Life, Work and Characters.* London: Cassell [1894?].

140 FITZGERALD, PERCY H. "Dickens and *Household Words.*" *Memoirs of an Author,* I:1-16. London: R. Bentley, 1894.

141 HURD, A. D. "Charles Dickens." *Munsey's Magazine* 10 (Mar. 1894): 647-60.

142 BENIGNUS, SIEGFRIED. *Studien über die Anfänge von Dickens.* Esslingen: W. Langgeth, 1895.

143 CHANCELLOR, EDWIN B. "Charles Dickens – Novelist," and "The Pathos of Dickens (A note)." *Literary Types,* 140-71. London: Macmillan, 1895.

144 HOWELLS, WILLIAM DEAN. "Dickens." *My Literary Passions,* 88-103. New York: Harper, 1895.

145 LILLY, WILLIAM S. "Dickens: the Humorist as Democrat." *Four English Humorists,* 1-33. London: John Murray, 1895. [Dickens, Thackeray, George Eliot, Carlyle.]

146 SAINTSBURY, GEORGE. "Charles Dickens." *Corrected Impressions: Essays on Victorian Writers,* 117-37. London: Heinemann, 1895.

147 HARRISON, FREDERICK. "Charles Dickens." *Forum* 18 (Jan. 1895): 545-53. Reprinted as "Dickens's Place in Literature." *Studies in Early Victorian Literature.* London: E. Arnold, 1895.

148 DICKENS, CHARLES Jr. "Glimpses of Charles Dickens." *North American Review* 160 (May 1895):525-37; (June 1895):677-84.

149 BARNARD, FREDERICK. *Character Sketches From Dickens.* London: Cassell, 1896.

150 McCARTHY, JUSTIN and JOHN R. ROBINSON. "Charles Dickens and His Staff." *The "Daily News" Jubilee,* 1-20. London: Sampson Low, Marston, 1896.

151 McCARTHY, JUSTIN and JOHN R. ROBINSON. "Retirement of Charles Dickens From the Editorship." *The "Daily News" Jubilee,* 21-36. London: Sampson Low, Marston, 1896.

152 RIDEAL, CHARLES F. *Charles Dickens' Heroines and Women-Folk.* London: Roxburghe Press, 1896.

153 SAINTSBURY, GEORGE. "Dickens." *A History of Nineteenth Century Literature 1780-1895*, 145-50. New York: Macmillan, 1896.

154 TRUMBLE, ALFRED. *In Jail with Charles Dickens*. London: Harper, 1896.

155 SCHOOLING, J. HOLT. "Charles Dickens's Manuscripts." *Strand Magazine* 11 (Jan. 1896):29-40.

156 LINTON, E. LYNN. "Landor, Dickens, Thackeray." *Bookman* 3 (Apr. 1896):125-33.

157 DICKENS, CHARLES Jr. "Notes on Some Dickens Places and People." *Pall Mall Magazine* 9 (July 1896):342-55.

158 GRIFFIN, MONTAGU. "An Estimate of Dickens as an Artist." *Irish Monthly* 24 (Sept. 1896):490-98; (Oct. 1896):539-49.

159 HALTON, LAURENCE. "Charles Dickens, 1812-1870." *Library of the World's Best Literature, Ancient and Modern,* ed. Charles D. Warner, VIII:4625-88. New York: R. S. Peale and J. A. Hill, 1896-99.

160 GRAHAM, RICHARD D. "Charles Dickens." *Masters of Victorian Literature, 1837-97,* 1-23. Edinburgh: J. Thin, 1897.

161 KITTON, FREDERIC G. *The Novels of Charles Dickens.* A bibliography and sketch. London: E. Stock, 1897.

162 DICKENS, MARY A. "A Child's Recollection at Gad's Hill." *Strand Magazine* 13 (Jan. 1897):69-74.

163 HOWELLS, WILLIAM DEAN. "My Favorite Novelist and His Best Book." *Munsey's Magazine* (Apr. 1897). Reprinted in *Criticism and Fiction and Other Essays by W. D. Howells.* New York: New York Univ. Press, 1959.

164 HOLYOAKE, MALTUS Q. "Memories of Charles Dickens." *Chambers' Journal* 14 (Nov. 1897):721-25.

165 McCARTHY, JUSTIN. "Dickens and Thackeray." *A History of Our Times,* II:255-59. New York: Harper, 1897-1905.

166 LANG, ANDREW. "Introductions, General Essay and Notes." *Works of Charles Dickens.* Gadshill edition. 36 vols. London: Chapman and Hall; New York: Scribner's, 1897-[1908].

167 CLARK, J. SCOTT. "Dickens." *A Study of English Prose Writers: A Laboratory Method,* 607-47. New York: Scribners, 1898.

168 GISSING, GEORGE. *Charles Dickens: A Critical Study.* London: Blackie, 1898. Reprinted as part of Imperial Edition of Dickens, 1901-3; as *Critical Studies of the Works of Charles Dickens,* with introduction and bibliography of Gissing by Temple Scott. New York: Greenberg, 1924; as *The Immortal Dickens,* ed. B. W. Matz. London: Palmer, 1925; and as *Critical Studies* etc. New York: Haskell House, 1965.

169 HEICHEN, PAUL H. *Charles Dickens: Sein Leben und seine Werke.* Naumberg: Albin Schirmer, 1898.

170 KITTON, FREDERIC G. "Introduction." *To Be Read at Dusk and Other Stories, Sketches and Essays.* London: G. Redway, 1898.

171 SCUDDER, VIDA D. "Social Pictures: Dickens and Thackeray." *Social Ideal in English Letters*, 128-42. Boston: Houghton Mifflin, 1898.

172 WILLIAMSON, EDMUND S. *Glimpses of Dickens.* Toronto: Bryant Press, 1898.

173 KITTON, FREDERIC G. "The Story of a Famous Society." *Gentleman's Magazine* 284 (Feb. 1898):118-27. [On the formation of "The Guild of Literature and Art."]

174 LANG, ANDREW. "Charles Dickens." *Fortnightly Review* 70 (Dec. 1898):944-60.

175 CROSS, WILLIAM L. "The Realistic Reaction (Dickens)." *The Development of the English Novel*, 168-96. New York: Macmillan, 1899.

176 KITTON, FREDERIC G. *Dickens and His Illustrators.* London: Redway, 1899.

177 WILSON, FRANK W. *Dickens in seinen Beziehungen zu den Humoristen Fielding und Smollet.* Leipzig: O. Schmidt, 1899.

178 HENLEY, WILLIAM E. "Some Notes on Charles Dickens." *Pall Mall Magazine* 18 (Aug. 1899):573-79. [Comments on Gadshill Edition.]

179 GARNETT, RICHARD. "Introductions." *Complete Works of Charles Dickens.* 30 vols. London: Chapman and Hall, 1900.

180 *The Bookman Extra Number. Charles Dickens.* London: Hodder and Stoughton, 1901.

181 HOWELLS, WILLIAM DEAN. "The Earlier Heroines of Charles Dickens." *Harper's Bazaar* 33 (Sept. 1900):1192-97. Reprinted in *Heroines of Fiction*, vol. 1. New York: Harper, 1901.

182 HOWELLS, WILLIAM DEAN. "Heroines of Dickens's Middle Period." *Harper's Bazaar* 33 (Sept. 1900):1287-92. Reprinted as "Heroines of Charles Dickens's Middle Period." *Heroines of Fiction*, vol. 1. New York: Harper, 1901.

183 HOWELLS, WILLIAM DEAN. "Later Heroines of Dickens." *Harper's Bazaar* 33 (Oct. 1900):1415-21. Reprinted as "Dickens's Later Heroines." *Heroines of Fiction*, vol. 1. New York: Harper, 1901.

184 GISSING, GEORGE. "Introductions." *Works of Charles Dickens.* 11 vols. Rochester edition. London: Methuen, 1900-1.

185 HUGHES, JAMES L. *Dickens as an Educator.* London: E. Arnold; New York: Appleton, 1901.

186 LANG, ANDREW, AMELIA E. BARR, and JAMES L. HUGHES. *Charles Dickens: His Life and Work.* Course VII: Booklovers Reading Club. Talks and lectures. Editorial notes by T. M. Parrott. Philadelph: Booklover Library, 1901.

187 CROSS, CONSTANCE. "Charles Dickens: A Memory." *New Liberal Review* 2 (Oct. 1901):392-98.

188 MATZ, BERTRAM W. "Dickens and his Illustrators." *Literature* (Dec. 1901):572-85. Reprinted in *The Critic* (Jan. 1902):43-51.

189 KITTON, FREDERIC G. *Charles Dickens, his Life, Writings and Personality.* London: T. C. and E. C. Jack, 1902.

190 MATZ, BERTRAM W. "Dickens: The Story of his Life and Writings." *Household Words* (June 14, 1902). Reprinted as *Charles Dickens: The Story of His Life and Writings.* London: Dickens Fellowship, 1902.

191 HOWELLS, WILLIAM DEAN. "Editor's Easy Chair." *Harper's Monthly Magazine* 105 (July 1902):308-12. [On the reputation of Dickens.]

192 SWINBURNE, ALGERNON C. "Charles Dickens." *Quarterly Review* 196 (July 1902):20-39. Reprinted with additions as *Charles Dickens,* ed. T. Watts-Dunton. London: Chatto and Windus, 1913.

193 MELVILLE, LEWIS. "Thackeray and Dickens." *Temple Bar* 126 (Oct. 1902):413-20.

194 WAUGH, ARTHUR. "Biographical Introductions." *Works of Charles Dickens.* Biographical edition. 18 vols. London: Chapman and Hall, 1902-3.

195 CHESTERTON, GILBERT K. and FREDERIC G. KITTON. *Charles Dickens.* London: Hodder and Stoughton, 1903.

196 GAUSSERON, B. H. *Lectures Littéraires. Dickens.* Paris: Colin, 1903. [Anthology with biographical and critical introduction.]

197 MAURICE, ARTHUR B. "Famous Novels and their Contemporary Critics." *Bookman* 17 (1903):130-38.

198 MEYNELL, ALICE. "Charles Dickens as a Man of Letters." *Atlantic Monthly* 91 (Jan. 1903):52-59. Reprinted in *The Dickens Critics,* ed. G. H. Ford and L. Lane, Jr., 1961 q.v.

199 PERUGINI, KATE DICKENS. "Dickens as a Lover of Art and Artist." *Magazine of Art* 27 (Jan. 1903):125-30; (Feb. 1903):164-69.

200 LORD, WALTER F. "Charles Dickens." *Nineteenth Century* 54 (Nov. 1903):765-81.

201 KITTON, FREDERIC G. "Annotations, bibliography and topograph: *The Complete Works of Charles Dickens.* 15 vols. Autograph edition. London: George G. Harrap, 1903-8. [Incomplete edition.]

202 BAGSTER, G. *Charles Dickens, ein Essay.* Stuttgart: 1904.

203 BARLOW, GEORGE. *The Genius of Dickens*. London: H. J. Glaisher, 1904. Reprinted in *The Contemporary Review* 94 (Nov. 1908):542-62.

204 HENLEY, WILLIAM E. "Introduction." *Reprinted Pieces*. Autograph edition. London: George G. Harrap, 1904.

205 JERROLD, WALTER. "Introduction." *The Holly-Tree*. Philadelphia: H. Altemus, 1904.

206 McSPADDEN, JOSEPH W. *Synopses of Dickens's Novels*. New York: Crowell, 1904.

207 SAUNDERS, MARGARET B. *The Philosophy of Dickens*. London: H. J. Glaisher, 1904.

208 SHORE, WILLIAM T. *Dickens*. London: G. Bell, 1904.

209 ROBINSON, SIR JOHN R. "Charles Dickens and the Guild of Literature and Art." *Cornhill Magazine* 16 (Jan. 1904):28-33.

210 BAILLIE-SAUNDERS, MARGARET E. *The Philosophy of Dickens: A Study of his Life and Teaching as a Social Reformer*. London: H. J. Glaisher, 1905.

211 BOWES, C. C. *The Associations of Dickens with Liverpool*. Liverpool: Lyceum Press, 1905. Introd. E. A. Browne.

212 DA COSTA, JOHN C. *Dickens Doctors*. Philadelphia: The Philobiblon Club, 1905.

213 DAWSON, WILLIAM J. "Charles Dickens." *The Makers of English Fiction*, 88-102. London: Hodder and Stoughton, 1905.

214 DAWSON, WILLIAM J. "The Greatness of Dickens." *The Makers of English Fiction*, 103-12. London: Hodder and Stoughton, 1905.

215 FITZGERALD, PERCY H. *Life of Charles Dickens: as Revealed in His Writings*. 2 vols. London: Chatto and Windus, 1905.

216 SAWIN, JAMES M. "Introduction." *A Christmas Carol*, and *The Cricket on the Hearth*. London: Macmillan, 1905.

217 FITZGERALD, PERCY H. "Scott and Dickens." *Dickensian* 1 (Jan. 1905):4-6.

218 DICKENS, SIR HENRY F. "The Social Influence of Dickens." *Dickensian* 1 (Mar. 1905):60-63.

219 MATZ, BERTRAM W. "*Sketches By Boz* – A Bibliographical Note." *Dickensian* 1 (Mar. 1905):64-65.

220 LEY, J. W. T. "Dickens and Children." *Dickensian* 1 (Apr. 1905): 87-90.

221 SOWRAY, WOODFORD. "Dickensian Humbugs." *Dickensian* 1 (May 1905):123-27 ["In General"] ; (June 1905):148-52 ["In Particular"] ; 2 (Aug. 1906):209-13 ["Uriah and Some Others"].

222 VAN RIPEN, J. F. "Charles Dickens: a Question of Caricature." *Dickensian* 5 (May 1905):122-25.

223 DOURLIAC, ARTHUR. "The Heroes of Dickens. From a French Point of View." *Dickensian* 1 (July 1905):171-73. [Translated from *Revue Idéaliste* (May 15, 1905).]

224 PAGAN, ISABELLE M. "The Dramatic Element in Dickens." *Dickensian* 1 (July 1905):178-82.

225 CROTCH, W. WALTER. "Dickens's Instinct for Reform." *Dickensian* 1 (Sept. 1905):227-31; (Oct. 1905):255-58.

226 MILNE, JAMES. "'Boz' and Others: Mr Percy Fitzgerald's Literary Reminiscenses." *Book Monthly* 3 (Oct. 1905):17-22.

227 CAINE, HALL. "Introduction." *The Cricket on the Hearth.* London: William Heinemann, 1906.

228 CHESTERTON, GILBERT K. *Charles Dickens.* London: Methuen, 1906. Reprinted as *Charles Dickens: A Critical Study.* London: Dodd, Mead, 1913; and as *Charles Dickens: the Last of the Great Men.* New York: The Press of the Readers Club, 1942.

229 GISSING, GEORGE. "Dickens." *Homes and Haunts of Famous Authors* [Gissing *et al.*], 107-20. London: Wells, Gardner, Darton, 1906.

230 HENLEY, WILLIAM E. "Dickens." *Views and Reviews: Essays in Appreciation,* 1-8. New York: Scribner's Sons, 1906.

231 RICKETT, ARTHUR C. "Charles Dickens: the Humorist." *Personal Forces in Modern Literature,* 143-85. London: Dent, 1906.

232 JOHNSON, R. BRIMLEY. "Dickens as Artist, or Genius and the Cry of 'Art for Art's Sake'." *Book Monthly* 3 (Jan. 1906):235-39.

233 MATCHETT, WILLOUGHBY. "Certain Lovers in Dickens." *Dickensian* 2 (Feb. 1906):33-36.

234 WELCH, DESHLER. "Dickens in Switzerland." *Harper's Monthly Magazine* 112 (Apr. 1906):714-19.

235 FRASER, W. A. "The Illustrators of Dickens." *Dickensian* 2 (May 1906):117-22 [George Cruikshank] ; (July 1906):176-83 [Hablôt K. Browne] ; (Sept. 1906):237-39 [George Cattermole] ; (Oct. 1906):263-66 [Marcus Stone] ; (Dec. 1906):330-33 [John Leech and the Christmas Books] .

236 LEY, J. W. T. "The Government Education Bill: Dickens's Views on Some of its Points." *Dickensian* 2 (May 1906):123-25.

237 HELM, W. H. "Dickens and Balzac." *Empire Review* 11 (June 1906):444-51.

238 FRASER, J. A. LOVAT. "Dickens and his Comparisons." *Dickensian* 2 (July 1906):185-86.

239 MILNE, JAMES. "How Dickens Sells: He Comes Next to the Bible and Shakespeare." *Book Monthly* 3 (Aug. 1906):773-76.

240 CHESTERTON, GILBERT K. "Introductions." *Works of Charles Dickens.* 22 vols. London: Dent; New York: Dutton, 1906-21. [Omits *Barnaby Rudge* and *A Tale of Two Cities.*]

241 BROWNE, JOHN H. BALFOUR. "Bleak House." *Essays Critical and Political,* I:111-22. London: Longmans, Green, 1907.

242 HOLLINGSHEAD, JOHN. "Charles Dickens As A Reader." [Introduction.] *Readings From the Works of Charles Dickens As Arranged and Read by Himself.* London: Chapman and Hall, 1907.

243 WILLIAMS, MARY. *The Dickens Concordance.* London: F. Griffiths, 1907.

244 FITZGERALD, PERCY H. "Boz's Publishers." [After Pt. 1 called "Boz and His Publishers."] *Dickensian* 3 (Jan. 1907):10-14 [Macrone and Others] ; (Feb. 1907):33-37; (Mar. 1907):70-73 [Richard Bentley and his *Miscellany*] ; (Apr. 1907):93-96; (May 1907):126-29 [From Richard Bentley to Chapman and Hall] · (June 1907):158-61 [Bradbury and Evans and some others] .

245 SIBBALD, WILLIAM A. "Charles Dickens Revisited." *Westminster Review* 167 (Jan. 1907):62-73.

246 SLOAN, J. M. "Robert Burns and Charles Dickens." *Fortnightly Review* 88 (Aug. 1907):269-82. Reprinted in *Living Age* 255 (Oct. 1907):8-18.

247 LEFFMAN, HENRY. "Dickens's Doctors." *Dickensian* 3 (Oct. 1907): 268-71.

248 WARD, JOSEPHINE (Mrs Wilfred). "The Realism of Dickens." *Dublin Review* 141 (Oct. 1907):285-95.

249 FITZGERALD, PERCY H. "Parallels Between Scott and Dickens." *Chambers' Journal* 10 (Nov. 1907):807-13.

250 MATZ, BERTRAM W. "Dickens and Hans Andersen." *Dickensian* 3 (Dec. 1907):329-32.

251 SAINTSBURY, GEORGE. "Dickens." *Cambridge History of English Literature,* ed. A. W. Ward and A. R. Waller, XIII,pt.2:303-39. Cambridge, Eng.: The University Press, 1907-16.

252 *The Bookman Extra Number. Charles Dickens.* London: Hodder and Stoughton, 1908.

253 ELLISON, OWEN. *Charles Dickens, Novelist.* London: Sisley's, 1908.

254 JACKSON, HOLBROOK. "Charles Dickens." *Great English Novelists,* 215-54. London: Grant Richards, 1908.

255 MORE, PAUL E. "The Praise of Dickens." *Shelburne Essays,* 5th series, 22-44. New York: Putnam, 1908.

256 MUNRO, WILLIAM A. *Charles Dickens et Alphonse Daudet: Romanciers de l'Enfant et des Humbles.* Toulouse: Edouard Privat, 1908.

257 PUGH, EDWIN. *Charles Dickens: the Apostle of the People.* London: New Age Press, 1908.

258 STEPHEN, SIR LESLIE. "Dickens, Charles." *Dictionary of National Biography* V:925-37. London: Smith, Elder, 1908.

259 ROBERTS, HELEN. "The Idea of Friendship (as Revealed in the Works of Dickens)." *Dickensian* 4 (Feb. 1908):38-40; (Mar. 1908): 72-73.

260 BOSWELL, CLARENCE. "Charles Dickens as an Artist." *Dickensian* 4 (Mar. 1908):69-72. [Dickens' sketches of characters, printed here for first time.]

261 MACHEN, ARTHUR. "The Art of Dickens." *Academy* 74 (Apr. 1908) 664-66.

262 "OLD FLEET." "Dickens's Women Characters." *Dickensian* 4 (Apr. 1908):92-95; (May 1908):127-29.

263 MATZ, BERTRAM W. "Dickens as a Journalist." *Fortnightly Review* 83 (May 1908):817-32.

264 LEFFMAN, HENRY. "German Appreciation of Dickens." *Dickensian* 4 (Oct. 1908):262-64; (Nov. 1908):295-97.

265 ASHBY-NORRIS, E. E. "The Domestic Atmosphere in Dickens's Novels." *Dickensian* 4 (Nov. 1908):288-90.

266 CHESTERTON, GILBERT K. "The Immortality of Dickens." *Dickensian* 4 (Nov. 1908):285-87.

267 EARLE, ANNE M. "Charles Dickens, 1812-1870, in London and Rochester." *Book News* 27 (Nov. 1908):155-62.

268 YEIGH, FRANK. "Popularity of Charles Dickens in Canada." *Book News* 27 (Nov. 1908):163-70.

269 BURTON, RICHARD. "Dickens." *Masters of the English Novel: a Study of Principles and Personalities,* 175-94. New York: Henry Holt, 1909.

270 CHESTERTON, GILBERT K. "Dickensian." *Tremendous Trifles,* 96-103. London: Methuen, 1909.

271 PHILIP, ALEX J. and W. L. GADD. *A Dickens Dictionary.* [The characters and scenes of the novels and miscellaneous works alphabetically arranged.] New York: Dutton, 1909. 2nd edition, revised and enlarged. London: Simpkin, Marshall, 1928.

272 SHORE, WILLIAM T. *Charles Dickens and His Friends.* London: Cassell, 1909.

273 DICKENS, MARY A. "England's Gratitude to Dickens." *Dickensian* 5 (Jan. 1909):9-12.

274 "Charles Dickens Acting in 'The Lighthouse'." *Dickensian* 5 (Apr. 1909):91-94. [A drama by Collins.]

275 MATCHETT, WILLOUGHBY. "Dickens in Bayham Street."
Dickensian 5 (June 1909):147-52; (July 1909):180-84. [Dickens'
first London home, the back room that figured in his writing,
especially *David Copperfield* and *A Christmas Carol.*]

276 YOUNG, R. T. "Dickens's Use of the Word 'Gentleman'." *Dickensian*
5 (June 1909):154-58.

277 "Dickens and the Law." *Dickensian* 5 (July 1909):185-86.

278 SUDDABY, JOHN. "A Theatrical Evening in 1838: 'Jim Crow,' 'Mr
Ferguson,' and 'Pickwickians'." *Dickensian* 5 (July 1909):173-78.
[Piracy of Dickens' works.]

279 W., M. "George Meredith and Dickens." *Dickensian* 5 (July 1909):179.

280 LEFFMAN, HENRY. "Charles Dickens as a Nature-Faker." *Dickensian*
5 (Aug. 1909):213-16. [Dickens' attitude to phenomena in nature,
especially animals.]

281 WELCH, DESHLER. "Dickens in Genoa." *Harper's Monthly Magazine*
119 (Aug. 1909):374-82.

282 HUNTER, R. W. G. "Charles Dickens and Bulwer Lytton." *Dickensian*
5 (Sept. 1909):245-47. [The influence of Dickens on the third and
last stage of Lytton's writing.]

283 DAVIS, GEORGE W. "Dickens and Birmingham." *Dickensian* 5
(Oct. 1909):260-61. [The role of Birmingham in Dickens' works and
in his life.]

284 MAURICE, ARTHUR B. "Dickens as an Editor." *Bookman* 30
(Oct. 1909):111-14.

285 *The Bookman Extra Number. Charles Dickens.* London: Hodder and
Stoughton, 1910.

286 CHAPMAN, E. M. "The Masters of Fiction – Dickens." *English
Literature in Account with Religion, 1800-1900*, 272-86. Boston:
Houghton, Mifflin, 1910.

287 FITZGERALD, S. J. ADAIR. *Dickens and the Drama.* New York:
Scribner, 1910.

288 FYFE, THOMAS A. *Charles Dickens and the Law.* London: Chapman
and Hall; Edinburgh: W. Hodge, 1910.

289 HAMMERTON, SIR JOHN A. *The Dickens Companion: A Book of
Anecdote and Reference.* Vol. 18 of *Works of Charles Dickens*, ed.
J. A. Hammerton. Library edition. 18 vols. London: Educational
Book Co., 1910. [Biographical narrative with extracts, list of
authorities, short-title bibliography, etc.]

290 HAMMERTON, SIR JOHN A. *The Dickens Picture Book: A Record
of Dickens Illustrators.* Vol. 17 of *Works of Charles Dickens*, ed. J. A.
Hammerton. Library edition. 18 vols. London: Educational Book Co.,
1910.

291 HARRIS, EDWIN. *Gad's Hill Place and Charles Dickens.* Rochester, Eng.: Edwin Harris, 1910.

292 SMITH, MABEL S., ed. *Studies in Dickens.* New York: Chautaqua Press, 1910. [Reviews, appreciations.]

293 DICKENS, SIR HENRY F. "Dickens at Work." *Lloyd's Weekly News* (Feb. 6, 1910).

294 CHESTERTON, GILBERT K. "Dickens and Snobbishness." *Dickensian* 6 (Mar. 1910):67-68.

295 STONE, MARCUS. "Some Recollections of Dickens." *Dickensian* 6 (Mar. 1910):61-64.

296 DOUGHTY, LADY. "Dickens's Child Characters." *Dickensian* 6 (Apr. 1910):89-91.

297 SUDDABY, JOHN. "The Wrecked Dying-Child Near Natal: Its Life-long Effects on Dickens." *Dickensian* 6 (Apr. 1910):92-98. [Of the East Indiaman, "Grosvenor" and the death of the only child on board.]

298 SUDDABY, JOHN. *"Master Humphrey's Clock."* *Dickensian* 6 (Sept. 1910):236-40.

299 DAVEY, HENRY. "Dickens at Brighton." *Dickensian* 6 (Oct. 1910): 257-61.

300 "MUSIKER." "Brothers and Sisters in Dickens." *Dickensian* 6 (Oct. 1910):268-70.

301 SNYDER, J. F. "Charles Dickens in Illinois." *Journal of the Illinois State Historical Society* 3 (Oct. 1910):7-22.

302 MATZ, BERTRAM W. "Charles Dickens and Reform." *Bookman* 39 (supplement, Nov. 1910):79-86. Reprinted in *The Bookman Extra Number* (1914):186-93.

303 BLATHWAYT, RAYMOND. "Reminiscences of Dickens: An Interview with Mr Alfred Tennyson Dickens." *Great Thoughts* 9 (Nov. 12, 1910):104-5.

304 MATCHETT, WILLOUGHBY. "The Lesson of 'Hunted Down.'" *Dickensian* 6 (Dec. 1910):316-18.

305 CANNING, ALBERT S. *Dickens and Thackeray Studied in Three Novels.* London: T. F. Unwin, 1911. [*Pickwick, Nickleby, Vanity Fair.*]

306 CHESTERTON, GILBERT K. *Appreciations and Criticisms of Charles Dickens.* New York: Dutton; London: Dent, 1911. Reprinted from the Everyman edition of the works of Dickens. Reprinted as *Criticisms and Appreciations of Dickens*, 1933.

307 GRECH, WYNDHAM L. *Charles Dickens in His Works.* Valetta, Malta: Daily Malta Chronicle Office, 1911.

308 HERVIER, PAUL-LOUIS. *Charles Dickens.* (The Anecdotal and Picturesque Life of the Great Writers.) Paris: Société des Éditions Louis-Michard, 1911.

309 "Introduction." *Works of Charles Dickens.* 25 vols. New York: Collier [1911].

310 KITTON, FREDERIC G. *The Dickens Country.* London: A. and C. Black, 1911.

311 MOSES, BELLE. *Charles Dickens and His Girl Heroines.* New York: Appleton, 1911.

312 WALTERS, J. CUMING. *Phases of Dickens: The Man, his Message, and his Mission.* London: Chapman and Hall, 1911.

313 WILKINS, W. GLYDE. *Charles Dickens in America.* London: Chapman and Hall, 1911.

314 MACKAY, WILLIAM. "Charles Dickens and Harrison Ainsworth." *Dickensian* 7 (Apr. 1911):91-92.

315 LANG, ANDREW. "A Mystery of Dickens." *Blackwood's Magazine* 189 (May 1911):670-81.

316 PERUGINI, KATE DICKENS. "My Father's Love for Children." *Dickensian* 7 (May 1911):117-19.

317 MATCHETT, WILLOUGHBY. "Dickens at Wellington House Academy." *Dickensian* 7 (June 1911):145-49; (July 1911):180-84; (Aug. 1911):212-15.

318 NORRIS, E. ASHBY. "Dickens and Children." *Dickensian* 7 (June 1911):151-53; (July 1911):190-93.

319 EDMONDS, W. E. "The Dramatic Power of Dickens." *Queen's Quarterly* 19 (July-Sept. 1911):31-38.

320 WALTERS, J. CUMING. "Some Notes on Plagiarism: Charles Reade and Charles Dickens on Patents." *Dickensian* 7 (July 1911):173-77.

321 PERUGINI, KATE DICKENS. "The Thackeray Celebrations: Thackeray and My Father." *Pall Mall Magazine* 48 (Aug. 1911): 213-19.

322 SUDDABY, JOHN. "Dickens's Pen Pictures of the Seasons." *Dickensian* 7 (Aug. 1911):201-5 (Pt. 1, "Time, The Year, and Their Changes"); (Sept. 1911):243-47 (Pt. 2, "The Passing of Time and the Year Described").

323 DICKENS, ALFRED T. "My Father and His Friends." *Nash's Magazine* 4 (Sept. 1911):627-41.

324 SALA, GEORGE A. "Recollections of Charles Dickens by A Schoolfellow and Friend." *Dickensian* 7 (Sept. 1911):229-31.

325 SHAW, J. "Dickens in Devonshire Terrace." *Dickensian* 7 (Sept. 1911): 233-36.

326 DICKENS, MARY A. "My Grandfather as I Knew Him." *Nash's Magazine* 5 (Oct. 1911):100-10.

327 SACK, O. "Charles Dickens and Bristol." *Dickensian* 7 (Oct. 1911): 260-64.

328 WILKINS, W. GLYDE. "Charles Dickens and Madame Celeste." *Dickensian* 7 (Oct. 1911):260-73. [Actess and danseuse who played Mme Defarge on stage.]

329 LAWRENSON, WINIFRED J. "Dickens's Objectionable Characters." *Dickensian* 7 (Nov. 1911):295-97.

330 RINGWALT, MAY C. "Charles Dickens – His Visits to America." *Americana* 6 (Nov. 1911):1062-66.

331 *The Bookman Extra Number. Charles Dickens.* London: Hodder and Stoughton, 1912. Reprinted 1914. [Special centenary issue of *The Bookman.*]

332 CANNING, ALBERT S. *Dickens Studied in Six Novels.* London: T. F Unwin, 1912. [*Oliver Twist, Old Curiosity Shop, Barnaby Rudge, Martin Chuzzlewit, David Copperfield, Edwin Drood.*]

333 EDWARDS, OSMAN. *The Value of Dickens.* London: F. J. Parsons, 1912.

334 EICHLER, M. M. "Dickens and the Jews." *Jewish Exponent* 54 (1912):9+.

335 FITZGERALD, PERCY H. "Some Memories of Dickens and *Household Words.*" *The Dickens Souvenir,* ed. Dion Clayton Calthrop and Max Pemberton, 22-28. London: Chapman and Hall, 1912.

336 FREYMOND, R. *Der Einfluss von Charles Dickens auf Gustav Freytag.* (Prager deutsche Studien 19). Prague: 1912.

337 JACKSON, JOSEPH. *Dickens in Philadelphia.* Philadelphia: W. J. Campbell, 1912.

338 IPSEN, ALFRED. *Charles Dickens: Hans Liv og Gerning.* København Nationale Forfatteres, 1912.

339 KOHUT, GEORGE A. *Charles Dickens and the Jews.* A Contribution to the Dickens' Centenary (February 7, 1912). Philadelphia: Dickens Fellowship, 1912.

340 LANG, ANDREW. "Dickens." *History of English Literature,* 612-16. London: Longmans, Green, 1912.

341 LIGHTWOOD, JAMES T. *Charles Dickens and Music.* London: Kelly 1912.

342 MATZ, BERTRAM W. "Introduction." *Gone Astray.* London: Chapman and Hall, 1912. ["Gone Astray" first published in *Household Words,* August 13, 1853.]

343 PUGH, EDWIN. *The Charles Dickens Originals.* London: T. N. Foulis; New York: Scribner's, 1912. [Some biography; chiefly a study of Dickens' fictional creations.]

344 RUTARI, A. *Charles Dickens.* Leipzig: Bielefeld, 1912.

345 SACK, O. "Charles Dickens and London." *The Bookman Extra Number* (1912):90-100.

346 SANDBERG, LEONARD. *Charles Dickens.* Oslo: Aschehoug, 1912.

347 SHORTER, CLEMENT. "Introductions." Pears' Centenary Edition of Charles Dickens' Christmas Books. [*A Christmas Carol, The Chimes, The Haunted Man, The Battle of Life.*] London: Pears, 1912.

348 SPAVENTA FILIPPI, SILVIO. *Carlo Dickens.* Modena: Formiggini, 1912. Revised edition. Rome: Formiggini, 1924. Reprinted in *L'Umorismo e gli Umoristi ed Altri Saggi.* Milan: Monammi, 1932.

349 SWINBURNE, ALGERNON C. "Dickens." *The Bookman Extra Number* (1912):83.

350 SWINBURNE, ALGERNON C. "The Greatness of Dickens." *The Bookman Extra Number* (1912):181-85.

351 THOMSON, W. R. *In Dickens Street.* Glasgow: John Smith; London: Chapman and Hall, 1912.

352 WATSON, WILLIAM. "The Centenary of Dickens." *The Bookman Extra Number* (1912):179-80.

353 WATTS-DUNTON, THEODORE. "Dickens Returns on Christmas Day." *The Bookman Extra Number* (1912):120-78.

354 WHIPPLE, EDWIN P. *Charles Dickens: The Man and his Work.* 2 vols. Introd. Arlo Bates. Boston: Houghton, Mifflin, 1912.

355 DEXTER, WALTER. "Charles Dickens, the Man and his Work." *England Illustrated* 46 (Jan. 1912):374-86.

356 DICKENS, ALFRED T. "New Chapters From the Life of Dickens." *Cosmopolitan Magazine* 52 (Jan. 1912):148-59.

357 DICKENS, MARY. "My Father in His Home Life." *Ladies' Home Journal* 29 (Jan. 1912):15.

358 ESCOTT, THOMAS H. S. "Charles Dickens: His Work, Age and Influence." *London Quarterly Review* 117 (Jan. 1912):29-47.

359 ESCOTT, THOMAS H. S. "Literature and Journalism." *Fortnightly Review* 91 (Jan. 1912):115-30. [Dickens' influence on Victorian taste.]

360 ORR, LYNDON. "Charles Dickens – His Love Affairs." *Munsey* 46 (Jan. 1912):490-96.

361 ANDERSON, KATE. "Scenery and the Weather in Dickens." *The Dial* 16 (Feb. 1912):115-16.

362 CROTHERS, SAMUEL M. "The Obviousness of Dickens." *Century Magazine* (Feb. 1912):560-74. Reprinted in *Humanly Speaking.* Boston: Houghton, Mifflin, 1912.

363 "Dickens and London." *Bookman* 41 (Feb. 1912):238-46.

364 FIGGIS, DARRELL. "Praise of Dickens." *Nineteenth Century* 71 (Feb. 1912):274-84; *Living Age* 272 (Mar. 1912):524-32. Reprinted in *Studies and Appreciations.* London: Dent, 1912.

365 LEY, J. W. T. "Charles Dickens: His Universal Appeal." *Dickensian* 8 (Feb. 1912):33-36.

366 JEROME, JEROME K. "Dickens." *Pall Mall Gazette* (Feb. 7, 1912).

367 CLUTTON-BROCK, A. "Dickens." *Times Literary Supplement* (Feb. 8, 1912):48-49. Reprinted in *Essays on Books.* London: Methuen, 1920.

368 "Articles Which Appeared on February 7, 1912." *Dickensian* 8 (Mar. 1912):81-82.

369 BENSON, ARTHUR C. "Charles Dickens." *North American Review* 195 (Mar. 1912):382-91.

370 "In Praise of Dickens: Some Centenary Tributes." *Dickensian* 8 (Mar. 1912):70-72.

371 MATZ, BERTRAM W. "Charles Dickens as Editor." *Dickensian* 8 (Mar. 1912):73-74.

372 RITCHIE, LADY ANNE THACKERAY. "Charles Dickens as I Remember Him." *Pall Mall Magazine* 49 (Mar. 1912):301-9.

373 DAVIES, MABEL R. "Some of Dickens's Good and Bad Men." *Dickensian* 8 (Apr. 1912):96-97; (May 1912):132-34.

374 LANSDEN, J. N. "Charles Dickens – His Visit to Cairo, Ill." *Illinois Historical Journal* 5 (Apr. 1912):30-40.

375 MEYNELL, ALICE. "Notes of a Reader of Dickens." *Dublin Review* 150 (Apr. 1912):370-84. Reprinted as "Dickens as Man of Letters" in *Hearts of Controversy.* London: Burns and Oates, 1917; and in *Living Age* 69 (May 1912):461-69.

376 NEALE, CHARLES M. "Did Dickens Learn Virgil?" *Dickensian* 8 (Apr. 1912):89-91; (May 1912):123-26.

377 BIRON, H. C. "The Plots of Dickens." *National Review* 59 (May 1912):514-23.

378 CHEVALIER, REV. W. A. C. "Charles Dickens at Gore House." *Dickensian* 8 (May 1912):127-31.

379 NABOKOFF, VLADIMIR. "Charles Dickens: A Russian Appreciation." *Dickensian* 8 (June 1912):145-48; (July 1912):173-76; (Aug. 1912): 201-4. [Father of the novelist, Vladimir Nabokov.]

380 ROBERTS, IDA L. "The Point of View." *Dickensian* 8 (June 1912): 153-54.

381 VAN DYKE, HENRY. "The Good Enchantment of Charles Dickens." *Scribner's Magazine* 51 (June 1912):656-65. Reprinted in *Companionable Books and Their Authors*. London: Hodder and Stoughton, 1922.

382 HUGHES, EILIAN. "Dickens and Love of the Beautiful." *Dickensian* 8 (July 1912):177-81.

383 ALLBUT, ROBERT. "Charles Dickens and Sir Edward Bulwer-Lytton." *Dickensian* 8 (Aug. 1912):204-9.

384 CORFIELD, WILMOT. "'At the Canal', Birmingham." *Dickensian* 8 (Sept. 1912):232-38. [Birmingham – its effects on Dickens' life and fiction.]

385 COPELAND, CHARLES T. "Dickens's Best Book." *Dickensian* 8 (Oct. 1912):268-70. [On the difference of opinion regarding Dickens' "best book".]

386 CROSS, WILBUR L. "The Return to Dickens." *Yale Review* 2 (Oct. 1912):142-62.

387 SHARP, HELENA. "Concerning the Marvellous Memory of Charles Dickens." *Dickensian* 8 (Oct. 1912):257-60.

388 MILLER, WILLIAM. "Charles Dickens and C. Edwards Lester." *Dickensian* 8 (Nov. 1912):295-96.

389 SACK, O. "'Mugby Junction' and the *Grand Magazine*." *Dickensian* 8 (Dec. 1912):323-25.

390 BROWNE, EDGAR. *Phiz and Dickens*. London: J. Nisbet, 1913; New York: Dodd, Mead, 1914.

391 CROTCH, W. WALTER. *Charles Dickens, Social Reformer*. London: Chapman and Hall, 1913.

392 FITZGERALD, PERCY H. *Memories of Charles Dickens*. With an account of *Household Words* and *All the Year Round* and of the contributors thereto. Bristol: J. W. Arrowsmith; London: Simpkin, Marshall, 1913.

393 KEIM, ALBERT and LOUIS LUMET. *Dickens*. Paris: Laffitte, 1913. Translated as *Charles Dickens*. New York: Frederick A. Stokes, 1914.

394 RENTON, RICHARD. "The Two Triumvirates: Concerning a Great Friendship." *John Forster and his Friendships*, 49-93. London: Chapman and Hall, 1913.

395 WALKER, HUGH. "Dickens and Thackeray." *The Literature of the Victorian Era*, 660-706. Cambridge, Eng.: The University Press, 1913.

396 WARNER, CHARLES D. *Charles Dickens: An Appreciation*. Newark, NJ: Carteret Book Club, 1913.

397   WILLIAMS, BRANSBY. *My Sketches From Dickens.* London: Chapman and Hall, 1913.

398   SUDDABY, JOHN. "Home and the Song 'Home! Sweet Home!' Their Enchantment of Dickens." *Dickensian* 9 (Jan. 1913):7-12.

399   WHITE, F. ASHFORD. "In France with Charles Dickens." *Dickensian* 9 (Feb. 1913):37-41; (Mar. 1913):64-68.

400   CROTCH, W. WALTER. "Sportsmen in Dickens' Works." *Windsor* 37 (Mar. 1913):549-59.

401   HANNAM-CLARK, FREDERIC. "The Didactic Humour of Dickens." *Dickensian* 9 (Apr. 1913):98-99; (May 1913):125-27.

402   PUGH, EDWIN. "Dickens Influences." *Dickensian* 9 (June 1913): 145-48.

403   LEY, J. W. T. "Dickens and Macready: an Undivided Friendship." *Dickensian* 9 (Aug. 1913):201-06; (Sept. 1913):237-43.

404   SPRIGGE, S. S. "Medicine of Charles Dickens." *Cornhill Magazine* 35 (Aug. 1913):258-67.

405   CROTCH, W. WALTER. "Lawyers in Dickens' Works." *Windsor* 38 (Sept. 1913):409-18.

406   WILKINS, W. GLYDE. "Dickens and His First American Publishers." *Dickensian* 9 (Oct. 1913):257-61.

407   LEY, J. W. T. "Dickens and Ainsworth: Boz's First Friend." *Dickensian* 9 (Nov. 1913):285-88; (Dec. 1913):315-18.

408   ROBERTS, HELEN. "Could Dickens Describe a Gentleman?" *Dickensian* 9 (Nov. 1913):292-95; (Dec. 1913):325-27.

409   MAXWELL, WILLIAM B. "Introduction." *American Notes.* Waverley Edition. London: Waverley Book Co., 1913-15.

410   RIDGE, W. PETT. "Introduction." *Uncommercial Traveller.* Waverley Edition. London: Waverley Book Co., 1913-15.

411   "Charles Dickens: Some Personal Recollections and Opinions." *The Bookman Extra Number* (1914):102-17.

412   CHESTERTON, GILBERT K. "Charles Dickens." *The Bookman Extra Number* (1914):7-11.

413   KITTON, FREDERIC G. "The Life and Works of Charles Dickens." *The Bookman Extra Number* (1914):12-19.

414   MATZ, BERTRAM W. "Charles Dickens: His Work and Personality." *The Bookman Extra Number* (1914):20-25.

415   NOYES, ALFRED. "Dickens and Mr Chesterton." *The Bookman Extra Number* (1914):194-202.

416   PHELPS, WILLIAM L. "Dickens." *Essays on Books,* 178-91. New York: Macmillan, 1914.

417 PUGH, EDWIN. "Dickens as Social and Literary Force." *Dickensian* 10 (Jan. 1914):5-9.

418 LEY, J. W. T. "Dickens and Talfourd: An Early and Deeply Rooted Acquaintance." *Dickensian* 10 (Apr. 1914):89-94.

419 CLARKE, E. "Law and Charles Dickens." *Cornhill Magazine* 36 (May 1914):637-49.

420 FREEMANTLE, W. T. "Charles Dickens and His Visits to Sheffield." *Dickensian* 10 (May 1914):117-22; (June 1914):152-57; (July 1914): 185-89.

421 SUDDABY, JOHN. "Tom Ellar Once Harlequin to Grimaldi: How Boz Declined to Edit His Life." *Dickensian* 10 (May 1914):123-27.

422 SHAW, GEORGE BERNARD. "On Dickens." *Dickensian* 10 (June 1914):150-51. Reprinted in *The Bookman Extra Number* (1914):103-4.

423 DICKENS, SIR HENRY F. "Chat About Dickens." *Harper's Magazine* 129 (July 1914):186-93.

424 LEY, J. W. T. "'Uncle Mark': Dickens's Friendship With Mark Lemon." *Dickensian* 10 (Aug. 1914):201-6.

425 WILKINS, W. GLYDE. "Dickens and Longfellow." *Dickensian* 10 (Sept. 1914):242-44; (Oct. 1914):273-76.

426 HILL, THOMAS W. "Charles Dickens and War." *Dickensian* 10 (Oct. 1914):257-62.

427 LEY, J. W. T. "'Dear Old Mac': The Friendship of Dickens and Maclise." *Dickensian* 10 (Nov. 1914):285-89; (Dec. 1914):315-18.

428 CROTCH, W. WALTER. *The Pageant of Dickens.* London: Chapman and Hall, 1915.

429 GEISSENDOERFER, JOHN T. *Dickens' Einfluss auf Ungern-Sternberg, Hesslein, Stolle, Raabe und Ebner-Eschenbach. Americana-Germanica* 19 (1915).

430 POWYS, JOHN C. "Dickens." *Visions and Revisions,* 119-31. New York: Shaw, 1915. Reprinted with new preface. London: Macdonald, 1955.

431 WILKINS, W. GLYDE, ed. *Report of the Dickens Dinner, June 25, 1841.* Cedar Rapids, Iowa: Privately printed, 1915. [Edited reprint of report of Dickens' speech as given by *Edinburgh Advertiser* (June 30, 1841).]

432 PEARSON, E. KENDALL. "Charles Dickens and Ross: When the American Reading Tour was Decided Upon." *Dickensian* 11 (Jan. 1915):5-9.

433 VAN NOORDEN, C. "Dickens as a Reporter." *Bookman* 47 (Feb. 1915):148-49.

434   LEACOCK, STEPHEN. "A Dickens Fireside Fantasy." *Bookman* (NY) 41 (Apr. 1915):169-78.

435   LITTLE, G. LEON. "Minor Characters of Dickens." *Dickensian* 11 (Apr. 1915):97-99; (May 1915):132-33.

436   WALTERS, J. CUMING. "Dickens' Secret." *Bookman* 48 (Apr. 1915): 20-21.

437   SUDDABY, JOHN. "Charles Dickens and Mary Elizabeth Braddon." *Dickensian* 11 (May 1915):117-20.

438   LEY, J. W. T. "Boz and Phiz: Centenary of Hablôt Knight Browne's Birth." *Dickensian* 11 (June 1915):145-53.

439   WALTERS, J. CUMING. "Foreign War or Home Reform? A Problem that Troubled Dickens." *Dickensian* 11 (Aug. 1915):201-8.

440   CROTCH, W. WALTER. "Dickens and War Muddles." *Dickensian* 11 (Sept. 1915):229-33.

441   SUDDABY, JOHN. "The Shaw Academy Trials." *Dickensian* 11 (Sept. 1915):260-69.

442   WILKINS, W. GLYDE. "Charles Dickens and Professor Felton." *Dickensian* 11 (Sept. 1915):243-44; (Oct. 1915):274-77.

443   HOOD, ARTHUR. "Charles Dickens and Love." *Dickensian* 11 (Oct. 1915):265-69.

444   MATCHETT, WILLOUGHBY. "Dickens and Some Modern Authors." *Dickensian* 11 (Oct. 1915):271-74; (Nov. 1915):299-301; (Dec. 1915): 322-23.

445   LEY, J. W. T. "Dickens and Our Allies." *Dickensian* 11 (Nov. 1915): 285-90.

446   WEBLING, PEGGY. "Dickens on Animals." *Dickensian* 11 (Nov. 1915):292-94.

447   CROTCH, W. WALTER. *The Soul of Dickens.* London: Chapman and Hall, 1916.

448   DIBELIUS, WILHELM. *Charles Dickens.* Leipzig, Berlin: Teubner, 1916. 2nd edition, 1926.

449   LEACOCK, STEPHEN. "Fiction and Reality: A Study of the Art of Charles Dickens." *Essays and Literary Studies,* 159-88. London: John Lane, 1916.

450   "Dickens and Social Reform." *Rice Institute Pamphlet* 3 (Jan. 1916): 3-22.

451   MATZ, BERTRAM, W. "Christina Weller: A Friend of Dickens." *Dickensian* 12 (Jan. 1916):8-13.

452   PUGH, EDWIN. "The Sailors and Soldiers of Dickens." *Dickensian* 12 (Feb. 1916):33-37.

453 PUGH, EDWIN. "Dickens as a Social Reformer." *Bookman* 49 (Mar. 1916):188-89.

454 HILL, THOMAS W. "A Dickensian's View of Shakespeare." *Dickensian* 12 (Apr. 1916):93-97.

455 PHILLIPS, T. M. "Dickens and the Comic Spirit." *Dickensian* 12 (Apr. 1916):100-3; (May 1916):130-32.

456 JEFFERY, SIDNEY. "Dickens and Peace." *Dickensian* 12 (May 1916):117-20.

457 LEY, J. W. T. "Dickens and Walter Savage Landor, a Much Esteemed Friend." *Dickensian* 12 (June 1916):145-54.

458 CROTCH, W. WALTER. "Dickens as Educational Reformer: A Fragment." *Dickensian* 12 (July 1916):177-78.

459 McNULTY, J. H. "The Dethronement of Dickens." *Dickensian* 12 (July 1916):185-88.

460 MATZ, BERTRAM W. "John Pritt Harley: One of Dickens's Actor Friends." *Dickensian* 12 (Aug. 1916):201-7.

461 WILKINS, W. GLYDE. "Charles Dickens and Washington Irving." *Dickensian* 12 (Aug. 1916):216-21; (Sept. 1916):246-49; (Oct. 1916): 274-77.

462 HILL, THOMAS W. "The Poetic Instinct of Dickens." *Dickensian* 12 (Oct. 1916):272-74; (Nov. 1916):293-96.

463 WILSON, JOHN (Christopher North, pseud.). "Charles Dickens." *Dickensian* 12 (Oct. 1916):257-62.

464 LEY, J. W. T. "Dickens and Carlyle." *Dickensian* 12 (Dec. 1916): 313-16.

465 GORDON, ELIZABETH H. *The Naming of Characters in the Works of Charles Dickens.* Lincoln: Univ. of Nebraska Press, 1917.

466 HUTTON, LAURENCE. "Charles Dickens 1812-1870." *Library of the World's Best Literature, Ancient and Modern,* ed. Charles D. Warner, VIII:4625-4688. New York: Warner Library Co., 1917.

467 SCHOLES, PERCY A. "Dickens and Music." *Everyman and His Music,* 114-17. London: Kegan, Paul, Trench, Trubner, 1917.

468 WILKINS, W. GLYDE. "Dickens and James T. Fields." *Dickensian* 13 (Mar. 1917):61-64; (Apr. 1917):101-03.

469 MATCHETT, WILLOUGHBY. "Dickens as a Master of Words." *Dickensian* 13 (Apr. 1917):89-91; (May 1917):129-30.

470 THRUSH, ARTHUR. "Dickens and Ben Jonson – A Comparison." *Dickensian* 13 (Apr. 1917):96-98.

471 FITZGERALD, S. J. ADAIR. "Dickens and the Stage." *Dickensian* 13 (May 1917):124-26.

472 LEY, J. W. T. "Dickens and Douglas Jerrold: A Well-Loved Friend."
     Dickensian 13 (May 1917):117-21; (June 1917):153-56.

473 MILLER, WILLIAM and THOMAS W. HILL. "Charles Dickens's
     Manuscripts." *Dickensian* 13 (July 1917):181-85; (Aug. 1917):
     217-19.

474 LEY, J. W. T. "John Leech: Dickens's Friendship With the Great
     Punch Artist." *Dickensian* 13 (Aug. 1917):202-7.

475 PALLEN, CONDÉ B. "Dickens the Realist." *Dickensian* 13
     (Sept. 1917):236-39.

476 CROTCH, W. WALTER. "Dickens and Ibsen: A Comparison and a
     Contrast." *Dickensian* 13 (Oct. 1917):258-60.

477 "Dickens in America, 1842." *Magazine of History* 25 (Nov.-Dec. 1917):
     152-53.

478 McNULTY, J. H. "Dickens and Meredith: A Comparison and
     Contrast." *Dickensian* 13 (Nov. 1917):292-95.

479 CLARK, CUMBERLAND. *Charles Dickens and His Jewish Characters.*
     London: Chiswick Press, 1918.

480 CLARK, CUMBERLAND. *Shakespeare and Dickens.* London:
     Chiswick Press, 1918.

481 CLARK, CUMBERLAND. *The Story of a Great Friendship: Dickens
     and Clarkson Stanfield.* With seven unpublished letters. London:
     Chiswick Press, 1918.

482 DAVIS, ELIZA, ed. *Charles Dickens and his Jewish Characters.*
     Introd. Cumberland Clark. London: Chiswick Press, 1918.

483 LEY, J. W. T. *The Dickens Circle.* London: Chapman and Hall, 1918.

484 LEY, J. W. T. "Dickens and Sir Arthur Helps." *Dickensian* 14
     (Feb. 1918):38-41.

485 WILKINS, W. GLYDE. "The Guild of Literature and Art." *Dickensian*
     14 (Mar. 1918):61-63; (Apr. 1918):98-101.

486 LEY, J. W. T. "Dickens and Lord Jeffrey: Great Critic's Affection
     for Boz." *Dickensian* 14 (Apr. 1918):93-96; (May 1918):124-26;
     (June 1918):161-63.

487 MATCHETT, WILLOUGHBY. "The Chopped-Up Murdered Man."
     Dickensian 14 (May 1918):117-19. [About Waterloo Bridge Mystery
     of 1857 to which Dickens refers in "Night Walks" in *The Uncommer-
     cial Traveller.*]

488 JACKSON, JOSEPH. "Poe's Signature to 'The Raven.'" *Sewanee
     Review* 26 (July-Sept. 1918):272-75.

489 LASKI, E. de. "The Psychological Attitude of Dickens Towards
     Surnames." *American Journal of Psychology* 29 (July 1918):337-46.

490 CREES, J. H. E. "Dickens and Meredith." *Dickensian* 14 (Sept. 1918):
     234-35.

491 WALTERS, J. CUMING. "Dickens and Captain Marryat." *Dickensian* 14 (Oct. 1918):265-68.

492 RALEIGH, SIR WALTER. "The Hypocrite: Shakespearian and Dickensian." *Dickensian* 14 (Nov. 1918):297.

493 SUDDABY, JOHN. "Was Dickens a Christmas Renegade?" *Dickensian* 14 (Nov. 1918):285-88; (Dec. 1918):326-30.

494 WALTERS, J. CUMING. "The Friends of Dickens." *Dickensian* 14 (Nov. 1918):289-91.

495 CROTCH, W. WALTER. "Dickens and Reconstruction." *Dickensian* 14 (Dec. 1918):316-19.

496 BROWNING, ELIZABETH BARRETT. *Charles Dickens and Other "Spirits of the Age" Discussed and Analysed.* London: T. J. Wise, 1919. [Two letters to R. H. Horne.]

497 BURTON, RICHARD. *Charles Dickens: How to Know Him.* Indianapolis: Bobbs-Merrill, 1919.

498 CLARK, CUMBERLAND. *Dickens and Talfourd.* London: Chiswick Press, 1919.

499 CROTCH, W. WALTER. *The Secret of Dickens.* London: Chapman and Hall, 1919.

500 DARK, SIDNEY. *Charles Dickens.* London: T. Nelson, 1919.

501 HAMILTON, WALTER J. *A Dickens Legend: An Interpretation.* London: Miller, 1919.

502 PHILLIPS, WALTER C. *Dickens, Reade and Collins, Sensation Novelists.* A Study in the Conditions and Theories of Novel Writing in Victorian England. New York: Columbia Univ. Press, 1919; New York: Russell and Russell, 1962.

503 CASTIEAU, JOHN B. "Dickens and His Critics." *Dickensian* 15 (Jan. 1919):30-36.

504 MATCHETT, WILLOUGHBY. "Dickens and Pinero." *Dickensian* 15 (Jan. 1919):19-23.

505 PEEKE, H. L. "Charles Dickens in Ohio in 1842." *Ohio State Archaeological and Historical Quarterly* 28 (Jan. 1919):72-81.

506 PHILLIPS, T. M. "Life and Art in Dickens and Henry James." *Manchester Quarterly* 38 (Jan. 1919):20-31.

507 WAUGH, ARTHUR. "Dickens's Lovers." *Dickensian* 15 (Jan. 1919): 8-18.

508 SWEETSER, KATE D. "Dining with Dickens at Delmonico's." *Bookman* 49 (Mar. 1919):20-28.

509 "Charles Dickens: An American View." *Dickensian* 15 (Apr. 1919): 86-89. [Reprinted from magazine, *Common Sense.*]

510 LEY, J. W. T. "Douglas Jerrold." *Dickensian* 15 (Apr. 1919):82-86.

511 WALTERS, J. CUMING. "The Humanism of Dickens." *Dickensian* 15 (Apr. 1919):78-80.

512 CROTCH, W. WALTER. "The Decline – and After!" *Dickensian* 15 (July 1919):121-27. [Reputation of Dickens.]

513 BIRON, H. C. "Dickens' Picture of the Legal World." *National Review* 73 (Aug. 1919):806-13.

514 CHESTERTON, GILBERT K. *Charles Dickens Fifty Years After.* London: C. Shorter, 1920.

515 CHESTERTON, GILBERT K. "Dickens Again." *Uses of Diversity,* 226-32. London: Methuen, 1920.

516 COOPER, THOMAS P. *Dickens Footsteps Series: The Real Micawber.* London: Simkin, Marshall, 1920.

517 CROTCH, W. WALTER. *The Touchstone of Dickens.* London: Chapman and Hall, 1920.

518 DARWIN, SIR FRANCIS. "Charles Dickens." *Springtime and Other Essays,* 199-229. London: J. Murray, 1920.

519 ELTON, OLIVER. "Charles Dickens." *Survey of English Literature: 1830-1880,* II:194-221. London: E. Arnold, 1920. Revised and reprinted in *Dickens and Thackeray.* London: E. Arnold, 1924.

520 HORNE, RICHARD H. *Notes and Comments on Certain Writings in Prose and Verse.* London: R. Clay, 1920.

521 WILLIAMSON, CLAUDE C. "The Humour of Dickens." *Writers of Three Centuries 1789-1914,* 185-91. London: G. Richards, 1920.

522 ZWEIG, STEFAN. *Drei Meister: Balzac, Dickens, Dostoievski.* (Baumeister der Welt 1.) Leipzig: Inselverlag, 1920. "Charles Dickens," trans. Kenneth Burke, *Dial* 74 (Jan. 1923):1-24. Reprinted in *Master Builders,* trans. Eden and Cedar Paul. New York: Viking, 1939.

523 CORELLI, MARIE. "Why Dickens is Popular." *Book Monthly* 15 (Feb. 1920):87-88.

524 CROTCH, W. WALTER. "Why Dickens is Popular." *Book Monthly* 15 (Feb. 1920):92-95.

525 DICKENS, SIR HENRY F. "Why Dickens is Popular." *Book Monthly* 15 (Feb. 1920):85-87.

526 WALTERS, J. CUMING. "Why Dickens is Popular." *Book Monthly* 15 (Feb. 1920):88-92.

527 FITZGERALD, S. J. ADAIR. "Charles Dickens and the St James's Theatre." *Dickensian* 16 (Apr. 1920):67-76.

528 DIBBLE, ROY F. "Charles Dickens: His Reading." *Modern Language Notes* 35 (June 1920):334-39.

529 KENT, W. "Critical Sketch." *Bookman* 58 (June 1920):107-10.

530 SHORTER, CLEMENT K. "Charles Dickens Fifty Years After." *Observer* (June 6), 1920.

531 QUAIL, JESSE. "Charles Dickens and the *Daily News.*" *Nineteenth Century* 88 (Oct. 1920):632-42.

532 ALLEMANDY, VICTOR H. *Notes on Dickens's Christmas Books.* London: Normal Press, 1921.

533 DOERNENBURG, EMIL and WILHELM FEHSE. *Raabe und Dickens: Ein Beitrag zur Erkenntnis der geistigen Gestalt Wilhelm Raabes.* Magdeburg: Creutz, 1921.

534 JOHNSON, NORMAN C. *The Life-Story of Charles Dickens.* London: Stead, 1921.

535 BENSLY, EDWARD. "Charles Dickens at Hazebrouck." *Notes and Queries* 8 (Mar. 1921):207-8.

536 MARKLAND, RUSSELL. "William Challinor: Birth Centenary of a Dickens' Link." *Notes and Queries* 8 (Mar. 1921):186-87.

537 VAN DYKE, CATHERINE. "A Talk With Charles Dickens's Office Boy." *Bookman* 53 (Mar. 1921):49-52.

538 ELLIS, M. A. "Mistranslation in Dickens." *Notes and Queries* 8 (June 1921):487.

539 WIDDEMER, MARGARET. "Dickens's Dolls." *Literary Review* 9 (June 18, 1921):1-2.

540 "Page Headings." *Notes and Queries* 9 (Sept. 1921):208.

541 "'The Beggar's Opera' in Dickens." *Notes and Queries* 9 (Oct. 1921): 309.

542 GROVE, J. S. P. "Dickens, Ramo Samee and the Three Potatoes." *Dickensian* 17 (Oct. 1921):211-14. Reprinted in *Living Age* 311 (Dec. 1921):608-10. [Re "An Unsettled Neighbourhood" in *Household Words*, Nov. 1854, and a source for "Ramo Samee."]

543 SANTAYANA, GEORGE. "Dickens." *Dial* 71 (Nov. 1921):537-49. Reprinted in *Soliloquies in England and Later Soliloquies.* Ann Arbor: Univ. of Michigan Press, 1967. Reprinted in *The Dickens Critics*, ed. G. H. Ford and L. Lane, Jr., 1961 q.v.

544 MABBOTT, THOMAS O. *Dickensian Inns and Taverns.* New York: Scribners, 1922.

545 MATZ, BERTRAM W. *Dickensian Inns and Taverns.* New York: Scribners, 1922.

546 RADLOV, ERNST L. *Čarl's Dikkens.* Berlin-Moscow: Izd. Z. I. Gržebina, 1922.

547 SHETTLE, GEORGE T. "Charles Dickens and the Church." *John Wycliffe and Other Essays*, 49-75. London: R. Jackson, 1922.

548 WOOLCOTT, ALEXANDER. *Mr. Dickens Goes to the Play.* The
     Dickensian Plays, Players, and the Theatre. New York: Putnam, 1922

549 DODDS, M. H. "'The Beggars' Opera' in Dickens." *Notes and Queries*
     10 (Jan. 1922):14,74; (June 1922):437,467; 11 (July 1922):13,27,
     54,71-74; (Aug. 1922):111-13,157; (Oct. 1922):314,356.

550 CHESTERTON, GILBERT K. "Charles Dickens." *Living Age* 312
     (Feb. 1922):480-85; *Dickensian* 18 (Jan. 1922):9-14.

551 "Charles Dickens, His Dislike for Law and Lawyers." *Chambers
     Journal* 12 (Mar. 1922):241-45.

552 HOWE, MARK A. DeWOLFE. "With Dickens in America: New Mate-
     rial From the Papers of Mrs J. T. Fields." *Harper's* 144 (May 1922):
     708-22; 145 (June 1922):110-20.

553 WEEKLEY, ERNEST. "Mrs Gamp and the King's English (Cockney).
     Cornhill Magazine 52 (May 1922):565-76.

554 MURRY, JOHN MIDDLETON. "The Dickens Revival." *Times* 19
     (May 1922):16.

555 WILSTACH, FRANK J. "Surtees and Charles Dickens." *New York
     Times Book Review* 23 (July 1922):13,26.

556 MOFFATT, JAMES. "Dickens and Meredith." *Hibbert Journal* 21
     (Oct. 1922):107-20.

557 STUART, E. A. G. "The Dickens Amateurs." *Notes and Queries* 11
     (Oct. 1922):308. [Jonson's *Every Man in His Humour* by Dickens
     and his friends: Sept. 1845, July 1847, Apr.-July 1848, 1850.]

558 WOOLCOTT, ALEXANDER. "Charles Dickens, the Side-tracked
     Actor." *North American Review* 216 (Oct. 1922):513-22. [Dickens'
     plays and readings.]

559 BROWN, T. H. *Charles Dickens, His Life and Work.* London: A. H.
     Stockwell, 1923.

560 CLARK, CUMBERLAND. *Dickens' London.* London: Wass, Pritchard
     1923.

561 COOPER, THOMAS P. *With Dickens in Yorkshire.* Introd. Bertram
     W. Matz. London: Ben Johnson, 1923.

562 DEXTER, WALTER. *The London of Dickens.* London: Palmer,
     1923; New York: Dutton, 1924.

563 HOPKINS, ALBERT A. and NEWBURY F. READ. *A Dickens Atlas:
     Including Twelve Walks in London with Charles Dickens.* New York:
     Hatton Garden Press; London: Spurr and Swift, 1923.

564 LUPTON, EDWARD B. *Dickens, the Immortal.* Kansas City, Mo.:
     A. Fowler; London: Bird, 1923.

565 NICOLL, SIR WILLIAM R. *Dickens's Own Story.* London: Chapman
     and Hall, 1923; New York: Stokes, 1924.

566 SPENCER, WALTER T. "Dickens' Illustrators." *Forty Years in My Bookshop,* 153-61. London: Constable, 1923.

567 HEARN, ARTHUR S. "Dickens' Links with the Town of Reading." *Dickensian* 19 (Jan. 1923):36-37. [Biography and sources for "Sleary" in *Hard Times* and Dotheboys Hall in *Nicholas Nickleby.*]

568 LEY, J. W. T. "A Sledge-Hammer Blow: How *The Chimes* Came to Be Written." *Dickensian* 19 (Apr. 1923):86-89.

569 WHIBLEY, CHARLES. "A Study of Charles Dickens." *Dickensian* 19 (Apr. 1923):65-70.

570 "Dickens at Gad's Hill Place." *Bookman* 64 (July 1923):183-84. [Duplicates 571.]

571 HOME, MAJOR GORDON. "Dickens at Gad's Hill Place." *Bookman* 64 (July 1923):183-84. [Duplicates 570.]

572 O'CONNOR, T. P. "The Genius of Dickens." *Dickensian* 19 (July 1923):121-22.

573 PUGH, EDWIN. "Dickens and Women." *Dickensian* 19 (July 1923): 123-27.

574 SIMONDS, C. H. "Peter Parley and Dickens." *Dickensian* 19 (July 1923):129-32. [No. 16 of Parley's Illuminated Library is a pirated edition of Dickens' *A Christmas Carol.*]

575 LUCY, SIR HENRY. "Charles Dickens: a Post-Mortem Interview." *Cornhill* 55 (Sept. 1923):295-99.

576 FITZGERALD, S. J. ADAIR. "Charles Dickens in the Fifties." *Dickensian* 19 (Oct. 1923):219-20.

577 TEETGEN, A. B. "Dickens and Some Modern Aspects of Penal Reform." *Contemporary Review* 124 (Oct. 1923):501-8.

578 BERESFORD, J. D. "The Successors of Charles Dickens." *The Nation and the Athenaeum* 34 (Dec. 1923):487.

579 CHANCELLOR, EDWIN B. *The London of Charles Dickens.* Being an account of the haunts of his characters, and the topographical setting of his novels. London: Richards, 1924.

580 DELATTRE, FLORIS. *Dickens.* Paris; Brussels: Renaissance du Livre, 1924.

581 DEXTER, WALTER. *The Kent of Dickens.* London: Palmer, 1924.

582 FRASER, CLAUD L. *Characters From Dickens.* London: T. C. and E. C. Jack, 1924.

583 FURNISS, HARRY. "Charles Dickens as an Actor." *Some Victorian Men,* 183-200. London: John Lane; New York: Dodd, Mead, 1924. [Dickens as actor, reader and speaker.]

584 HAYWARD, ARTHUR L. *The Dickens Encyclopedia.* New York: Dutton; London: Routledge, 1924. Reprinted 1969. [A dictionary of references to characters and places in Dickens' fiction with explanatory notes on obscure allusions and phrases.]

585 LANGSTAFF, JOHN B. David Copperfield's *Library*. Prologue by Sir O. Seaman and epilogue by Alfred Noyes. London: Allen and Unwin, 1924.

586 MATZ, BERTRAM W. *Character Sketches From Dickens*. Introd. Mrs Perugini (Kate Dickens). London: Tuck, 1924.

587 MILLER, LEONARD. *References in the Works of Charles Dickens to Rochester, Chatham and Neighbourhood, and to Persons Resident Therein*. Bath, Eng.: Herald Press, for the Dickens Fellowship, 1924.

588 PERUGINI, KATE DICKENS. "Introduction." *Character Sketches from Dickens*. Comp. B. W. Matz. London: Tuck, 1924. [Selection of incidents and stories.]

589 WILKINS, W. GLYDE. *Dickens in Cartoon and Caricature*. Introd. Bertram W. Matz. Boston: Boston Bibliophile Society, 1924. [Facsimiles with notes and comment.]

590 TYRRELL, T. W. "Charles Dickens, Miss Weller and Mr Birrell." *Notes and Queries* 147 (Nov. 1924):338-39.

591 SMITH, HARRY B. "How Charles Dickens Wrote His Books." *Harper* 150 (Dec. 1924):50-60. Reprinted in *Strand Magazine* (Feb. 1925).

592 CROTHERS, SAMUEL M. *The Children of Dickens*. New York: Scribner, 1925. [Study of child-characters.]

593 DEXTER, WALTER. *The England of Charles Dickens*. London: Palmer, 1925.

594 GRAN, GERHARD VON DER LIPPE. *Charles Dickens*. Oslo: H. Aschebourg, 1925. [In Norwegian.]

595 QUILLER-COUCH, SIR ARTHUR T. *Charles Dickens and Other Victorians*. Cambridge, Eng.: Cambridge Univ. Press, 1925. [See 596.]

596 QUILLER-COUCH, SIR ARTHUR T. "Dickens." *Charles Dickens and Other Victorians*, 1-100. Cambridge, Eng.:Cambridge Univ. Press; New York: Putnam, 1925.

597 STEVENS, JAMES S. "Dickens's Use of the English Bible." *Dickensian* 21 (Jan. 1925):32-34; (Apr. 1925):93-95; (July 1925):152-57; (Oct. 1925):214-18.

598 LEY, J. W. T. "Robert Seymour and Mr. Pickwick." *Dickensian* 21 (July 1925):122-27.

599 WEBER, JESSIE P. "Charles Dickens – Visits to Illinois by Himself and his Sons." *Illinois Historical Journal* 18 (July 1925):390-92.

600 DEXTER, WALTER. "Dickens, the Watsons and Rockingham Castle." *Dickensian* 21 (Oct. 1925):199-204.

601 HUGHES, JAMES L. "Personal Reminiscences Relating to Dickens." *Journal of Education* 101 (Dec. 1925):672-?

602 AMERONGEN, JUDA B. van. *The Actor in Dickens: A Study of the Histrionic and Dramatic Elements in the Novelist's Life and Works.* London: Palmer, 1926; New York: D. Appleton, 1927.

603 APOSTOLOV, NIKOLAY. "Tolstoy and Dickens." *Family Views of Tolstoy,* trans. Maude Aylmer, 71-84. London: Allen and Unwin, 1926.

604 CARLTON, WILLIAM J. *Charles Dickens; Shorthand Writer: The 'Prentice Days of a Master Craftsman.* London: Palmer, 1926. [Dickens as a reporter.]

605 CHARLES, EDWIN. *Some Dickens Women.* Foreword G. K. Chesterton. New York: Stokes; London: T. W. Laurie, 1926.

606 BROWNE, C. L. "Are They Caricatures?" *Papers of the Manchester Literary Club* 52 (1926):34-53.

607 HAYWARD, ARTHUR L. *The Days of Dickens: A Glance at Some Aspects of Early Victorian Life in London.* London: Routledge, 1926.

608 HUMPHREYS, ARTHUR. *Charles Dickens and his First Schoolmaster.* Manchester, 1926. [Identifying him with William Giles, Baptist Minister, the younger, rather than his father.]

609 KENT, WILLIAM R. *With Charles Dickens in the Borough.* London: Hamerland Assn., 1926.

610 PHELPS, WILLIAM L. "Preface." *The Lamplighter. A Farce in One Act and As a Short Story.* New York: Appleton, 1926.

611 DEXTER, WALTER. "Dickens' School Days in London." *Dickensian* 22 (Jan. 1926):45-47.

612 LEY, J. W. T. "History of *The Dickensian.*" *Dickensian* 22 (Jan. 1926): 11-22, 121-29.

613 PEARSON, E. KENDALL. "The Reality of Dickens." *Dickensian* 22 (Jan. 1926):38-42.

614 RAINEY, LILLIAN F. "Dickens Up To Date." *Century* 3 (Feb. 1926): 504-6.

615 WALMSLEY, ELIZABETH. "'New Lamps for Old': Charles Dickens on Art." *Cornhill Magazine* 60 (Feb. 1926):203-12.

616 "DEORAD." "A Mosaic: First Square – The Drama in Dickens. Second Square – The End of Chapter. Third Square – The Poetry of Dickens." *Dickensian* 22 (Apr. 1926):93-95.

617 SADLEIR, MICHAEL. "The Intimacy of Dickens." *Dickensian* 22 (Apr. 1926):106-09.

618 LEY, J. W. T. "Captain Marryat and Dickens." *Dickensian* 22 (Jul.-Sept. 1926):164-67.

619 CASON, CLARENCE E. "Charles Dickens in America Today." *Literary Digest International Book Review* 4 (Sept. 1926):603-7.

620 B., T. J. "Notes on Some Allusions in Dickens." *Dickensian* 22 (Oct. 1926):242-44.

621 GRAY, W. FORBES. "The Edinburgh Relatives and Friends of Dickens." *Dickensian* 22 (Oct. 1926):218-23; 23 (Dec. 1926):17-22. Reprinted as *The Edinburgh Relatives and Friends of Dickens.* Londc Dickens Fellowship, 1927.

622 HOPKINS, ALBERT A. "Eating and Drinking in Dickens." *Dickensia* 22 (Oct. 1926):228-29.

623 STUART-YOUNG, J. M. "On Eyes and Ugliness." *Dickensian* 22 (Oct. 1926):214-17.

624 DU SOIR, A. P. "The Elfin Quality in Dickens." *Dickensian* 23 (Dec. 1926):47-51.

625 SANDERS, H. S. "Imagination." *Dickensian* 23 (Dec. 1926):35-37.

626 WILD, SIR ERNEST. "The Durability of Dickens." *Dickensian* 23 (Dec. 1926):9-11.

627 CONWAY, EUSTACE. "My Dickens Episode." *Anthony Munday and Other Essays,* 100-4. New York: Privately printed, 1927.

628 DELATTRE, FLORIS. *Dickens et la France: Etude d'une Interaction Littéraire Anglo-Française.* Paris: Librairie Universitaire, 1927.

629 DEXTER, WALTER. *Dickens: The Story of the Life of the World's Favourite Author.* London: Dickens Fellowship, 1927.

630 DEXTER, WALTER. *Some Rogues and Vagabonds of Charles Dicker* London: Palmer; Philadelphia: Lippincott, 1927.

631 GALSWORTHY, JOHN. "Six Novelists in Profile." *Castles in Spain and Other Screeds,* 201-35. New York: Scribner, 1927. Reprinted in *Candelabra.* New York: Scribner, 1933.

632 MAUROIS, ANDRÉ. *Un Essai sur Dickens.* Paris: Grasset, 1927. Reprinted in *L'Angleterre Romantique.* Paris: Gallimard, 1953.

633 PAYNE, EDWARD F. *Dickens' Days in Boston: a Record of Daily Events.* Boston: Houghton, Mifflin, 1927.

634 PHELPS, WILLIAM L. "Introduction." *A Christmas Tree* and *What Christmas Is As We Grow Older.* New York: Rimington and Hooper, 1927.

635 BELLOC, HILAIRE. "Dickens Revisited." *New Statesman* 28 (Jan. 1927):444-45.

636 CROSS, A. E. BROOKES. "The Fascination of the Footlights." *Dickensian* 23 (Mar. 1927):85-91.

637 KELLY, KATHARINE. "A Few Remarks on Household Duties [in the Works of Dickens.]" *Dickensian* 23 (Mar. 1927):108-9.

638 BERGER, FRANCESCO. "Memories of Dickens." *Living Age* 332 (Apr. 1927):628-34. [From the *Manchester Guardian* Feb. 7, 1927.]

639 FISHER, W. J. "Influence of Carlyle." *Dickensian* 23 (June 1927): 197-99.

640 PEDRICK, F. G. "Newspaper Instinct." *Dickensian* 23 (June 1927): 167-69.

641 BIBBY, HAROLD. "Charles Dickens – Two Pictures of English Life." *Queen's Quarterly* 35 (July-Sept. 1927):71-81.

642 KIDD, H. H. "Is Dickens Still A Hero." *South Atlantic Quarterly* 26 (July 1927):280-89.

643 ELIOT, T. S. "Wilkie Collins and Dickens." *Times Literary Supplement* (Aug. 4, 1927):525-26. Reprinted in *Selected Essays, 1917-1932.* New York: Harcourt, Brace, 1932; new edition, New York: Harcourt, Brace, 1950; and in *The Dickens Critics,* ed. G. H. Ford and L. Lane, Jr., 1961 q.v.

644 "Dickens as a Reader." *Dickensian* 23 (Sept. 1927):270-76.

645 NOLIN, JOSEPH. "The Appreciation of Dickens by His French Contemporaries." *Dickensian* 23 (Autumn 1927):235-39.

646 WHITING, MARY B. "Mrs Trollope and an Unpublished Letter From Charles Dickens." *Bookman* 73 (Nov. 1927):104-06. [On Mrs. Trollope's novels alongside those of Dickens, with letters from Dickens.]

647 CROWTHER, J. H. "Dickens as a Public Speaker." *Dickensian* 24 (Dec. 1927):46-47.

648 DEXTER, WALTER. "London and Dickens." *Dickensian* 24 (Dec. 1927):67-68.

649 COR, R. *Un Romancier de la Vertu et un Peintre du Vice: Charles Dickens et M. Proust.* Paris: Editions du Capitole, 1928.

650 DICKENS, SIR HENRY F. *Memories of My Father.* London: Gollancz, 1928; New York: Duffield, 1929.

651 DICKENS, MARY. *New Year's Eve Frolic, Twelfth Night Festivities.* Recollections of Charles Dickens by his daughter "Mamie" Dickens. New York: Harmon and Irwin, 1928.

652 HOLDSWORTH, WILLIAM S. *Charles Dickens as a Legal Historian.* New Haven, Conn.: Yale Univ. Press; London: Milford, 1928. [Storrs lectures delivered before the Law School of Yale University, 1927.]

653 MASSON, DAVID. "Dickens and Thackeray." *British Novelists and Their Styles: Being a Critical Sketch of the History of British Prose Fiction.* Boston: W. Small, 1928. Reprinted in *The Dickens Critics,* ed. G. H. Ford and L. Lane, Jr., 1961 q.v.

654 ROBERTS, C. E. BECHHOFER (Ephesian, pseud.). *This Side Idolatry.* London: Mills and Boon, 1928.

655 STRAUS, RALPH. *Charles Dickens: a Biography from New Sources.* New York: Cosmopolitan Book Corp., 1928.

656 STRAUS, RALPH. *Charles Dickens: a Portrait in Pencil.* London: Gollancz, 1928. Reprinted in 1938 as *A Portrait of Dickens.*

657 WIERSTRA, FRANK D. *Smollett and Dickens.* Amsterdam: C. De Boer, 1928.

658 "Dickens's Audiences: Extracts From His Letters." *Dickensian* 24 (Mar.-Sept. 1928):122,199,318; 25 (Dec. 1928):20.

659 "Early Work of Dickens." *Dickensian* 24 (Mar. 1928):147-54.

660 WHITTAKER, RUTH. "Trammels of Passion." *Dickensian* 24 (Mar. 1928):112-15. [Dickens' lovers.]

661 "Dickens's Last Ten Years." *Dickensian* 24 (June 1928):215-22.

662 PAUL, CLAIRE. "Threatened Modernisation of Dickens." *Dickensian* 24 (June 1928):192-94.

663 DICKENS, SIR HENRY F. "Dickens as His Son Remembers Him." *New York Times Magazine* (June 10, 1928):3,16.

664 DICKENS, SIR HENRY F. "Home Life at Gad's Hill." *Times* (June 11, 1928):9.

665 ROE, FRANK G. "Dickens, Thackeray, and the Silhouette." *Connoisseur* 81 (Aug. 1928):231-34.

666 "Berlin Professor's [Wilhelm Dibelius's] Criticism and a Canadian Professor's [F. J. Cross's] Reply." *Dickensian* 24 (Sept. 1928):303-0

667 "First Four Years of Fame." *Dickensian* 24 (Sept. 1928):319-24.

668 PORTER, A. "Dickens and the *Spectator.*" *Spectator* 141 (Sept. 192 320.

669 WALTERS, J. CUMING. "Mr Knag and his Brethren." *Dickensian* 24 (Sept. 1928):279-82.

670 MAUROIS, ANDRÉ. "The Youth of Dickens." *Forum* 80 (Oct. 1928 562-74.

671 CHESTERTON, GILBERT K. "The Popularity of Dickens." *Spectat* 141 (Nov. 1928, Centenary no.):43-44. Reprinted in *Sidelights on New London and Newer York.* New York: Dodd, 1932.

672 FORMAN, W. COURTHOPE. "The Baptism of Charles Dickens." *Notes and Queries* 155 (Nov. 1928):345-46.

673 HAIGHT, SHERMAN P. "George Cruikshank." *Publishers' Weekly* 114 (Nov. 1928):2059-63.

674 MAUROIS, ANDRÉ. "Dickens as a Novelist." *Forum* 80 (Nov. 1928 707-18.

675 DEXTER, WALTER. "[Reply to C. E. Bechhofer Roberts's *This Sid Idolatry*]." *Dickensian* 25 (Dec. 1928):1-18.

676 MACY, JOHN. "Charles Dickens. Household Word." *American Bookman* 68 (Dec. 1928):420-28.

677 WHITTAKER, RUTH. "Joy in Heaven." *Dickensian* 25 (Dec. 1928): 37-39. [Dickens' fools.]

678 BARNES, ALBERT W. *A Dickens Guide.* London: J. Bale, 1929.

679 CHESTERTON, GILBERT K. "Women in Dickens." *GKC as MC,* ed. J. P. de Fonseka, 208-12. London: Methuen, 1929.

680 JEANS, SAMUEL. *Charles Dickens.* London: A. and C. Black, 1929.

681 MORELAND, ARTHUR. *Dickens in London.* Forty-seven drawings with descriptive notes. Introd. Frank S. Johnson. London: Palmer, 1929.

682 PAYNE, EDWARD F. and HENRY H. HARPER. *The Charity of Charles Dickens.* Boston: Bibliophile Society, 1929.

683 PAYNE, EDWARD F. and HENRY H. HARPER. *The Romance of Charles Dickens and Maria Beadnell Winter.* Boston: Bibliophile Society, 1929.

684 PRIESTLEY, J. B. "Dickens." *English Humour,* 150-62. London: Longmans, Green, 1929.

685 STEVENS, JAMES S. *Quotations and References in Charles Dickens.* Boston: Christopher, 1929.

686 WAGENKNECHT, EDWARD. *The Man Charles Dickens: A Victorian Portrait.* Boston: Houghton Mifflin, 1929. Revised edition. Norman: Univ. of Oklahoma Press, 1966.

687 MAUROIS, ANDRÉ. "The Philosophy of Dickens." *Forum* 81 (Jan. 1929):54-59.

688 WAGENKNECHT, EDWARD. "Dickens Himself." *Virginia Quarterly Review* 5 (Jan. 1929):115-32. [Biography, with comments on *This Side Idolatry,* by C. E. Bechhofer Roberts, a novel based on the life of Dickens.]

689 CAMMAERTS, EMILE. "Dickens and Balzac." *Contemporary Review* 135 (Mar. 1929):331-39.

690 SMITH, HARRY B. "Dickens as Don Quixote." *Scribner's* 85 (Apr. 1929):395-404.

691 EDGAR, HERMAN L. and R. G. W. VAIL. "Early American Editions of the Works of Charles Dickens." *Bulletin of the New York Public Library* 33 (May 1929):302-19.

692 WAGENKNECHT, EDWARD. "Dickens and Katherine Mansfield." *Dickensian* 26 (Winter 1929-30):15-23. Reprinted in *Dickens and the Scandalmongers,* 1965 q.v.

693 CLARK, CUMBERLAND. *Dickens and Democracy and Other Studies.* London: Palmer, 1930.

694 DARWIN, BERNARD, ed. *The Dickens Advertiser.* A collection of the advertisements in the original parts of novels by Charles Dickens. London: Mathews and Marrot; New York: Macmillan, 1930.

695 GARRETT, JOHN W. P., ed. *Dickens and Daudet.* London: Dent, 1930.

696 KENT, WILLIAM R. *Dickens and Religion.* London: Watts, 1930.

697 LINDSTROM, E. *Charles Dickens.* Stockholm: Hugo Gebers, 1930.

698 PROCTOR, WILLIAM C. *Christian Teaching in the Novels of Charles Dickens.* London: H. R. Allenson, 1930.

699 SAWYER, C. J. and F. J. H. D. *Dickens v. Barabbas, Forster Intervening.* London: C. J. Sawyer, 1930. [Re some unpublished letters of Forster's.]

700 CIOLKOWSKA, M. "Proust and Dickens." *Times Literary Supplement* (Feb. 19, 1930):135.

701 WAGENKNECHT, EDWARD. "Dickens and Fechter." *Dickensian* 26 (Spring 1930):138-39. Reprinted in *Dickens and the Scandalmongers.* 1965 q.v.

702 YEIGH, FRANK. "Scott, Carlyle, Dickens and Canada." *Queen's Quarterly* 37 (Spring 1930):335-47.

703 ADAMS, MABEL ELLERY. "Dickens's Influence on Education." *Dickensian* 26 (Summer 1930):177-81.

704 DOBBIE, SIR JOSEPH. "Burns and Dickens – the Men and Their Mission." *Dickensian* 26 (Summer 1930):213-18.

705 LEY, J. W. T. "Some Comic Songs that Dickens Knew." *Dickensian* 26 (Summer 1930):189-97; 26 (Autumn 1930):289-95; 27 (Winter 1930-31):33-38.

706 JERROLD, SIDNEY. "Dickens and E. L. Blanchard." *Times Literary Supplement* (July 3, 1930):554.

707 SUMMERS, MONTAGUE. "A Note on Mrs Behn and a Dickens Parallel." *Notes and Queries* 159 (Oct. 1930):274-75.

708 CARDEN, PERCY T. "Roundabout Doctors' Commons." *Dickensian* 27 (Winter 1930-31):7-17.

709 LEY, J. W. T. "Dickens and Surtees." *Dickensian* 27 (Winter 1930-31): 66-68.

710 CHESTERTON, GILBERT K. "On Dickens and After." *Come to Think of It,* 250-60. New York: Dodd, Mead, 1931.

711 LUNACHARSKY, A. and R. ŠOR. *Dikkens.* Moscow-Leningrad: Goslitizdat, 1931.

712 STONEHOUSE, JOHN H. *Green Leaves: New Chapters in the Life of Charles Dickens.* Revised and enlarged. London: Piccadilly Fountain Press, 1931.

713 WAGENKNECHT, EDWARD. "Introduction." *The Chimes.* London: Printed by George W. Jones for the members of the Limited Editions Club, 1931.

714 LEY, J. W. T. "Some Hymns and Songs of Childhood." *Dickensian* 27 (Spring 1931):121-26.

715 LEY, J. W. T. "The Sea Songs of Dickens." *Dickensian* 27 (Autumn 1931):255-66.

716 SITWELL, SIR OSBERT. "A Note on Charles Dickens." *Week-End Review* 4 (Nov. 1931):643.

717 LEY, J. W. T. "More Songs of Dickens's Day." *Dickensian* 28 (Winter 1931-32):15-26; 28 (Spring 1932):97-104.

718 SURVEYER, EDOUARD FABRE. "Dickens in France." *Dickensian* 28 (Winter 1931-32):46-56; 28 (Spring 1932):122-29; 28 (Summer 1932):197-201.

719 BEACH, JOSEPH W. *The Twentieth-Century Novel.* New York: Century, 1932.

720 CHANCELLOR, EDWIN B. *Dickens and His Times.* London: Richards, 1932.

721 CHARLES, EDWIN. *Some Dickens Men.* Foreword Philip Gibbs. London: Richard and Cowan, 1932.

722 CHESTERTON, GILBERT K. "The Great Gusto." *The Great Victorians,* ed. H. J. and Hugh Massingham, 163-71. London: Nicholson and Watson; New York: Doubleday, Doran, 1932. Reprinted in *Handful of Authors,* ed. Dorothy Collins. London: Sheed and Ward, 1953.

723 KÖNIG, KARLA. *Dickens und das Theater.* Stettin, 1932.

724 LOVETT, R. M. and H. S. HUGHES. "Dickens and his School. Charles Dickens (1812-1870)." *The History of the Novel in England,* 221-55. Boston: Houghton Mifflin, 1932.

725 SITWELL, SIR OSBERT. *Dickens.* London: Chatto and Windus, 1932.

726 PARTINGTON, WILFRED. "Swinburne, Dickens and the Lovely Circus Rider." *American Bookman* 75 (June-July 1932):292-93.

727 LEY, J. W. T. "The Sporting Songs of Dickens." *Dickensian* 28 (Summer 1932):187-89.

728 LEY, J. W. T. "Dickens's Hypnotic Power." *Dickensian* 28 (Sept. 1932):322-24.

729 LEY, J. W. T. "Fair Play for Buss." *Dickensian* 28 (Sept. 1932): 258-64. [Robert William Buss, the illustrator of *Pickwick.*]

730 LEY, J. W. T. "Sentimental Songs in Dickens." *Dickensian* 28 (Autumn 1932):313-21; 29 (Winter 1932-33):43-52.

731 MACEY, MARY A. "Dickens, Southwood Smith and the First Nursing Home." *Dickensian* 28 (Autumn 1932):271-76.

732 WILKINS, EVA I. "The Influence of Foreign Travel on Dickens's Novels." *Dickensian* 28 (Autumn 1932):277-80.

733 "Dickens and his French Publisher." *Dickensian* 29 (Dec. 1932):7-10.

734 LASKI, HAROLD. "In Praise of Dickens." *Daily Herald* (Dec. 24, 1932).

735 FREWER, L. B., *et al.* "The Influence of Dickens; Collected from Recent Books." *Dickensian* 28 (Winter 1932):40-45, and in successive issues from 28 (Spring 1932) to 33 (Autumn 1937).

736 GUSEV, N. "Dickens and Tolstoy." *Dickensian* 28 (Winter 1932): 63-64.

737 COLLINS, NORMAN. "Charles Dickens." *The Facts of Fiction,* 155-65. New York: Dutton, 1933.

738 DARTON, F. J. HARVEY. *Dickens: Positively the First Appearance: A Centenary Review With a Bibliography of Sketches by Boz.* London: Argonaut Press, 1933.

739 DARWIN, BERNARD. *Dickens.* London: Duckworth; New York: Macmillan, 1933.

740 DE LA MARE, WALTER. "Introduction." *The Cricket on the Hearth* Waltham St. Lawrence, Eng.: Golden Cockerel Press for members of Limited Editions Club, 1933.

741 DENT, H. C. *The Life and Characters of Charles Dickens.* London: Odhams Press, 1933.

742 DEXTER, WALTER. *Days in Dickensland.* London: Methuen, 1933.

743 GREEN, FRANK. *As Dickens Saw Them: A Commentary on the Characters Created by Dickens.* London: Stockwell, 1933.

744 LEACOCK, STEPHEN. *Charles Dickens: His Life and Work.* London: Davies, 1933; New York: Doubleday, Doran, 1934.

745 McNULTY, J. H. *Concerning Dickens and Other Literary Characters.* London: the Author, 1933.

746 NEWTON, A. E. "Charles Dickens." *End Papers,* 196-208. Boston: Little, Brown, 1933.

747 WICKARDT, WOLFGANG. *Die Formen der Perspektive in Charles Dickens' Romanen, ihr sprachlicher Ausdruck und ihre strukturelle Bedeutung.* (Neue Forschungen Bd. 22.) Berlin: Junker und Dümmhaupt, 1933.

748 WINTERICH, JOHN T. *An American Friend of Dickens.* New York: T. F. Madigan, 1933. [Elisha Bartlett. Includes facsimile reproductions of Dickens' letter to Dr Bartlett.]

749 MACHEN, ARTHUR. "Lost Books (by Dickens and Sir Walter Scott). *American Bookman* 76 (Feb. 1933):134-36.

750 DEXTER, WALTER. "A Necessary Correction. Some Mistakes from America." *Dickensian* 29 (Mar. 1933):127-30.

751 PARTINGTON, WILFRED. "Dickens, Thackeray and Yates: with an Unknown 'Indiscretion' by Trollope." *Saturday Review* 155 (Mar. 11, 1933):243-45.

752 MATTHEWS, T. S. "Dickens' Sacred Dust." *New Republic* 76 (Sept. 1933):129-30.

753 McNULTY, J. H. "Dickens' Opening Chapters." *Dickensian* 29 (Autumn 1933):289-92.

754 DEXTER, WALTER. "Dickens. Positively the First Appearance." *Times Literary Supplement* (Oct. 5, 1933):671.

755 CHESTER, AUSTIN. "Christmas with Dickens." *Windsor Magazine* 79 (Dec. 1933):33-48.

756 PHELPS, WILLIAM L. "Charles Dickens." *Saturday Review of Literature* 10 (Dec. 1933):319-20.

757 SADLEIR, MICHAEL. "John Macrone, Charles Dickens and *The Thief*." *Times Literary Supplement* (Dec. 28, 1933):924. [Comments re F. J. Harvey Darton's book *Dickens: Positively the First Appearance*.]

758 CECIL, LORD DAVID. "Charles Dickens." *Early Victorian Novelists*, 27-63. London: Constable, 1934; Indianapolis, Ind.: Bobbs-Merrill, 1935. Reprinted in *Victorian Novelists: Essays in Revaluation*. Chicago: Chicago Univ. Press, 1958.

759 DICKENS, SIR HENRY F. *The Recollections of Sir Henry Dickens, K.C.* London: Heinemann, 1934.

760 LEACOCK, STEPHEN. *The Greatest Pages of Charles Dickens*. Garden City, NY: Doubleday Doran, 1934.

761 LUNN, HUGH KINGSMILL (Hugh Kingsmill, pseud.). *The Sentimental Journey: a Life of Charles Dickens*. London: Wishart, 1934.

762 MAUROIS, ANDRÉ. *Dickens, his Life and Work*. Trans. Hamish Miles. London: J. Lane, 1934. [Translation of pp. 14-88 of *Etudes Anglaises*. Paris: Grasset, 1927.]

763 PHILIP, ALEX J. *Dickens' Honeymoon and Where He Spent It*. Gravesend, Kent: the Author, 1934.

764 RUBENS, CHARLES. *The Dummy Library of Charles Dickens at Gad's Hill Place*. Chicago: Privately printed by T. Rubovits, 1934.

765 SIMON and SCHUSTER. "Publishers' Foreword." *The Life of Our Lord*, 3-8. New York: Simon and Schuster, 1934.

766 DARTON, F. J. HARVEY. "Dickens the Beginner: 1833-1836." *Quarterly Review* 262 (Jan. 1934):52-69.

767 SHEPARD, WILLIAM. "A Mockingbird and Dickens." *William and Mary College Quarterly* 14 (Jan. 1934):22-23. [Re a contemporary anonymous letter on the Dickens' readings in New York.]

768 SILVER, ROLLO G. "Whitman and Dickens." *American Literature* 5 (Jan. 1934):370-71.

769 DARTON, F. J. HARVEY. "Macrone, Brydges, Dickens, *The Thief.*" *Times Literary Supplement* (Jan. 4, 1934):16. [Re Darton's article, "Dickens: Positively the First Appearance," concerning *The Thief* of 1834.]

770 SCRIBNER, HENRY S. "A Study in Contrast: The Broken Friendship of Dickens and Thackeray." *Scholastic* 24 (Feb. 3, 1934):9+.

771 DEXTER, WALTER. "The Genesis of Sketches by Boz." *Dickensian* 30 (Mar. 1934):105-11.

772 FANTHAM, HAROLD B. "Charles Dickens: A Biological Study of His Personality." *Character and Personality* 2 (Mar. 1934):222-30.

773 WRIGHT, THOMAS. "Charles Dickens Began his Honeymoon." *Daily Express* (Apr. 3, 1934).

774 ROUSE, W. H. D. "Dickens and Jorrocks." *Times Literary Supplement* (Apr. 19, 1934):282.

775 HOWE, MARK A. DeWOLFE. "Georgina Hogarth's Letter [About Dickens's *Life of Our Lord.*]" *Saturday Review of Literature* 10 (May 1934):700.

776 DEXTER, WALTER. "Charles Dickens: Journalist." *Nineteenth Century* 115 (June 1934):705-16.

777 YOUNG, R. T. "Doctors and Diseases in Dickens." *Cornhill Magazine* 75 (June 1934):709-15.

778 WRIGHT, C. HAGBERG. "'Dickens: Positively the First Appearance'" *Times Literary Supplement* (June 7, 1934):408. [A short letter on tracing a copy of the *London Weekly Magazine* which contained "A Dinner at Poplar Walk".]

779 STONEHOUSE, JOHN H. "Dickens's Library." *Times Literary Supplement* (June 21, 1934):443.

780 WAGENKNECHT, EDWARD. "Review of Recent Dickens Literature." *Virginia Quarterly Review* 10 (July 1934):455-59.

781 TYRRELL, T. W. "Dickens and the 'Gong-Donkey'." *Notes and Queries* 167 (Sept. 1934):231. ["The Lazy Tour of Two Idle Apprentices," *Household Words* (Oct. 3-31, 1857).]

782 LEACOCK, STEPHEN. "Two Humorists: Charles Dickens and Mark Twain." *Yale Review* 24 (Autumn 1934):118-29.

783 DICKENS, CHARLES Jr. "Personal Reminiscences of My Father." *Windsor Magazine* 81 (Dec. 1934, Christmas Supplement):1-32.

784 MORLEY, E. J. "Dickens's First Contribution to *The Morning Chronicle.*" *Dickensian* 31 (Dec. 1934):5-10.

785 PAYNE, EDWARD F. "Dexter Bust." *Dickensian* 16 (Winter 1934): 23-25.

786 EDGAR, HERMAN L. "Dickens's Friendship with the Coldens." *Dickensian* 31 (Winter 1934-35):11-22.

787 BOARMAN, JOSEPH C. and JAMES L. HARTE. *"Boz": An Intimate Biography of Charles Dickens.* Boston: Stratford, 1935.

788 CRUSE, AMY. "Dickens." *The Victorians and Their Reading,* 151-73. Boston: Houghton Mifflin, 1935. Published as *Victorians and Their Books.* London: G. Allen and Unwin, 1935.

789 FIELD, RACHEL L. *People From Dickens: A Presentation of Leading Characters From the Books of Charles Dickens.* New York: Scribner, 1935.

790 HESSELAA, PEDER. "Dickens' Skaebne i den Kritiske Litteratur fra 1870 til vore Dage." *Fetskrift til Valdemar Vedel fra Venner og Elever,* 132-47. Udgivet med Understöttelse af Carlsbergfondet. Under Redaktion af K. F. Plesner. Copenhagen: Gyldendal, 1935. [Critical reputation and treatment.]

791 KENT, WILLIAM R. *London for Dickens Lovers.* London: Methuen, 1935.

792 MAUROIS, ANDRÉ. *Dickens.* Paris: Ferenczi, 1935.

793 WRIGHT, THOMAS. *The Life of Charles Dickens.* London: H. Jenkins, 1935.

794 DEXTER, WALTER. "Contemporary Opinion of Dickens's Earliest Work." *Dickensian* 31 (Mar. 1935):105-8.

795 EVANS, MABEL. "Dickens the Satirist." *Dickensian* 31 (Spring 1935): 111-16.

796 ROE, FRANK G. "Surnames in Dickens." *Dickensian* 31 (Spring 1935):83-90.

797 "Libraries of Dickens and Thackeray." *Times Literary Supplement* (Apr. 18, 1935):260.

798 DARWIN, BERNARD. "New Discoveries of Charles Dickens. His Earliest Writings in Maria Beadnell's Album." *Strand* 89 (June 1935): 574-79.

799 GRAY, W. FORBES. "Dickens's Debt to Scotland." *Dickensian* 31 (June 1935):177-91.

800 SUZANNET, ALAIN de. "Maria Beadnell's Album." *Dickensian* 31 (June 1935):161-68.

801 HEWARD, A. H. "Dickens in 1867." *Saturday Review of Literature* 12 (Sept. 7, 1935):9.

802 DEXTER, WALTER. *"Dickensian* Peeps into *Punch* I." *Dickensian* 31 (Autumn 1935):264-66.

803 BENSLY, EDWARD. "Dickens and Turgenev." *Notes and Queries* 169 (Oct. 1935):276.

804 R., V. "Lucretian: Dickens." *Notes and Queries* 169 (Nov. 1935):312.

805 "The Centenary of Boz." *Times Literary Supplement* (Dec. 28, 1935) 885.

806 CHARTIER, EMILE. "A French Appreciation of Dickens." *Dickensian* 31 (Winter 1935):52-58.

807 D., W. "The Reception of Dickens's First Book." *Dickensian* 32 (Winter 1935-36):43-50. [On *Sketches by Boz.*] [Duplicates 808.]

808 DEXTER, WALTER. "The Reception of Dickens's First Book." *Dickensian* 32 (Winter 1935-36):43-50. [Duplicates 807.]

809 LEY, J. W. T. "What the Soldier Said – Scandal Articulate at Last – Mr Thomas Wright's 'Life' of Dickens." *Dickensian* 32 (Winter 1935-36):15-21.

810 DYBOSKI, ROMAN. *Charles Dickens: Życie i Twórczość.* Warsaw, 1936. [*Charles Dickens: Life and Works.*]

811 HARPER, HENRY H. and MARGUERITE. *This Thing Called Fame: Dramatic Episodes in the Private Life of a Literary Genius.* Cedar Rapids, Ia.: Torch Press, 1936.

812 O'FAOLÁIN, SÉAN. "Charles Dickens and W. M. Thackeray." *The English Novelists: A Survey of the Novel by Twenty Contemporary Novelists,* ed. Derek Verschoyle, 141-51. London: Chatto and Windus 1936.

813 SENNEWALD, CHARLOTTE. *Die Namengebung bei Dickens. Eine Studie über Lautsymbolik.* (Palaestra 203) Leipzig: Mayer und Müller, 1936.

814 STRAUS, RALPH. *Dickens: The Man and the Book.* London: Nelson, 1936.

815 WRIGHT, THOMAS. *Thomas Wright of Olney.* London: H. Jenkins, 1936.

816 SQUIRES, PAUL C. "The Case of Dickens as Viewed by Biology and Psychology." *Journal of Abnormal Psychology* 30 (Jan.-Mar. 1936): 468-73.

817 WILLIAMS, P. CLAXTON. "A Defence of Dickens's Detectives." *Dickensian* 32 (Mar. 1936):144-47.

818 BRADLEY, T. J. "'Fielding' in Dickens." *Notes and Queries* 170 (Apr. 1936):244.

819 BUCK, PEARL S. "A Debt to Dickens." *Saturday Review of Literature* 13 (Apr. 4, 1936):11+; *English Review* 62 (Apr. 1936):408-12. Reprinted in *Essay Annual, 1937,* ed. E. A. Walter. New York: Scott, 1937.

820 BOLL, ERNEST M. "The Sketches of Boz." *University of Pennsylvania General Magazine and Historical Chronicle* 38 (July 1936):380-85.

821 "CANTAB." "Dickens, Cambridge and Modern Languages." *Notes and Queries* 171 (July 1936):4-5. [Dickens on education.]

822 R., V. "The Wooden Legs in Dickens." *Notes and Queries* 171 (Aug. 1936):74-76.

823 CURTOYS, W. F. D. "Tobias Smollett's Influence on Dickens." *Dickensian* 32 (Autumn 1936):249-54.

824 "Dickens's Instructions to 'Phiz' for the *Pickwick* Illustrations." *Dickensian* 32 (Autumn 1936):266-68, 283.

825 F., A. W. "The Wooden Legs in Dickens." *Notes and Queries* 171 (Oct. 1936):246-47.

826 ERICKSON, EFFIE L. "The Influence of Charles Dickens on the Novels of Benito Pérez Galdós." *Hispania* 19 (Dec. 1936):421-30.

827 LEY, J. W. T. "More of What the Soldier Said – Further 'Disclosures' of Mr Thomas Wright." *Dickensian* 33 (Winter 1936-37):47-51.

828 ANDERSEN, HANS CHRISTIAN. *Hans Christian Andersen's Visits to Charles Dickens as Described in His Letters.* With six of Dickens' letters in facsimile. Ed. Ejnar Munksgaard. Copenhagen: Levin and Munksgaard, 1937.

829 JACKSON, THOMAS A. *Charles Dickens: The Progress of a Radical.* London: Lawrence and Wishart, 1937; New York: International, 1938.

R830 [JACKSON, THOMAS A. *Charles Dickens: the Progress of a Radical,* 1937 q.v.] COWLEY, MALCOLM. "Dickens and the Revolution." *New Republic* 96 (Aug. 24, 1938):81.

R831 [JACKSON, THOMAS A. *Charles Dickens: the Progress of a Radical,* 1937 q.v.] GEISMAR, MAXWELL. "Dickens – in the Flat." *Nation* 147 (Aug. 6, 1938):132.

832 MASON, JOHN E. *Charles Dickens.* Exeter, Eng.: A. Wheaton, 1937.

833 RICKETT, ARTHUR C. "Dickens Once Again." *Portraits and Personalities,* 171-84. London: Selwyn and Blount, 1937.

834 WAUGH, ARTHUR. "Charles Dickens and His Illustrators." *The Nonesuch Dickens. Retrospectus and Prospectus,* 1-52. London: Nonesuch Press, 1937.

835 YOUNG, GEORGE M. "Mr and Mrs Dickens." *Daylight and Champaign,* 26-30. London: J. Cape, 1937.

836 JONES, G. W. "Cruikshank Drawings." *Times Literary Supplement* (Feb. 6, 1937):92.

837 BACON, J. "Waxwork." *Dickensian* 33 (Mar. 1937):111-12.

838 BARKER, W. C. "Letters of Sydney Smith to Charles Dickens." *Dickensian* 33 (Mar. 1937):91-92.

839 DEXTER, WALTER. "*The Metropolitan Magazine* and Dickens's Early Work." *Dickensian* 33 (Mar. 1937):93-96.

840 DEXTER, WALTER. "A Stage Aside. Dickens's Early Dramatic Productions." *Dickensian* 33 (Mar. 1937):81-85 [*The Strange Gentleman,* Sept. 1836] ; (June 1937):163-69 [*The Village Coquettes,* Dec. 1836] ; (Sept. 1937):254-56 [*Is She His Wife?,* Mar. 1837] ; 34 (Dec. 1937):36 [*The Lamplighter*] .

841 MILLHAUSER, M. "Dickens and De Quincey." *Notes and Queries* 172 (Mar. 1937):224-25.

842 O'CONNELL, R. J. "Dickens and the Sea." *Dickensian* 33 (Mar. 1937) 113-16.

843 WILLIAMS, PHILIP C. "Dickens's Comic Detectives." *Dickensian* 33 (Mar. 1937):97-100.

844 CALLUM, K. H. "Women and the Home." *Dickensian* 33 (June 1937) 240-41.

845 DEXTER, WALTER. "Macrone and the Reissue of *Sketches by Boz.*" *Dickensian* 33 (June 1937):173-76.

846 FISHER, JAMES. "Reform as a Dickens Background." *Dickensian* 33 (June 1937):181-86.

847 LEY, J. W. T. "The Double Tragedy of Mary Hogarth." *Dickensian* 33 (June 1937):205-10.

848 R., S. J. "The Tenancy Agreement for 48 Doughty Street." *Dickensian* (June 1937):213-16.

849 TYLEE, F. "A Man of Letters." *Dickensian* 33 (June 1937):155-61. [Dickens as letter-writer.]

850 "The Agreements with Richard Bentley." *Dickensian* 33 (Summer 1937):199-204. [One of a series of agreements (legal documents) between Dickens and Bentley, one of his early publishers.]

851 MILLER, A. G. SCHAW. "Dickens's *The Battle of Life.*" *Times Literary Supplement* (July 31, 1937):564.

852 AITKEN, D. F. "Did Dickens Exaggerate?" *Listener* 18 (Aug. 1937): 299-301. [Not in his descriptions.]

853 TINKER, EDWARD L. "New Editions, Fine and Otherwise." *New York Times Book Review* 42 (Aug. 29, 1937):20.

854 DEXTER, WALTER. "*Bentley's Miscellany.*" *Dickensian* 33 (Sept. 1937):232-38.

855 MacMAHON, W. P. D. "Honoured in His Own Country." *Dickensian* 33 (Sept. 1937):229-31.

856 PAYNE, EDWARD F. "Dickens in Boston in 1842." *Dickensian* 33 (Sept. 1937):252-53.

857 PENDERED, MARY L. "The Firm of Human Interest Bros." *Dickensian* 33 (Sept. 1937):245-51.

858 SKOTTOWE, P. F. "Dickens and the Weather." *Dickensian* 33 (Sept. 1937):257-59.

859 SPENCE, L. "The Secret of Charles Dickens." *Dickensian* 33 (Sept. 1937):279-87. [Dickens' genius.]

860 STAPLES, LESLIE C. "Reflections of An Innkeeper." *Dickensian* 33 (Sept. 1937):288-90. [The "George" Inn in London and its restoration.]

861 STRANGE, E. H. "The Memoirs of Grimaldi: A Bibliographical Note." *Dickensian* 33 (Sept. 1937):239-40.

862 C., T. C. "'Stipendiary'." *Notes and Queries* 175 (Oct. 1937):298.

863 CROSS, A. E. BROOKES. "The Influence of Dickens on the Contemporary Stage." *Dickensian* 34 (Dec. 1937):55-62.

864 DAVIES, E. M. "In Christmas Story-Book Land." *Dickensian* 34 (Dec. 1937):37-40.

865 MASON, LEO. "Aunt Sophy and John Macrone." *Dickensian* 34 (Dec. 1937):14.

866 SPENCE, L. "In the Highlands – 1841." *Dickensian* 34 (Dec. 1937): 63-65.

867 WOOLLIAMS, W. P. "Social Reform: a Rejoinder." *Dickensian* 34 (Dec. 1937):33-35.

868 BRUSSEL, JAMES A. "Charles Dickens: Child Psychologist and Sociologist." *Psychiatric Quarterly Supplement* 12, Supplement 1 (1938):163-74.

869 NEELY, ROBERT D. *The Lawyers of Dickens and Their Clerks.* Boston: Christopher Publishing House, 1938.

870 POWYS, JOHN C. "Dickens." *Enjoyment of Literature,* 321-41. New York: Simon and Schuster, 1938. Published in England as *Pleasures of Literature.* London: Cassel, 1938.

871 SITWELL, SIR OSBERT. "Dickens and the Modern Novel." *Trio: Dissertations on Some Aspects of National Genius,* 1-45. London: Macmillan, 1938.

872 CONNELL, J. M. "The Religion of Charles Dickens." *Hibbert Journal* 36 (Jan. 1938):225-34.

873 DEAN, F. R. "Dickens and Manchester." *Dickensian* 34 (Spring 1938): 111-18.

874 GUMMER, ELLIS N. "Dickens and Germany." *Modern Language Review* 33 (Apr. 1938):240-47.

875 CROSS, A. E. BROOKES. "Albert Smith, Charles Dickens and 'Christopher Tadpole'." *Dickensian* 34 (Summer 1938):157-63. [Albert Smith's work, *The Adventures of Christopher Tadpole* (1848) and the works of Dickens as part of "newly-born art of the novel."]

876 SQUIRES, PAUL C. "Charles Dickens as Criminologist." *Journal of the American Institute of Criminal Law and Criminology* 29 (July-Aug. 1938):170-201.

877 "Our Aristophanes." *Times Literary Supplement* (Aug. 27, 1938):555.

878 NIELSEN, HILMER. "Some observations on *Sketches by Boz.*" *Dickensian* 34 (Autumn 1938):243-45. [Bibliographical.]

879 DEXTER, WALTER. "Dickensian Peeps into *Punch.*" *Dickensian* 35 (Dec. 1938):49-53; (Mar. 1939):117-22; (June 1939):175-79.

880 "The Extraordinary Gazette." *Dickensian* 34 (Dec. 1938):45-47. [Re three page leaflet meant to advertise the novel *Oliver Twist* – reproduced.]

881 CHRISTIE, O. F. *Dickens and His Age.* London: H. Cranton, 1939.

882 JOHNSON, DAVID D. "Fear of Death in Victorian Fiction." *West Virginia Univ. Bulletin: Philological Studies* 3 (1939):3-11.

883 NEELY, ROBERT D. *Doctors, Nurses and Dickens.* Boston: Christopher, 1939.

884 RAND, FRANK H. *Les Adaptations Théâtrales des Romans de Dickens en Angleterre 1837-1870.* Paris: Lipshutz, 1939.

885 STOREY, GLADYS. *Dickens and Daughter.* London: Müller, 1939. [Based on conversations between the author and Mrs Katherine Perugini, daughter of Dickens.]

886 WAGENKNECHT, EDWARD. "Explaining Dickens." *Saturday Review of Literature* 19 (Jan. 14, 1939):9.

887 BOAS, GUY. "Charles Dickens To-day." *Blackwood's Magazine* 245 (Mar. 1939):314-26.

888 HAIGHT, ANNE L. "Charles Dickens Tries to Remain Anonymous. Notes on 'The Loving Ballad of Lord Bateman,' Together with a Reprint of the Poem." *Colophon* 1 (Mar. 1939):39-[66].

889 MALVERN, MURIEL M. "When Dickens put the Question." *Dickensian* 35 (Mar. 1939):92-94. [Dickens as match-maker in his novels.]

890 MOORE, WINNIFRED. "A Visit to Some Landladies." *Dickensian* 35 (Mar. 1939):96-100. [Landladies from *Sketches by Boz, Pickwick Papers, David Copperfield.*]

891 SAROLEA, CHARLES. "Dickens and the Slogans of 'Democracy'." *Dickensian* 35 (Mar. 1939):13-16.

892 WILLIAMS, CHARLES R. "The Personal Relations of Dickens and Thackeray." *Dickensian* 35 (Mar. 1939):75-91.

893 YOUNGER, G. W. "Thames-side Taverns." *Dickensian* 35 (Mar. 1939): 123-25.

894 LEACOCK, STEPHEN. "Charles Dickens and Canada." *Queens Quarterly* 46 (Spring 1939):28-37.

895 H., S. S. "Dickens in Twentieth-Century Fiction." *Notes and Queries* 176 (Apr. 1939):279.

896 DEXTER, WALTER. "Some of the Earliest Compositions of Dickens." *Dickensian* 35 (June 1939):196-97.

897 DRURY, W. P. "'Eyes Left' for Dickens." *Dickensian* 35 (June 1939): 147-48. [A memorial.]

898 NOYES, ALFRED. "The Value of Dickens, Here and Now." *Dickensian* 35 (June 1939):189-93. Reprinted as "Dickens," in *Pageant of Letters.* New York: Shead, 1940.

899 PIRIE, WALTER. "The Return of the Native: Dickens's Readings at Portsmouth." *Dickensian* 35 (June 1939):205-07.

900 POWER, WILLIAM. "Universal Dickens." *Dickensian* 35 (June 1939): 167-71.

901 SHAW, GEORGE BERNARD. "Dickens and Mrs Perugini." *Times Literary Supplement* (July 29, 1939):453.

902 FORSE, EDWARD J. "Dickens as a Plagiarist." *Notes and Queries* 177 (Aug. 1939):118.

903 DEXTER, WALTER. "For One Night Only. Dickens's Appearance as an Amateur Actor." *Dickensian* 35 (Sept. 1939):231-42; 36 (Dec. 1939):20-30; (Mar. 1939):91-102; (June 1939):131-35; (Sept. 1939):195-201; 37 (Dec. 1940):7-11.

904 DODDS, M. H. "Dickens in Twentieth-Century Fiction." *Notes and Queries* 177 (Sept. 1939):249-50.

905 MONRO, DOROTHY A. "The Dickens Orchestra." *Dickensian* 35 (Sept. 1939):263-64. ["The deep sad music of humanity" as played by Dickens in his novels.]

906 PENDERED, MARY L. "Soul Drama." *Dickensian* 35 (Sept. 1939): 243-49. [On "pure emotion drama" in Dickens' fiction.]

907 DEARSLEY, R. L. "The Education of the Poor." *Dickensian* 36 (Dec. 1939):47-54.

908 FOSTER, FRANK. "Transatlantic Astigmatism in the Sixties." *Dickensian* 35 (Dec. 1939):13-14.

909 PATERSON, ANDREW. "Two of a Kind." *Dickensian* 35 (Dec. 1939): 54-57. [Dickens and Burns.]

910 PENDERED, MARY L. "Stipendiary Girls and Spinsters." *Dickensian* 35 (Dec. 1939):23-28. [On the "distinct personalities" of minor characters in Dickens' fiction.]

911 PIKE, JAMES S. "Dickens, Carlyle and Tennyson." *Atlantic Monthly* 164 (Dec. 1939):810-19.

912 R., V. "At Christmas. Ibsen and Dickens." *Notes and Queries* 177 (Dec. 1939):474-75.

913 RUST, S. J. "Treasures at the Dickens House." *Dickensian* 35 (Dec. 1939):32-36.

914 WILLIAMS, PHILIP C. "Dickens's Literary Caricatures." *Dickensian* 36 (Dec. 1939):9-11.

915 BRADBY, M. K. "An Explanation of George Silverman's Explanation." *Dickensian* 34 (Winter 1939-40):13-18.

916 BECKER, MAY L. *Introducing Charles Dickens.* New York: Dodd, Mead, 1940.

917 DARWIN, BERNARD. "A Little Dickens." *Life is Sweet Brother,* 183-96. London: Collins, 1940.

918 GURIAN, O. "Dickens and his Illustrators." *Literature for Children* (USSR) 8 (1940):44-48.

919 MASON, LEO. *A Tale of Three Authors, and Poe and the Messenger.* London: Dickens Fellowship, 1940. [Dickens, Ainsworth, Poe.]

920 ORWELL, GEORGE. "Charles Dickens." *Inside the Whale,* 9-85. London: Gollancz, 1940. Reprinted in *Critical Essays.* London: Secker and Warburg, 1946 [published in US as *Dickens, Dali and Others.* New York: Reynal and Hitchcock, 1946] ; *A Collection of Essays.* New York: Doubleday, 1954; *Collected Essays.* London: Secker and Warburg, 1961; *An Age Like This, 1920-1940,* ed. Sonia Orwell and Ian Angus (The Collected Essays, Journalism and Letters of George Orwell 1). New York: Harcourt Brace, 1968; *Discussions of Charles Dickens,* ed. W. R. Clark, 1961 q.v.; *The Dickens Critics,* ed. G. H. Ford and L. Lane, Jr., 1961 q.v.

R921 [ORWELL, GEORGE. *Dickens, Dali and Others,* 1946.] BENTLEY, ERIC. "Young Man Out of His Time." *Saturday Review of Literature* (May 11, 1946):11.

R922 [ORWELL, GEORGE. *Dickens, Dali and Others,* 1946.] HAMPSHIRE STUART. "A Redoubtable Critic." *Spectator* (Mar. 8, 1946):250.

R923 [ORWELL, GEORGE. *Inside the Whale,* 1940 q.v.] HOUSE, HUMPHRY. "Dickens, Billy Bunter and Jonah." *Spectator* (Mar. 15, 1940):382.

R924 [ORWELL, GEORGE. *Dickens, Dali and Others,* 1946.] LA DRIÈVE CRAIG. *Journal of Aesthetics* 5 (Mar. 1947):231.

R925 [ORWELL, GEORGE. *Dickens, Dali and Others,* 1946.] PRITCHETT V. S. "The Rebel." *New Statesman and Nation* (Feb. 16, 1946):124.

926 PATTEE, FRED L. "The Shadow of Dickens." *The Feminine Fifties,* 68-81. New York: Appleton-Century, 1940.

927 SHASKOLSKAYA, T. "Dickens and Carlyle." *Transactions of the State Pedagogical Institute of Foreign Languages in Kharkov* (USSR) 29 (1940):113-20.

928 D., M. H. "At Christmas: Ibsen and Dickens." *Notes and Queries* 178 (Jan. 1940):68-69.

929 DARWIN, BERNARD. "Return to Dickens." *St. Martin's Review* (Jan. 1940):30-33.

930 GASELEE, STEPHEN. "At Christmas: Ibsen and Dickens." *Notes and Queries* 178 (Jan. 1940):51.

931 BOLL, ERNEST M. *"The Sketches by 'Boz'." Dickensian* 36 (Mar. 1940):69-73.

932 DAVIS, EARLE R. "Dickens and the Evolution of Caricature." *PMLA* 55 (Mar. 1940):231-40.

933 HILL, THOMAS W. "Let's Talk of – Epitaphs." *Dickensian* 36 (Mar. 1940):79-84. [Epitaphs composed by Dickens.]

934 MASON, LEO. "A Tale of Three Authors." *Dickensian* 36 (Mar. 1940): 109-19. [Charles Dickens, William Harrison Ainsworth, and Edgar Allan Poe.] Reprinted in *A Tale of Three Authors and Poe and the Messenger,* 1940 q.v.

935 WILSON, EDMUND. "Dickens: The Two Scrooges." *New Republic* 102 (Mar. 1940):297-300, 339-42. Reprinted [revised and enlarged] in *The Wound and the Bow.* Boston: Houghton, Mifflin, 1941; *Eight Essays.* New York: Doubleday, 1954.

R936 [WILSON, EDMUND. *The Wound and the Bow,* 1941 q.v.] DE VANE, W. "Eight Wounds: Eight Bows." *Yale Review* 31 (Dec. 1941): 384-87.

R937 [WILSON, EDMUND. *The Wound and the Bow,* 1941 q.v.] LEAVIS, F. R. "An American Critic." *Scrutiny* 11 (Summer 1942): 72-73.

938 WILSON, EDMUND. "Dickens and the Marshalsea Prison." *Atlantic Monthly* 165 (Apr. 1940):473-83; (May 1940):681-91.

939 "A Dickens Diary." *Dickensian* 36 (June 1940):151-62; (Sept. 1940): 221-31; 37 (Dec. 1940):19-23.

940 GADD, W. LAURENCE. "The Dickens Touch." *Dickensian* 36 (June 1940):181-85.

941 HILL, THOMAS W. "The Oyster: A Close-up." *Dickensian* 36 (June 1940):139-46. [The oyster in Dickens' writings.]

942 LUCAS, AUDREY. "Some Dickens Women." *Yale Review* 29 (June 1940):706-28.

943 MASON, LEO. "Poe and the *Messenger.*" *Dickensian* 36 (June 1940): 163-68. Reprinted in *A Tale of Three Authors and Poe and the Messenger,* 1940 q.v.

944 SUZANNET, ALAIN de. "Sloman's; Another Dickens Original." *Dickensian* 36 (June 1940):180.

945 WOOLLEN, C. J. "Some Thoughts on Dickens's Women." *Dickensian* 36 (June 1940):178-80.

946 BURTON, G. S. "More Secrets." *Dickensian* 36 (Sept. 1940):235-37.

947 GRUBB, GERALD G. "Dickens's First Experience as a Parliamentary Reporter." *Dickensian* 36 (Sept. 1940):211-18.

948 HAMILTON, ROBERT. "Dickens and Boz." *Dickensian* 36 (Sept. 1940):242-44.

949 "Dickens in Russia." *Times Literary Supplement* (Sept. 7, 1940):459.

950 HILL, THOMAS W. "A Unique Collection of Music." *Dickensian* 37 (Dec. 1940):43-54. [The William Miller collection of Dickensian music located in the library of Dickens House.]

951 BECKER, MAY L. "Foreword." *Christmas Tales.* New York: Dodd, Mead, 1941.

952 BODELSEN, CARL A. *To Radioforedrag om Dickens.* Copenhagen: Haase, 1941.

953 HOUSE, HUMPHRY. *The Dickens World.* London: Oxford Univ. Press, 1941.

R954 [HOUSE, HUMPHRY. *The Dickens World,* 1941 q.v.] BUTT, JOHN] *Review of English Studies* 20 (Jan. 1944):88-90.

R955 [HOUSE, HUMPHRY. *The Dickens World,* 1941 q.v.] CHURCHILL, R. C. "Dickens as Journalist." *Scrutiny* 10 (Jan. 1942):304-7.

R956 [HOUSE, HUMPHRY. *The Dickens World,* 1941 q.v.] NEFF, EMER` *Modern Language Notes* 58 (Apr. 1943):325-26.

R957 [HOUSE, HUMPHRY. *The Dickens World,* 1941 q.v.] YOUNG, GEORGE M. "Two Worlds." *Dickensian* 38 (Dec. 1941):61-62.

R958 [HOUSE, HUMPHRY. *The Dickens World,* 1941 q.v.] ZABEL, MORTON D. "Dickens as Historian and Reformer." *Nation* 154 (Apr. 11, 1942):434-36.

959 ZECH, ADOLPH. "Wilhelm Dilthey's Analysis of Charles Dickens." *Stanford Studies in Language and Literature, 1941,* ed. Hardin Craig, 321-35. Stanford, Calif.: Stanford University School of Letters, 1941. [On Dilthey, the German philosopher and his reading of Dickens in "Charles Dickens und das Genie des erzählenden Kunstlers *Westermanns Illustriarte Deutsche Monatshefte* 41 (1877):482-89, 586-602.]

960 DEXTER, WALTER. "For One Night Only. Part Two: An Account of the Famous Readings." *Dickensian* 37 (Mar. 1941):106-9.

961 DEXTER, WALTER (L. A. Kennethe, pseud.). "Memorials of Friendship." *Dickensian* 37 (Mar. 1941):89-98. [Dedications in Dickens' novels.]

962 HOUTCHENS, LAWRENCE H. "Charles Dickens and International Copyright." *American Literature* 13 (Mar. 1941):18-28.

963 DEXTER, WALTER. "Mr Charles Dickens Will Read." *Dickensian* 37 (June 1941):133-39; (Sept. 1941):201-3; 38 (Dec. 1941):41-43; (June 1942):158-60; (Sept. 1942):231-34; 39 (Mar. 1943):93-94.

964 HILL, THOMAS W. "The Dickens Dietary: I. Breakfast, II. Domestic Meals and Little Feasts, III. Special Occasions, IV. Teas, V. Cookery and Cooks." *Dickensian* 37 (June 1941):145-51; (Sept. 1941):191-99; 38 (Dec. 1941):23-31; (Mar. 1942):95-101; (June 1942):167-71; (Sept. 1942):197-205; 39 (Dec. 1943):5-15.

965 STAPLES, LESLIE C. "A Kensal Green Circle." *Dickensian* 37 (June 1941):129-32. [The "circle" of intimate friends buried at Kensal Green Cemetery: Maclise, Stanfield, Cruikshank, Lover, Shirley Brooks, Dyer, Forster.]

966 SAVAGE, OLIVER D. "The First Dickens Sale." *Dickensian* 37 (Sept. 1941):227-29. [A report in *Chambers' Journal* for Aug. 6, 1870 entitled "At Dickens's Sale" as evidence of his contemporary fame.]

967 STAPLES, LESLIE C. "Tom Hill." *Dickensian* 37 (Sept. 1941): 185-90.

968 THOMAS, R. E. "Dickens's Characters." *Notes and Queries* 181 (Nov. 1941):303.

969 DEXTER, WALTER, ed. "America 1842. A Dickens Diary One Hundred Years Ago." *Dickensian* 38 (Dec. 1941):53-60; (Mar. 1942): 87-94; (June 1942):172-77.

970 GADD, W. LAURENCE. "Fact and Fiction of America." *Dickensian* 38 (Dec. 1941):49-52.

971 McKENZIE, GORDON. "Dickens and Daumier." *Studies in the Comic, University of California Publications in English* 8 (Dec. 1941):273-98.

972 PATERSON, ANDREW. "Dickensian Mysteries from Montreal." *Dickensian* 38 (Dec. 1941):17-22.

973 PAYNE, EDWARD F. "Dickens's First Look at America." *Dickensian* 38 (Dec. 1941):7-13.

974 DANA, HENRY WADSWORTH LONGFELLOW. "Longfellow and Dickens: The Story of a Trans-Atlantic Friendship." *Cambridge Historical Society Papers* 28 (1942):55-104.

975 GEROULD, GORDON H. "Dickens and Bulwer-Lytton." *The Pattern of English and American Fiction: a History*, 255-79. Boston: Little, Brown, 1942.

976 BRAIN, SIR RUSSELL. "Charles Dickens: Neuro-Psychiatrist." *London Hospital Gazette* 45 (Jan. 1942):32-35.

977 "The Amateur Theatricals in Montreal. Contemporary Criticism of Dickens's First Public Appearances as an Actor." *Dickensian* 38 (Mar. 1942):72-74.

978 HILL, THOMAS W. (T. Kent Brumleigh, pseud.) "Relicts and Relics." *Dickensian* 38 (Mar. 1942):103-12.

979 PATERSON, ANDREW. "The Montreal Theatre and Another Mystery." *Dickensian* 38 (Mar. 1942):85-86. [Dickens' performance in Montreal.]

980 YOUNG, GEORGE F. "Old Highgate Re-visited." *Dickensian* 38 (Mar. 1942):80-83.

981 CHURCHILL, R. C. "Dickens, Drama and Tradition." *Scrutiny* 10 (Apr. 1942):358-75. Reprinted in *The Importance of Scrutiny*, ed. Eric Bentley. New York: Stewart, 1948.

982 GRUBB, GERALD G. "Dickens's Pattern of Weekly Serialization." *English Literary History* 9 (June 1942):141-56.

983 HILL, THOMAS W. "The Staplehurst Railway Accident." *Dickensian* 38 (June 1942):147-52.

984 STAPLES, LESLIE C. "Fanny Kelly." *Dickensian* 38 (June 1942): 153-58. [Frances Maria Kelly, actress and friend of Dickens, 1790-1882.]

985 STOLL, ELMER E. "Heroes and Villains: Shakespeare, Middleton, Byron, Dickens." *Review of English Studies* 18 (July 1942):257-69. Reprinted in *From Shakespeare to Joyce*. New York: Doubleday, Doran, 1944.

986 PRICE, R. "Boz Reports on Ohio." *Ohio State Archaeological and Historical Quarterly* 51 (July-Sept. 1942):195-202.

987 ERVINE, ST. JOHN. "On Re-reading Dickens." *English Digest* 11 (Nov. 1942):31-32.

988 MASON, LEO. "More About Poe and Dickens." *Dickensian* 39 (Dec. 1942):21-28.

989 GORDAN, JOHN D. "The Secret of Dickens' Memoranda." *Bookman's Holiday: Notes and Studies Written and Gathered in Tribute to Harry Miller Lydenberg*, 188-95. New York: New York Public Library, 1943.

990 JOHNSON, DAVID D. "'Without Benefit of Clergy' in Victorian Fiction." *West Virginia Univ. Bulletin: Philological Studies* 4 (1943): 15-21.

991 SIMPSON, EVELYN M. "Jonson and Dickens: A Study in the Comic Genius of London." *Essays and Studies* 29 (1943):82-92.

992 WAGENKNECHT, EDWARD. "White Magic." *Cavalcade of the English Novel,* 173-268. New York: Holt, Rinehart and Winston, 1943.

993 WELLS, JAMES M. "The Artist in the English Novel, 1850-1919." *West Virginia Univ. Bulletin: Philological Studies* 4 (1943):77-80.

994 GRUBB, GERALD G. "Dickens's Editorial Methods." *Studies in Philology* 40 (Jan. 1943):79-100.

995 JOHNSON, LOUISE H. "The Source of the Chapter on Slavery in Dickens's *American Notes." American Literature* 14 (Jan. 1943): 427-30.

996 J., W. H. "Dickens in the *DNB." Notes and Queries* 184 (Feb. 1943): 92-93.

997 DAVIDS, E. I. GORE. "A Fourteenth-Century Dickens." *Dickensian* 39 (Mar. 1943):70-74. [The Dickens' spirit in 14th century writers – Langland, Chaucer, and Lydgate.]

998 DEXTER, WALTER (L. A. Kennethe, pseud.). "The Unique Reading Books." *Dickensian* 39 (Mar. 1943):75-78.

999 FOSTER, FRANK. "Reflections on Waistcoats." *Dickensian* 39 (Mar. 1943):89-91.

1000 J., W. H. "The Dead Hand: Dickens and Scott." *Notes and Queries* 184 (Mar. 1943):191-92. [Dickens edits and selects, *Religious Opinions of the late Chauncy Hare Townshend.*]

1001 STAFF, FRANK J. "Dickens the Conjurer, and a Mystery Solved." *Dickensian* 39 (Mar. 1943):61-63. [Biography.]

1002 C., D. "Dickens and His Wife." *Notes and Queries* 184 (Apr. 1943): 244-46.

1003 C., D. "Mrs Lynn Linton and Dickens." *Notes and Queries* 184 (Apr. 1943):216-17.

1004 LEACOCK, STEPHEN. "Dickens Distilled: How to Lose Size Without Losing Stature." *Saturday Review of Literature* 26 (Apr. 17, 1943): 16-18.

1005 C., D. "Thomas Wright and Dickens." *Notes and Queries* 184 (May 1943):287-88.

1006 "A Dickens Diary, 1843. Compiled from Authoritative Sources." *Dickensian* 39 (June 1943):155-56.

1007 DEXTER, WALTER. (L. A. Kennethe, pseud.). "The Cheap Edition." *Dickensian* 39 (June 1943):112-14.

1008 DEXTER, WALTER. "Thomas Wright and Dickens." *Notes and Queries* 184 (June 1943):351-52.

1009 GARLEY, GRANVILLE. "Small Fry Folk. Tributes to Some of the Less Famous." *Dickensian* 39 (June 1943):147-48; (Sept. 1943): 203-04; 40 (Dec. 1943):45-46; (Mar. 1944):64; (June 1944):159-60. [Minor characters in Dickens.]

1010 GRUBB, GERALD G. "A Hogarth Influence on Dickens." *Dickensian* 39 (June 1943):144-45.

1011 HILL, THOMAS W. (T. Kent Brumleigh, pseud.). "Autoplagiarism." *Dickensian* 39 (June 1943):115-18; (Sept. 1943):169-73; 40 (Dec. 1943):9-11.

1012 WILLIAMS, PHILIP C. "The Art That Failed." *Dickensian* 39 (June 1943):145-46.

1013 STEVENSON, LIONEL. "Dickens' Dark Novels, 1851-7." *Sewanee Review* 51 (Summer 1943):398-409.

1014 WRIGHT, ANGELINA. "Thomas Wright and Dickens." *Notes and Queries* 185 (Aug. 1943):115.

1015 YOUNGER, G. W. "Greenwich Taverns." *Dickensian* 39 (Sept. 1943) 193-96.

1016 C., H. H. "Three Christmases. I. The Dickens Feast." *Times Literary Supplement* (Nov. 13, 1943):541.

1017 "Christmas Once and Now." *Times Literary Supplement* (Nov. 13, 1943):547. [A nostalgic wartime article on Christmas.]

1018 GRUBB, GERALD G. "The Editorial Policies of Charles Dickens." *PMLA* 58 (Dec. 1943):1110-24.

1019 MABBOTT, THOMAS O. "Dickens, Sala and S. C. Hall." *Notes and Queries* 185 (Dec. 1943):347. [Comments by Dickens and Sala on a book by S. C. Hall, *A Memory of Thomas Moore.*]

1020 WATT, WILLIAM W. "Christmas 1943 – A Dickens Centenary." *Saturday Review of Literature* 26 (Dec. 4, 1943):16-18.

1021 RANTAVAARA, IRMA. *Dickens in the Light of English Criticism.* (Suomalaisen Tiedeakalemian Toimituksia. sarja B. nid. 53. no. 1.) Helsinki, 1944.

1022 HOUTCHENS, CAROLYN W. and LAWRENCE H. "Three Early Works Attributed to Dickens." *PMLA* 59 (Mar. 1944):226-35. [Works incorrectly attributed to Dickens: "Some Passages in the Life of Francis Looseflesh," "My First Song," "Reminiscences of a Good-Natured Man," and "Hobbledehoys," – the last three published in the *New York Mirror,* and given here.]

1023 PRIESTLEY, J. B. "New Judgment." *Dickensian* 40 (Mar. 1944): 61-63.

1024 RIGG, RONALD E. "The Fascination of the Sea." *Dickensian* 40 (Mar. 1944):89-96; (June 1944):151-58.

1025 "Actor or Play." *Times Literary Supplement* (May 6, 1944):223. [Ninetta Crummles, the Infant Phenomenon, was drawn (or distorted) by Dickens from Jean Davenport (1829-1903).]

1026 DEXTER, WALTER. "The 'Library,' 'People's' and 'Charles Dickens' Editions." *Dickensian* 40 (Sept. 1944):186-87.

1027 McNULTY, J. H. "Leacock on Dickens. A Canadian's View." *Dickensian* 40 (Sept. 1944):205-06.

1028 BOLL, ERNEST M. "Dickens and Washington Irving." *Modern Language Quarterly* 5 (Dec. 1944):453-67.

1029 GREAVES, JOHN. "Fireside Reflections." *Dickensian* 41 (Dec. 1944): 43-47. [The role of fires and firesides.]

1039 GREEN, ROGER L. "Andrew Lang: Critic and Dickensian." *Dickensian* 41 (Dec. 1944):10-14.

1031 WILLIAMS, PHILIP C. "The Soldier in Dickens." *Dickensian* 41 (Dec. 1944):48-51.

1032 CHARTIER, EMILE ("ALAIN," pseud.). *En Lisant Dickens.* Paris: Gallimard, 1945. Translated excerpt reprinted in *The Dickens Critics*, ed. G. H. Ford and L. Lane Jr., 1961, q.v.

1033 DAVIS, EARLE R. *Charles Dickens and Wilkie Collins.* Wichita, Kans.: Municipal Univ. of Wichita, 1945. [Same as *Municipal Univ. of Wichita Bulletin* 20 (June 1945).]

1034 POPE-HENNESSY, UNA. *Charles Dickens, 1812-70.* London: Chatto and Windus, 1945.

1035 PACEY, W. C. DESMOND. "Washington Irving and Charles Dickens." *American Literature* 16 (Jan. 1945):332-39.

1036 BRAYBROOKE, PATRICK. "Chesterton and Charles Dickens." *Dickensian* 41 (Mar. 1945):77-80.

1037 HILL, THOMAS W. (Kentley Bromhill, pseud.) "Names and Labels." *Dickensian* 41 (Mar. 1945):92-93.

1038 "A New Dickens Bibliography." *Dickensian* 41 (Mar. 1945):82-83; (Sept. 1945):206-7.

1039 POPE-HENNESSY, UNA. "The Gad's Hill Library." *Dickensian* 41 (Mar. 1945):60-64.

1040 STAPLES, LESLIE C. "Mrs Dickens, Dietitian." *Dickensian* 41 (Mar. 1945):94-95. ["The Cookery Book" published by Mrs Charles Dickens in 1851 and again in 1852 entitled "What Shall We Have For Dinner?"]

1041 CARLTON, WILLIAM J. "Dickens and O'Connell." *Notes and Queries* 188 (Apr. 1945):147. [The effect on Dickens of a moving speech in the House.]

1042 DODDS, M. H. "George Eliot and Charles Dickens." *Notes and Queries* 190 (Apr. 1945):143-45.

1043 MILLICAN, JOHN N. "Dickens Illustrations." *Times Literary Supplement* (Apr. 7, 1945):163. [For replies to the letter above objecting to illustrations, see Douglas G. Browne, *et al., Times Literary Supplement* (Apr. 28, 1945):199; Oliver Millar and R. L. Hayne, *Times Literary Supplement* (May 5, 1945):211; Herbert Brown, *et al., Times Literary Supplement* (May 12, 1945):223; Shane Leslie, *Times Literary Supplement* (May 19, 1945):235.]

1044 CROYDON, JOHN. "Film Prospecting Among the Yorkshire Schools." *Dickensian* 41 (June 1945):121-25.

1045 EASTON, EDWARD R. "Doctors in Dickens." *Dickensian* 41 (June 1945):150-56.

1046 HOUTCHENS, CAROLYN W. and LAWRENCE H. "Contributions of Early American Journals to the Study of Charles Dickens." *Modern Language Quarterly* 6 (June 1945):211-17.

1047 McNULTY, J. H. "The Weather." *Dickensian* 41 (June 1945):138-42. ["High wind," "snowfall," and "great fog" in Dickens.]

1048 STAFF, FRANK J. "Nightcaps." *Dickensian* 41 (June 1945):148-49. [In the novels.]

1049 WILLIAMS, PHILIP C. "Murder Most Foul." *Dickensian* 41 (June 1945):145-48. [Murders in Dickens' novels.]

1050 KIDDLE, MARGARET. "Caroline Chisholm and Charles Dickens." *Historical Studies. Australia & New Zealand* 3 (July 1945):77-94. [Immigrants' rights and *Household Words.*]

1051 STEVENSON, LIONEL. "The Second Birth of the English Novel." *Univ. of Toronto Quarterly* 14 (July 1945):366-74.

1052 CLARKE, GEORGE H. "Dickens Now." *Queen's Quarterly* 52 (Autumn 1945):280-87.

1053 CLARKE, GEORGE H. "The Theater Influence in His [Dickens] Work." *Queen's Quarterly* 52 (Autumn 1945):280-87.

1054 GRUBB, GERALD G. "Dickens' Influence as an Editor." *Studies in Philology* 42 (Oct. 1945):811-23.

1055 WHITE, FREDERIC C. "Dickens and His Children." *Notes and Queries* 189 (Oct. 1945):168.

1056 R., V. "Dickens and a Baronetcy." *Notes and Queries* 189 (Nov. 1945): 212.

1057 KENT, W. and G. W. SAUNDERS. "Dickens and His Children." *Notes and Queries* 189 (Dec. 1945):261. [Followed by a letter from Dickens.]

1058 McNULTY, J. H. "*The Haunted Man* (A New Version)." *Dickensian* 42 (Dec. 1945):6-11.

1059 YARRE, d'A. P. "Dickens Without Phiz?" *Dickensian* 42 (Dec. 1945): 32-34.

1060 BECKER, MAY L. "Introduction." *Christmas Stories: A Christmas Carol. The Chimes. The Cricket on the Hearth.* Cleveland; New York: World, 1946.

1061 LAIRD, JOHN. "Philosophy in the Works of Dickens." *Philosophical Incursions into English Literature,* 136-60. New York: Russell and Russell, 1946.

1062 LANN, EUGENY. *Dikkens.* Moscow: Gosudarstvennoe Izdatel'stvo Xudožestvennoj Literatury, 1946. [A fictional biography.]

1063 LEMONNIER, LEON. *Dickens.* Paris: Albin Michel, 1946.

1064 McCULLOUGH, BRUCE. "The Comedy of Character: Charles Dickens." *Representative English Novelists: Defoe to Conrad,* 131-51. New York: Harper, 1946.

1065 MONOD, SYLVÈRE. "Critical Introduction." *Nouveaux Contes de Noël de Dickens.* Paris: Union Bibliophile de France, 1946.

1066 POPPER, RUDOLF (Rudolph Vasata, pseud.). "*Amerika* and Charles Dickens." *The Kafka Problem,* ed. Angel Flores, 134-39. New York: New Directions, 1946.

1067 WARNER, REX. "On Reading Dickens." *The Cult of Power,* 21-38. London: J. Lane, 1946. Reprinted in *The Dickens Critics,* ed. G. H. Ford and L. Lane, Jr., 1961 q.v.

1068 DICKINS, MARY G. "Dickens Self-Revealed." *Dickensian* 42 (Mar. 1946):65-71; (June 1946):129-33.

1069 STAPLES, LESLIE C. "Dickens and Australian Immigration." *Dickensian* 42 (Mar. 1946):75-77.

1070 SUMMERS, MONTAGUE. "Dickens and the Decadent." *Dickensian* 42 (Mar. 1946):61-64. [Jorris-Karl Huysmans.]

1071 WEGELIN, CHRISTOF. "Dickens and Irving: The Problem of Influence." *Modern Language Quarterly* 7 (Mar. 1946):83-91.

1072 WILLIAMS, PHILIP C. "In the Beginning ..." *Dickensian* 42 (Mar. 1946):99-101. [On the first chapter in the Dickens novel.]

1073 VANDIVER, EDWARD P., Jr. "Dickens' Knowledge of Shakespeare." *Shakespeare Association Bulletin* 21 (July 1946):124-28.

1074 HOPKINS, ANNETTE B. "Dickens and Mrs Gaskell." *Huntington Library Quarterly* 9 (Aug. 1946):357-85.

1075 BOLL, ERNEST M. "The Infusion of Dickens in Trollope." *Trollopian* 1 (Sept. 1946):11-24.

1076 HEILMAN, ROBERT B. "The New World in Charles Dickens's Writings." *Trollopian* 1 (Sept. 1946):25-43; (Mar. 1947):11-26.

1077 RANDALL, DAVID A. "Charles Dickens and Richard Bentley." *Times Literary Supplement* (Oct. 12, 1946):496.

1078 RUCKMINI, M. A. "The Didactic in the Art of Dickens." *Aryan Path* 17 (Nov. 1946):419-22.

1079 POPE-HENNESSY, UNA. "[Charles] Dickens and [Richard] Bentley." *Times Literary Supplement* (Nov. 2, 1946):535.

1080 GERSON, ARMAND J. *These Dickens Folk.* Philadelphia: Dorrance, 1947.

1081 KIRKBY, JOHN. *Unpopular Dickens.* Dedicated, as the spur is dedicated to the horse, to the Dickens Fellowship. London: the Author, 1947.

1082 LAMM, MARTIN. *Dickens och Hans Romaner.* Stockholm: Bonnier, 1947.

1083 LAWSON, McEWAN. *Challenge to Oppression: the Story of Charles Dickens.* Toronto: Macmillan; London: SCM Press; New York: Student, 1947.

1084 MITCHELL, EDWIN V. "Introduction." *Best Short Stories of Charles Dickens.* New York: Scribner's, 1947.

1085 MONOD, SYLVÈRE. "Critical Introduction." *Autres Contes de Noël de Dickens.* Paris: Union Bibliophile de France, 1947.

1086 PRIESTLEY, J. B. "Introduction." *Scenes of London Life from* Sketches by Boz. London: Pan Books, 1947.

1087 HOUSE, HUMPHRY. "Two Aspects of Dickens." *Listener* (Jan. 23, 1947).

1088 CHRISTIAN, MILDRED G. "Carlyle's Influence Upon the Social Theory of Dickens. Pt. 1, Their Personal Relationship; Pt. 2, Their Literary Relationship." *Trollopian* 1 (Mar. 1947):27-35; 2 (June 1947):11-26.

1089 GIBSON, FRANK A. "Dickens and Germany." *Dickensian* 43 (Mar. 1947):69-74. [The novels in Germany.]

1090 MILLER, WILLIAM. "Dickens Reads at the British Museum." *Dickensian* 43 (Mar. 1947):83-84.

1091 SANDERS, FREDERICK. "The Spirit of Dickens: Gad's Hill Mysteries." *Dickensian* 43 (Mar. 1947):94-96.

1092 WENGER, JARED. "Character-Types of Scott, Balzac, Dickens, and Zola." *PMLA* 62 (Mar. 1947):213-32.

1093 GIBSON, FRANK A. "*The Child's History.*" *Dickensian* 43 (June 1947):127-31.

1094 MASON, LEO. "Charlotte Bronte and Charles Dickens." *Dickensian* 43 (June 1947):118-24.

1095 EATON, WALTER P. "Little Less Than a God." *Pacific Spectator* 1 (Summer 1947):265-71.

1096 HAMILTON, ROBERT. "Dickens in His Characters." *Nineteenth Century* 142 (July 1947):40-49.

1097 PARTINGTON, WILFRED. "Should a Biographer Tell?" *Atlantic Monthly* 180 (Aug. 1947):56-63. Reprinted in *Dickensian* 43 (Sept. 1947):193-200; 44 (Dec. 1947):14-23. [The story of Dickens's denunciation of Thomas Powell's forgeries.]

1098 ATKINS, STEWART. "A Possible Dickens Influence in Zola." *Modern Language Quarterly* 8 (Sept. 1947):302-8.

1099 MILLER, WILLIAM. "Contemporary Views of Dickens." *Dickensian* 43 (Sept. 1947):200-2.

1100 STEVENSON, LIONEL. "Dickens and the Origin of *The Warden.*" *Trollopian* 2 (Sept. 1947):83-89.

1101 MURPHY, THERESA and RICHARD. "Dickens as a Professional Reader." *Quarterly Journal of Speech* 33 (Oct. 1947):299-307.

1102 ALDINGTON, RICHARD. "The Underworld of Young Dickens." *Four English Portraits, 1801-1851,* 147-89. London: Evans, 1948.

1103 ANDERSEN, HANS CHRISTIAN. *Et Besøg hos Charles Dickens. Tegninger af des Asmusen.* Copenhagen: Korch, 1948.

1104 AYDELOTTE, WILLIAM O. "The England of Marx and Mill as Reflected in Fiction." *The Tasks of Economic History* 8 (1948):42-58 (Supplemental issue of *The Journal of Economic History*).

1105 GOMME, G. J. L. "The Interpolation of Thomas Bailey Aldrich's *The Flight of the Goddess* in Charles Dickens' *Household Words.*" *Papers of the Bibliographical Society of America* 42 (First quarter 1948):70-72.

1106 MONOD, SYLVÈRE. "Critical Preface." *Martin Chuzzlewit.* Paris: Stock, 1948. [French translation.]

1107 SIL'MAN, TAMARA I. *Dikkens. (Očerki Tvorčestva).* Moscow-Leningrad: Goslitizdat, 1948. [*Dickens. (Sketches of His Creative Work).*]

1108 CARLTON, WILLIAM J. "'Mr Powell'." *Dickensian* 44 (Mar. 1948): 104-5. ["Powell" and "Mr Powell" in Dickens' letters.]

1109 PARTINGTON, WILFRED. "The Problem of a Powell Dossier Elucidated." *Dickensian* 44 (Mar. 1948):102-03.

1110 SHYVERS, W. GIBSON. "'Positively the First Appearance'." *Dickensian* 44 (Mar. 1948):89-93. [The earliest known portrait of Dickens by Miss Millington.]

1111 STAPLES, LESLIE C. "Dickens and Macready's 'Lear'." *Dickensian* 44 (Mar. 1948):78-80.

1112 FORD, GEORGE H. "The Governor Eyre Case in England." *University of Toronto Quarterly* 17 (Apr. 1948):219-33.

1113 BUTT, JOHN E. "Dickens at Work." *Durham University Journal* N.S. 9 (June 1948):65-77.

1114 MAJOR, GWEN. "'The City of the Absent'." *Dickensian* 44 (June 1948):130-35. [City churchyards discussed by THE UNCOMMERCIAL TRAVELLER in 1866.]

1115 MORLEY, MALCOLM. "Early Dickens Drama in America." *Dickensian* 44 (June 1948):153-57.

1116 O'SULLIVAN, D. "Charles Dickens and Thomas Moore." *Studies* (Dublin) 37 (June 1948):169-78.

1117 CARLTON, WILLIAM J. "Dickens in Shorthand." *Dickensian* 44 (Sept. 1948):205-8. [Shorthand editions of Dickens' novels.]

1118 MASON, LEO. "Condensed Novels." *Dickensian* 44 (Sept. 1948): 198-99.

1119 MORLEY, MALCOLM. "American Theatrical Notes and Boz." *Dickensian* 44 (Sept. 1948):187-93.

1120 WINTERS, WARRINGTON. "Dickens and the Psychology of Dreams." *PMLA* 63 (Sept. 1948):984-1006.

1121 JOHNSON, EDGAR. "Dickens and the Bluenose Legislator." *American Scholar* 17 (Autumn 1948):450-58.

1122 GIBSON, FRANK A. "Dickens's Unique Book: A Bibliographical Causerie." *Dickensian* 44 (Dec. 1948):44-48. [*Master Humphrey's Clock.*]

1123 MORLEY, MALCOLM. "Theatre Royal, Montreal." *Dickensian* 45 (Dec. 1948):39-44.

1124 MUSGRAVE, OLIVETTE. "Dickens Still Lives – A Christmas Communique." *New York Times Book Review* (Dec. 19, 1948):15.

1125 CRUIKSHANK, ROBERT J. *Charles Dickens and Early Victorian England*. London: Pitman, 1949; New York: Chanticleer Press, 1950.

1126 EISENSTEIN, SERGEI. "Dickens, Griffith and the Film Today." *Film Form*. New York: Harcourt, Brace, 1949. Reprinted in *Film Form and the Film Sense*, 195-255. Cleveland: World, 1957.

1127 ELLING, CHRISTIAN. *Man Laeser Dickens*. Copenhagen: Gyldendalske Boghandel, 1949.

1128 HIGHET, GILBERT. "Dickens as a Dramatist." *People, Places and Books*, 69-76. New York: Oxford Univ. Press, 1949, 1953.

1129 PEARSON, HESKETH. *Dickens: His Character, Comedy and Career*. London: Methuen; New York: Harper, 1949.

1130 HILL, THOMAS W. "Books That Dickens Read." *Dickensian* 45 (Mar. 1949):81-90; (Sept. 1949):201-7.

1131 STAPLES, LESLIE C. "The Dickens Ancestry: Some New Discoverie Being Notes on the Unpublished Work of the Late A. T. Butler, MVO

MC, FSA and the Late Arthur Campling, FSA. Together With an Introductory Note by Ralph Straus." *Dickensian* 45 (Mar. 1949): 64-73; (Sept. 1949):179-88.

1132 STAPLES, LESLIE C. "Dickens in Broadstairs." *Dickensian* 45 (Mar. 1949):91-96.

1133 BUTT, JOHN E. "Dickens's Notes for His Serial Parts." *Dickensian* 45 (June 1949):129-38.

1134 ALTICK, RICHARD D. "Dickens and America." *Pennsylvania Magazine of History and Biography* 73 (July 1949):326-36.

1135 ZABEL, MORTON D. "Dickens: The Reputation Revised." *Nation* 169 (Sept. 1949):279-81. Reprinted in *Craft and Character in Modern Fiction*. New York: Viking, 1957; *Discussions of Charles Dickens*, ed. W. R. Clark, 1961 q.v.

1136 JOHNSON, EDGAR. "Dickens Clashes with His Publisher. Adapted From a Forthcoming Biography, *Charles Dickens: His Tragedy and Triumph.*" *Dickensian* 46 (Dec. 1949):10-17; (Mar. 1950):76-83.

1137 ROLFE, FRANKLIN P. "Dickens and the Ternans." *Nineteenth Century Fiction* 4 (Dec. 1949):243-44.

1138 SHUCKBURGH, SIR JOHN. "The Villain of the Piece." *Dickensian* 46 (Dec. 1949):18-23. [On characters most odious in Dickens' fiction.]

1139 BREDEL, WILLI. *Sieben Dichter.* Schwerin: Petermänken-Verlag, 1950.

1140 GRUBB, GERALD G. *Dickens and the* Daily News: *The Origins of the Idea.* Chapel Hill: Univ. of North Carolina Press, 1950.

1141 LINDSAY, JACK. *Charles Dickens: A Biographical and Critical Study.* New York: Philosophical Library; London: Dakers; Toronto: McLeod, 1950.

1142 YAMAMOTO, TADAO. *Growth and System of the Language of Dickens.* An Introduction to a Dickens Lexicon. Osaka: Kohansha, 1950.

1143 JOHNSON, EDGAR. "Dickens, Fagin and Mr Riah, the Intention of the Novelist." *Commentary* 9 (Jan. 1950):47-50.

1144 ALLEN, WALTER. "The English Novel – V: The World of Dickens' Imagination." *Listener* (Feb. 16, 1950):302-3.

1145 ASHLEY, ROBERT P. "Wilkie Collins Reconsidered." *Nineteenth Century Fiction* 4 (Mar. 1950):265-73. [In relation to Dickens.]

1146 BOEGE, FRED W. "Point of View in Dickens." *PMLA* 65 (Mar. 1950): 90-105.

1147 STAPLES, LESLIE C. "Pictures From Genoa." *Dickensian* 46 (Mar. 1950):84-89.

1148 VIVIAN, CHARLES H. "Dickens, the *True Sun* and Samuel Laman Blanchard." *Nineteenth Century Fiction* 4 (Mar. 1950):328-30.

1149 WAGENKNECHT, EDWARD. "Dickens and the Scandalmongers." *College English* 11 (Apr. 1950):373-82. Reprinted in *Dickens and the Scandalmongers*, 1965 q.v.

1150 MACKENZIE, COMPTON. "Charles Dickens." *Irish Library Bulletin* N.S. 11 (Apr.-May 1950):71-72.

1151 WILSON, ANGUS. "Dickens and the Divided Conscience." *The Mon* 189 (May 1950):349-60.

1152 GRUBB, GERALD G. "The Personal and Literary Relationships of Dickens and Poe." *Nineteenth Century Fiction* 5 (June 1950):1-22; (Sept. 1950):101-20; (Dec. 1950):209-21.

1153 R., V. "Dickens: Two Curious Idioms." *Notes and Queries* 195 (June 1950):279.

1154 SULLIVAN, A. E. "Soldiers of the Queen – and of Charles Dickens.' *Dickensian* 46 (June 1950):138-43. [Source for soldiers in *Pickwick Papers, Bleak House, Barnaby Rudge.*]

1155 FIELDING, KENNETH J. "A New Article by Dickens. Scott and his Publishers from *The Examiner*, Sept. 2nd. 1838. With a note by K. J Fielding." *Dickensian* 46 (Summer 1950):122-27.

1156 NISBET, ADA B. "Dickens Loses an Election." *Princeton University Library Chronicle* 11 (Summer 1950):157-76. [For Rector of Glasgo University.]

1157 VAN GHENT, DOROTHY. "The Dickens World: A View From Todgers'." *Sewanee Review* 58 (Summer 1950):419-38. Reprinted in *The Dickens Critics*, ed. G. H. Ford and L. Lane, Jr., 1961 q.v.; *Dickens: A Collection of Critical Essays*, ed. M. Price, 1967 q.v.

1158 H., A. "Dickens: Two Curious Idioms." *Notes and Queries* 195 (Aug. 1950):372.

1159 HILL, THOMAS W. "Dickens and His 'Ugly Duckling'." *Dickensian* 46 (Sept. 1950):190-96. [*The Village Coquettes.*]

1160 HILL, THOMAS W. "Notes on *Sketches by Boz*." *Dickensian* 46 (Sept. 1950):206-13; 47 (Dec. 1950):41-48; (Mar. 1951):102-07; (June 1951):154-58; (Sept. 1951):210-18; 48 (Dec. 1951):32-37; (Mar. 1952):90-94.

1161 ROUSE, H. BLAIR. "Charles Dickens and Henry James: Two Approaches to the Art of Fiction." *Nineteenth Century Fiction* 5 (Sept. 1950):151-57.

1162 BUCKLER, WILLIAM E. "Dickens's Success with *Household Words*. *Dickensian* 46 (Autumn 1950):197-203.

1163 FIEDLER, LESLIE. "William Faulkner: An American Dickens." *Commentary* 10 (Oct. 1950):384-87.

1164 HAMILTON, LOUIS. "Dickens in Canada." *Dalhousie Review* 30 (Oct. 1950):279-86.

1165 HILL, THOMAS W. "Dickensian Biography from Forster to the Present Day." *Dickensian* 47 (Dec. 1950):10-15; (Mar. 1951):72-79.

1166 MORLEY, MALCOLM. "Jim Crow and Boz's Juba." *Dickensian* 47 (Dec. 1950):28-32. [Young negro dancer who performed between acts of plays.]

1167 WATSON, Mrs R. "Sidelight on a Great Friendship." *Dickensian* 47 (Dec. 1950):16-21.

1168 BREDSDORFF, ELIAS L. *H. C. Andersen og Charles Dickens, et venskab og dets opløsning.* Med gengivelse af H. C. Andersens dagbog fra besøget hos Dickens i sommeren 1857 og brevvekslingen mellem H. C. Andersen og Dickens i årene 1847-62, samt en raekke hidtil utrykte dokumenter og breve. København: Rosenkilde og Bagger, 1951. Trans. as *Hans Andersen and Charles Dickens: a Friendship and its Dissolution.* Copenhagen: Rosenkilde and Bagger; Cambridge, Eng.: Heffer, 1956.

1169 BUCKLER, WILLIAM E. "*Household Words* in America." *Papers of the Bibliographical Society of America* 45 (Second Quarter 1951): 160-66.

1170 DeLANGE, D. *Het Verschijnsel Charles Dickens. Een Poging tot Begrijpen.* Utrecht, Antwerp: Spectrum, 1951.

1171 GREEN, FRANK. *London Homes of Dickens.* Introd. Walter Dexter. Illus. Charles Pearce. London: W. and R. Chambers, 1951.

1172 ROBINSON, KENNETH. "The Dickens Circle." *Wilkie Collins,* 59-72. London: Bodley Head; New York: Macmillan, 1951.

1173 ROOKE, ELEANOR. "Fathers and Sons in Dickens." *Essays and Studies* 4 (1951):53-69.

1174 STAPLES, LESLIE C. *The Dickens Ancestry.* Some new discoveries, being notes on the unpublished work of the late A. T. Butler ... and the late Arthur Campling. With an introd. by Ralph Straus. With an account of the Barrows of Bristol by William J. Carlton. London: the Author, 1951.

1175 SYMONS, JULIAN. *Charles Dickens.* New York: Roy; London: Barker; Toronto: McClelland and Stewart, 1951.

1176 YAMAMOTO, TADAO. *Dickens' English.* Tokyo: Kenkyusha, 1951.

1177 GREGORY, S. E. "Dickens and the Royal Academy." *Notes and Queries* 196 (Jan. 1951):42. [Reply to a question in *Notes and Queries* 195 (Sept. 1950):414 re the date and occasion of Dickens' political squib attacking certain Royal Academicians.]

1178 GRUBB, GERALD G. "Dickens' Western Tour and the Cairo Legend." *Studies in Philology* 48 (Jan. 1951):87-97.

1179 MAXWELL, J. C. "Mrs Christian's Reminiscences of Dickens."
      Review of English Studies N.S. 2 (Jan. 1951):59-63.

1180 CARLTON, WILLIAM J. "'The Story Without a Beginning'. An
      Unrecorded Contribution by Boz to the *Morning Chronicle.*"
      Dickensian 47 (Mar. 1951):67-70.

1181 FIELDING, KENNETH J. "Charles Dickens and Thomas C. Evans.
      A Proposed Reading Tour in the U.S.A. – 1859." *Notes and Queries*
      196 (Mar. 1951):123-24.

1182 NISBET, ADA B. "New Light on the Dickens-Poe Relationship."
      Nineteenth Century Fiction 5 (Mar. 1951):295-302.

1183 FIELDING, KENNETH J. "'Women in the Home'. An Article Which
      Dickens Did *Not* Write." *Dickensian* 47 (June 1951):140-42.

1184 HILL, THOMAS W. "Dickens and the 1851 Exhibition." *Dickensian*
      47 (June 1951):119-24. [Re *Household Words* and Dickens' reaction
      to the 1851 Exhibition.]

1185 DAVIS, ROBERT G. "The Sense of the Real in English Fiction."
      Comparative Literature 3 (Summer 1951):200-17.

1186 CARLTON, WILLIAM J. "Dickens and the Two Tennysons."
      Dickensian 47 (Sept. 1951):173-77.

1187 ENKVIST, NILS E. "Charles Dickens in the Witness Box." *Dickensian*
      47 (Sept. 1951):201.

1188 FIELDING, KENNETH J. "Dickens and Maria Goodluck." *Notes and
      Queries* 196 (Sept. 1951):430-31.

1189 HILL, THOMAS W. "A Lawyer's Black Boxes: Light on the Guild of
      Literature and Art and the Douglas Jerrold Fund." *Dickensian* 47
      (Sept. 1951):178-89.

1190 MASON, LEO. "Poe and Dickens." *Dickensian* 47 (Sept. 1951):
      207-10.

1191 MORLEY, MALCOLM. "Ring Up *The Chimes.*" *Dickensian* 47
      (Sept. 1951):202-6.

1192 POSTLETHWAITE, AMELIA. "My Favorite Men Characters."
      Dickensian 47 (Sept. 1951):196-97.

1193 STAPLES, LESLIE C. "Two Early London Homes of Charles
      Dickens." *Dickensian* 47 (Sept. 1951):198-200.

1194 HILL, THOMAS W. "Organs." *Notes and Queries* 196 (Oct. 1951):
      460.

1195 HOUSE, HUMPHRY. "A New Edition of Dickens's Letters."
      Listener 46 (Oct. 1951):637-38; *Dickensian* 48 (Mar. 1952):65-69.
      Reprinted in *All In Due Time.* London: Hart-Davis, 1955.

1196 HUDSON, RICHARD B. "The Dickens Affair Again." *College
      English* 13 (Nov. 1951):111-13.

1197 BUCKLER, WILLIAM E. "Dickens the Paymaster." *PMLA* 66
(Dec. 1951):1177-80.

1198 CARLTON, WILLIAM J. "The Barber of Dean Street." *Dickensian*
48 (Dec. 1951):8-12.

1199 GRUBB, GERALD G. "Dickens and the *Daily News:* Preliminaries
to Publication." *Nineteenth Century Fiction* 6 (Dec. 1951):174-94;
(Mar. 1952):234-46; 7 (June 1952):19-38.

1200 MORLEY, MALCOLM. "'The Cricket' on the Stage." *Dickensian* 48
(Dec. 1951):17-24.

1201 SAVAGE, OLIVER D. "Johnson and Dickens: A Comparison."
Dickensian 48 (Dec. 1951):42-44.

1202 CRUIKSHANK, ROBERT J., ed. *The Humour of Dickens.* London:
News Chronicle, 1952.

1203 FAWCETT, FRANK D. *Dickens the Dramatist, on Stage, Screen and
Radio.* London: Allen, 1952.

1204 HOPKINS, ANNETTE B. "Dickens: North and South and the Difficulties of Serial Publication." *Elizabeth Gaskell Her Life and Work,*
135-57. London: John Lehmann, 1952.

1205 JOHNSON, EDGAR. *Charles Dickens, His Tragedy and Triumph.*
2 vols. New York: Simon and Shuster; Toronto: Musson, 1952.

R1206 [JOHNSON, EDGAR. *Charles Dickens, His Tragedy and Triumph,*
1952 q.v.] BUTT, JOHN E. "*Charles Dickens: His Tragedy and
Triumph.*" *Nineteenth Century Fiction* 8 (Sept. 1953):151-53.

R1207 [JOHNSON, EDGAR. *Charles Dickens, His Tragedy and Triumph,*
1952 q.v.] CARLTON, WILLIAM J. "Charles Dickens – A Full-Scale
Biography." *Dickensian* 49 (Dec. 1952):53-58.

R1208 [JOHNSON, EDGAR. *Charles Dickens, His Tragedy and Triumph,*
1952 q.v.] FERGUSON, DELANAY. "Superman and the Blacking
Works." *Saturday Review of Literature* (Jan. 10, 1953):10-12.

R1209 [JOHNSON, EDGAR. *Charles Dickens, His Tragedy and Triumph,*
1952 q.v.] MUIR, EDWIN. "*Charles Dickens, His Tragedy and
Triumph.*" *Observer* (Sept. 27, 1953):11.

R1210 [JOHNSON, EDGAR. *Charles Dickens, His Tragedy and Triumph,*
1952 q.v.] WEST, ANTHONY. "Books." *New Yorker* 28
(Jan. 10, 1953):81+. Reprinted as "Charles Dickens" in *Principles
and Persuasions.* New York: Harcourt, 1957.

1211 NISBET, ADA B. *Dickens and Ellen Ternan.* Foreword by Edmund
Wilson. Berkeley; Los Angeles: Univ. of California Press, 1952.

R1212 [NISBET, ADA B. *Dickens and Ellan Ternan,* 1952 q.v.] EATON,
EVELYN. "For the Love of Nelly." *New York Times Book Review*
(Dec. 21, 1952):4.

R1213 [NISBET, ADA B. *Dickens and Ellan Ternan*, 1952 q.v.] FIELDING, KENNETH J. *Review of English Studies* N.S. 5 (July 1954):322-25.

R1214 [NISBET, ADA B. *Dickens and Ellan Ternan*, 1952 q.v.] GRUBB, GERALD G. *"Dickens and Ellan Ternan."* Dickensian 49 (June 1953): 121-29.

R1215 [NISBET, ADA B. *Dickens and Ellan Ternan*, 1952 q.v.] JOHNSON, EDGAR. "Ada Nisbet's *Dickens and Ellan Ternan.*" *Nineteenth Century Fiction* 7 (Mar. 1953):296-98.

R1216 [NISBET, ADA. *Dickens and Ellan Ternan*, 1952 q.v.] WAGENKNECHT, EDWARD. "Ellan Ternan." *Dickensian* 50 (Dec. 1953):28-34.

1217 WAGENKNECHT, EDWARD, ed. *Introduction to Dickens.* New York: Scott, Foresman, 1952.

1218 BUTT, JOHN E. "New Light on Charles Dickens." *Listener* 51 (Feb. 1952):341-42.

1219 FIELDING, KENNETH J. "John Henry Barrow and the Royal Literary Fund." *Dickensian* 48 (Mar. 1952):61-64.

1220 HILL, THOMAS W. (T. Kent Brumleigh, pseud.) "Journalistics." *Dickensian* 48 (Mar. 1952):82-89.

1221 HOUTCHENS, LAWRENCE H. "The Spirit of the Times and a 'New Work by Boz'." *PMLA* 67 (Mar. 1952):94-100. [A hoax.]

1222 MORLEY, MALCOLM. "*The Battle of Life* in the Theatre." *Dickensian* 48 (Mar. 1952):76-81.

1223 FIELDING, KENNETH J. "Charles Whitehead and Dickens." *Review of English Studies* N.S. 3 (Apr. 1952):141-54.

1224 ADRIAN, ARTHUR A. "Dickens on American Slavery: A Carlylean Stint." *PMLA* 67 (June 1952):315-29.

1225 GRUBB, GERALD G. "Personal and Business Relations of Charles Dickens and Thomas Coke Evans." *Dickensian* 48 (June 1952): 106-13; (Sept. 1952):168-73.

1226 FIELDING, KENNETH J. "The MS of the *Cricket on the Hearth.*" *Notes and Queries* 197 (July 1952):324-25.

1227 CARLTON, WILLIAM J. "Mr Blackmore Engages an Office Boy." *Dickensian* 48 (Sept. 1952):162-67.

1228 FIELDING, KENNETH J. "Charles Dickens and Colin Rae Brown." *Nineteenth Century Fiction* 7 (Sept. 1952):103-10.

1229 MORLEY, MALCOLM. "Pepper and *The Haunted Man.*" *Dickensian* 48 (Sept. 1952):185-90.

1230 JOHNSON, EDGAR. "The Scope of Dickens." *Saturday Review of Literature* 35 (Nov. 29, 1952):13-14, 44-48.

1231 FIELDING, KENNETH J. "'Dickens and Scott: An Unusual Borrowing' Queried." *Nineteenth Century Fiction* 7 (Dec. 1952): 223-24.

1232 AUSTIN, JAMES C. "Charles Dickens and Charles Reade." *Fields of* The Atlantic Monthly, 379-94. Los Angeles: Anderson, Ritchie and Simon, 1953.

1233 CARTER, FREDERICK A. *Haywire Dickens.* (French's Monologue Series 59) London: S. French, 1953. [Characters in Dickens.]

1234 FIELDING, KENNETH J. *Charles Dickens.* (Writers and Their Work 37) London: Longmans, Green, 1953. Revised edition. London: Longmans, Green, 1960.

1235 HARRISON, MICHAEL. *Charles Dickens: A Sentimental Journey in Search of an Unvarnished Portrait.* London: Cassell, 1953.

1236 MONOD, SYLVÈRE. *Dickens Romancier: Étude sur la Création Littéraire dans les Romans de Charles Dickens.* Paris: Hatchett, 1953.

1237 PATTERSON, CLARA B. "Friendship with Dickens." *Angela Burdett-Coutts and the Victorians,* 142-77. London: John Murray, 1953.

1238 NICHOLS, LEWIS. "Talk with Edgar Johnson." *New York Times Book Review* 18 (Jan. 1953):18.

1239 ADRIAN, ARTHUR A. "A Note on the Dickens-Collins Friendship." *Huntington Library Quarterly* 16 (Feb. 1953):211-13.

1240 ASHLEY, ROBERT P. "Wilkie Collins and the Dickensians." *Dickensian* 49 (Mar. 1953):59-65. [Collins, a novelist in his own right. He was "the only Victorian novelist to influence Dickens' art," and few Dickens biographers have given him his due.]

1241 GIBSON, PRISCILLA. "Dickens's Use of Animism." *Nineteenth Century Fiction* 7 (Mar. 1953):283-91.

1242 HOUSE, HUMPHRY. "A Dickens Letter. A Copy or a Forgery?" *Dickensian* 49 (Mar. 1953):69-73.

1243 CARLTON, WILLIAM J. "When the Cholera Raged at Chatham. A Reminiscence of Dickens's Youth." *Dickensian* 49 (June 1953): 113-18.

1244 FIELDING, KENNETH J. "Dickens and Wilkie Collins: A Reply." *Dickensian* 49 (June 1953):130-36.

1245 FIELDING, KENNETH J. "A Great Friendship (Miss Burdett Coutts)." *Dickensian* 49 (June 1953):102-7.

1246 CARLTON, WILLIAM J. "'The Old Lady' in *Sketches by Boz.*" *Dickensian* 49 (Sept. 1953):149-52.

1247 GRUBB, GERALD G. "Dickens's Quarrel with John A. Overs." *Dickensian* 49 (Sept. 1953):164-68.

1248 HOUSE, HUMPHRY. "The Dickens Story." *Listener* 50 (Oct. 1953): 693-94. Reprinted in *All In Due Time*. London: Hart-Davis, 1955.

1249 WEITENKAMPF, FRANK. "American Illustrators of Dickens." *Boston Public Library Quarterly* 5 (Oct. 1953):189-94.

1250 FIELDING, KENNETH J. "Dickens Since Forster." *Times Literary Supplement* (Oct. 9, 1953):637-38.

1251 LINDSAY, JACK. "Charles Dickens and Women." *Twentieth Century* 154 (Nov. 1953):375-86.

1252 BOEGE, FRED W. "Recent Criticism of Dickens." *Nineteenth Century Fiction* 8 (Dec. 1953):171-87.

1253 CARLTON, WILLIAM J. "A Companion of the *Copperfield* Days." *Dickensian* 50 (Dec. 1953):7-16. [James E. Roney.]

1254 FIELDING, KENNETH J. "Dickens and Cave. A Theatrical Anecdote." *Dickensian* 50 (Dec. 1953):24-27.

1255 MORLEY, MALCOLM. "'No Thoroughfare' Back Stage." *Dickensian* 50 (Dec. 1953):37-42. [The Christmas number of *All the Year Round* for 1867.]

1256 WAGENKNECHT, EDWARD. "Ellen Ternan." *Dickensian* 50 (Dec. 1953):28-34.

1257 FARJEON, ELEANOR. "Introduction." *Christmas Books.* (New Oxford Illustrated Dickens.) London: Oxford Univ. Press, 1954.

1258 GRAHAM, ELEANOR. *The Story of Charles Dickens.* Illus. with plates from the original editions of his works, and with additional drawings by Norman Meredith. New York: Abelard-Schuman, 1954.

1259 IVAŠEVA, V. V. *Tvorčestvo Dikkensa.* Moscow: Izdatel'stvo Moskovskogo Universiteta, 1954. [*Dickens' Works.*]

1260 IZZO, CARLO. *Autobiografismo di Charles Dickens.* Venezia: Neri Pozza Editore, 1954.

1261 SELIVESTROV, M. L. *Dikkens i Tekkerej v Ocenke Černyševskogo.* Frunze: Kirkiz, 1954. [*Dickens and Thackeray as Judged by Chernyshevsky.*]

1262 WILLIAMS, EMLYN. *Readings From Dickens.* Introd. Bernard Darwin. London: Heinemann, 1954. [Adaptations.]

1263 HAMILTON, ROBERT. "Dickens Triumphant." *Quarterly Review* 292 (Jan. 1954):46-58. [Review article of Johnson Biography.]

1264 FIELDING, KENNETH J. "Bradbury v. Dickens." *Dickensian* 50 (Mar. 1954):73-82. [*Household Words.*]

1265 GIBSON, FRANK A. "Discomforts in Dickens." *Dickensian* 50 (Mar. 1954):86-89. [Examples of lack of control and inconsistency.]

1266 HAMILTON, ROBERT. "Chesterton and Dickens." *Dickensian* 50 (Mar. 1954):83-85.

1267 CARLTON, WILLIAM J. "Portraits in 'A Parliamentary Sketch'."
Dickensian 50 (June 1954):100-9.

1268 GRUBB, GERALD G. "Charles Dickens and His Brother Fred."
Dickensian 50 (June 1954):123-31.

1269 PRITCHETT, V. S. "The Humour of Dickens." *Listener* 51
(June 1954):970-73. Reprinted as "The Comic World of Dickens."
Avon Book of Modern Writing. New York: Berkley Publishing Corp.,
1955; *The Dickens Critics,* ed. G. H. Ford and L. Lane, Jr., 1961 q.v.

1270 JOHNSON, EDGAR. "The Paradox of Dickens. Address to the
Boston Branch of the Dickens Fellowship, 142nd Birthday Anniversary Dinner, Feb. 10th, 1954." *Dickensian* 50 (Sept. 1954):149-58.

1271 PATERSON, ANDREW. "Grandfather Thomson." *Dickensian* 50
(Sept. 1954):173-74. [George Thomson, grandfather of Catherine
Hogarth.]

1272 RAY, GORDON N. "Dickens Versus Thackeray: The Garrick Club
Affair." *PMLA* 69 (Sept. 1954):815-32.

1273 WHIPPLE, WILLIAM. "Poe's Two-edged Satiric Tale." *Nineteenth
Century Fiction* 9 (Sept. 1954):121-33.

1274 FIELDING, KENNETH J. "Dickens and the Royal Literary Fund
1855." *Times Literary Supplement* (Oct. 15, 1954):664;
(Oct. 22, 1954):680.

1275 FIELDING, KENNETH J. "Carlyle, Charles Dickens, and William
Maccall." *Notes and Queries* N.S. 1 (Nov. 1954):488-90.

1276 AYLMER, FELIX. "John Forster and Dickens's Book of Memoranda."
Dickensian 51 (Dec. 1954):19-23.

1277 FIELDING, KENNETH J. "Dickens's Novels and Miss Burdett-Coutts."
Dickensian 51 (Dec. 1954):30-34.

1278 DAIX, PIERRE. "A Critical Introduction." *Martin Chuzzlewit.*
Paris: Editeurs Français Réunis, 1954-56. [French translation.]

1279 ADDISON, WILLIAM. *In the Steps of Charles Dickens.* London:
Rich and Cowan, 1955.

1280 ALLEN, WALTER. "Charles Dickens." *Six Great Novelists: Defoe,
Fielding, Scott, Dickens, Stevenson, Conrad,* 95-125. London:
Hamish Hamilton, 1955.

1281 EBUKE, SHUNJI. *Charles Dickens.* Tokyo: Kenkyusha, 1955.

1282 FORD, GEORGE H. *Dickens and His Readers: Aspects of Novel
Criticism Since 1836.* Princeton, NJ: Princeton Univ. Press, 1955;
New York: Norton, 1965.

R1283 [FORD, GEORGE H. *Dickens and His Readers,* 1955 q.v.] AMIS,
KINGSLEY. "The Cockney's Homer." *Spectator* 196 (Jan. 1956):
22-23.

R1284 [FORD, GEORGE H. *Dickens and His Readers,* 1955 q.v.]
JOHNSON, EDGAR. "Turning Tides." *Virginia Quarterly Review* 31
(Autumn 1955):644-48.

R1285 [FORD, GEORGE H. *Dickens and His Readers,* 1955 q.v.] ROSS,
MALCOLM. "The Editor's Shelf." *Queen's Quarterly* 62
(Autumn 1955):469

R1286 [FORD, GEORGE H. *Dickens and His Readers,* 1955 q.v.] STONE,
EDWARD. *College English* 17 (Nov. 1955):124-25.

R1287 [FORD, GEORGE H. *Dickens and His Readers,* 1955 q.v.]
TILLOTSON, GEOFFREY. "Victorian Novelists and Near-Novelists."
Sewanee Review 64 (Fall 1956):671-73.

R1288 [FORD, GEORGE H. *Dickens and His Readers,* 1955 q.v.] WILSON,
ANGUS. "Novels and Highbrows." *Encounter* 31 (Apr. 1956):75-77.

1289 HOUSE, HUMPHRY. "The Macabre Dickens." *All In Due Time,*
183-89. London: Hart-Davis, 1955. Reprinted in *The Dickens Critics,*
ed. G. H. Ford and L. Lane, Jr., 1961 q.v.

1290 LANE, LAURIAT, Jr. *The Collings-Mennen Extra-illustrated Copy
of John Forster's LIFE OF CHARLES DICKENS.* Ithaca, NY:
Cornell Univ. Library Associates, 1955. Reprinted in *Cornell Library
Journal* 8 (Spring 1969).

1291 MAJUT, RUDOLF. "Some Literary Affiliations of Georg Büchner
with England." *Modern Language Review* 50 (Jan. 1955):30-43.
[Including Dickens.]

1292 ROUTH, C. R. N. "A Cruikshank Caricature." *Times Literary
Supplement* (Jan. 7, 1955):9.

1293 CARLTON, WILLIAM J. "Dickens and the Ross Family." *Dickensian*
51 (Mar. 1955):58-66.

1294 GRUBB, GERALD G. "Dickens the Paymaster Once More."
Dickensian 51 (Mar. 1955):72-78.

1295 HULSE, BRYAN F. "Dostoevsky for Dickensians." *Dickensian* 51
(Mar. 1955):66-71.

1296 NISBET, ADA B. "Poe and Dickens." *Nineteenth Century Fiction*
9 (Mar. 1955):313-14.

1297 MANHEIM, LEONARD F. "The Law as Father." *American Imago*
12 (Spring 1955):17-23.

1298 JOHNSON, EDGAR. "The Present State of Dickensian Studies."
Victorian Newsletter 7 (Apr. 1955):4-9.

1299 BIRCH, DENNIS. "A Forgotten Book; Extracts from a Talk on
A Child's History of England Given to Dickens Fellowship in
London." *Dickensian* 51 (June 1955):121-26; (Sept. 1955):154-57.

1300 CARLTON, WILLIAM J. "Dickens's Insurance Policies." *Dickensian*
51 (June 1955):133-37.

1301 CHAPLIN, CHARLES. "The Immortal Memory of Charles Dickens."
     Dickensian 51 (June 1955):111-14.

1302 COLLINS, PHILIP A. W. "A Note on Dickens and Froebel." *National
     Froebel Foundation Bulletin* 94 (June 1955):15-18.

1303 FIELDING, KENNETH J. "Dickens and The Hogarth Scandal."
     Nineteenth Century Fiction 10 (June 1955):64-74.

1304 GIBSON, FRANK A. "Hats in Dickens." *Dickensian* 51 (June 1955):
     108-10.

1305 MORLEY, MALCOLM. "Plays from the Christmas Numbers of
     Household Words." *Dickensian* 51 (June 1955):127-32; (Sept. 1955):
     169-73.

1306 WALKER, SAXON. "The Artistry of Dickens as an English Novelist."
     Dickensian 51 (June 1955):102-8.

1307 FIELDING, KENNETH J. "Charles Dickens and His Wife: Fact or
     Forgery?" *Études Anglaises* 8 (July-Sept. 1955):212-22.

1308 ENGEL, MONROE. "Dickens on Art." *Modern Philology* 53
     (Aug. 1955):25-38. Reprinted in *The Maturity of Dickens,* 1959 q.v.
     [Fiction as art.]

1309 ADRIAN, ARTHUR A. "The Demise of 'The Strange Gentleman'."
     Dickensian 51 (Sept. 1955):158-60.

1310 CARLTON, WILLIAM J. "Who Was Dickens's French Employer?"
     Dickensian 51 (Sept. 1955):149-54.

1311 COLLINS, PHILIP A. W. "Bruce Castle; A School Dickens Admired."
     Dickensian 51 (Sept. 1955):174-81.

1312 BROWN, T. J. "English Literary Autographs 15: Charles Dickens
     1812-1870." *Book Collector* 4 (Autumn 1955):237. [Analysis of
     his handwriting.]

1313 LEAVIS, Q. D. "A Note on Literary Indebtedness: Dickens, George
     Eliot, Henry James." *Hudson Review* 8 (Autumn 1955):423-28.

1314 FIELDING, KENNETH J. "Dickens and the Royal Literary Fund –
     1858." *Review of English Studies* N.S. 6 (Oct. 1955):383-94.

1315 MURPHY, THERESA. "Interpretation in the Dickens Period."
     Quarterly Journal of Speech 41 (Oct. 1955):243-49.

1316 ADRIAN, ARTHUR A. "Dickens and the Brick-and-Mortar Sects."
     Nineteenth Century Fiction 10 (Dec. 1955):188-201.

1317 WAGENKNECHT, EDWARD. "Dickens in Longfellow's Letters and
     Journals." *Dickensian* 52 (Dec. 1955):7-19. Reprinted in *Dickens and
     the Scandalmongers,* 1965 q.v.

1318 BRAIN, SIR RUSSELL. "Dickensian Diagnoses." *British Medical
     Journal* (Dec. 24, 1955):1553-56. Reprinted in *Some Reflections on
     Genius and Other Essays.* London: Pitman, 1960. [Dickens'
     psychiatric insight.]

1319 MUIR, P. H. "Note No. 55. Dickens and Tauchnitz." *Book Collector* 4 (Winter 1955):329.

1320 BOWEN, WILLIAM H. *Charles Dickens and His Family. A Sympathetic Study.* Cambridge: W. Heffer, 1956.

1321 FUTRELL, MICHAEL H. "Dostoevsky and Dickens." *English Miscellany* 7 (1956):41-89.

1322 JOHANNSEN, ALBERT. *Phiz: Illustrations From the Novels of Charles Dickens.* Chicago: Univ. of Chicago Press, 1956.

1323 LANE, MARGARET. "Introduction." *Christmas Stories.* New Oxford Illustrated Dickens. London: Oxford Univ. Press, 1956.

1324 PRAZ, MARIO. "Charles Dickens." *The Hero in Eclipse in Victorian Fiction*, 127-88. Trans. Angus Davidson. London; New York: Oxford Univ. Press, 1956. [Translation of *La Crisi dell'eroe nel romanzo vittoriano.* Firenze: Sansoni, 1952.]

1325 SIMONS, JACOB B. *The Romance and Humanity of Dickens.* Southport, Eng.: A. Downie, 1956.

1326 THALMANN, LISELOTTE. *Charles Dickens in seinen Beziehungen zum Ausland.* (ZüricherBeiträge zur vergleichenden Literaturgeschichte 6.) Zürich: Juris Verlag, 1956.

1327 TRILLING, LIONEL. "The Dickens of Our Day." *A Gathering of Fugitives*, 41-48. London: Secker and Warburg, 1956.

1328 CARLTON, WILLIAM J. "Dickens in the Jury Box." *Dickensian* 52 (Mar. 1956):65-69.

1329 GIBSON, FRANK A. "The Idyllic in Dickens." *Dickensian* 52 (Mar. 1956):59-64.

1330 GRUBB, GERALD G. "Dickens Rejects." *Dickensian* 52 (Mar. 1956): 89-90.

1331 HAIGHT, GORDON S. "Dickens and Lewes." *PMLA* 71 (Mar. 1956): 166-79.

1332 MATTHEWS, VERY REV. W. R. "Religious Movements in the Lifetime of Charles Dickens." *Dickensian* 52 (Mar. 1956):52-59.

1333 MORLEY, MALCOLM. "Plays and Sketches by Boz." *Dickensian* 52 (Mar. 1956):81-88.

1334 SCHOEK, R. J. "Acton on Dickens." *Dickensian* 52 (Mar. 1956): 77-80.

1335 STAPLES, LESLIE C. "The Ghost of a French *Hamlet.*" *Dickensian* 52 (Mar. 1956):71-76. [Dickens' French friend, Charles Fechter.]

1336 TILLOTSON, KATHLEEN. "Dickens and a Story by John Poole." *Dickensian* 52 (Mar. 1956):69-70. [Dickens' story, "A Dinner at Poplar Walk."]

1337 PASCAL, ROY. "Dickens and Kafka." *Listener* 55 (Apr. 1956):
504-6.

1338 COLLINS, PHILIP A. W. "'Keep *Household Words* Imaginative!'"
Dickensian 52 (June 1956):117-23.

1339 FUTRELL, MICHAEL H. "Gogol and Dickens." *Slavonic and East
European Review* 34 (June 1956):443-59.

1340 GRUBB, GERALD G. "Dickens and Chorley." *Dickensian* 52
(June 1956):100-09.

1341 MANNING, JOHN. "Dickens and the Glasgow System." *School and
Society* 83 (June 1956):202-6.

1342 MORLEY, MALCOLM. "*All the Year Round* Plays." *Dickensian* 52
(June 1956):128-31; (Sept. 1956):177-80.

1343 ADRIAN, ARTHUR A. "Charles Dickens and Dean Stanley."
Dickensian 52 (Sept. 1956):152-56.

1344 DuCANN, CHARLES G. "Dickens on the Death Penalty." *Dickensian*
52 (Sept. 1956):149-51. [Continued effort to abolish hanging by the
Dickens Fellowship following Dickens' stand.]

1345 MURPHY, THOMAS D. "*A Child's History of England.*" *Dickensian*
52 (Sept. 1956):157-61.

1346 PECHEY, R. F. "Dickensian Nomenclature." *Dickensian* 52
(Sept. 1956):180-82.

1347 CLARK, WILLIAM R. "The Hungry Mr Dickens." *Dalhousie Review*
26 (Autumn 1956):250-57. Reprinted in *Discussions of Charles
Dickens,* 1961 q.v.

1348 CLARK, WILLIAM R. "The Rationale of Dickens' Death Rate."
Boston University Studies in English 2 (Autumn 1956):125-39.

1349 BURNS, WAYNE. "The Genuine and the Counterfeit: A Study in
Victorian and Modern Fiction." *College English* 18 (Dec. 1956):
143-50.

1350 ENGEL, MONROE. "The Politics of Dickens' Novels." *PMLA* 71
(Dec. 1956):945-74. Reprinted in *The Maturity of Dickens*, 1959 q.v.

1351 FIELDING, KENNETH J. "The Recent Reviews – Dickens in 1858."
Dickensian 52 (Dec. 1956):25-32.

1352 FLEMING, ROY F. "Charles Dickens Visits the Great Lakes."
Inland Seas 12 (Winter 1956):301-03.

1353 ADRIAN, ARTHUR A. *Georgina Hogarth and The Dickens Circle.*
London: Oxford Univ. Press, 1957.

1354 BODELSEN, CARL A. *Dickens og Hans Bøger.* Copenhagen:
Aschehoug, 1957.

1355 BUTT, JOHN E. and KATHLEEN TILLOTSON. *Dickens at Work.*
London: Methuen, 1957.

R1356 [BUTT, JOHN E. and KATHLEEN TILLOTSON. *Dickens at Work,* 1957 q.v.] CARNALL, GEOFFREY. "Reviews." *Modern Language Review* 53 (Oct. 1958):574-75.

R1357 [BUTT, JOHN E. and KATHLEEN TILLOTSON. *Dickens at Work,* 1957 q.v.] ENGEL, MONROE. "Book Reviews." *Victorian Studies* 1 (Mar. 1958):288-89.

R1358 [BUTT, JOHN E. and KATHLEEN TILLOTSON. *Dickens at Work,* 1957 q.v.] FIELDING, KENNETH J. "The Novelist at Work." *Dickensian* 65 (Jan. 1969):49-51.

R1359 [BUTT, JOHN E. and KATHLEEN TILLOTSON. *Dickens at Work,* 1957 q.v.] LANE, LAURIAT, Jr. *Modern Language Notes* 74 (June 1959):543-46.

1360 COVENEY, PETER. "The Child in Dickens." *Poor Monkey: the Child in Literature,* 71-119. London: Rockliff, 1957. *The Image of Childhood.* Introd. F. R. Leavis, Baltimore: Peregrine, 1967.

1361 HOLME, THEA. "Introduction." *Sketches by Boz.* (New Oxford Illustrated Dickens.) London: Oxford Univ. Press, 1957.

1362 MILNER, IAN. "The Nature of the Hero in Dickens and the Eighteenth Century Tradition." *Philologica* (Foreign Language Supplement to *Časopis Pro Moderni Filologii*) 9 (1957):57-67.

1363 NERSESOVA, MAGDALINA A. *Tvorčestvo Čarl'za Dikkensa.* Moscow: "Znanie," 1957. [*The Works of Charles Dickens.*]

1364 O'DONOVAN, MICHAEL (Frank O'Connor, pseud.). "Dickens: The Intrusion of the Audience." *Mirror in the Roadway,* 70-82. London: H. Hamilton, 1957.

1365 SITWELL, SACHEVERELL. "Introduction." *American Notes and Pictures From Italy.* New Oxford Illustrated Dickens. London: Oxford Univ. Press, 1957.

1366 CARLTON, WILLIAM J. "John Dickens, Journalist." *Dickensian* 53 (Jan. 1957):5-11.

1367 FINLAY, IAN F. "Dickens's Influence on Dutch Literature." *Dickensian* 53 (Jan. 1957):40-42.

1368 HUNTER, RICHARD A. and IDA MACALPINE. "A Note on Dickens' Psychiatric Reading." *Dickensian* 53 (Jan. 1957):49-51.

1369 RIGBY, STEPHEN. "Olfactory Gleanings." *Dickensian* 53 (Jan. 1957): 36-38.

1370 ROCKMAN, ROBERT E. "Dickens and Shaw: Another Parallel." *Shaw Bulletin* 2 (Jan. 1957):8-10.

1371 SHUSTERMAN, DAVID. "Peter Cunningham, Friend of Dickens." *Dickensian* 53 (Jan. 1957):20-35.

1372 STONE, HARRY. "Dickens's Knowledge of Thackeray's Writings." *Dickensian* 53 (Jan. 1957):42-45.

1373 TROUGHTON, MARION. "Dickens as Editor." *Contemporary Review* 191 (Feb. 1957):87-91.

1374 PEARSON, GABRIEL. "Dickens and his Readers." *Universities and Left Review* 1 (Spring 1957):52-56.

1375 COCKSHUT, A. O. J. "Sentimentality in Fiction." *Twentieth Century* 161 (Apr. 1957):354-64.

1376 CARLTON, WILLIAM J. "Captain Morgan – *Alias* Jorgan." *Dickensian* 53 (May 1957):75-82.

1377 DICKINS, LOUIS G. "The Friendship of Dickens and Carlyle." *Dickensian* 53 (May 1957):98-106.

1378 PEYROUTON, NOEL C. "Dickens Breakfasts with Longfellow." *Dickensian* 53 (May 1957):85-92.

1379 STAPLES, LESLIE C. "The Honeymoon Village of Chalk." *Dickensian* 53 (May 1957):110-11. [The three houses laying claim to sheltering the honeymooning Dickenses in 1836.]

1380 STONE, HARRY. "Dickens and Wilkie Collins." *Dickensian* 53 (May 1957):112-14. [Re N. P. Davis's book *The Life of Wilkie Collins.*]

1381 CARLTON, WILLIAM J. "Fanny Dickens, Pianist and Vocalist." *Dickensian* 53 (Sept. 1957):133-43.

1382 GIBSON, FRANK A. "Dogs in Dickens." *Dickensian* 53 (Sept. 1957): 145-52.

1383 KARL, FREDERICK R. "Conrad's Debt to Dickens." *Notes and Queries* N.S. 4 (Sept. 1957):398-400.

1384 PEYROUTON, NOEL C. "Dickens, Dolby and Dolliver: An American Note." *Dickensian* 53 (Sept. 1957):153-59.

1385 MANNING, JOHN. "Charles Dickens and the Oswego System." *Journal of the History of Ideas* 18 (Oct. 1957):580-86.

1386 CARLTON, WILLIAM J. "The Third Man at Newgate." *Review of English Studies* 8 (Nov. 1957):402-7. [Material for "A Visit to Newgate" in *Sketches by Boz.*]

1387 JAMES, G. INGLI. "Dickens: an Essay in Christian Evaluation." *Blackfriars* 38 (Nov. 1957):466-73.

1388 NISBET, ADA B. "The Boz Ball." *American Heritage* 9 (Dec. 1957): 10-11, 112-13. [In New York to welcome Dickens, 1842.]

1389 STONE, HARRY. "Charles Dickens and Harriet Beecher Stowe." *Nineteenth Century Fiction* 12 (Dec. 1957):188-202. [Duplicates 1390.]

1390 STONE, HARRY. "Dickens and Harriet Beecher Stowe." *Nineteenth Century Fiction* 12 (Dec. 1957):188-202. [Duplicates 1389.]

1391 JOHNSON, EDGAR. "Dickens and Shaw: Critics of Society." *Virginia Quarterly Review* 33 (Winter 1957):66-79.

1392 BUSH, DOUGLAS. "A Note on Dickens' Humor." *From Jane Austen to Joseph Conrad; Essays Collected in Memory of James T. Hillhouse,* ed. Robert C. Rathburn and Martin Steinmann, Jr., 82-91. Minneapolis: Univ. of Minnesota Press, 1958. Reprinted in *Discussions of Charles Dickens,* ed. W. R. Clark, 1961 q.v.; and in *Engaged and Disengaged,* by Douglas Bush. Cambridge, Mass.: Harvard Univ. Press, 1966.

1393 CHURCHILL, R. C. "Charles Dickens." *From Dickens to Hardy,* ed. Boris Ford, 119-43. Harmondsworth: Penguin, 1958.

1394 COX, C. B. "In Defense of Dickens." *Essays and Studies* 11 (1958): 86-100. Reprinted in *Dickens: Modern Judgements,* ed. A. E. Dyson, 1968 q.v.

1395 FIELDING, KENNETH J. *Charles Dickens: A Critical Introduction.* London: Longmans, Green, 1958. 2nd. edition revised and enlarged. London: Longmans, Green, 1965.

1396 HUDSON, DEREK. "Introduction." *Master Humphrey's Clock and A Child's History of England.* New Oxford Illustrated Dickens. London: Oxford Univ. Press, 1958.

1397 MILLER, J. HILLIS. *Charles Dickens: the World of His Novels.* Cambridge, Mass.: Harvard Univ. Press, 1958; Bloomington: Indiana Univ. Press, 1969.

R1398 [MILLER, J. HILLIS. *Charles Dickens: The World of His Novels,* 1958 q.v.] JOHNSON, EDGAR. "In a World They Never Made." *Saturday Review* 41 (Aug. 30, 1958):17-18.

R1399 [MILLER, J. HILLIS. *Charles Dickens: The World of His Novels,* 1958 q.v.] McMASTER, ROWLAND D. "Dickens, Jung, and Coleridge." *Dalhousie Review* 38 (Winter 1959):512-16.

R1400 [MILLER, J. HILLIS. *Charles Dickens: The World of His Novels,* 1958 q.v.] MONOD, SYLVÈRE. "J. Hillis Miller's *Charles Dickens: The World of His Novels.*" *Nineteenth Century Fiction* 13 (Mar. 1959):360-63.

R1401 [MILLER, J. HILLIS. *Charles Dickens: The World of His Novels,* 1958 q.v.] MOYNAHAN, JULIAN. "Book Reviews." *Victorian Studies* 2 (Dec. 1958):170-72.

R1402 [MILLER, J. HILLIS. *Charles Dickens: The World of His Novels,* 1958 q.v.] STEVENSON, LIONEL. *South Atlantic Quarterly* 58 (Summer 1959):478-79.

R1403 [MILLER, J. HILLIS. *Charles Dickens: The World of His Novels,* 1958 q.v.] TILLOTSON, KATHLEEN. *Modern Language Notes* 75 (May 1960):439-42.

1404 MITCHELL, ROSAMOND J. and MARY D. R. LEYS. "Charles Dickens's London." *History of London Life,* 253-69. New York: Longmans, Green, 1958.

1405 MONOD, SYLVÈRE. *Charles Dickens.* (Ecrivains d'Hier et
      Aujourd'Hui.) Paris: Seghers, 1958.

1406 STAPLES, LESLIE C. "Introduction." *The Uncommercial Traveller
      and Reprinted Pieces, Etc.* New Oxford Illustrated Dickens. London:
      Oxford Univ. Press, 1958.

1407 CARLTON, WILLIAM J. "Dickens's 'Old Stage-Coaching House'."
      Dickensian 54 (Jan. 1958):13-20. [Dickens' visits to Newbury.]

1408 "Dummy Books at Gad's Hill Place." *Dickensian* 54 (Jan. 1958):46-7.

1409 FIELDING, KENNETH J. "The Monthly Serialization of Dickens's
      Novels." *Dickensian* 54 (Jan. 1958):4-11.

1410 GOODHEART, EUGENE. "Dickens's Method of Characterization."
      Dickensian 54 (Jan. 1958):35-37.

1411 MORLEY, MALCOLM. "The Theatrical Ternans." *Dickensian* 54
      (Jan. 1958):38-43; (May 1958):95-106; (Sept. 1958):155-63; 55
      (Jan. 1959):36-44; (May 1959):109-17; (Sept. 1959):159-68; 56
      (Jan. 1960):41-46; (May 1960):76-83; (Sept. 1960):153-57; 57
      (Jan. 1961):29-35.

1412 OLLÉ, JAMES G. "Dickens and Dolby." *Dickensian* 54 (Jan. 1958):
      27-35.

1413 STONE, HARRY. "Dickens and Melville Go to Chapel." *Dickensian*
      54 (Jan. 1958):50-52.

1414 STONE, HARRY. "Dickens's Tragic Universe: 'George Silverman's
      Explanation'." *Studies in Philology* 55 (Jan. 1958):86-97.

1415 TILLOTSON, KATHLEEN. "Seymour Illustrating Dickens in 1834."
      Dickensian 54 (Jan. 1958):11-12.

1416 LANE, LAURIAT, Jr. "Dickens' Archetypal Jew." *PMLA* 73
      (Mar. 1958):94-100.

1417 McMASTER, ROWLAND D. "Dickens and the Horrific." *Dalhousie
      Review* 38 (Spring 1958):18-28.

1418 "Charles Dickens Looks at the News Trade." *The Library Journal* 83
      (Apr. 1958):1151-52.

1419 FIEDLER, LESLIE. "Good Good Girl and Good Bad Boy." *New
      Leader* (Apr. 14, 1958):22-25. Reprinted in *No! in Thunder: Essays
      on Myth and Literature.* Boston: Beacon Press, 1960.

1420 CARLTON, WILLIAM J. "Captain Morgan Again." *Dickensian* 54
      (May 1958):88-93.

1421 COLBURN, WILLIAM E. "Dickens and the 'Life-Illusion'."
      Dickensian 54 (May 1958):110-18.

1422 FINLAY, IAN F. "Dickens in the Cinema." *Dickensian* 54 (May 1958):
      106-9. [Lists films of Dickens' writings 1902-1958.]

1423 WOODALL, ROBERT. "The Dickens Readings." *Contemporary Review* 194 (May 1958):248-51.

1424 FIEDLER, LESLIE. "From Redemption to Initiation." *New Leader* (May 26, 1958):20-23. Reprinted in *No! in Thunder: Essays on Myth and Literature.* Boston: Beacon Press, 1960.

1425 STEADMAN, JOHN M. "Dickens' Typography and the Dragon's Teeth." *Notes and Queries* N.S. 5 (June 1958):256-57.

1426 CARLTON, WILLIAM J. "Who Wrote 'Mr Robert Bolton'?" *Dickensian* 54 (Sept. 1958):178-81.

1427 FIELDING, KENNETH J. "The Weekly Serialization of Dickens's Novels." *Dickensian* 54 (Sept. 1958):134-41.

1428 PEYROUTON, NOEL C. "The Gurney Photographs." *Dickensian* 54 (Sept. 1958):145-55. [14 plates of photographs of Dickens by J. Gurney and Son.]

1429 RALEIGH, JOHN H. "Dickens and the Sense of Time." *Nineteenth Century Fiction* 13 (Sept. 1958):127-37. Reprinted in *Time, Place and Idea: Essays on the Novel.* Carbondale: Southern Illinois Univ. Press, 1968.

1430 FIELDING, KENNETH J. "Charles Dickens." *Victorian Newsletter* 14 (Fall 1958):22-23. [Guide to research materials.]

1431 AYLMER, FELIX. *Dickens Incognito.* London: R. Hart-Davis, 1959. [Dickens and Ellen Ternan, based on evidence in Dickens' diary, with facsimilies.] Extracts reprinted in *The Sunday Times* (London) 22 (Nov. 1959):5, 33.

1432 BRUNNER, KARL. "Dickens and Mark Twain in Italian." *Festschrift für Walter Fischer*, 112-16. Heidelberg: C. Winter, 1959.

1433 CAHOON, HERBERT. "News and Note." *Papers of the Bibliographical Society of America* 53 (1st quarter 1959):78; (3rd quarter 1959): 274; 54 (4th quarter 1960):299. [On the progress of an edition of Dickens' letters.]

1434 ENGEL, MONROE. *The Maturity of Dickens.* Cambridge, Mass.: Harvard Univ. Press; London: Oxford Univ. Press, 1959.

R1435 [ENGEL, MONROE. *The Maturity of Dickens,* 1959 q.v.] "Keys to the House of Fiction." *Times Literary Supplement* (Nov. 20, 1959):678.

R1436 [ENGEL, MONROE. *The Maturity of Dickens,* 1959 q.v.] BUTT, JOHN E. *Review of English Studies* N.S. 11 (Nov. 1960):440-43.

R1437 [ENGEL, MONROE. *The Maturity of Dickens,* 1959 q.v.] JOHNSON, EDGAR. "Engel's *The Maturity of Dickens.*" *Nineteenth Century Fiction* 14 (June 1959):182-84.

R1438 [ENGEL, MONROE. *The Maturity of Dickens*, 1959 q.v.]
STEVENSON, LIONEL. "Book Reviews." *Journal of English and Germanic Philology* 59 (2nd quarter):308-10.

1439 HORSMAN, ERNEST A. *Dickens and the Structure of the Novel.* An Inaugural Lecture delivered before the University of Otago on Aug. 9, 1957. Dunedin, NZ: Univ. of Otago Press, 1959.

1440 KIRK, CLARA M. and RUDOLPH, eds. "Dickens and Thackeray." *Criticism and Fiction and Other Essays By W. D. Howells*, 93-97. New York: New York Univ. Press, 1959.

1441 MANNING, JOHN. *Dickens on Education.* Toronto: Univ. of Toronto Press, 1959.

1442 MIXAL'SKAJA, N. P. *Čarl'z Dikkens. (Očerk Žizni i Tvorčestva).* Moscow: Gosudarstvennoe Učebno-Pedagogičeskoe Izdatel'stvo, 1959. [*Charles Dickens. (A Sketch of His Life and Work).*]

1443 MIYAZAKI, KOICHI. *Charles Dickens.* Tokyo: Kenkyusha, 1959.

1444 PEARE, CATHERINE O. *Charles Dickens: His Life.* New York: Holt, 1959; London: D. Dobson, 1962.

1445 PRINGLE, PATRICK. *The Young Dickens.* (Famous Childhood Series) London: M. Parrish; New York: Roy, 1959.

1446 QUIRK, RANDOLPH. *Charles Dickens and Appropriate Language.* Inaugural lecture. Durham, Eng.: Univ. of Durham, 1959.

1447 SCHILLING, BERNARD N., ed. *The Comic World of Dickens: the Wellers, Mrs Gamp, Mr Chuzzlewit.* London: J. Murray, 1959.

1448 SCHMIDT-HIDDING, WOLFGANG. *Sieben Meister des literarischen Humors in England und Amerika.* Heidelberg: Quelle und Meyer, 1959.

1449 SMITH, SHEILA M. "Anti-Mechanism and the Comic in the Writings of Charles Dickens." *Renaissance and Modern Studies* 3 (1959): 131-44.

1450 STANG, RICHARD. "Bulwer and Dickens – The Attack on Realism." *The Theory of the Novel in England 1850-1870*, 153-59. New York: Columbia Univ. Press; London: Routledge and K. Paul, 1959.

1451 STANG, RICHARD. "Dickens and Charles Reade." *The Theory of the Novel in England 1850-1870*, 19-29. New York: Columbia Univ. Press; London: Routledge and K. Paul, 1959.

1452 ZABEL, MORTON D. "Introduction." *Best Stories of Charles Dickens.* Garden City, NY: Hanover House, 1959.

1453 CARLTON, WILLIAM J. "Dickens's Debut in America." *Dickensian* 55 (Jan. 1959):55-56.

1454 LANE, LAURIAT, Jr. "Dickens and the Double." *Dickensian* 55 (Jan. 1959):47-55. [Dickens' use of double figures in Chuzzlewit, Bradley Headstone and John Jasper.]

1455 PEYROUTON, NOEL C. "Rapping the Rappers: More Grist for the
Biographer's Mill." *Dickensian* 55 (Jan. 1959):19-30; (May 1959):
75-89. [Dickens's struggle with the spiritualists.]

1456 STAPLES, LESLIE C. "48 Doughty Street: Dickens Negotiates."
Dickensian 55 (Jan. 1959):5-9.

1457 STONE, HARRY. "Dickens and Interior Monologue." *Philological
Quarterly* 38 (Jan. 1959):52-65.

1458 VERKOREN, L. "Dickens in Holland." *Dickensian* 55 (Jan. 1959):
44-46. [Reputation.]

1459 PRAZ, MARIO. "Donne and Dickens." *Times Literary Supplement*
(Feb. 20, 1959):97.

1460 HARDER, KELSIE B. "Charles Dickens Names his Characters."
Names 7 (Mar. 1959):35-42.

1461 COX, C. B. "Comic Viewpoints in *Sketches by Boz*." *English* 12
(Spring 1959):132-35.

1462 WILSON, ARTHUR H. "The Great Theme in Charles Dickens."
Susquehanna University Studies 6 (Apr.-June 1959):422-57.

1463 CARLTON, WILLIAM J. "A Five-Year-Old Critic of *Nicholas
Nickleby*." *Dickensian* 55 (May 1959):89-93. [William Hastings
Hughes, son of Dr John Hughes.]

1464 COLLINS, PHILIP A. W. "Dickens and the Ragged Schools."
Dickensian 55 (May 1959):94-109.

1465 "Dickens Birthday Dinner at the House of Commons." *Dickensian* 55
(May 1959):118-22.

1466 STONE, HARRY. "Dickens's 'Call Slips'." *Times Literary Supplement* (June 12, 1959):360.

1467 CARLTON, WILLIAM J. "The Dickens Diaries." *Dickensian* 55
(Sept. 1959):134-39.

1468 MAJOR, GWEN. "'No Thoroughfare'." *Dickensian* 55 (Autumn 1959)
175-78. [A Christmas story of Wilding and Co., Wine Merchants.]

1469 PAKENHAM, PANSY. "Dickens and the Class Question." *Victorian
Newsletter* 16 (Fall 1959):30.

1470 SPILKA, MARK. "Kafka's Sources for 'The Metamorphosis'."
Comparative Literature 11 (Fall 1959):289-307.

1471 COLLINS, PHILIP A. W. "Dickens Educates his Sons." *Educational
Review* (Nov. 1959).

1472 BODELSEN, CARL A. "Some Notes on Dickens' Symbolism."
English Studies 40 (Dec. 1959):420-31. Reprinted in *Essays and
Papers*. Copenhagen: Nature Method Centre, 1964.

1473 WRIGG, WILLIAM. "Dickens' Message of Christmas." *English
Journal* 48 (Dec. 1959):537-39.

1474 STOREY, GRAHAM. "'Dickens Incognito': New Evidence." *The Sunday Times* (London) (Dec. 13, 1959):6.

1475 LLOYD, J. D. K. "Dickens and the Railway." *Times Literary Supplement* (Dec. 18, 1959):741.

1476 PEYROUTON, NOEL C. "The Eytinge Portrait." *Dickensian* 55 (Winter 1959):9-11.

1477 BLOOM, URSULA. *The Romance of Charles Dickens.* London: R. Hale, 1960. [A biographical novel.]

1478 DUPEE, F. W. "Introduction." *The Selected Letters of Charles Dickens.* New York: Farrar, Straus and Cudahy, 1960.

1479 FIELDING, KENNETH J., ed. *The Speeches of Charles Dickens.* Oxford: Clarendon Press, 1960.

1480 KATARSKIJ, I. M. *Dikkens. (Kritiko-Biografičeskij Očerk).* Moscow: Goslitizdat, 1960. [*Dickens. (A Critical-Biographical Sketch).*]

1481 KORG, JACOB, comp. *London in Dickens's Day.* Englewood Cliffs, NJ: Prentice-Hall, 1960.

1482 MARIANI, GIULIANNA. *La Crítica Social en las Novelas de Dickens.* Lima, Peru: Impreso en los Talleres de Artes Gráficas de la Tipografia Peruana S. A. Rávaejo e Hijos, Enrique Isabel La Católica 99, 1960.

1483 MOERS, ELLEN. "Dickens." *The Dandy: Brummell to Beerbohm,* 215-50. London: Secker and Warburg; New York: Viking, 1960.

1484 MONOD, SYLVÈRE. "Critical Preface." *Hard Times.* Paris: Club Français du Livre, 1960. [French translation.]

1485 REES, RICHARD. "Dickens, or the Intelligence of the Heart." *For Love or Money, Studies in Personality and Essence,* 89-112. London: Secker and Warburg, 1960.

1486 SÜKÖSD, MIHÁLY. *Dickens.* Budapest: Gondolat, 1960.

1487 YAMAMOTO, TADAO. *Dickens's Style.* Tokyo: Nanundo, 1960.

1488 CAPON, R. LAWRENCE. "Gamaliel Bradford and Charles Dickens." *Dickensian* 56 (Jan. 1960):34-40. [Bradford's criticism.]

1489 CARLTON, WILLIAM J. "Charles Dickens, Dramatic Critic." *Dickensian* 56 (Jan. 1960):11-27.

1490 ROSENBERG, MARVIN. "The Dramatist in Dickens." *Journal of English and Germanic Philology* 59 (Jan. 1960):1-12.

1491 BOMANS, GODFRIED. "Dickens and the Railway." *Times Literary Supplement* 1 (Jan. 1960):7.

1492 WAGENKNECHT, EDWARD. "Mrs Hawthorne on Dickens." *Boston Public Library Quarterly* 12 (Apr. 1960):120-21.

1493 ADRIAN, ARTHUR A. "Dickens Faces a Libel Suit." *Dickensian* 56 (May 1960):114-16.

1494 COLLINS, PHILIP A. W. "Dickens as Editor: Some Uncollected
      Fragments." *Dickensian* 56 (May 1960):85-96.

1495 DUNSTAN, J. LESLIE. "The Ministers in Dickens." *Dickensian* 56
      (May 1960):103-13.

1496 FIELDING, KENNETH J. "Two Prologues for the Amateur Players."
      Dickensian 56 (May 1960):100-2.

1497 LASCELLES, T. S. "The Signalman's Story: Had Dickens Any
      Particular Tunnel in Mind?" *Dickensian* 56 (May 1960):84.

1498 STEWART, D. H. "Dickens' Contribution, Then and Now."
      Dickensian 56 (May 1960):71-75.

1499 STONE, HARRY. "A Note on 'Dickens' Archetypal Jew'." *Victorian
      Studies* 3 (June 1960):459-60.

1500 WEBB, HOWARD W., JR. "A Further Note on the Dickens-Poe
      Relationship." *Nineteenth Century Fiction* 15 (June 1960):80-82.

1501 WILSON, ANGUS. "Charles Dickens: A Haunting." *Critical Quarterly*
      2 (Summer 1960):101-8. Reprinted in *The Dickens Critics,* ed.
      G. H. Ford and L. Lane, Jr., 1961 q.v.; *Dickens: Modern Judgements,*
      ed. A. E. Dyson, 1968 q.v.

1502 WALLER, JOHN O. "Charles Dickens and the American Civil War."
      Studies in Philology 57 (July 1960):535-48.

1503 COLLINS, PHILIP A. W. "Dickens and the Maimed Boy." *Dickensian*
      56 (Sept. 1960):185-86. [Records an 1877 anecdote by Rev C. J.
      Whitmore.]

1504 FIELDING, KENNETH J. "Dickens and the Novel." *Dickensian* 56
      (Sept. 1960):160-64.

1505 GIBSON, FRANK A. "Mysteries in Dickens." *Dickensian* 56
      (Sept. 1960):176-78.

1506 PEYROUTON, NOEL C. "A Postscript on Pirates." *Dickensian* 56
      (Sept. 1960):179-81. [On literary piracy with a few letters by
      Dickens.]

1507 STAPLES, LESLIE C. "Tavistock House Theatricals." *Dickensian* 56
      (Sept. 1960):158-59.

1508 BOWKETT, C. E. "Charles Dickens Commemoration Sermon."
      Dickensian 56 (Autumn 1960):182-84. [Dickens' attitude towards
      the Christian Church.]

1509 COOLIDGE, ARCHIBALD C., Jr. "Dickens' Humor." *Victorian
      Newsletter* 18 (Fall 1960):8-15.

1510 PRITCHETT, V. S. "The Great Reformist." *New Statesman* 60
      (Oct. 1960):489.

1511 ADRIAN, ARTHUR A. "Charles Dickens as Verse Editor." *Modern
      Philology* 58 (Nov. 1960):99-107.

1512 MACKANESS, GEORGE. "'Hunted Down': A Dickens Link with America." *American Book Collector* 11 (Nov. 1960):6-10. [Biographical data concerning Thomas G. Wainewright.]

1513 DUPEE, F. W. "The Other Dickens." *Partisan Review* 27 (Winter 1960):111-22. Reprinted as the "Introduction" to *Selected Letters of Charles Dickens.* New York: Farrar, Straus, 1960.

1514 ANDERSON, DAVID D. "Charles Dickens on Lake Erie." *Inland Seas* 17 (1961):25-30.

1515 BUTT, JOHN E. "Editing a Nineteenth Century Novelist (Proposals for an Edition of Dickens)." *English Studies Today,* 2nd. series, 187-95. The Fourth Conference of the Intl. Assoc. of U. Profs. of English at Lausanne and Berne, Switzerland, Aug. 1959. Bern: Francke, 1961.

1516 CLARK, WILLIAM R., ed. *Discussions of Charles Dickens.* Boston: Heath, 1961.

1517 COCKSHUT, A. O. J. *The Imagination of Charles Dickens.* London: Collins, 1961; New York: New York Univ. Press, 1962.

R1518 [COCKSHUT, A. O. J. *The Imagination of Charles Dickens,* 1961 q.v.] BAYLEY, JOHN. "Sleep-Walking Genius." *Spectator* 207 (Sept. 8, 1961):328-29.

R1519 [COCKSHUT, A. O. J. *The Imagination of Charles Dickens,* 1961 q.v.] FIELDING, KENNETH J. "*The Imagination of Charles Dickens.*" *Dickensian* 58 (Jan. 1962):21-22.

R1520 [COCKSHUT, A. O. J. *The Imagination of Charles Dickens,* 1961 q.v.] MARCUS, STEVEN. "The Lame, The Halt and the Blind." *New Statesman and Nation* 62 (Sept. 1, 1961):278-79.

R1521 [COCKSHUT, A. O. J. *The Imagination of Charles Dickens,* 1961 q.v.] MILLER, J. HILLIS. "Book Reviews." *Victorian Studies* 5 (Dec. 1961):174-76.

1522 COLLINS, PHILIP A. W. "Dickens and the Trained Schoolmaster." *University of Leeds Institute of Education Researches and Studies* 22 (1961):1-13.

1523 DuCANN, CHARLES G. *The Love Lives of Charles Dickens.* London: Muller, 1961.

1524 FORD, GEORGE H. and LAURIAT LANE, Jr., eds. *The Dickens Critics.* Ithaca, NY: Cornell Univ. Press, 1961.

R1525 [FORD, GEORGE H. and LAURIAT LANE, Jr., eds. *The Dickens Critics,* 1961 q.v.] FIELDING, KENNETH J. "Dickens and the Critics." *Dickensian* 58 (Sept. 1962):150-51.

R1526 [FORD, GEORGE H. and LAURIAT LANE, Jr., eds. *The Dickens Critics,* 1961 q.v.] GARIS, ROBERT E. "Dickens Criticism." *Victorian Studies* 7 (Mar. 1964):375-86.

R1527 [FORD, GEORGE H. and LAURIAT LANE, Jr., eds. *The Dickens Critics*, 1961 q.v.] HODGART, MATTHEW. "*The Dickens Critics.*" *New Statesman* 64 (Nov. 1962):744-45.

R1528 [FORD, GEORGE H. and LAURIAT LANE, Jr., eds. *The Dickens Critics*, 1961 q.v.] JUMP, JOHN D. "*The Dickens Critics.*" *Critical Quarterly* 4 (Winter 1962):371-72.

R1529 [FORD, GEORGE H. and LAURIAT LANE, Jr., eds. *The Dickens Critics*, 1961 q.v.] REINHOLD, HEINZ. "*The Dickens Critics.*" *Anglia* 80 (1962):352-54.

1530 HOFF, RHODA. "Charles Dickens 1812-1870." *Why They Wrote: Dickens, Thoreau, Flaubert, Clemens, Stevenson*, 1-30. New York: Walck, 1961.

1531 KETTLE, ARNOLD. "Dickens and the Popular Tradition." *Zeitschrift für Anglistik und Amerikanistik* 9 (1961):229-52. Reprinted in *Carleton Miscellany* 3 (1961).

1532 LASCH, CHRISTOPHER. "Introduction." *American Notes.* Greenwich, Conn.: Fawcett, 1961.

1533 PRIESTLEY, J. B. *Charles Dickens: A Pictorial Biography.* London: Thames and Hudson, 1961; New York: Viking, 1962. French edition, *Dickens*, translated by Anne Rousseau. Paris: Hachette, 1964.

1534 QUIRK, RANDOLPH. "The Language of Dickens." *Langue et Littérature*, 322-23. Paris: Belles Lettres, 1961. [Proceedings of the 8th Congress of the Fédération Internationale des Langues et Littératures Modernes, Liège, Sept. 1960.]

1535 SEEHASE, GEORG. *Charles Dickens: zu einer Besonderheit seines Realismus.* Halle a. d. Saale: Max Niemeyer, 1961.

1536 COLLINS, PHILIP A. W. "Dickens and the Prison Governor George Laval Chesterton." *Dickensian* 57 (Jan. 1961):11-26.

1537 GIBSON, FRANK A. "On Not Reading Dickens." *Dickensian* 57 (Jan. 1961):26-28.

1538 GILENSON, BORIS. "Dickens in Russia." *Dickensian* 57 (Jan. 1961): 56-58.

1539 PEYROUTON, NOEL C. "Dickens and the Other Hughes." *Dickensian* 57 (Jan. 1961):36-42. [On Dickens' influence on Thomas Hughes, future author of *Tom Brown's Schooldays*.]

1540 ATTHILL, ROBIN. "Dickens and the Railway." *English* 13 (Spring 1961):130-35. [The railway in Dickens' fiction.]

1541 NELSON, HARLAND S. "Dickens' Plots: 'The Ways of Providence' or Influence of Collins?" *Victorian Newsletter* 19 (Spring 1961):11-14.

1542 COLLINS, PHILIP A. W. "Queen Mab's Chariot Among the Steam Engines: Dickens and 'Fancy'." *English Studies* 42 (Apr. 1961):78-90.

1543 MILLER, MELVIN H. "Charles Dickens at the English Charity Dinner." *Quarterly Journal of Speech* 47 (Apr. 1961):143-49.

1544 MOYNAHAN, JULIAN. "Dickens Criticism." *Essays in Criticism* 11 (Apr. 1961):239-41. [Reply to criticism of his article "The Hero's Guilt," (Jan. 1960) q.v.]

1545 CARLTON, WILLIAM J. "'Captain Holland' Identified." *Dickensian* 57 (May 1961):69-77.

1546 COLLINS, PHILIP A. W. "Dickens on the Education of Girls." *Dickensian* 57 (May 1961):86-96.

1547 DRAYTON, W. H. *"The Uncommercial Traveller* and the Royal Commercial Travellers' Schools." *Dickensian* 57 (May 1961):

1548 FIELDING, KENNETH J. "Dickens and Miss Burdett-Coutts: The Last Phase." *Dickensian* 57 (May 1961):97-105.

1549 GREEN, ROGER L. "Andrew Lang – Real Reader of Dickens." *Dickensian* 57 (May 1961):124-27.

1550 MORLEY, MALCOLM. "Messrs Four, Two and One." *Dickensian* 57 (May 1961):78-81. [A character in Dickens's satire from *Bentley's Magazine* of Feb. 1837.]

1551 BODELSEN, CARL A. "'The Physiognomy of the Name.'" *Review of English Literature* 2 (July 1961):39-48. Reprinted in *Essays and Papers.* Copenhagen: Nature Method Centre, 1964. [On Dickens' choice of names.]

1552 COLLINS, PHILIP A. W. "The Significance of Dickens's Periodicals." *Review of English Literature* 2 (July 1961):55-64.

1553 GRANT, DOUGLAS. "A Sketch of Charles Dickens." *Review of English Literature* 2 (July 1961):50-51.

1554 JEFFARES, A. NORMAN, ed. *A Review of English Literature* 2 (July 1961). London: Longman's, 1961. [Special Dickens Issue.]

1555 MONOD, SYLVÈRE. "A French View of Dickens's Humour." *Review of English Literature* 2 (July 1961):29-38.

1556 QUIRK, RANDOLPH. "Some Observations on the Language of Dickens." *Review of English Literature* 2 (July 1961):19-28.

1557 SPILKA, MARK. "Dickens and Kafka: 'The Technique of the Grotesque'." *Minnesota Review* 1 (July 1961):441-58.

1558 THOMSON, D. CLEGHORN. "Francis Jeffrey: Charles Dickens's Friend and Critic." *Review of English Literature* 2 (July 1961):52-54.

1559 WILSON, ANGUS. "The Heroes and Heroines of Dickens." *Review of English Literature* 2 (July 1961):9-18. Reprinted in *Dickens and the Twentieth Century,* ed. J. Gross and G. Pearson, 1962 q.v.; *Dickens: A Collection of Critical Essays,* ed. M. Price, 1967 q.v.;

British Victorian Literature: Recent Revaluations, ed. Shio K. Kumar. New York: New York Univ. Press, 1968.

1560 HOUSE, MADELINE, PHILIP A. W. COLLINS, and GRAHAM STOREY. "Dickens's Letters." *Times Literary Supplement* (July 21, 1961):449.

1561 HARVEY, P. D. A. "Charles Dickens as Playwright." *British Museum Quarterly* 24 (Aug. 1961):22-25.

1562 HUNTER, RICHARD A. and IDA MACALPINE. "Dickens and Connolly: An Embarrassed Editor's Disclaimer." *Times Literary Supplement* (Aug. 11, 1961):534-35. [See COLLINS, PHILIP A. W. "Dickens and Connolly" (Aug. 18, 1961) q.v.]

1563 COLLINS, PHILIP A. W. "Dickens and Connolly." *Times Literary Supplement* (Aug. 18, 1961):549.

1564 COOLIDGE, ARCHIBALD C., Jr. "Dickens's Complex Plots." *Dickensian* 57 (Sept. 1961):174-82.

1565 HARDY, BARBARA. "The Change of Heart in Dickens' Novels." *Victorian Studies* 5 (Sept. 1961):49-67. Partially reprinted in *Assessing Great Expectations,* ed. R. Lettis and W. E. Morris, 1960 q.v., and completely in *Dickens: A Collection of Critical Essays,* ed. M. Price, 1967 q.v.

1566 KELTY, JEAN M. "The Modern Tone of Charles Dickens." *Dickensian* 57 (Sept. 1961):160-65.

1567 WALBANK, ALAN. "With A Blush Retire." *Dickensian* 57 (Sept. 1961):166-73. [Dickens' treatment of death.]

1568 CARLTON, WILLIAM J. "Dickens Periodicals." *Times Literary Supplement* (Sept. 22, 1961):629.

1569 COOLIDGE, ARCHIBALD C., Jr. "Dickens and the Heart as Hope for Heaven." *Victorian Newsletter* 20 (Fall 1961):6-13. [See 1571.]

1570 COOLIDGE, ARCHIBALD C., Jr. "Dickens and the Philosophic Basis of Melodrama." *Victorian Newsletter* 20 (Fall 1961):1-6. [See 1571.]

1571 COOLIDGE, ARCHIBALD C., Jr. "Two Commentaries on Dickens. A. Dickens and the Philosophic Basis of Melodrama. B. Dickens and the Heart as the Hope for Heaven: A Study of the Philosophic Basis of Sensational Literary Technique." *Victorian Newsletter* 20 (Fall 1961):1-6 (A); 6-13 (B).

1572 BROWNING, ROBERT. "Sketches by Boz." *Dickens and the Twentieth Century,* ed. J. Gross and G. Pearson, 19-34. London: Routledge and K. Paul, 1962.

1573 COLLINS, PHILIP A. W. *Dickens and Adult Education.* Leicester, Eng.: University Dept. of Education, 1962.

1574 COLLINS, PHILIP A. W. *Dickens and Crime.* London: Macmillan; New York: St. Martin's Press, 1962.

R1575 [COLLINS, PHILIP A. W. *Dickens and Crime*, 1962 q.v.] ANON. "Mr Fang and Mr Creakle." *Times Literary Supplement* (Aug. 17, 1962):627.

R1576 [COLLINS, PHILIP A. W. *Dickens and Crime*, 1962 q.v.] BUTT, JOHN E. *"Dickens and Crime."* *Dickensian* 59 (Jan. 1963):44-45.

R1577 [COLLINS, PHILIP A. W. *Dickens and Crime*, 1962 q.v.] FIELDING, KENNETH J. *Review of English Studies* N.S. 14 (Aug. 1963):308-9.

R1578 [COLLINS, PHILIP A. W. *Dickens and Crime*, 1962 q.v.] GROSS, JOHN. "Dickens of Dock Green." *New Statesman* N.S. 64 (Aug. 1962):234.

R1579 [COLLINS, PHILIP A. W. *Dickens and Crime*, 1962 q.v.] JOHNSON, PAMELA H. *Listener* 68 (Aug. 1962):218.

R1580 [COLLINS, PHILIP A. W. *Dickens and Crime*, 1962 q.v.] MacINNES, COLIN. "Tempted into Virtue." *Spectator* 209 (Aug. 1962):277-78.

1581 EMPSON, WILLIAM. "The Symbolism of Dickens." *Dickens and the Twentieth Century*, ed. J. Gross and G. Pearson, 13-15. London: Routledge and K. Paul, 1962.

1582 FORD, GEORGE H., EDGAR JOHNSON, J. HILLIS MILLER, SYLVERE MONOD, and NOEL C. PEYROUTON. *Dickens Criticism, Past, Present, and Future Directions.* A Symposium at the 56th Annual Conference of the Dickens Fellowship, Northeastern University, Boston, Mass., June 10, 1962. Cambridge, Mass.: Charles Dickens Reference Center, 1962.

1583 GROSS, JOHN. "Dickens: Some Recent Approaches." *Dickens and the Twentieth Century*, ed. J. Gross and G. Pearson, ix-xvi. London: Routledge and K. Paul, 1962.

1584 GROSS, JOHN and GABRIEL PEARSON, eds. *Dickens and the Twentieth Century.* London: Routledge and K. Paul, 1962.

R1585 [GROSS, JOHN and GABRIEL PEARSON, eds. *Dickens and the Twentieth Century*, 1962 q.v.] FIELDING, KENNETH J. *"Dickens and the Twentieth Century."* *Dickensian* 59 (Jan. 1963):45-47.

R1586 [GROSS, JOHN and GABRIEL PEARSON, eds. *Dickens and the Twentieth Century*, 1962 q.v.] GARIS, ROBERT E. "Dickens Criticism." *Victorian Studies* 7 (Mar. 1964):375-86.

R1587 [GROSS, JOHN and GABRIEL PEARSON, eds. *Dickens and the Twentieth Century*, 1962 q.v.] JOHNSON, EDGAR. *English Language Notes* 2 (June 1965):308-13.

R1588 [GROSS, JOHN and GABRIEL PEARSON, eds. *Dickens and the Twentieth Century*, 1962 q.v.] LANE, LAURIAT, Jr. *Nineteenth Century Fiction* 18 (Sept. 1963):200-2.

R1589 [GROSS, JOHN and GABRIEL PEARSON, eds. *Dickens and the Twentieth Century*, 1962 q.v.] McMASTER, ROWLAND D. "Book Reviews." *Dalhousie Review* 43 (Winter 1963-64):552-54.

1590 LAURITZEN, HENRY. *Jul med Dickens*. Aalborg, Denmark: A. Schølins bogtr., 1962. [Christmas in Dickens.]

1591 PEARSON, GABRIEL. "Dickens: The Present Position." *Dickens and the Twentieth Century*, ed. J. Gross and G. Pearson, xvii-xxiv. London: Routledge and K. Paul, 1962.

1592 REID, JOHN C. *The Hidden World of Charles Dickens*. (Macmillan Brown Lectures 1961. Auckland Univ. Bulletin 61. English Series 10) Auckland: Univ. of Auckland Press, 1962.

1593 CARLTON, WILLIAM J. "'Boz' and the Beards." *Dickensian* 58 (Jan. 1962):9-21.

1594 COLLINS, PHILIP A. W. "Dickens and the Whiston Case." *Dickensian* 58 (Jan. 1962):47-49.

1595 COOLIDGE, ARCHIBALD C., Jr. "The Unremoved Thorn: A Study in Dickens' Narrative Methods." *North Dakota Quarterly* 30 (Jan. 1962):8-13.

1596 FIELDING, KENNETH J. "The Imagination of Charles Dickens." *Dickensian* 58 (Jan. 1962):21-22.

1597 GIBSON, FRANK A. "Nature's Possible: A Reconsideration of *The Battle of Life*." *Dickensian* 58 (Jan. 1962):43-46.

1598 PEYROUTON, NOEL C. "Boz-Town Conference." *Dickensian* 58 (Jan. 1962):7-8. [On Dickens' visits to Boston.]

1599 BIRKETT, LORD. "The Versatility of Charles Dickens." *Listener* 67 (Feb. 1962):282.

1600 JOHNSON, EDGAR. "Dickens and His Critics." *Saturday Review* 45 (Feb. 10, 1962):31, 69.

1601 COOLIDGE, ARCHIBALD C., Jr. "Dickens' Use of Hazlitt's Principle of the Sympathetic Imagination." *Mississippi Quarterly* 15 (Spring 1962):68-73.

1602 PERRY, JOHN O. "The Popular Tradition of Melodrama in Dickens." *Carleton Miscellany* 3 (Spring 1962):105-10.

1603 BUTT, JOHN E. "Dickens's Manuscripts." *Yale University Library Gazette* 36 (Apr. 1962):149-61.

1604 McMASTER, ROWLAND D. "Man Into Beast in Dickensian Caricature." *University of Toronto Quarterly* 31 (Apr. 1962):354-61.

1605 CARLTON, WILLIAM J. "Postscripts to Forster." *Dickensian* 58 (May 1962):87-92. [Letters addressed to Forster.]

1606 COOLIDGE, ARCHIBALD C., Jr. "Charles Dickens and Mrs Radcliffe: A Farewell to Wilkie Collins." *Dickensian* 58 (May 1962):112-16.

1607 FIELDING, KENNETH J. "Comprehensive Education." *Dickensian* 58 (May 1962):119.

1608 FIELDING, KENNETH J. "Dickens' Novels and the Discovery of Soul." *Aryan Path* 33 (May 1962):210-14.

1609 GIBSON, FRANK A. "A Trifle on Titles." *Dickensian* 58 (May 1962): 117-19. [Titles of *Sketches by Boz, Pickwick Papers, Old Curiosity Shop, David Copperfield, Martin Chuzzlewit, Oliver Twist, Nicholas Nickleby.*]

1610 LASCELLES, T. S. "Transport in the Dickensian Era. (A Lecture Delivered to the Dickens Fellowship in London on Jan. 21st., 1960)." *Dickensian* 58 (May 1962):75-86; (Sept. 1962):152-60.

1611 LOHRLI, ANNE. "Dickens's *Household Words* on American English." *American Speech* 37 (May 1962):83-94.

1612 MORLEY, MALCOLM. "Dickens' Contributions to *Sweeney Todd.*" *Dickensian* 58 (May 1962):92-95. [Dickens and the Victorian Melodrama.]

1613 "One Hundred and Fiftieth Anniversary of the Birth of Charles Dickens." *Dickensian* 58 (May 1962):69-74. [Deals with dinner at Dorchester, London, and an after-dinner speech presented by Lord Birkett. It is reproduced here.]

1614 PEYROUTON, NOEL C. "Charles Dickens and the Christian Social-ists: The Kingsley-Dickens Myth." *Dickensian* 58 (May 1962):96-109.

1615 COOLIDGE, ARCHIBALD, C., Jr. "Dickens' Use of Character as Novelty." *South Atlantic Quarterly* 61 (Summer 1962):405-10.

1616 FIELDING, KENNETH J. "Dickens and International Copyright." *Bulletin of the British Association for American Studies* N.S. 4 (Aug. 1962):29-35.

1617 MORLEY, MALCOLM. "Fiction or Fact." *Dickensian* 58 (Sept. 1962):180-81. [Dickens and the theatre.]

1618 STEDMAN, JANE W. "Boz and Bab." *Dickensian* 58 (Sept. 1962): 171-78. [Sir William Schwenk Gilbert, consciously imitative of Dickens with Bab.]

1619 VOSS-MOETON, J. F. G. HEERMA van. "Tears in Literature: Particularly in Dickens." *Dickensian* 58 (Sept. 1962):182-87.

1620 ZIEGLER, ALBERT F. "The Haunted Man." *Dickensian* 58 (Sept. 1962):145-48.

1621 GIMBEL, RICHARD. "An Exhibition of 150 Manuscripts, Illustra-tions, and First Editions of Charles Dickens to Commemorate the 150th Anniversary of his Birth." *Yale Library Gazette* 37 (Oct. 1962): 46-96.

1622 VIEBROCK, HELMUT. "The Knocker: Physiognomical Aspects of a Motif in Hoffmann and Dickens." *English Studies* 43 (Oct. 1962): 396-402.

1623 COLLINS, PHILIP A. W. "John Forster's Diary." *Times Literary Supplement* (Nov. 30, 1962):937.

1624 CALHOUN, PHILO. "Charles Dickens in Maine." *Colby Library Quarterly* 6 (Dec. 1962):137-48.

1625 MACKANESS, GEORGE. "A Dickens Link with Australia." *Journal and Proceedings of the Royal Australian Historical Society* 48 (Dec. 1962):370-77.

1626 BROADBENT, CLAIRENE R. "Dickens, You Say?" *Dickensian* 58 (Winter 1962):54-57. [Malpractices of the US press.]

1627 BROWN, IVOR. *Dickens in His Time.* London: Nelson, 1963.

1628 CLAIR, COLIN. *Charles Dickens: Life and Characters.* Leavesden, Eng.: Bruce and Gawthorn, 1963.

1629 COLLINS, PHILIP A. W. *Dickens and Education.* New York: St. Martin's; London: Macmillan, 1963.

R1630 [COLLINS, PHILIP A. W. *Dickens and Education,* 1963 q.v.] BLOUNT, TREVOR. *Review of English Studies* 17 (1966):219-21.

R1631 [COLLINS, PHILIP A. W. *Dickens and Education,* 1963 q.v.] ENGEL, MONROE. *Victorian Studies* 7 (Sept. 1963):105-6.

R1632 [COLLINS, PHILIP A. W. *Dickens and Education,* 1963 q.v.] HILL, A. G. "The Real World of Charles Dickens." *Critical Quarterly* 7 (Winter 1965):374-83.

R1633 [COLLINS. PHILIP A. W. *Dickens and Education,* 1963 q.v.] McMASTER, ROWLAND D. *Nineteenth Century Fiction* 19 (Dec. 1964):306-8.

R1634 [COLLINS, PHILIP A. W. *Dickens and Education,* 1963 q.v.] RICKS, CHRISTOPHER. "Squeers and Co." *Listener* 70 (Nov. 7, 1963):756, 759.

R1635 [COLLINS, PHILIP A. W. *Dickens and Education,* 1963 q.v.] STONE, HARRY. *Victorian Studies* 8 (Mar. 1965):371-72.

1636 DAVIS, EARLE R. *The Flint and the Flame: The Artistry of Charles Dickens.* Columbia: Univ. of Missouri Press, 1963.

1637 ELSNA, HEBE. *Unwanted Wife: A Defense of Mrs Charles Dickens.* London: Jarrolds, 1963.

1638 JAMES, LOUIS. "Plagiarisms of Dickens." *Fiction for the Working Man 1830-1850,* 45-71. London: Oxford Univ. Press, 1963.

1639 JOHNSON, EDGAR. "Afterword." *A Tale of Two Cities.* New York: New American Library, 1963.

1640 MORSIANI, YAMILÈ. *Dickens e l'America.* Bologna: Patron, 1963.

1641 SPILKA, MARK. *Dickens and Kafka: A Mutual Interpretation.* Bloomington: Indiana Univ. Press, 1963.

R1642 [SPILKA, MARK. *Dickens and Kafka,* 1963 q.v.] HILL, A. G. "The Real World of Charles Dickens." *Critical Quarterly* 7 (Winter 1965): 374-83.

R1643 [SPILKA, MARK. *Dickens and Kafka,* 1963 q.v.] HOUK, MIM ANN. "Book Reviews." *Literature and Psychology* 14 (Winter 1964):37-39.

R1644 [SPILKA, MARK. *Dickens and Kafka,* 1963 q.v.] MATEER, RUTH. "Improbable Metamorphosis." *Essays in Criticism* 15 (Apr. 1965): 224-29.

R1645 [SPILKA, MARK. *Dickens and Kafka,* 1963 q.v.] MILLER, J. HILLIS. "Notes and Reviews." *Nineteenth Century Fiction* 18 (Mar. 1964):404-7.

1646 TRACY, G. M. *Les Anglais au Temps de Dickens.* Paris: Palatine, 1963.

1647 CARLTON, WILLIAM J. "Dickens Studies French." *Dickensian* 59 (Jan. 1963):21-27.

1648 COLLINS, PHILIP A. W. "Dickens on Ghosts: An Uncollected Article, with Introduction and Notes." *Dickensian* 59 (Jan. 1963):5-14.

1649 COOLIDGE, ARCHIBALD C., Jr. "Charles Dickens' Creation of Story From Character." *North Dakota Quarterly* 31 (Jan. 1963): 8-11.

1650 COOLIDGE, ARCHIBALD C., Jr. "Dickens and Latitudinarian Christianity." *Dickensian* 59 (Jan. 1963):57-60.

1651 PHILLIPS, GEORGE L. "Dickens and the Chimney Sweepers." *Dickensian* 59 (Jan. 1963):28-44. [Dickens' championship of them in life and fiction.]

1652 LEAVIS, F. R. "Dickens and the Critics." *Spectator* 211 (Jan. 4, 1963):15.

1653 CROSS, BARBARA M. "Comedy and Drama in Dickens." *Western Humanities Review* 17 (Spring 1963):143-49.

1654 WINTERS, WARRINGTON. "Charles Dickens: The Pursuers and the Pursued." *Victorian Newsletter* 23 (Spring 1963):23-24.

1655 PLAYFAIR, LYON. "'Dear Gentle Little Fellow': On Augustus Egg." *Listener* 69 (Apr. 1963):716-17. [Dickens' friend.]

1656 BROOKS, HAROLD F. and JEAN R. "Dickens in Shaw." *Dickensian* 59 (May 1963):93-99.

1657 CARLTON, WILLIAM J. "George Hogarth – A Link with Scott and Dickens." *Dickensian* 59 (May 1963):78-89.

1658 COLLINS, PHILIP A. W. "Dickens and the 'Edinburgh Review'." *Review of English Studies* 14 (May 1963):167-72.

1659 COLLINS, PHILIP A. W. "Dickens on Chatham: An Uncollected Piece, with Introduction and Notes." *Dickensian* 59 (May 1963): 69-73.

1660 MORLEY, MALCOLM. "Private Theatres and Boz." *Dickensian* 59 (May 1963):119-23. [The private playhouses satirized by Boz in "Private Theatres" – sources.]

1661 PEYROUTON, NOEL C. "THE LIFE OF OUR LORD: Some Notes of Explication." *Dickensian* 59 (May 1963):102-12.

1662 PHILLIPS, GEORGE L. "'The Poor Chimney Sweep of Windsor': A Philanthropist Without a Name." *Dickensian* 59 (May 1963):91-92.

1663 STEDMAN, JANE W. "Child-Wives of Dickens." *Dickensian* 59 (May 1963):112-18.

1664 WARD, W. A. "Language and Charles Dickens." *Listener* 69 (May 1963):870-71, 874.

1665 STONE, HARRY. "Dark Corners of the Mind: Dickens' Childhood Reading." *Horn Book Magazine* 39 (June 1963):306-21.

1666 CARTER, JOHN A., Jr. "T. J. Wise and the Technique of Promotion." *Book Collector* 12 (Summer 1963):202. [On J. C. Thomson's Dickens bibliography (1904).]

1667 CARLTON, WILLIAM J. "'Old Nick' at Devonshire Terrace: Dickens Through French Eyes in 1843." *Dickensian* 59 (Sept. 1963):138-44.

1668 COLLINS, PHILIP A. W. "Dickens in Conversation." *Dickensian* 59 (Sept. 1963):145-55.

1669 GIBSON, FRANK A. "Hard on the Lawyers?" *Dickensian* 59 (Sept. 1963):160-64.

1670 MORLEY, MALCOLM. "Dickens Goes to the Theatre." *Dickensian* 59 (Sept. 1963):165-71.

1671 PEYROUTON, NOEL C. "Mr 'Q,' Dickens's American Secretary." *Dickensian* 59 (Sept. 1963):156-59. [On George Washington Putnam, 1812-1896.]

1672 DENTON, C. R. "Charles Dickens' Lakeland Excursion." *Country Life* 134 (Sept. 19, 1963):685-86.

1673 CARY, RICHARD. "Robinson on Dickens." *American Notes and Queries* 2 (Nov. 1963):35-36. [Edward Arlington Robinson's attitude toward Dickens.]

1674 NOLAND, RICHARD W. "A Letter from Basil Hall to Charles Dickens." *Journal of Rutgers University Library* 27 (Dec. 1963): 19-23.

1675 BODELSEN, CARL A. "Dickens, The Social Critic." *Essays and Papers,* 39-74. Copenhagen: Nature Method Centre, 1964.

1676 BREDSDORFF, ELIAS L. "Hans Christian Andersen and Charles Dickens." *Annali Instituto Universitario Orientale, Napoli, Sezione Germanica* 7 (1964):5-20.

1677 HUTCHINGS, RICHARD J. *Dickens at Winterbourne, Bonchurch.* Shanklin, Isle of Wight: B. G. Saunders for R. J. H., 1964.

1678 JOHNSON, EDGAR. *Dickens Theatrical Reader.* Boston: Little, Brown, 1964. [Duplicates 1679.]

1679 JOHNSON, EDGAR and ELEANOR, eds. *The Dickens Theatrical Reader.* With prologue and notes. Boston: Little, Brown; London: Gollancz, 1964. [Duplicates 1678.]

1680 PETRINI, ENZO. *Dickens.* Brescia: La Scuola Editrice, 1964.

1681 RYAN, J. S. "The Australian Materials in *Household Words.*" *Proceedings of the Ninth Congress of the Australasian Universities' Languages and Literature Association, August 19th to 26th, 1964,* 57-59. Melbourne: Univ. of Melbourne, 1964.

1682 YAMAMOTO, TADAO. "Historical Studies in English Literature with Special Reference to Dickens's Works." *Studies in English Literature* (English Literary Society of Japan, Univ. of Tokyo) (1964):23-35.

1683 BORT, BARRY D. "George Silverman's Explanation." *Dickensian* 60 (Jan. 1964):48-51.

1684 BROWN, F. J. "Those Dickens Christmases." *Dickensian* 60 (Jan. 1964):17-19.

1685 CARLTON, WILLIAM J. "In the Blacking Warehouse." *Dickensian* 60 (Jan. 1964):11-16.

1686 COLLINS, PHILIP A. W. "Dickens on Keeley the Comedian: An Uncollected Piece, with Introduction and Notes." *Dickensian* 60 (Jan. 1964):5-10.

1687 HELDRING, E. "Some European Reactions to Dickens." *Dickensian* 60 (Jan. 1964):55-56.

1688 PEYROUTON, NOEL C. "Some Boston Abolitionists on Boz: A Lost American Note." *Dickensian* 60 (Jan. 1964):20-26.

1689 SMITH, TIMOTHY d'A. "The Penny Dreadful." *Dickensian* 60 (Jan. 1964):44-46.

1690 WARNER, JOHN R. "Dickens Looks At Homer." *Dickensian* 60 (Jan. 1964):52-54.

1691 DARROLL, G. M. H. "A Note on Dickens and Maria Beadnell, and Dickens's Comic Genius." *English Studies in Africa* 7 (Mar. 1964): 82-87.

1692 CARLTON, WILLIAM J. "'Who was the Lady?' Mrs Christian's Reminiscences of Dickens." *Dickensian* 60 (Spring 1964):68-77.

1693 EASSON, ANGUS. "Dickens's *Household Words,* and a Double Standard." *Dickensian* 60 (Spring 1964):104-14.

1694 GRYLLS, R. GLYNN. "Dickens and Holman Hunt." *Texas Studies in Literature and Language* 6 (Spring 1964):76-79. [Re. Hunt's charge that he was caricatured in a story, "Calmuck," in *Household Words* (Apr. 3, 1858).]

1695 MORLEY, MALCOLM. "Revelry by Night." *Dickensian* 60 (Spring 1964):97-101. [On Boz's sketch, "Making a Night of It."]

1696 JOHNSON, PAUL. "Garrick at War." *New Statesman* 67 (Apr. 1964) 595-96. [Garrick Club row between Dickens and Thackeray.]

1697 PEYROUTON, NOEL C. "Dickens and the Chartists." *Dickensian* 60 (May 1964):78-88; (Sept. 1964):152-61.

1698 GARIS, ROBERT E. "Dickens Criticism." *Victorian Studies* 7 (June 1964):375-86.

1699 SMITH, SHEILA M. "An Unpublished Letter from Dickens to Disraeli." *Notes and Queries* 11 (June 1964):233.

1700 MACKENZIE, COMPTON. "Intimate of Every Household." *Horizon* 6 (Summer 1964):108-15.

1701 WARD, J. A. "Dining With The Novelists." *Personalist* 45 (July 1964) 399-411. [Dickens, et al.]

1702 BROOK, G. L. "The Language of Dickens." *Bulletin of the John Rylands Library* 47 (Sept. 1964):32-48.

1703 COLLINS, PHILIP A. W. "Dickens's Reading." *Dickensian* 60 (Sept. 1964):136-51.

1704 LOHRLI, ANNE. "*Household Words* and Its 'Office Book'." *Princeton University Library Chronicle* 26 (Autumn 1964):27-47.

1705 WILLIAMS, RAYMOND. "Social Criticism in Dickens: Some Problems of Method and Approach." *Critical Quarterly* 6 (Autumn 1964):214-27.

1706 CHAUDHRY, GHULAM ALI. "Dickens and Hawthorne." *Essex Institute Historical Collections* 100 (Oct. 1964):256-73. [Special Hawthorne issue.]

1707 FIELDING, KENNETH J. "*American Notes* and Some English Reviewers." *Modern Language Review* 59 (Oct. 1964):527-37.

1708 FLEISSNER, ROBERT F. "Lear's 'Poor Fool' and Dickens." *Essays in Criticism* 14 (Oct. 1964):425.

1709 FIELDING, KENNETH J. "Dickens and Education." *Dickensian* 60 (Winter 1964):38-39.

1710 GROB, SHIRLEY. "Dickens and Some Motifs of the Fairy Tale." *Texas Studies in Literature and Language* 5 (Winter 1964):567-79. Reprinted in *Myth and Literature,* ed. John B. Vickery. Lincoln: Univ. of Nebraska Press, 1966.

1711 HAMBLEN, ABIGAIL A. "The American Scene: Dickens and Mark Twain." *Mark Twain Journal* 12 (Winter 1964):9-11.

1712 CLAYBOROUGH, ARTHUR. "Dickens: A Circle of Stage Fire." *The Grotesque in English Literature,* 201-51. Oxford: Clarendon, 1965.

1713 DAVIE, DONALD. "Dickens in Russia." *Russian Literature and Modern English Fiction*, 117-19. Chicago: Univ. of Chicago Press, 1965.

1714 FANGER, DONALD L. "Dickens: Realism, Subjunctive and Indicative." *Dostoevsky and Romantic Realism: a Study of Dostoevsky in Relation to Balzac, Dickens and Gogol*, 65-100. (Harvard Studies in Comparative Literature 27) Cambridge, Mass.: Harvard Univ. Press, 1965.

1715 FLEISSNER, ROBERT F. *Dickens and Shakespeare*. A Study in Histrionic Contrasts. New York: Haskell House, 1965.

1716 GARIS, ROBERT E. *The Dickens Theatre: A Reassessment of the Novels.* Oxford: Clarendon Press, 1965.

R1717 [GARIS, ROBERT E. *The Dickens Theatre*, 1965 q.v.] FORD, GEORGE H. "Portrait of a Novelist, But." *Dickens Studies* 2 (May 1966):96-101.

R1718 [GARIS, ROBERT E. *The Dickens Theatre*, 1965 q.v.] GREEN, MARTIN. "The Problems of Fictional Theatre." *Kenyon Review* 27 (Summer 1965):510-16.

R1719 [GARIS, ROBERT E. *The Dickens Theatre*, 1965 q.v.] HERRING, PAUL D. "*The Dickens Theatre: A Reassessment of the Novels.*" *Modern Philology* 65 (Feb. 1968):259-63.

R1720 [GARIS, ROBERT E. *The Dickens Theatre*, 1965 q.v.] JOHNSON, EDGAR. "*The Dickens Theatre and Dickens: From* Pickwick *to* Dombey." *Nineteenth Century Fiction* 20 (Mar. 1966):395-402.

R1721 [GARIS, ROBERT E. *The Dickens Theatre*, 1965 q.v.] WILLIAMSON, C. F. "Dickensians." *Essays in Criticism* 16 (Apr. 1966):228-37.

1722 HARDWICK, MICHAEL and MOLLIE. *The Charles Dickens Companion.* London: J. Murray; Toronto: Macmillan, 1965.

1723 KOROLENKO, V. G. "My First Encounter with Dickens." *Russian Literature and Modern English Fiction*, ed. D. Davie, 107-16. Chicago: Univ. of Chicago Press, 1965.

1724 MARCUS, STEVEN. *Dickens: From* Pickwick *to* Dombey. New York: Basic Books; London: Chatto and Windus, 1965.

R1725 [MARCUS, STEVEN. *Dickens: From* Pickwick *to* Dombey, 1965 q.v.] FIELDING, KENNETH J. "The Marcus Dickens." *Dickens Studies* 1 (Sept. 1965):145-48.

R1726 [MARCUS, STEVEN. *Dickens: From* Pickwick *to* Dombey, 1965 q.v.] JOHNSON, EDGAR. "*The Dickens Theatre* and *Dickens: From* Pickwick *to* Dombey." *Nineteenth Century Fiction* 20 (Mar. 1966): 395-402.

R1727 [MARCUS, STEVEN. *Dickens: From* Pickwick *to* Dombey, 1965 q.v.] MOYNAHAN, JULIAN. "Early Dickens." *Encounter* 24 (May 1965):84-87.

R1728 [MARCUS, STEVEN. *Dickens: From* Pickwick *to* Dombey, 1965 q.v.] STONE, HARRY. "Critic of the Hour." *Kenyon Review* 27 (Summer 1965):516-23.

R1729 [MARCUS, STEVEN. *Dickens: From* Pickwick *to* Dombey, 1965 q.v.] WILLIAMSON, C. F. "Dickensians." *Essays in Criticism* 16 (Apr. 1966):228-37.

1730 MUIR, EDWIN. "The Dark Felicities of Charles Dickens." *Essays on Literature and Society,* 206-14. Cambridge, Mass.: Harvard Univ. Press, 1965.

1731 PEACHE, LAWRENCE D. *Charles Dickens.* Loughborough, Eng.: Wills and Hepworth, 1965. [A children's biography.]

1732 [A Russian Correspondent.] "Dickens in Russia, a Moral Educator." *Russian Literature and Modern English Fiction,* ed. D. Davie, 117-19. Chicago: University of Chicago Press, 1965.

1733 RYAN, J. S., ed. *Charles Dickens and New Zealand: A Colonial Image.* Selected from the periodical publications of Charles Dickens, with historical and biographical notes, Wellington, NZ: A. H. and A. W. Reed for the Dunedin Public Library; San Francisco: Tri-Ocean, 1965.

1734 STOEHR, TAYLOR. *Dickens: The Dreamer's Stance.* Ithaca, NY: Cornell Univ. Press, 1965.

R1735 [STOEHR, TAYLOR. *Dickens: The Dreamer's Stance,* 1965 q.v.] FIELDING, KENNETH J. *"Dickens – The Dreamer's Stance." Dickensian* 62 (Jan. 1966):22-24.

R1736 [STOEHR, TAYLOR. *Dickens: The Dreamer's Stance,* 1965 q.v.] HARDY, BARBARA. *Modern Language Quarterly* 27 (June 1966): 230-33.

R1737 [STOEHR, TAYLOR. *Dickens: The Dreamer's Stance,* 1965 q.v.] HERRING, PAUL D. *"Dickens: The Dreamer's Stance." Modern Philology* 65 (Feb. 1968):259-63.

R1738 [STOEHR, TAYLOR. *Dickens: The Dreamer's Stance,* 1965 q.v.] STEIG, MICHAEL. "Article-Review on Five Dickens Studies." *Literature and Psychology* 15 (Fall 1965):230-37.

R1739 [STOEHR, TAYLOR. *Dickens: The Dreamer's Stance,* 1965 q.v.] STONE, HARRY. *"Dickens: The Dreamer's Stance." Nineteenth Century Fiction* 20 (Mar. 1966):402-6.

1740 WAGENKNECHT, EDWARD. "Dickens and Ellen Glasgow." *Dickens and the Scandal-Mongers,* 95-98. Norman: Univ. of Oklahoma Press, 1965.

1741 WAGENKNECHT, EDWARD. "Dickens and the Marxians." *Dickens and the Scandal-Mongers,* 109-13. Norman: Univ. of Oklahoma Press, 1965.

1742 WAGENKNECHT, EDWARD. *Dickens and the Scandal-Mongers: Essays in Defense and Criticism.* Norman: Univ. of Oklahoma Press, 1965.

1743 WAGENKNECHT, EDWARD. "Dickens at Work: *The Chimes.*" *Dickens and the Scandal-Mongers,* 50-70. Norman: Univ. of Oklahoma Press, 1965.

1744 WAGENKNECHT, EDWARD. "Edmund Wilson on Dickens." *Dickens and the Scandal-Mongers,* 114-20. Norman: Univ. of Oklahoma Press, 1965.

1745 CARLTON, WILLIAM J. "An Early Home of Dickens in Kensington." *Dickensian* 61 (Jan. 1965):20-25.

1746 COLLINS, PHILIP A. W. "Dickens and Popular Amusements." *Dickensian* 61 (Jan. 1965):7-19.

1747 DUNN, RICHARD J. "Dickens's Mastery of the Macabre." *Dickens Studies* 1 (Jan. 1965):33-39.

1748 GERSON, STANLEY. "Dickens's Use of Malapropisms." *Dickensian* 61 (Jan. 1965):40-45.

1749 GREAVES, JOHN. "The Thirsty Woman of Tutbury." *Dickensian* 61 (Jan. 1965):51-52. [Cf. short footnote added to Greaves' comments by Michael Slater, *Dickensian* 61 (Sept. 1965):181.]

1750 WALL, STEPHEN. "Dickens' Plot of Fortune." *Review of English Literature* 6 (Jan. 1965):56-67.

1751 HOLLOWAY, JOHN. "Dickens's Vision of Society." *Listener* 73 (Feb. 1965):287-89. Reprinted in *The Novelist as Innovator* [Holloway *et al.*]. London: British Broadcasting Corp., 1965.

1752 "Hard Words; Dickens at His Post." *Times Literary Supplement* (Feb. 11, 1965):97-99.

1753 JOHNSON, EDGAR. "Scott and Dickens: Realist and Romantic." *Victorian Newsletter* 27 (Spring 1965):9-11.

1754 DUTT, R. PALME. "The Young Dickens." *Listener* 73 (Apr. 1965): 492.

1755 CARLTON, WILLIAM J. "Dickens's Literary Mentor (John Henry Barrow)." *Dickens Studies* 1 (May 1965):54-64.

1756 CARLTON, WILLIAM J. "Dickens Studies Italian." *Dickensian* 61 (May 1965):101-8.

1757 COLLINS, PHILIP A. W. "'Inky Fishing Nets': Dickens as Editor." *Dickensian* 61 (May 1965):120-25.

1758 FIELDING, KENNETH J. "Dickens in Victorian Fiction." *Dickensian* 61 (May 1965):126-28.

1759 FIELDING, KENNETH J. "Dickens's Work with Miss Coutts." *Dickensian* 61 (May 1965):112-19; (Sept. 1965):155-60.

1760 HUTCHINGS, RICHARD J. "Dickens at Bonchurch." *Dickensian* 61 (May 1965):79-100.

1761 McCABE, BERNARD. "Taking Dickens Seriously." *Commonweal* 82 (May 1965):244-47.

1762 CHAPELL, MARIAN C. "The Man Who Drew for Dickens." *Country Life* 137 (June 1965):1447-48.

1763 BIZAM, LENKE. "The Imagery of Dickens and Proust." *New Hungarian Quarterly* 6 (Summer 1965):174-80.

1764 MANHEIM, LEONARD F. "Floras and Doras: The Women in Dickens' Novels." *Texas Studies in Literature and Language* 7 (Summer 1965):181-200.

1765 CARLTON, WILLIAM J. "Dickens or Forster? Some *King Lear* Criticisms Re-Examined." *Dickensian* 61 (Sept. 1965):133-40. [On Macready's *Lear.*]

1766 COUSTILLAS, PIERRE. "Gissing's Writings on Dickens: A Bio-Bibliographical Survey." *Dickensian* 61 (Sept. 1965):168-79.

1767 SENELICK, LAURENCE. "'Charl'z Dikkens' and the Russian Encyclopedias." *Dickens Studies* 1 (Sept. 1965):129-44.

1768 STEDMAN, JANE W. "Good Spirits: Dickens's Childhood Reading." *Dickensian* 61 (Sept. 1965):150-54.

1769 BUTTS, DENNIS. "Dickens and Children." *Use of English* 17 (Autumn 1965):43-45. [Children as Dickensians.]

1770 HONAN, PARK. "Metrical Prose in Dickens." *Victorian Newsletter* 28 (Fall 1965):1-3.

1771 SLACK, ROBERT C. "A Comment on Recent Victorian Scholarship." *Pennsylvania Council of Teachers of English Bulletin* 12 (Dec. 1965):19-30.

1772 HILL, A. G. "The Real World of Charles Dickens." *Critical Quarterly* 7 (Winter 1965):374-83.

1773 RILEY, ANTHONY W. "Notes on Thomas Mann and English and American Literature." *Comparative Literature* 17 (Winter 1965): 57-72. [Humour and the grotesque, etc. including refs. to Dickens.]

1774 CARROW, G. D. "An Informal Call on Charles Dickens by a Philadelphia Clergyman." *University: A Princeton Quarterly* 27 (Winter 1965-66):14-17. Reprinted in *Dickensian* 63 (May 1967).

1775 ALLEN, M. L. "The Black Veil: Three Versions of a Symbol." *English Studies* 47 (1966):286-89. [In Dickens, Hawthorne, and Radcliffe.]

1776 AXTON, WILLIAM F. *Circle of Fire: Dickens Vision and Style and the Popular Victorian Theatre.* Lexington: Univ. of Kentucky Press, 1966.

R1777 [AXTON, WILLIAM F. *Circle of Fire*, 1966 q.v.] FORD, GEORGE H. *Cithara* 7 (Nov. 1967):75-77.

R1778 [AXTON, WILLIAM F. *Circle of Fire*, 1966 q.v.] STAPLES, LESLIE C. "Dickens and the Theatre, II." *Dickensian* 63 (May 1967): 124.

R1779 [AXTON, WILLIAM F. *Circle of Fire*, 1966 q.v.] WARING, WALTER W. *Library Journal* 91 (Dec. 1966):6087.

R1780 [AXTON, WILLIAM F. *Circle of Fire*, 1966 q.v.] WORTH, KATHERINE J. "*Circle of Fire: Dickens' Vision and Style and the Popular Victorian Theater.*" *Victorian Studies* 11 (Mar. 1968):416-17.

1781 BRANNAN, ROBERT L., ed. *Under the Management of Mr Charles Dickens: His Production of "The Frozen Deep."* Ithaca, NY: Cornell Univ. Press, 1966.

1782 DUNLOP, AGNES M. R. (Elisabeth Kyle, pseud.) *The Boy Who Asked for More: The Early Life of Dickens.* London: Evans, 1966. [Juvenile.]

1783 JOHNSON, EDGAR. "Dickens and the Spirit of the Age." *Bibliotheca Bucnellensis* 4 (1966):1-13. Reprinted in *Victorian Essays, A Symposium: Essays on the Occasion of the Centennial of the College of Wooster in Honor of Emeritus Professor Waldo H. Dunn*, ed. Warren D. Anderson and Thomas D. Clareson. Kent, Ohio: Kent State Univ. Press, 1967.

1784 KATARSKIJ, I. M. *Dikkens v Rossii.* Moscow: Akademija Nauk SSSR, 1966. [*Dickens in Russia.*]

1785 MADDEN, WILLIAM A. "The Search for Forgiveness in Some Nineteenth Century English Novelists." *Comparative Literature Studies* 3 (1966):139-53.

1786 MANHEIM, LEONARD F. "Thanatos: The Death Instinct in Dickens' Later Novels." *Hidden Patterns; Studies in Psychoanalytic Literary Criticism*, ed. with introd. by Leonard and Eleanor Manheim, 113-31. New York: Macmillan, 1966.

1787 MILLER J. HILLIS. "Some Implications of Form in Victorian Fiction." *Comparative Literature Studies* 3 (1966):109-18.

1788 MONOD, SYLVÈRE. "John Forster's 'Life of Dickens' and Literary Criticism." *English Studies Today*, 4th series, 357-73. Rome: Edizioni di Storia e Letteratura, 1966.

1789 STIRLING, MONICA. "A Visit to Dickens, 1857," *The Wild Swan: The Life and Times of Hans Christian Andersen*, 269-81. New York: Harcourt, Brace, 1966.

1790 VALLANCE, ROSALIND. "Introduction." *Dickens' London.* [Essays from *Sketches by Boz* and *The Uncommercial Traveller*.] London: Folio Society, 1966.

1791 WILSON, ANGUS. "The Artist as Your Enemy is Your Only Friend." *Southern Review* N.S. 2 (1966):101-14. [Univ. of Adelaide.]

1792 DUNLOP, JOSEPH R. "A Fourth Christmas: Calculation and Commentary." *Dickensian* 62 (Jan. 1966):57-61.

1793 FIELDING, KENNETH J. "Two Sketches by Maclise: The Dickens Children and *The Chimes* Reading." *Dickens Studies* 2 (Jan. 1966): 7-17.

1794 GIBSON, FRANK A. "John Hollingshead – A Notable Victorian." *Dickensian* 62 (Jan. 1966):37-46.

1795 GREAVES, JOHN. "The Birmingham and Midland Institute." *Dickensian* 62 (Jan. 1966):34-36.

1796 LOHRLI, ANNE. "Andersen, Dickens and 'Herr von Müffe'." *Dickensian* 62 (Jan. 1966):5-13.

1797 PASSERINI, EDWARD M. "Hawthornesque Dickens." *Dickens Studies* 2 (Jan. 1966):18-25.

1798 PEYROUTON, NOEL C. "Dickens and the *Judy* Magazine." *Dickensian* 62 (Jan. 1966):14-20. [Burlesques in *Judy* concerning Dickens.]

1799 VALLANCE, ROSALIND. "From Boz to the Uncommercial." *Dickensian* 62 (Jan. 1966):27-33.

1800 LOHRLI, ANNE. "Greek Slave Mystery." *Notes and Queries* 13 (Feb. 1966):58-60.

1801 TODD, WILLIAM B. "Dickens's *Battle of Life:* Round Six." *Book Collector* 15 (Spring 1966):48-54.

1802 WINTERS, WARRINGTON. "The Death Hug in Charles Dickens." *Literature and Psychology* 16 (Spring 1966):109-15.

1803 STONE, HARRY. "Dickens, Browning and the Mysterious Letter." *Pacific Coast Philology* 1 (Apr. 1966):42-47.

1804 CARLTON, WILLIAM J. "Dickens's Forgotten Retreat in France." *Dickensian* 62 (May 1966):69-86.

1805 COLLINS, PHILIP A. W. "W. C. Macready and Dickens: Some Family Recollections." *Dickens Studies* 2 (May 1966):51-56.

1806 DUNN, RICHARD J. "But We Grow Affecting: Let Us Proceed." *Dickensian* 62 (May 1966):53-55.

1807 HARDWICK, MOLLIE. "Born Under Aquarius." *Dickensian* 62 (May 1966):86-95.

1808 HORN, ROBERT D. "Dickens and the Patent Bramah Lock." *Dickensian* 62 (May 1966):100-5.

1809 SCRUTTON, CANON T. B. "'The State of the Prisons' as Seen by John Howard and Charles Dickens." *Dickensian* 62 (May 1966): 112-17.

1810 STAPLES, LESLIE C. "The Dexter Bust of Dickens." *Dickensian* 62 (May 1966):120-22.

1811 LANSBURY, CORAL. "Charles Dickens and his Australia." *Royal Australian Historical Society Journal* 52 (June 1966):115-28.

1812 MAUSKOPF, CHARLES. "Thackeray's Attitude Toward Dickens's Writings." *Nineteenth Century Fiction* 21 (June 1966):21-23.

1813 SMITH, ANGELA. "Dickens's Integrity." *New Statesman* N.S. 72 (July 1, 1966):17.

1814 CARTER, JOHN A., Jr. (J. H. Siddons, pseud.) "Memories of 'Charlie Wag'." *Dickensian* 62 (Sept. 1966):147-51. [*Souvenirs of Charles Dickens,* an account of an early friendship by J. H. Stocqueler, is reprinted.]

1815 GIBSON, FRANK A. "Letter to the Editor: Dickens's Forgotten Retreat in France." *Dickensian* 62 (Sept. 1966):184.

1816 GREAVES, JOHN. "Dickens Was Right." *Dickensian* 62 (Sept. 1966): 156-57.

1817 SLATER, MICHAEL. "Dickens (and Forster) at Work on *The Chimes.*" *Dickens Studies* 2 (Sept. 1966):106-40.

1818 WILDEN, ELDRED J. "Enjoy Dickens With Me." *Dickensian* 62 (Sept. 1966):185-87.

1819 BROOK, G. L. "Dickens as a Literary Craftsman." *Bulletin of the John Rylands Library* 49 (Autumn 1966):47-68.

1820 STOTT, R. TOOLE. "Boz's Memoirs of Joseph Grimaldi, 1838." *Book Collector* 15 (Autumn 1966):354-56.

1821 HENLEY, ELTON F. "Charles Dickens on Aesthetic Distance and a Possible Dickens Influence." *Language Quarterly of the University of South Florida* 5 (Fall-Winter 1966):2-4. [Influence on Ortega.]

1822 "The Clarendon Dickens: Aim to Present Text Readers Were Meant to See." *Bookseller* (Oct. 8, 1966):1928-34.

1823 GERLACH, W. H. "An Interview with Charles Dickens on Scientific Methodology." *Journal of Politics* 28 (Nov. 1966):831-35.

1824 PRICE, MARTIN. "Dickens and George Eliot: The Necessary Ancestors." *Yale Review* 55 (Winter 1966):291-96.

1825 BELL, ALDON D. *London in the Age of Dickens.* Norman: Univ. of Oklahoma Press, 1967.

1826 COOLIDGE, ARCHIBALD C., Jr. *Charles Dickens as Serial Novelist.* Ames: Iowa State Univ. Press, 1967.

R1827 [COOLIDGE, ARCHIBALD C., Jr. *Charles Dickens as Serial Novelist,* 1967 q.v.] *Choice* 4 (Jan. 1968):1240.

R1828 [COOLIDGE, ARCHIBALD C., Jr. *Charles Dickens as Serial Novelist,* 1967 q.v.] FIELDING, KENNETH J. "Dickens as a Serial Novelist." *Dickensian* 63 (Sept. 1967):156-57.

R1829 [COOLIDGE, ARCHIBALD C., Jr. *Charles Dickens as Serial Novelist,* 1967 q.v.] HALE, OSBORNE. *North Dakota Quarterly* 35 (Spring 1967):55-56.

R1830 [COOLIDGE, ARCHIBALD C., Jr. *Charles Dickens as Serial Novelist,* 1967 q.v.] SUTHERLAND, J. A. "*Charles Dickens as Serial Novelist.* *Dickens Studies* 4 (Mar. 1968):95-98.

1831 DABNEY, ROSS H. *Love and Property in the Novels of Dickens.* London: Chatto and Windus; Berkeley: Univ. of California Press, 1967.

R1832 [DABNEY, ROSS H. *Love and Property in the Novels of Dickens,* 1967 q.v.] HAMILTON, ROBERT. "Dickens and Mercenary Marriage." *Dickensian* 63 (May 1967):110.

R1833 [DABNEY, ROSS H. *Love and Property in the Novels of Dickens,* 1967 q.v.] KETTLE, ARNOLD. "*Love and Property in the Novels of Dickens.*" *Victorian Studies* 11 (Dec. 1967):249.

R1834 [DABNEY, ROSS H. *Love and Property in the Novels of Dickens,* 1967 q.v.] LANE, LAURIAT, Jr. "On Stage-Off Stage, and Behind the Scenes." *Dickens Studies* 3 (Oct. 1967):170-75.

1835 GERSON, STANLEY. *Sound and Symbol in the Dialogue of the Works of Charles Dickens.* (Stockholm Studies in English 19) Stockholm: Almquist and Wiksell, 1967.

1836 HIBBERT, CHRISTOPHER. *The Making of Charles Dickens.* London Longmans, Green, 1967.

1837 JARMUTH, SYLVIA L. *Dickens Use of Women in His Novels.* New York: Excelsior, 1967.

1838 MORLEY, MALCOLM. *Margate and Its Theatres.* London: Museum Press, 1967. [Theatre of Dickens' day and his summer visits from Broadstairs.]

1839 NAUMOV, NIČIFOR. *Dikens Kod Srba i Hrvata.* Belgrade: Univerzitet. Filoški Fakultet. Monografije, Knj. 9, 1967. [*Dickens Among the Serbs and Croats.*]

1840 PRICE, MARTIN, ed. *Dickens: A Collection of Critical Essays.* Englewood Cliffs, NJ: Prentice-Hall, 1967.

1841 PRICE, MARTIN. "Introduction." *Dickens: A Collection of Critical Essays,* 1-15. Englewood Cliffs, NJ: Prentice-Hall, 1967.

1842 TAYLOR, BARRY. *Dickens.* London: Outposts, 1967.

1843 ZHEGALOV, NIKOLAI. "Dickens in Russia." *Soviet Literature* 5 (1967):168-75.

1844 ARNOLD, BETH R. "Disraeli and Dickens on Young England." *Dickensian* 63 (Jan. 1967):26-31.

1845 CARLTON, WILLIAM J. "Dickens and the Artists' Benevolent Funds." *Dickensian* 63 (Jan. 1967):8-13.

1846 WILSON, ROSS. "The Dickens of a Drink." *Dickensian* 63 (Jan. 1967):46-61. [Alcoholic beverages.]

1847 COLLINS, PHILIP A. W. "Dickens and *Punch*." *Dickens Studies* 3 (Mar. 1967):4-21.

1848 PEYROUTON, NOEL C. "Boz and the American Phreno-Mesmerists." *Dickens Studies* 3 (Mar. 1967):38-50.

1849 STONE, HARRY. "Dickens and Composite Writing." *Dickens Studies* 3 (Mar. 1967):68-79. [Most of the composite pieces date from the first three years (1850-53) of *Household Words*.]

1850 WILSON ANGUS. "Evil in The English Novel." *Kenyon Review* 29 (Mar. 1967):167-94.

1851 GRIGG, JOHN. "Next to Shakespeare." *Guardian* (Mar. 20, 1967):14.

1852 KIRKPATRICK, LARRY. "The Gothic Flame of Charles Dickens." *Victorian Newsletter* 31 (Spring 1967):20-24.

1853 SMITH, WILBUR J. "Boz's *Memoirs of Joseph Grimaldi, 1838*." *Book Collector* 16 (Spring 1967):80. [Describes a first edition.]

1854 CARLTON, WILLIAM J. "The Death of Mary Hogarth – Before and After." *Dickensian* 63 (May 1967):68-74.

1855 GREAVES, JOHN. "Dickens Today." *Dickensian* 63 (May 1967):111. [Review of talks about Dickens on BBC.]

1856 GREAVES, JOHN. "Historic Additions to the Dickens House Museum." *Dickensian* 63 (May 1967):81.

1857 LEON, H. C. "The Birthday Dinner in London." *Dickensian* 63 (May 1967):95-99. [On Dickens as a legal and social reformer.]

1858 STONE, HARRY. "Dickens and the Idea of a Periodical: A History of the Triumphant Will." *Western Humanities Review* 21 (Summer 1967):237-56.

1859 KILLHAM, JOHN. "Autonomy Versus Mimesis." *British Journal of Aesthetics* 7 (July 1967):274-85. [Partly on Dickens.]

1860 MACINTYRE, ALASDAIR. "Sociology and the Novel." *Times Literary Supplement* (July 27, 1967):657-58.

1861 ANDRE, ROBERT. "Un Grand Ecrivain Populaire." *Nouvelle Revue Francaise* 15 (Aug. 1967):306-11.

1862 BANTA, MARTHA. "Charles Dickens's Warning to England." *Dickensian* 63 (Sept. 1967):166-75. [The neglected child.]

1863 BRICE, ALEC W. "Ignorance and Its Victims: Another New Article by Dickens." *Dickensian* 63 (Sept. 1967):143-47.

1864 CARLTON, WILLIAM J. "Dickens and the Royal Society of Arts."
Dickensian 63 (Sept. 1967):138-42.

1865 GIBSON, FRANK A. "If-and Maria." *Dickensian* 63 (Sept. 1967):
162-65. [Beadnell.]

1866 NOWELL-SMITH, SIMON. "The 'Cheap Edition' of Dickens's Works
[First Series] 1847-1852." *Library* 22 (Sept. 1967):245-51.

1867 PEYROUTON, NOEL C. "When Nast Drew Dickens: An Historical
Note and Correction." *Dickensian* 63 (Sept. 1967):154-55.

1868 THALE, JEROME. "The Imagination of Charles Dickens: Some
Preliminary Discriminations." *Nineteenth Century Fiction* 22
(Sept. 1967):127-43.

1869 STONE, HARRY. "New Writings By Dickens." *Dalhousie Review* 47
(Autumn 1967):305-25. [Dickens' "composite articles," written in
collaboration with colleagues, published in *Household Words.*]

1870 AXTON, WILLIAM F. "'Keystone' Structure in Dickens' Serial
Novels." *Univ. Toronto Quarterly* 37 (Oct. 1967):31-50.

1871 BARTON, H. M. *Dickens and his Works.* London: Methuen, 1968.
[Biography, plot summaries, basic critical comments, etc.]

1872 BLOUNT, TREVOR. *Dickens: The Early Novels.* (Writers and Their
Work 204.) London: Longmans, Green, 1968.

1873 DONOVAN, FRANK. *Dickens and Youth.* New York: Dodd, Mead,
1968.

1874 DYSON, A. E., ed. *Dickens: Modern Judgements.* Toronto: Macmillan,
1968.

1875 FIDO, MARTIN. *Charles Dickens.* London: Routledge and K. Paul,
1968.

1876 FIELDING, KENNETH J. "Dickens and the Past: The Novelist of
Memory." *Experience in the Novel,* ed. Roy H. Pearce, 107-31.
New York: Columbia Univ. Press, 1968.

1877 FRYE, NORTHROP. "Dickens and the Comedy of Humours."
Experience in the Novel, ed. Roy H. Pearce, 49-81. New York:
Columbia Univ. Press, 1968.

1878 HARDWICK, MOLLIE. "Introduction." *Stories from Dickens.*
London: E. Arnold, 1968.

1879 HARDY, BARBARA. *Dickens: The Later Novels.* (Writers and Their
Work 205.) London: Longmans, Green, 1968.

1880 DUNLOP, AGNES M. R. (Elisabeth Kyle, pseud.). *Great Ambitions,
A Story of the Early Years of Charles Dickens.* New York: Holt, 1968.
[An introduction for children.]

1881 MONOD, SYLVÈRE. *Dickens the Novelist.* Introd. Edward
Wagenknecht. Norman: Univ. of Oklahoma Press, 1968.

R1882 [MONOD, SYLVÈRE. *Dickens the Novelist,* 1968 q.v.] ALLEN, WALTER. *New York Times Book Review* (May 5, 1968):22.

R1883 [MONOD, SYLVÈRE. *Dickens the Novelist,* 1968 q.v.] FIELDING, KENNETH J. "The Novelist at Work." *Dickensian* 65 (Jan. 1969): 49-51.

R1884 [MONOD, SYLVÈRE. *Dickens the Novelist,* 1968 q.v.] McMASTER, ROWLAND D. "Sylvère Monod: *Dickens the Novelist.*" *Nineteenth Century Fiction* 23 (Dec. 1968):359-61.

1885 STONE, HARRY. "Introduction." *Charles Dickens' Uncollected Writings from* Household Words *(1850-1859),* I, 3-68. Bloomington: Indiana Univ. Press, 1968; London: Allen Lane, Penguin Press, 1969.

1886 STONE, HARRY, ed. *Uncollected Writings of Charles Dickens:* Household Words *(1850-59).* 2 vols. Bloomington: Indiana Univ. Press, 1968; London: Allen Lane, Penguin Press, 1969. [With 132 illus. from contemporary sources.]

1887 SUSSMAN, HERBERT L. "The Industrial Novel and the Machine: Charles Dickens." *Victorians and the Machine: the Literary Response to Technology,* 41-76. Cambridge, Mass.: Harvard Univ. Press, 1968.

1888 COLLINS, PHILIP A. W. "Dickens's Weeklies." *Victorian Periodicals Newsletter* 1 (Jan. 1968):18-19.

1889 GIFFORD, HENRY. "Dickens in Russia: The Initial Phase." *Forum for Modern Language Studies* 4 (Jan. 1968):45-52.

1890 HAMILTON, ROBERT. "The Creative Eye: Dickens as Essayist." *Dickensian* 64 (Jan. 1968):36-42.

1891 MAJOR, GWEN. "Into the Shadowy Past." *Dickensian* 64 (Jan. 1968): 28-33. [London locales in Dickens and their present condition.]

1892 "The Amateur Contribution." *Times Literary Supplement* (Feb. 15, 1968):157. [On the *Dickensian.*]

1893 DAVIS, PAUL B. "Dickens and the American Press, 1842." *Dickens Studies* 4 (Mar. 1968):32-77.

1894 KREUTZ, IRVING W. "Sly of Manner, Sharp of Tooth: A Study of Dickens's Villains." *Nineteenth Century Fiction* 22 (Mar. 1968): 331-48.

1895 PEYROUTON, NOEL C. "Bozmania vs. Bozphobia: A Yankee Pot-pourri." *Dickens Studies* 4 (Mar. 1968):78-94.

1896 PEYROUTON, NOEL C. "Re: Memoir of an *American Notes* Original." *Dickens Studies* 4 (Mar. 1968):23-31. [Observations of a fellow passenger on the "Brittania," 1842.]

1897 RALEIGH, JOHN H. "The Novel and the City: England and America in the Nineteenth Century." *Victorian Studies* 11 (Mar. 1968): 291-328.

1898 STEVENS, JOAN. "A Note on Thackeray's 'Manager of the Performance'." *Nineteenth Century Fiction* 22 (Mar. 1968):391-97.

1899 TICK, STANLEY. "On Not Being Charles Dickens." *Bucknell Review* 16 (Mar. 1968):85-95.

1900 WELSH, ALEXANDER. "Satire and History: The City of Dickens." *Victorian Studies* 11 (Mar. 1968):379-400.

1901 DUNN, RICHARD J. "Dickens and the Mormons." *Brigham Young University Studies* 8 (Spring 1968):325-34.

1902 DUNN, RICHARD J. "The Unnoticed Uncommercial Traveller." *Dickensian* 64 (May 1968):103-4. [Biographical background to Dickens' *Uncommercial Traveller* essay for July 4, 1863: "Bound for the Great Salt Lake."]

1903 SLATER, MICHAEL. "On 'Selling' Dickens." *Dickensian* 64 (May 1968):101-2. [Misleading descriptions of Dickens' writings.]

1904 STONE, HARRY. "Dickens 'Conducts' *Household Words*." *Dickensian* 64 (May 1968):71-85.

1905 STANGE, G. ROBERT. "The Victorian City and the Frightened Poets." *Victorian Studies* 11 (Summer 1968):627-40.

1906 BOWN, DEREK. "Feeding the Robber Fancy: Dickens for Schools." *Dickensian* 64 (Sept. 1968):166-68.

1907 FIELDING, KENNETH J. and ALEC W. BRICE. "Charles Dickens on 'The Exclusion of Evidence' – I." *Dickensian* 64 (Sept. 1968): 131-40. [On Court Procedure.]

1908 PENNER, TALBOT. "Dickens: An Early Influence." *Dickensian* 64 (Sept. 1968):157-62. [John Barrow.]

1909 REID, JOHN C. "Mr Tringham of Slough." *Dickensian* 64 (Sept. 1968):164-65. [Dickens' whereabouts from Jan. 1866 to June 1867, and use of name Tringham.]

1910 GANZ, MARGARET. "Humor's Alchemy: The Lesson of *Sketches by Boz*." *Genre* 1 (Oct. 1968):290-306.

1911 BRICE, A. W. C. and KENNETH J. FIELDING. "Dickens and the Tooting Disaster." *Victorian Studies* 12 (Dec. 1968):227-44.

1912 IFKOVIC, EDWARD. "'I Took a Jaunt': Dickens's *American Notes* and Whitman's *Franklin Evans*." *Walt Whitman Review* 14 (Dec. 1968):171-74.

1913 LAMB, CEDRIC. "Love and Self-Interest in Dickens' Novels." *Paunch* 33 (Dec. 1968):32-47.

1914 BENTLEY, NICOLAS. "Dickens and his Illustrators." *Charles Dickens 1812-1870*, ed. E. W. F. Tomlin, 205-27. London: Weidenfeld and Nicolson, 1969. Partially reprinted in *Dickensian* 65 (Sept. 1969): 148-62.

1915 BROWN, IVOR. "Dickens as Social Reformer." *Charles Dickens 1812-1870*, ed. E. W. F. Tomlin, 141-67. London: Weidenfeld and Nicolson, 1969.

1916 BUTT, JOHN E. "Dickens' Christmas Books." *Pope, Dickens, and Others*, 127-48. Edinburgh: University Press, 1969.

1917 FLETCHER, GEOFFREY. *Dickens' London*. London: *The Daily Telegraph*, 1969.

1918 HIBBERT, CHRISTOPHER. "Dickens's London." *Charles Dickens 1812-1870*, ed. E. W. F. Tomlin, 73-99. London: Weidenfeld and Nicolson, 1969.

1919 JOHNSON, E. D. H. *Charles Dickens: An Introduction to the Reading of His Novels*. New York: Random House, 1969.

1920 JOHNSON, EDGAR. "Dickens: The Dark Pilgrimage." *Charles Dickens 1812-1870*, ed. E. W. F. Tomlin, 41-63. London: Weidenfeld and Nicolson, 1969.

1921 LEE, JAMES W., ed. *Studies in the Novel* 1 (Summer 1969). Denton, Texas: North Texas State Univ., 1969. [Charles Dickens Special Number.]

1922 MIYOSHI, MASAO. "Broken Music: 1870, VII." *The Divided Self*, 265-78. New York: New York Univ. Press; London: Univ. of London Press, 1969.

1923 PRIESTLEY, J. B. "The Great Inimitable." *Charles Dickens 1812-1870*, ed. E. W. F. Tomlin, 13-31. London: Weidenfeld and Nicolson, 1969.

1924 REINHOLD, HEINZ, ed. *Charles Dickens. Sein Werk im Lichte neuer deutscher Forschung*. With contributions by Horst Oppel, Helmut Viebrock, Ludwig Borinski, and Wilhelm Füger. Heidelberg, 1969.

1925 SMITH, GRAHAME. *Dickens, Money and Society*. Berkeley: Univ. of California Press, 1969.

1926 TOMLIN, ERIC W. F., ed. *Charles Dickens 1812-1870; A Centenary Volume*. London: Weidenfeld and Nicolson, 1969.

1927 TOMLIN, ERIC W. F. "Dickens's Reputation: a Reassessment." *Charles Dickens 1812-1870*, 237-63. London: Weidenfeld and Nicolson, 1969.

1928 WILLIAMS, EMLYN. "Dickens and the Theatre." *Charles Dickens 1812-1870*, ed. E. W. F. Tomlin, 177-95. London: Weidenfeld and Nicolson, 1969.

1929 WING, GEORGE D. *Dickens*. (Writers and Critics Series.) Edinburgh: Oliver and Boyd, 1969.

1930 FIELDING, KENNETH J. and ALEC W. BRICE. "Charles Dickens on 'The Exclusion of Evidence' – Concluded." *Dickensian* 65 (Jan. 1969):35-41. [On Court Procedures.]

1931 GARDNER, JOSEPH H. "Mark Twain and Dickens." *PMLA* 84 (Jan. 1969):90-101.

1932 GREAVES, JOHN. "When Dickens Went on Strike." *Dickensian* 65 (Jan. 1969):12-16. [Dickens' reacting to poor hotel accommodation by reading poorly. Berwick, 1861.]

1933 SLATER, MICHAEL. "The Christmas Books." *Dickensian* 65 (Jan. 1969):17-24.

1934 TASKER, CANON DEREK. "Dickens Commemoration Sermon." *Dickensian* 65 (Jan. 1969):56-58.

1935 GOLD, JOSEPH. "Charles Dickens and Today's Reader." *English Journal* 58 (Feb. 1969):205-11.

1936 WALTON, JAMES. "Conrad, Dickens, and the Detective Novel." *Nineteenth Century Fiction* 23 (Mar. 1969):446-62.

1937 GOLD, JOSEPH. "Dickens and Faulkner: The Uses of Influence." *Dalhousie Review* 49 (Spring 1969):69-79.

1938 COHEN, JANE R. "All-of-a Twist: The Relationship of George Cruikshank and Charles Dickens." *Harvard Library Bulletin* 17 (Apr. 1969):169-94.

1939 CARLTON, WILLIAM J. "Dickens Reports O'Connell: A Legend Examined." *Dickensian* 65 (May 1969):95-99.

1940 STONE, HARRY. "Dickens' England." *Dickensian* 65 (May 1969): 135-38.

1941 TILLOTSON, KATHLEEN and NINA BURGIS. "Dickens at Drury Lane." *Dickensian* 65 (May 1969):81-83. [Comments on and reprint of review by Dickens in *Examiner* Oct. 21, 1843 of operas: *La Favorita* and *My Wife's Come.*]

1942 COLLINS, PHILIP A. W. "Dickens' Public Readings: The Performer and the Novelist." *Studies in the Novel* 1 (Summer 1969):118-32.

1943 DUNN, RICHARD J. "Dickens and the Tragi-Comic Grotesque." *Studies in the Novel* 1 (Summer 1969):147-56.

1944 LANE, LAURIAT, Jr. "Dickens Studies, 1958-1968: An Overview." *Studies in the Novel* 1 (Summer 1969):240-54.

1945 LEVINE, RICHARD A. "Dickens, the Two Nations, and Individual Possibility." *Studies in the Novel* 1 (Summer 1969):157-80.

1946 McMASTER, ROWLAND D. "Dickens, the Dandy, and the Savage: A Victorian View of the Romantic." *Studies in the Novel* 1 (Summer 1969):133-46.

1947 MANHEIM, LEONARD F. "The Dickens Hero as Child." *Studies in the Novel* 1 (Summer 1969):189-95.

1948 STEIG, MICHAEL. "Dickens, Hablôt Browne, and the Tradition of English Caricature." *Criticism* 11 (Summer 1969):219-33.

Books, essays and articles
on single novels
and on A Christmas Carol,
and letters

Mr Carker in his hour of triumph. *Dombey and Son*, drawn by Phiz

1949 *"The Uncommercial Traveller* and *The Pickwick Papers." Saturday Review* 11 (Feb. 23, 1861):194-96.

1950 "History of *Pickwick." Athenaeum* (Mar. 31, 1866):430. Correction to "History of *Pickwick*": (Apr. 7, 1866):464. [On the Seymour claims.]

1951 BESANT, WALTER. "The Calverley Examination in *Pickwick* at Cambridge, 1857." *The Posthumous Papers of the Pickwick Club,* ed. Charles Dickens the Younger. (Jubilee Edition) 2 vols. London: Macmillan, 1886. Reprinted in *Dickensian* 32 (Winter 1935-36):51-54.

1952 FITZGERALD, PERCY H. *The History of* Pickwick. An account of its characters, localities, allusions and illustrations with a bibliography. London: Chapman and Hall, 1891.

1953 LUBBOCK, SIR JOHN. "Introduction." *The Posthumous Papers of the Pickwick Club.* London: G. Routledge, 1891.

1954 LOCKWOOD, SIR FRANK. *The Law and Lawyers of* Pickwick. London: Roxburghe Press, 1894.

1955 FITZGERALD, PERCY H. *Pickwickian Manners and Customs.* London: Chapman and Hall, 1897.

1956 NEALE, CHARLES M. *An Index to* Pickwick. London: J. Hitchcock, 1897.

1957 GREGO, JOSEPH. *Pictorial Pickwickiana: Dickens and his Illustrators.* 2 vols. London: Chapman and Hall, 1899. [With illus. by artists who illus. original or early editions of Dickens. Commentary and bibliographical notes not confined to the *Pickwick Papers*.]

1958 SEYMOUR, MRS ROBERT. *An Account of the Origin of the* Pickwick Papers. London: the Author, 1901.

1959 FITZGERALD, PERCY H. "Introduction." *Posthumous Papers of the Pickwick Club.* 3 vols. Autograph edition. London: George G. Harrap, 1903.

1960 BAILEY, SIR WILLIAM H. "Wellerisms and Wit." *Dickensian* 1 (Feb. 1905):31-34.

1961 ALLBUT, ROBERT. "Sam Weller: A Character Sketch." *Dickensian* 2 (Apr. 1906):89-92.

1962 LEY, J. W. T. "Is Sudbury Eatanswill?" *Dickensian* 3 (May 1907): 117-21.

1963 BERNDT, ARNOLD. "Entstehungsgeschichte der *Pickwick Papers*." Greifswald, 1908. [Dissertation.]

1964 NEALE, CHARLES M. "A Few More *Pickwick* References." *Dickensian* 4 (Aug. 1908):246-48.

1965 BEISIEGEL, MARY K. *Notes on Dickens'* Pickwick Papers. London: Normal Press, 1910.

1966 NEALE, CHARLES M. "*Pickwick* and Charles Lamb." *Dickensian* 6 (Feb. 1910):41-44, 76-78; (Apr. 1910):125-28.

1967 FITZGERALD, PERCY H. Pickwick *Riddles and Perplexities.* London: Gay and Hancock, 1912.

1968 LANG, ANDREW. "Introduction." *Pickwick Papers.* Waverley edition. London: Waverley Book Co., 1913-15.

1969 SUDDABY, JOHN. "The Anonymous Hot-Pieman in *Pickwick.*" *Dickensian* 10 (Aug. 1914):209-13.

1970 BOWEN, C. M. "*Dead Souls* and *Pickwick Papers.*" *Athenaeum* 4606 (June 1916):269-70.

1971 RIDDELL, WILLIAM R. "The Famous Case of Bardell v. Pickwick." *Dalhousie Review* 2 (July 1922):200-7.

1972 HUSE, WILLIAM W., Jr. "Pickle and *Pickwick.*" *Washington Univ. Studies* 10 (Oct. 1922):143-54.

1973 BENNETT, ARCHIBALD S. "Chronology of Pickwick with Some Anachronisms." *Dickensian* 19 (Jan. 1923):26-31.

1974 POTTER, GEORGE R. "Mr Pickwick, Eminent Scientist, and His Theory of Tittlebats." *Philological Quarterly* 2 (Jan. 1923):48-55.

1975 LAMBERT, SAMUEL W. *When Mr Pickwick Went Fishing.* New York: Brick Row Book Shop, 1924. [Dickens-Seymour controversy.]

1976 DEXTER, WALTER. *Mr Pickwick's Pilgrimage.* Illustrations from the original drawings by Phiz and photographs by the author. London: Chapman and Hall, 1926; Philadelphia: Lippincott, 1927.

1977 FORSYTHE, R. S. "The 'Ode to an Expiring Frog'." *Philological Quarterly* 5 (Apr. 1926):180-82.

1978 MacKINNON, THE HON. MR JUSTICE F. D. "The Chronology of *Pickwick.*" *Cornhill Magazine* 60 (May 1926):537-48.

1979 WALTERS, J. CUMING. "The Place of *Pickwick* in Literature." *Dickensian* 23 (Winter 1926-27):93-99; (Summer 1927):149-51.

1980 ROE, FRANK G. "Seymour, the 'Inventor' of *Pickwick.*" *Connoisseur* 77 (Feb. 1927):67-71.

1981 "The Shades of Mr Pickwick." *Outlook* 146 (June 1927):270-71.

1982 ZABEL, MORTON D. "A *Pickwick* Holiday." *Commonweal* 6 (June 1927):122-23.

1983 BRADLEY, T. J. "How Dickens Wrote His Description of Bath." *Dickensian* 23 (Summer 1927):181-84.

1984 CHESTERTON, GILBERT K. "*Pickwick.*" *Empire Review* 46 (July 1927):44-48.

1985 KRUTCH, JOSEPH W. "Pickwick Redivivus." *Nation* 125 (Sept. 1927):320.

1986 LEFFMAN, HENRY. "Defence of Messrs Dodson and Fogg." *Dickensian* 24 (Dec. 1927):49-52.

1987 DAVIS, GEORGE W. *The Posthumous Papers of the Pickwick Club.* New bibliographical discoveries. London: Marks, 1928.

1988 ECKEL, JOHN C. *Prime* Pickwicks *in Parts, Census with Complete Collation, Comparison and Comment.* With a foreword by A. Edward Newton. New York: E. H. Wells; London: C. J. Sawyer, 1928.

1989 HOLDSWORTH, WILLIAM S. "*Pickwick* and the Procedure of the Common Law." *Charles Dickens as a Legal Historian,* 117-48. New Haven: Yale Univ. Press, 1928.

1990 HEWART, BARON GORDON. "Bardell v. Pickwick." *Times* (Feb. 14, 1928):15-16.

1991 HAGBERG, KNUT. "Samuel Pickwick." *Personalities and Powers,* 201-11. London: John Lane, 1930.

1992 DEXTER, WALTER. "*Pickwick Papers* in the *Dickensian* 1905-29." *Dickensian* 26 (Summer 1930):204-6; 26 (Autumn 1930):273-74.

1993 STONEHOUSE, JOHN H. "Introduction." *Pickwick Papers.* Lombard Street edition. London: Piccadilly Fountain Press, 1931-32. [Reprint of original text issued in monthly parts.]

1994 RAILO, EINO. "Mr Pickwick." *Valvoja-Aika* (Helsingfors) (1932): 257-69.

1995 SUZANNET, ALAIN de. "The Original Manuscript of *Pickwick Papers.*" *Dickensian* 28 (Summer 1932):193-96.

1996 MILLER, WILLIAM and E. H. STRANGE. "The Original *Pickwick Papers:* the Collation of a Perfect First Edition." *Dickensian* 29 (Sept. 1933):303-9; 30 (Dec. 1933):31-37; (Mar. 1934):121-24; (June 1934):177-80; (Sept. 1934);249-59; 31 (Dec. 1934):35-40; (Mar. 1935):95-99; (June 1935):219-22; (Sept. 1935):284-86.

1997 ROE, FRANK G. "Sam Weller's Scrap Book." *Bookman* 87 (Oct. 1934):45-47.

1998 LUNACHARSKY, A. "Foreword." *The Posthumous Papers of the Pickwick Club.* Moscow: Co-operative Publishing Society of Foreign Workers in the USSR, 1935.

1999 D., W. "The *Pickwick* Dedications and Prefaces." *Dickensian* 32 (Winter 1935-36):61-64. [Duplicates 2001.]

2000 DEXTER, WALTER. "*Dickensian* Peeps into *Punch* II, III." *Dickensian* 32 (Winter 1935-36):37-42; (Spring 1936):110-16.

2001 DEXTER, WALTER. "The *Pickwick* Dedications and Prefaces." Dickensian 32 (Winter 1935-36):61-64. [Duplicates 1999.]

2002 MILLER, WILLIAM. "Imitations of *Pickwick.*" *Dickensian* 32 (Winter 1935-36):4-5.

2003 WAUGH, ARTHUR. "The Birth of *Pickwick." Dickensian* 32 (Winter 1935-36):7-14.

2004 CLENDENING, LOGAN. *A Handbook to* Pickwick Papers. New York: Knopf, 1936.

2005 DARWIN, BERNARD. "Mr Pickwick's Birthday." *English* 1 (1936): 112-14.

2006 DEXTER, WALTER, ed. *A Pickwick Portrait Gallery.* London: Chapman and Hall, 1936. [Duplicates 2010.]

2007 DEXTER, WALTER and J. W. T. LEY. *The Origin of* Pickwick: *New Facts Now First Published in the Year of the Centenary.* London: Chapman and Hall, 1936.

2008 MILLER, WILLIAM and STRANGE, E. H. *A Centenary Bibliography of* The Pickwick Papers. London: Argonaut; Toronto: S. J. R. Saunders, 1936.

2009 NEVINSON, HENRY W. "Another Humorist." *Between the Wars,* 50-56. London: Hutchinson, 1936.

2010 *A* Pickwick *Portrait Gallery.* From the pens of divers admirers of the illustrious members of the Pickwick Club, their friends and enemies. London: Chapman and Hall; New York: Scribners, 1936. [Duplicates 2006.]

2011 DEXTER, WALTER. "How Press and Public Received *The Pickwick Papers." Nineteenth Century* 119 (Mar. 1936):318-29.

2012 FORSE, EDWARD J. "Dickens: *The Pickwick Papers." Notes and Queries* 170 (Mar. 1936):179.

2013 HAVELOCK, ERIC. "Nomina Rerum." *Classical Journal* 31 (Mar. 1936):8-9.

2014 BENSLY, EDWARD. "'Lights in the Sun, John'." *Times Literary Supplement* (Mar. 28, 1936):278.

2015 D., A. H. "The Pickwick Exhibition [A 'Pikewike' of 1274]." *Times Literary Supplement* (Mar. 28, 1936):278.

2016 CARDEN, PERCY T. "Speculations on the Source of Bardell versus Pickwick." *Dickensian* 32 (Spring 1936):105-9.

2017 DEXTER, WALTER. "Books About *Pickwick." Dickensian* 32 (Spring 1936):116.

2018 DEXTER, WALTER. "The English Editions of *Pickwick." Dickensian* 32 (Spring 1936):126-28.

2019 LEY, J. W. T. "Buss's *Pickwick* Pictures: An Important Letter." *Dickensian* 32 (Spring 1936):101-4. [Letter from R. W. Buss to Forster, Dec. 11, 1871.]

2020 "The *Pickwick* Advertisements and Other Addresses to the Public." *Dickensian* 32 (Spring 1936):86-90.

2021 "Some Dickens Letters About *Pickwick*." *Dickensian* 32 (Spring 1936):118-25.

2022 CLENDENING, LOGAN. "Mr Pickwick's Birthday." *Atlantic Monthly* 157 (Apr. 1936):463-72.

2023 HOPKINS, FREDERICK M. "*Pickwick Papers* Centenary." *Publishers' Weekly* 129 (Apr. 1936):1627-30.

2024 R., V. "A Few Words More on *Pickwick*." *Notes and Queries* 170 (May 1936):385-87.

2025 DEXTER, WALTER. "The Rise to Fame." *Dickensian* 32 (Summer 1936):193-202. [Dickens' rise to fame with P.P.]

2026 DEXTER, WALTER. "Some Early Reviews of *Pickwick*." *Dickensian* 32 (Summer 1936):216-18; (Autumn 1936):284-85.

2027 BERRY, J. G. "One Hundred Years of Mr Pickwick." *Dalhousie Review* 16 (July 1936):177-84.

2028 STEVENSON, LIONEL. "Names in *Pickwick*." *Dickensian* 32 (Sept. 1936):241-44.

2029 HEWART, BARON GORDON. "The Centenary of *Pickwick*." *Not Without Prejudice,* 17-22. London: Hutchinson, 1937.

2030 MITCHELL, E. J. "Jarndyce v. Jarndyce ... Bardell v. Pickwick: A Comparison." *Dickensian* 34 (Spring 1938):85-95.

2031 PARTINGTON, WILFRED. "The Blacking Laureate: the Identity of Mr Slum." *Dickensian* 34 (Summer 1938):199-202.

2032 LANN, EUGENY. "Dickens' Style and the Translation of *The Posthumous Papers of the Pickwick Club*." *The Literary Critic* (USSR) 1 (1940):156-71.

2033 G., W. W. "'In a Pickwickian Sense'." *Notes and Queries* 179 (July 1940):63.

2034 IGNOTO. "*Pickwick*: Two Queries." *Notes and Queries* 179 (Aug. 1940):137.

2035 B., E. G. "*Pickwick*: Two Queries." *Notes and Queries* 179 (Sept. 1940):197

2036 SENEX. "*Pickwick*: Two Queries." *Notes and Queries* 179 (Oct. 1940):302-3.

2037 C., T. C. "*Pickwick*: Two Queries." *Notes and Queries* 179 (Nov. 1940):358-59.

2038 ROE, FRANK G. "*Pickwick* in America." *Connoisseur* 107 (Mar. 1941):111-14. [On plagiarisms of *Pickwick*.]

2039 McNULTY, J. H. "The Overture." *Dickensian* 37 (June 1941):141-44.

2040 "*Pickwick* in America." *Dickensian* 38 (Dec. 1941):33-34.

2041 LEWIS, E. A. "A Defense of Mrs Bardell." *Dickensian* 38
      (Sept. 1942):208-9.

2042 D., W. "A Note on the Payment for *Pickwick.*" *Dickensian* 40
      (June 1944):118-19.

2043 "Bogus Pickwickiana." *Dickensian* 41 (Mar. 1945):74-76.

2044 HOWARTH, S. F. D. "The Second Court on the Right Hand Side."
      Dickensian 42 (Dec. 1945):45-48.

2045 WOOD, FREDERICK T. "Sam Weller's Cockneyisms." *Notes and
      Queries* 190 (June 1946):234-35.

2046 MORLEY, MALCOLM. "Pickwick Makes His Stage Debut."
      Dickensian 42 (Sept. 1946):204-6.

2047 HILL, THOMAS W. "Notes on the *Pickwick Papers.*" *Dickensian* 44
      (Dec. 1947):29-36, 105 [entitled *"Pickwick* Notes."] ; (Mar. 1948):
      81-88; (June 1948):145-62; (Sept. 1948):193-98; 45 (Dec. 1948):
      27-33.

2048 DARWIN, BERNARD. "Introduction." *The Posthumous Papers of
      the Pickwick Club.* New Oxford Illustrated Dickens. London:
      Oxford Univ. Press, 1948.

2049 CARLTON, WILLIAM J. "Sergeant Buzfuz." *Dickensian* 45
      (Dec. 1948):21-22.

2050 FADIMAN, CLIFTON. "Introduction." *Pickwick Papers.* New York:
      Simon and Schuster, 1949. Reprinted as "Pickwick and Dickens," in
      Party of One. Cleveland: World, 1955.

2051 FADIMAN, CLIFTON. "Pickwick Lives Forever." *Atlantic Monthly*
      184 (Dec. 1949):23-29.

2052 TIDWELL, JAMES N. "Wellerisms in *Alexander's Weekly Messenger,*
      1837-39." *Western Folklore* 9 (July 1950):257-62.

2053 BENTLEY, ERIC. "Pickwick in Love." *New Republic* 127
      (Oct. 6, 1952):30-31.

2054 WAUGH, ALEC. "Introduction." *Pickwick Papers.* London: Collins,
      1953. [Edition date.]

2055 LANE, WILLIAM S. *"Pickwick* Resartus." *Dickensian* 50
      (Dec. 1953):42-43.

2056 MacLEAN, H. N. "Mr Pickwick and the Seven Deadly Sins."
      Nineteenth Century Fiction 8 (Dec. 1953):198-212.

2057 CLINTON-BADDELEY, V. C. "Stiggins." *Dickensian* 50
      (Mar. 1954):53-56.

2058 DREW, ARNOLD P. *"Pygmalion* and *Pickwick.*" *Notes and Queries*
      N.S. 2 (May 1955):221-22.

2059 CARLTON, WILLIAM J. "A 'Pickwick' Lawsuit in 1837."
      Dickensian 52 (Dec. 1955):33-38.

2060 BOVILL, E. W. "Tony Weller's Trade." *Notes and Queries* N.S. 3 (Aug. 1956):324-28; 3 (Dec. 1956):527-31; 4 (Apr. 1957):155-59; 4 (June 1957):260-63; 4 (Oct. 1957):451-53.

2061 R., V. "An American *Pickwick*." *Notes and Queries* N.S. 4 (Mar. 1957):123-24.

2062 TILLOTSON, KATHLEEN. "Dickens's Count Smorltork." *Times Literary Supplement* (Nov. 22, 1957):712. [Original of.]

2063 LANE, LAURIAT, Jr. "Mr Pickwick and *The Dance of Death*." *Nineteenth Century Fiction* 14 (Sept. 1959):171-72.

2064 MERSAND, JOSEPH. "Introduction." *The Pickwick Papers*. New York: Washington Square Press, 1960.

2065 STONE, HARRY. "Dickens and the Naming of Sam Weller." *Dickensian* 56 (Jan. 1960):47-49.

2066 TILLOTSON, KATHLEEN. "*Pickwick* and Edward Jesse." *Times Literary Supplement* (Apr. 1, 1960):214.

2067 BEVINGTON, DAVID M. "Seasonal Relevance in *The Pickwick Papers*." *Nineteenth Century Fiction* 16 (Dec. 1961):219-30.

2068 AUDEN, W. H. "Dingley Dell and the Fleet." *The Dyer's Hand, and Other Essays*, 407-28. New York: Random House; London: Faber and Faber, 1962. Reprinted in *Dickens: A Collection of Critical Essays*, ed. M. Price, 1967 q.v.

2069 KILLHAM, JOHN. "*Pickwick*, Dickens and the Art of Fiction." *Dickens and the Twentieth Century*, ed. J. Gross and G. Pearson, 35-47. London: Routledge and Paul, 1962.

2070 GREAVES, JOHN. "Eatanswill?" *Dickensian* 58 (May 1962):110-11.

2071 GIBSON, FRANK A. "Why Those Papers?" *Dickensian* 59 (May 1963):99-101. [Influence of *Pickwick Papers* on subsequent works.]

2072 ASHFORTH, A. "When Pickwick Went to Vanity Fair." *New York Times Magazine* (Dec. 22, 1963):8+.

2073 JOHNSON, EDGAR. "Introduction." *Pickwick Papers*. New York: Dell, 1964.

2074 MARCUS, STEVEN. "Afterword." *The Pickwick Papers*. New York: New American Library, 1964.

2075 MORLEY, MALCOLM. "Pickwick on Horseback." *Dickensian* 60 (Jan. 1964):33-38.

2076 AXTON, WILLIAM F. "Unity and Coherence in *The Pickwick Papers*." *Studies in English Literature* 5 (1965):663-76.

2077 GREAVES, JOHN. "Blues, Buffs, and Others." *Dickensian* 61 (Jan. 1965):25-27.

2078 PATTEN, ROBERT L. "The Interpolated Tales in *Pickwick Papers*." *Dickens Studies* 1 (May 1965):86-89.

2079 "What the Dickens." *Newsweek* 66 (Oct. 18, 1965):114.

2080 NICHOLAS, CONSTANCE. "Mrs Raddle and Mistress Quickly." *Dickensian* 62 (Jan. 1966):55-56.

2081 ASKEW, H. "Dickens: *The Pickwick Papers*." *Notes and Queries* 170 (Feb. 1966):142-43.

2082 WILLIAMS, GWENLLIAN L. "Sam Weller." *Trivium* 1 (May 1966): 88-101.

2083 GERSON, STANLEY. "I Spells it with a 'V'." *Dickensian* 62 (Sept. 1966):138-46.

2084 JELLEY, F. R. "Romance and Reality at Blossoms." *Dickensian* 62 (Sept. 1966):179-81.

2085 LANE, MARGARET. "Resisting Mr Pickwick." *Dickensian* 62 (Sept. 1966):133-37.

2086 BECKER, MAY L. "Foreword." *The Posthumous Papers of the Pickwick Club*. New York: Dodd, Mead, 1967.

2087 WELSH, ALEXANDER. "Waverley, Pickwick, and Don Quixote." *Nineteenth Century Fiction* 22 (June 1967):19-30.

2088 PATTEN, ROBERT L. "The Art of *Pickwick*'s Interpolated Tales." *ELH* 34 (Sept. 1967):349-66.

2089 COLWELL, MARY. "Organization in *Pickwick Papers*." *Dickens Studies* 3 (Oct. 1967):90-110.

2090 LEVY, HERMAN M., Jr. and WILLIAM RUFF. "The Interpolated Tales in *Pickwick Papers*, a Further Note." *Dickens Studies* 3 (Oct. 1967):122-25.

2091 GILL, STEPHEN C. "'Pickwick Papers' and the 'Chroniclers by the Line': A Note on Style." *Modern Language Review* 63 (Jan. 1968): 33-36.

2092 LEVY, HERMAN M., Jr. and WILLIAM RUFF. "Who Tells the Story of a Queer Client?" *Dickensian* 64 (Jan. 1968):19-21.

2093 EASSON, ANGUS. "Imprisonment for Debt in *Pickwick Papers*." *Dickensian* 64 (May 1968):105-12.

2094 REINHOLD, HEINZ. "'The Stroller's Tale' in *Pickwick*." Trans. Margaret Jury. *Dickensian* 64 (Sept. 1968):141-51.

OLIVER TWIST

2095 FORSTER, JOHN. "Review of *Oliver Twist*." *The Examiner* (Sept. 10, 1837). Reprinted as "Forster's Review of Oliver Twist, Reprinted for the First Time." *Dickensian* 34 (Dec. 1937):29-32.

2096 CRUIKSHANK, GEORGE. *The Artist and the Author*. London: Bell and Daldy, 1872.

2097 WHIPPLE, EDWIN P. *"Oliver Twist." Atlantic Monthly* 38 (Oct. 1876):474.

2098 PHILIPSON, DAVID. *The Jew in English Fiction*. Cincinnati: R. Clarke, 1889.

2099 FITZGERALD, PERCY. "Dickens in his Books." *Harper's Monthly Magazine* 104 (Apr. 1902):700-7.

2100 CHANDLER, FRANK W. "The Rogue in His Social Environment." *The Literature of Roguery*, II:411-27. Boston: Houghton, Mifflin, 1907.

2101 FIEDLER, FRITZ. "Entstehungsgeschichte von Charles Dickens' *Oliver Twist*." Halle, 1912. [Dissertation.]

2102 BENSON, ARTHUR C. "Introduction." *Oliver Twist*. Waverley edition. London: Waverley Book Co., 1913-15.

2103 PINE, FRANK W. "Introduction." *The Adventures of Oliver Twist*. New York: Macmillan, 1918.

2104 STONEHOUSE, JOHN H. "Introduction." *Sikes and Nancy: A Reading by Charles Dickens*. London: H. Lotheran, 1921. [Transcript of the Dickens' Reading.]

2105 LAW, MARIE H. "The Indebtedness of *Oliver Twist* to Defoe's *History of the Devil*." *PMLA* 40 (Dec. 1925):892-97.

2106 LANDA, MYER J. "The Original of Fagin." *The Jew in Drama*, 159-69. London: P. J. King, 1926; Port Washington, NY: Kennikat Press, 1968.

2107 HANSON, JOHN L. *Notes on Dickens'* Oliver Twist. London: Normal Press, 1928.

2108 DAVIS, HELEN I. "When Charles Dickens Atoned: the Story of his Sinister Character Fagin Which he Offset with the Benign Figure of Riah." *American Hebrew* 122 (May 1928):980, 1008, 1024-25.

2109 BRAYBROOKE, PATRICK. "Oliver Twist." *Great Children in Literature*, 139-60. London: A. Rivers, 1929.

2110 SYMONS, ARTHUR. *"Oliver Twist." Essays of the Year*, comp. Frederick J. H. Darton, 252-67. London: Argonaut Press, 1930.

2111 RIDDELL, WILLIAM R. "A Lawyer Reads *Oliver Twist*." *Dickensian* 30 (Winter 1933-34):27-30.

2112 DEXTER, WALTER. "Dickens's Agreements with Bentley." *Dickensian* 31 (Sept. 1935):241-54.

2113 DEXTER, WALTER. *"Dickensian* Peeps into *Punch* IV." *Dickensian* 32 (Summer 1936):181-84.

2114 "A Contemporary American Estimate of *Oliver Twist.*" *Dickensian* 33 (Mar. 1937):87-90.

2115 BOLL, THEOPHILUS E. "*Oliver Twist,* Centenarian." *General Magazine and Historical Chronicle* (Univ. of Pennsylvania) 40 (1938): 156-63.

2116 DEXTER, WALTER. "Author and Artist." *Dickensian* 34 (Spring 1938):97-100.

2117 MILLER, WILLIAM. "Fang and Laing Again." *Dickensian* 34 (Spring 1938):84.

2118 LECK, A. SIMPSON. "Some Weaknesses of *Oliver Twist.*" *Dickensian* 34 (Summer 1938):194-98.

2119 BOLL, ERNEST M. "Charles Dickens in *Oliver Twist.*" *Psychoanalytic Review* 27 (Apr. 1940):133-43.

2120 BECKER, MAY L. "Introduction." *Oliver Twist.* New York: Dodd, Mead, 1941.

2121 GRUBB, GERALD G. "On the Serial Publication of *Oliver Twist.*" *Modern Language Notes* 56 (Apr. 1941):290-94.

2122 SACKVILLE-WEST, EDWARD (Lionel Cranfield, pseud.). "Books in General." *New Statesman and Nation* 29 (Feb. 1945):95-96. Reprinted as part of "Dickens and the World of Childhood." *Inclinations.* London: Secker and Warburg, 1949.

2123 MORLEY, MALCOLM. "Early Dramas of *Oliver Twist.*" *Dickensian* 43 (Mar. 1947):74-79.

2124 BROGAN, COLIN. "*Oliver Twist* Re-examined." *Listener* 40 (Aug. 26, 1948):310-11.

2125 STAPLES, LESLIE C. "David Lean's *Oliver Twist.*" *Dickensian* 44 (Sept. 1948):203-5. [Film version.]

2126 HOUSE, HUMPHRY. "Introduction." *Oliver Twist.* New Oxford Illustrated Dickens. London: Oxford Univ. Press, 1949. Reprinted in *All In Due Time.* London: Hart-Davis, 1955.

2127 FIEDLER, LESLIE. "What Can We Do About Fagin?" *Commentary* 7 (May 1949):411-18.

2128 GREENE, GRAHAM. "Introduction." *Oliver Twist.* London: H. Hamilton, 1950. Reprinted as "The Young Dickens." *The Lost Childhood and Other Essays.* London: Eyre and Spottiswoode, 1951; *The Dickens Critics,* ed. G. H. Ford and L. Lane, Jr., 1961 q.v.; and in *Dickens: Modern Judgements,* ed. A. E. Dyson, 1968 q.v.

2129 PRITCHETT, V. S. "*Oliver Twist.*" *New Statesman* 39 (Mar. 1950): 344-45. Reprinted in *Books in General.* London: Chatto and Windus, 1953.

2130 HILL, THOMAS W. "Notes on *Oliver Twist.*" *Dickensian* 46 (Summer 1950):146-56.

2131 KETTLE, ARNOLD. "Oliver Twist." *An Introduction to the English Novel, I:*123-38. London: Hutchinson, 1951. Reprinted in *The Dickens Critics,* ed. G. H. Ford and L. Lane. Jr.. 1961 q.v.

2132 FIELDING, KENNETH J. "Sir Francis Burdett and *Oliver Twist.*" *Review of English Studies* N.S. 2 (Apr. 1951):154-57.

2133 LANE, LAURIAT, Jr. "*Oliver Twist*: A Revision." *Times Literary Supplement* (July 20, 1951):460.

2134 YOUNG, VERNON. "Dickens Without Holly: David Lean's *Oliver Twist.*" *New Mexico Quarterly* 22 (Winter 1952):425-30. [Film version.]

2135 AUDEN, W. H. "Huck and Oliver." *Listener* (Oct. 1, 1953):540-41.

2136 LUCAS, ALEC. "*Oliver Twist* and the Newgate Novel." *Dalhousie Review* 34 (Spring 1954):381-87.

2137 HAYENS, KENNETH. "Introduction." *Oliver Twist.* London: Collins, 1955. [Edition date.]

2138 LANE, WILLIAM G. "R.H. Barham and Dickens's Clergyman of *Oliver Twist.*" *Nineteenth Century Fiction* 10 (Sept. 1955):159-62.

2139 LANE, LAURIAT, Jr. "The Devil in *Oliver Twist.*" *Dickensian* 52 (June 1956):132-36.

2140 MONOD, SYLVÈRE. "Introduction." *Oliver Twist.* Paris: Garnier Frères, 1957. [French translation.]

2141 EOFF, SHERMAN. "*Oliver Twist* and the Spanish Picaresque Novel." *Studies in Philology* 54 (July 1957):440-47.

2142 TILLOTSON, KATHLEEN. "Oliver Twist." *Essays and Studies* 12 (1959):87-105.

2143 STONE, HARRY. "Dickens and the Jews." *Victorian Studies* 2 (Mar. 1959):223-53; 3 (June 1960):459-60.

2144 BISHOP, JONATHAN. "The Hero-Villain of *Oliver Twist.*" *Victorian Newsletter* 15 (Spring 1959):14-16.

2145 ROSENBERG, EDGAR. "The Jew as Bogey: Dickens." *From Shylock to Svengali: Jewish Stereotypes in English Fiction,* 116-37. Stanford, Calif.: Stanford Univ. Press, 1960.

2146 JOHNSON, EDGAR. "Introduction." *Oliver Twist.* New York: Washington Square Press, 1961.

2147 LE COMTE, EDWARD. "Afterword." *Oliver Twist.* New York: New American Library, 1961.

2148 TARTELLA, VINCENT P. "Charles Dickens's *Oliver Twist*: Moral Realism and the Uses of Style." *DA* 22 (1961):1616-17 (Notre Dame). [Dissertation.]

2149 BAYLEY, JOHN. *"Oliver Twist:* 'Things as they really are'." *Dickens and the Twentieth Century,* ed. J. Gross and G. Pearson, 49-64. London: Routledge and K. Paul, 1962. Reprinted in *Dickens: A Collection of Critical Essays,* ed. M. Price, 1967 q.v.

2150 MILLER, J. HILLIS. "Introduction." *The Adventures of Oliver Twist.* New York: Holt, Rinehart and Winston, 1962.

2151 MARCUS, STEVEN. "Who is Fagin?" *Commentary* 34 (July 1962): 48-59. Reprinted in *Dickens: From* Pickwick *to* Dombey, 1965 q.v.

2152 HOLLINGSWORTH, KEITH. "Date of the Action of *Oliver Twist.*" *The Newgate Novel 1830-1847,* 232-33. Detroit: Wayne State Univ. Press, 1963.

2153 HOLLINGSWORTH, KEITH. "The 'Real' World of *Oliver Twist.*" *The Newgate Novel 1830-1847,* 111-31. Detroit: Wayne State Univ. Press, 1963.

2154 TILLOTSON, KATHLEEN. *"Oliver Twist* in Three Volumes." *Library* 18 (June 1963):113-32.

2155 TOMKINS, A. R. "Introduction." *Oliver Twist.* London: Blackie and Son, 1965.

2156 ROBB, BRIAN. "George Cruikshank's Etchings for *Oliver Twist.*" *Listener* 74 (July 1965):130-31.

2157 SCHWEITZER, JOAN. "The Chapter Numbering in *Oliver Twist.*" *Papers of the Bibliographical Society of America* 60 (1966):337-43.

2158 TILLOTSON, KATHLEEN. "Introduction and annotation." *Oliver Twist.* Clarendon Dickens 1. Oxford: Clarendon Press, 1966.

R2159 [TILLOTSON, KATHLEEN, ed. *Oliver Twist,* 1966 q.v.] FURBANK, P. N. "Still Asking." *The Listener* 76 (Dec. 22, 1966):935.

R2160 [TILLOTSON, KATHLEEN, ed. *Oliver Twist,* 1966 q.v.] McMASTER, ROWLAND D. "Book Reviews." *Dalhousie Review* 47 (Spring 1967): 100-1.

R2161 [TILLOTSON, KATHLEEN, ed. *Oliver Twist,* 1966 q.v.] MUIR, KENNETH. "Reviews." *Modern Language Review* 63 (July 1968): 687-88.

R2162 [TILLOTSON, KATHLEEN, ed. *Oliver Twist,* 1966 q.v.] PATTEN, ROBERT L. "'So Much Pains About One Chalk-faced Kid': The Clarendon *Oliver Twist.*" *Dickens Studies* 3 (Oct. 1967):160-68.

2163 WILSON, ANGUS. "Introduction." *Oliver Twist.* Harmondsworth: Penguin, 1966.

2164 FINKEL, ROBERT J. "Another Boy Brought Up 'By Hand'." *Nineteenth Century Fiction* 20 (Mar. 1966):389-90.

2165 FREDERICK, KENNETH C. "The Cold, Cold Hearth: Domestic Strife in *Oliver Twist.*" *College English* 27 (Mar. 1966):465-70.

2166 PREEN, D. W. "Plays in Production, 10, *Oliver Twist.*" *Use of English* 17 (Spring 1966):213-16.

2167 COLBY, ROBERT A. "*Oliver Twist:* the Fortunate Foundling." *Fiction with a Purpose – Major and Minor Nineteenth Century Novels,* 105-37. Bloomington: Univ. of Indiana Press, 1967.

2168 McLEAN, ROBERT S. "Fagin: An Early View of Evil." *Lock Haven Review* (Lock Haven State Coll., Pa.) 9 (1967):29-36.

2169 WILLIAMSON, COLIN. "Two Missing Links in *Oliver Twist.*" *Nineteenth Century Fiction* 22 (Dec. 1967):225-34.

2170 KINCAID, JAMES R. "Laughter and *Oliver Twist.*" *PMLA* 83 (Mar. 1968):63-70.

2171 DUFFY, JOSEPH M. Jr. "Another Version of Pastoral: *Oliver Twist.*" *English Literary History* 35 (Sept. 1968):403-21.

2172 GOLD, JOSEPH. "Dickens' Exemplary Aliens: Bumble the Beadle and Fagin the Fence." *Mosaic* 2 (Fall 1968):77-89.

2173 PAGE, NORMAN. "'A language fit for heroes': Speech in *Oliver Twist* and *Our Mutual Friend.*" *Dickensian* 65 (May 1969):100-7.

2174 PATTEN, ROBERT L. "Capital and Compassion in *Oliver Twist.*" *Studies in the Novel* 1 (Summer 1969):207-21.

2175 TOBIAS, J. J. "Ikey Solomons – a real-life Fagin." *Dickensian* 65 (Sept. 1969):171-75.

NICHOLAS NICKLEBY

2176 HAYHURST, T. H. *An Appreciative Estimate of the Grant Brothers of Ramsbottom – the "Brothers Cheeryble."* London: T. Crompton, 1884.

2177 SUDDABY, JOHN. "The Dramatic Piracy of *Nicholas Nickleby.*" *Dickensian* 7 (Mar. 1911):64-68.

2178 BROUGHTON, R. J. "Squeers and Dotheboys Hall." *Dickensian* 7 (June 1911):154-56.

2179 THOMSON, W. R. "Mrs Nickleby's Tender Mindedness." *Dickensian* 9 (May 1913):117-20.

2180 BENSON, EDWARD F. "Introduction." *Nicholas Nickleby.* Waverley edition. London: Waverley Book Co., 1913-15.

2181 CLARK, CUMBERLAND. *Charles Dickens and the Yorkshire Schools.* London: Chiswick Press, 1918.

2182 DARTON, F. J. HARVEY, arr. *Vincent Crummles: His Theatre and His Times.* With an historical introductory note, and appendices from *Nicholas Nickleby* by Charles Dickens. London: Wells, Gardner, 1926.

2183 ROE, FRANK G. "New Light on *Nicholas Nickleby.*" *Connoisseur* (Feb. 1926):77-80.

2184 PRIESTLEY, J. B. "Note on Crummles." *Saturday Review* 23 (July 1927):126-27.

2185 GAWTHORP, WALTER E. "*Nicholas Nickleby:* A Strange Misprint." *Notes and Queries* 155 (Nov. 1928):365.

2186 FAWCETT, J. W. "The Prototype of Smike." *Notes and Queries* 166 (Jan. 1934):50.

2187 ASKEW, H. "Edward Smith, the Prototype of Smike." *Notes and Queries* 165 (Dec. 1934):402.

2188 PATERSON, ANDREW. "A Word for Wackford Squeers." *Dickensian* 39 (Mar. 1943):95-97.

2189 DISHER, M. WILLSON. "Playbills of the Crummleses." *Times Literary Supplement* (May 6, 1944):228.

2190 DISHER, M. WILLSON. "The Crummleses." *Times Literary Supplement* (May 27, 1944):259.

2191 R., D. A. P. "Nicholas Slips." *Dickensian* 41 (Mar. 1945):84-86.

2192 ADRIAN, ARTHUR A. "Charles Dickens: *The Life and Adventures of Nicholas Nickleby.*" Western Reserve, 1946. [Dissertation.]

2193 MORLEY, MALCOLM. "*Nicholas Nickleby.* On the Boards." *Dickensian* 43 (June 1947):137-41.

2194 SUZANNET, ALAIN de. "The Original Manuscript of *Nicholas Nickleby.*" *Dickensian* 43 (Sept. 1947):189-92.

2195 GRAHAM, W. H. "The Cherrybles and the Cogglesbys." *Dickensian* 45 (Dec. 1948):23-25.

2196 HILL, THOMAS W. "Notes on *Nicholas Nickleby.*" *Dickensian* 45 (Mar. 1949):98-102; 45 (June 1949):163-66; 46 (Dec. 1949):42-48; 46 (Mar. 1950):99-104.

2197 ADRIAN, ARTHUR A. "*Nicholas Nickleby* and Educational Reform." *Nineteenth Century Fiction* 4 (Dec. 1949):237-41.

2198 THORNDIKE, DAME SYBIL. "Introduction." *Nicholas Nickleby.* New Oxford Illustrated Dickens. London: Oxford Univ. Press, 1950.

2199 OLLÉ, JAMES G. "Where Crummles Played." *Dickensian* 47 (June 1951):143-47.

2200 BROMLEY, L. W. "A Guildford Link with Crummles." *Dickensian* 48 (Mar. 1952):75.

2201 WAUGH, ALEC. "Introduction." *Nicholas Nickleby.* London: Collins, 1953. [Edition date.]

2202 CLINTON-BADDELEY, V. C. "Benevolent Teachers of Youth." *Cornhill Magazine* 169 (Aug. 1957):361-82.

2203 CLINTON-BADDELEY, V. C. "Snevellici." *Dickensian* 57 (Jan. 1961):43-52.

2204 BERGONZI, BERNARD. *"Nicholas Nickleby." Dickens and the Twentieth Century,* ed. J. Gross and G. Pearson, 65-76. London: Routledge and K. Paul, 1962.

2205 CARTER, JOHN A., Jr. "The World of Squeers and the World of Crummles." *Dickensian* 58 (Jan. 1962):50-53.

2206 MORLEY, MALCOLM. "Where Crummles Played." *Dickensian* 58 (Jan. 1962):23-29. [T. D. Davenport, the original Crummles, and Westminister Theatre.]

2207 ALDERSON, B. R. *"Nicholas Nickleby* Illustrated." *Genealogists' Magazine* 14 (Dec. 1962):101-7. [Introd. by Kenneth J. Fielding. Burial data for a Yorkshire school.]

2208 MORLEY, MALCOLM. "More About Crummles." *Dickensian* 59 (Jan. 1963):51-56.

2209 ROULET, ANN. "A Comparative Study of *Nicholas Nickleby* and *Bleak House." Dickensian* 60 (Spring 1964):117-24.

2210 BALL, ROY A. "The Development of Smike." *Dickensian* 62 (May 1966):125-28.

2211 LEVY, HERMAN M., Jr. "An Omission Unnoticed: *Nickleby* Forgotten." *Dickensian* 63 (Jan. 1967):41.

2212 REED, JOHN R. "Some Indefinable Resemblance: Moral Form in Dickens' *Nicholas Nickleby." Papers on Language and Literature* 3 (Spring 1967):134-47.

2213 WING, GEORGE D. "A Part To Tear A Cat In." *Dickensian* 64 (Jan. 1968):10-19. [Ralph Nickleby.]

2214 THOMPSON, LESLIE M. "Mrs Nickleby's Monologue: The Dichotomy of Pessimism and Optimism in *Nicholas Nickleby." Studies in the Novel* 1 (Summer 1969):222-29.

THE OLD CURIOSITY SHOP

2215 POE, EDGAR ALLAN. "The Old Curiosity Shop." *Graham's Magazine* 18 (May 1841):248-51. Reprinted in *The Dickens Critics,* ed. G. H. Ford and L. Lane Jr., 1961 q.v.

2216 HAMMOND, R. A. *The Life and Writings of Charles Dickens; a Memorial Volume.* Toronto: A. H. Hovey, 1871.

2217 *"The Old Curiosity Shop." Pall Mall Gazette* (Jan. 1, 1884):11-12.

2218 SAINTSBURY, GEORGE. "Introduction." *The Old Curiosity Shop.* 2 vols. (Autograph edition.) London: George G. Harrap, 1904.

2219 ALLBUT, ROBERT, "F," and C. T. ROADE. "Old Curiosity Shop." *Dickensian* 6 (Feb. 1910):44-47. [Whether the house on Portsmouth Street is Dickens' Old Curiosity Shop or not.]

2220 POLACK, ERNEST E. "Humorous Villains: Comparison Between Daniel Quilp and Shakespeare's Richard the Third." *Dickensian* 6 (July 1910):182-84.

2221 BEISIEGEL, MARY K. *Notes on Dickens'* Old Curiosity Shop, *etc.* London: Normal Press, 1912.

2222 ROGERS, FREDERICK. "'Little Bethel'." *Dickensian* 9 (Sept. 1913):233-35.

2223 CORFIELD, WILMOT. "Where was 'Little Bethel'?" *Dickensian* 9 (Oct. 1913):268-71.

2224 FITZGERALD, PERCY H. "A Dickens Perplexity." *Dickensian* 12 (Feb. 1916):42-46 [Pt. 1, "Lady Dedlock's Flight"]. (Mar. 1916): 72-73 [Pt. 2, "Little Nell's Travels"].

2225 MINCK, J. MURRAY. "Daniel Quilp." *Dickensian* 13 (Mar. 1917): 73-76.

2226 HOOD, THOMAS. "*Master Humphrey's Clock* and Little Nell." *Dickensian* 13 (Sept. 1917):229-32; (Oct. 1917):271-73.

2227 SHARP, HELENA. "In Defence Of Little Nell." *Dickensian* 14 (Apr. 1918):89-92.

2228 DEXTER, WALTER. "Little Nell's Journey." *Dickensian* 20 (Oct. 1924):196-201.

2229 BRAYBROOKE, PATRICK. "Little Nell." *Great Children in Literature*, 195-215. London: A. Rivers, 1929.

2230 HUXLEY, ALDOUS. "The Vulgarity of Little Nell." *Vulgarity in Literature*, 54-59. London: Chatto and Windus, 1930. Reprinted in *Music at Night and Other Essays*. London: Chatto and Windus, 1931; and in *The Dickens Critics*, ed. G. H. Ford and L. Lane, Jr., 1961 q.v.

2231 LEY, J. W. T. "The Songs Dick Swiveller Knew." *Dickensian* 27 (Summer 1931):205-18.

2232 DEXTER, WALTER. *"The Old Curiosity Shop." Times Literary Supplement* (Dec. 12, 1936):1035.

2233 PARTINGTON, WILFRED. *The Identity of Mr Slum: Charles Dickens and the Blacking Laureate.* London: privately printed, 1937.

2234 KITCHEN, PAUL C. "Little Nell." *Times Literary Supplement* (Sept. 4, 1937):640.

2235 BENNETT, WILLIAM C. "The Marchioness and Little Nell." *Dickensian* 36 (Dec. 1939):7-8.

2236 S., D. M. *"The Old Curiosity Shop*: Dickens and Disney." *Times Literary Supplement* (Apr. 6, 1940):167.

2237 BENNETT, WILLIAM C. "The Mystery of the Marchioness." *Dickensian* 36 (Sept. 1940):205-8.

2238 WINTERICH, JOHN T. "How This Book Came to Be." *The Old Curiosity Shop.* New York: Heritage Press, 1941.

2239 HILL, THOMAS W. (T. Kent Brumleigh, pseud.). "On the Road with the Trents." *Dickensian* 37 (Sept. 1941):231-35; 38 (Dec. 1941): 14-16.

2240 "Dickens's Circus: Astley and English Literature." *Times Literary Supplement* (Jan. 10, 1942):20.

2241 BECKER, MAY L. "Introductory Sketch." *The Old Curiosity Shop.* New York: Dodd, Mead, 1943.

2242 "A New Dickens Bibliography. *The Old Curiosity Shop.*" *Dickensian* 40 (Mar. 1944):78.

2243 SACKVILLE-WEST, EDWARD (Lionel Cranfield, pseud.). "Books in General." *New Statesman and Nation* 29 (Feb. 1945):95-96. Reprinted as part of "Dickens and the World of Childhood." *Inclinations.* London: Secker and Warburg, 1949.

2244 ROBINSON, LENNOX. "A Defense of Little Nell." *Irish Times* (Mar. 31, 1945).

2245 COTTERELL, T. STURGE. "The Original of Quilp." *Dickensian* 43 (Dec. 1946):39-40.

2246 MORLEY, MALCOLM. "Plays in *Master Humphrey's Clock.*" *Dickensian* 43 (Sept. 1947):202-5.

2247 WICKLOW, EARL OF. "Introduction." *The Old Curiosity Shop.* New Oxford Illustrated Dickens. London: Oxford Univ. Press, 1951.

2248 JOHNSON, R. BRIMLEY. "Introduction." *The Old Curiosity Shop.* London: Collins, 1953. [Edition date.]

2249 GRUBB, GERALD G. "Dickens' Marchioness Identified." *Modern Language Notes* 68 (Mar. 1953):162-65.

2250 HILL, THOMAS W. "Notes on *The Old Curiosity Shop.*" *Dickensian* 49 (Mar. 1953):86-93; (June 1953):137-42; (Sept. 1953):183-91.

2251 STAPLES, LESLIE C. "Shavings From Dickens's Workshop. Unpublished Fragments from the Novels." Pt. 4, *The Old Curiosity Shop.* *Dickensian* 50 (Dec. 1953):17-23; (Mar. 1954):63-66; (June 1954): 132-36. [Cancelled passages from the proofs.]

2252 BARNETT, GEORGE L. "Corporal Trim's Hat." *Notes and Queries* N.S. 2 (Sept. 1955):403-4.

2253 GIBSON, FRANK A. "A 17th Century Kit Nubbles." *Dickensian* 53 (Jan. 1957):12-15.

2254 SPILKA, MARK. "Little Nell Revisited." *Papers of the Michigan Academy of Science, Arts and Letters* 45 (1960):427-37.

2255 PEARSON, GABRIEL. "*The Old Curiosity Shop.*" *Dickens and the Twentieth Century*, ed. J. Gross and G. Pearson, 77-90. London: Routledge and K. Paul, 1962.

2256 REID, JOHN C. "*The Old Curiosity Shop.*" *The Hidden World of Charles Dickens*, 34-47. (Macmillan Brown Lecture 3. Auckland Univ.

Bulletin 61. English Series 10.) Auckland: Univ. of Auckland Press, 1962.

2257 FLEISSNER, ROBERT F. "Fancy's Knell." *Dickensian* 58 (May 1962):125-27. [Cordelia in *King Lear* and Little Nell.]

2258 GIBSON, JOHN W. "*The Old Curiosity Shop*: The Critical Allegory." *Dickensian* 60 (Sept. 1964):178-83.

2259 STEIG, MICHAEL. "The Central Action of *The Old Curiosity Shop*, or Little Nell Revisited Again." *Literature and Psychology* 15 (Summer 1965):163-70.

2260 DYSON, A. E. "The *Old Curiosity Shop*: Innocence and the Grotesque." *Critical Quarterly* 8 (Summer 1966):111-30. Reprinted in *Dickens: Modern Judgements,* ed. A. E. Dyson, 1968 q.v.

2261 STEIG, MICHAEL. "Phiz's Marchioness." *Dickens Studies* 2 (Sept. 1966):141-46. [With illustrations and plates.]

2262 STEVENS, JOAN. "'Woodcuts Dropped into the Text': The Illustrations in *The Old Curiosity Shop* and *Barnaby Rudge*." *Studies in Bibliography: Papers of the Bibliographical Society of the University of Virginia* 20 (Jan. 1967):113-34.

2263 WINTERS, WARRINGTON. "*The Old Curiosity Shop*: A Consummation Devoutly to Be Wished." *Dickensian* 63 (Sept. 1967):176-80.

2264 SENELICK, LAURENCE. "Little Nell and the Prurience of Sentimentality." *Dickens Studies* 3 (Oct. 1967):146-59.

2265 McLEAN, ROBERT S. "Putting Quilp to Rest." *Victorian Newsletter* 34 (Fall 1968):29-33.

BARNABY RUDGE

2266 POE, EDGAR ALLAN. "*Barnaby Rudge*: The Original Review." *Philadelphia Saturday Post* (May 1, 1841). Reprinted in *Dickensian* 9 (July 1913):174-78.

2267 HOOD, THOMAS. "Review of *Barnaby Rudge*." *Athenaeum* (Jan. 22, 1842):77-79. Reprinted in *Works.* London: E. Moyon, 1862-63.

2268 POE, EDGAR ALLAN. *"Barnaby Rudge." Graham's Magazine* 20 (Feb. 1842):124-29. [One of "Review of New Books" articles.]

2269 DOBSON, AUSTIN. "Introduction." *Barnaby Rudge.* 3 vols. (Autograph edition.) London: George G. Harrap, 1905.

2270 BARTER, A. A. "Introduction." *Barnaby Rudge.* London: Adam and Charles Black, 1906. [Revised reprint from Soho Edition of the works 1903-4.]

2271 JERROLD, WALTER. "Introduction." *Barnaby Rudge.* London: Dent; New York: Dutton, 1906.

2272 FRASER, J. A. LOVAT. "Gashford and his Prototype." *Dickensian* 2 (Feb. 1906):39-41.

2273 MACLEOD, JOHN A. "The Personality of Barnaby Rudge."
     Dickensian 5 (Oct. 1909):262-66; (Nov. 1909):291-93.

2274 POLACK, ERNEST E. "Was Barnaby Rudge Mad?" *Dickensian* 7
     (Nov. 1911):298-99.

2275 REES, MRS BARTON. "The Polished Villain and the Uncouth
     Villain." *Dickensian* 8 (June 1912):158-59.

2276 WILKINS, W. GLYDE. "*Barnaby Rudge* and the Gordon Riots."
     Dickensian 8 (July 1912):185-87.

2277 "Edgar Allan Poe on *Barnaby Rudge*." *Dickensian* 9 (July 1913):
     173-74.

2278 WINTERSGILL, A. T. "*Barnaby Rudge* and Chigwell." *Dickensian*
     23 (Mar. 1927):122-26.

2279 ULRICH, ALFRED. "Studien zu Dickens' Roman *Barnaby Rudge*."
     Jena, 1931. [Dissertation.]

2280 GRAY, W. FORBES. "The Prototype of 'Gashford' in *Barnaby
     Rudge*." *Dickensian* 29 (June 1933):175-83.

2281 PEARSON, E. KENDALL. "Facts About the Gordon Riots – Dickens'
     Use of Newspaper Reports." *Dickensian* 30 (Dec. 1933):43-47.

2282 BRUSH, LILLIAN H. "A Psychological Study of *Barnaby Rudge*."
     Dickensian 31 (Winter 1934-35):24-30.

2283 LUCAS, JOHN P. Jr. "To John Landseer, Esquire: A Note From
     Charles Dickens." *South Atlantic Quarterly* 39 (Oct. 1940):448-53.

2284 BECKER, MAY L. "Foreword." *Barnaby Rudge*. New York: Dodd,
     Mead, 1945.

2285 GIBSON, FRANK A. "The Trial of George Gordon." *Dickensian* 42
     (Dec. 1945):12-20.

2286 JONES-EVANS, ERIC. *In the Footsteps of* Barnaby Rudge.
     London: S. French, 1947.

2287 GIBSON, FRANK A. "Gashford and Gordon." *Dickensian* 44
     (June 1948):124-29.

2288 LILLISHAW, A. M. "The Case of *Barnaby Rudge*." *Dickensian* 44
     (June 1948):141-44.

2289 LANE, LAURIAT, Jr. "Dickens and Scott: An Unusual Borrowing."
     Nineteenth Century Fiction 6 (Dec. 1951):223-24.

2290 LANE, LAURIAT, Jr. "Dickens and Scott: A Reply to Mr Fielding."
     Nineteenth Century Fiction 8 (June 1953):78.

2291 HAYENS, KENNETH. "Introduction." *Barnaby Rudge*. London:
     Collins, 1954. [Edition date.]

2292 TILLOTSON, KATHLEEN. "Introduction." *Barnaby Rudge*. (New
     Oxford Illustrated Dickens. London: Oxford Univ. Press, 1954.

2293 HILL, THOMAS W. "Notes on *Barnaby Rudge." Dickensian* 50
(Mar. 1954):91-94; 51 (Mar. 1955):93-96; (June 1955):137-41; 52
(June 1956):136-40; (Sept. 1956):185-88; 53 (Jan. 1957):52-57.

2294 AUBERON, FRANCIS. "Dickens *versus* Gissing: *In Re* Varden: Mr
Justice Stareleigh's Summing-Up." *Dickensian* 53 (May 1957):82-84.
[Gissing's misrepresentation of Mrs Varden, in his *Charles Dickens, a
Critical Study,* 1898 q.v.]

2295 HIBBERT, CHRISTOPHER. *King Mob.* The Story of Lord George
Gordon and the London riots of 1780. Cleveland: World, 1958.

2296 GIBSON, FRANK A. "The Love Interest in *Barnaby Rudge."
Dickensian* 54 (Jan. 1958):21-23.

2297 POSTLETHWAITE, ANGELA. "Poor Sir John!" *Dickensian* 54
(May 1958):83-87. [John Chester.]

2298 ZIEGLER, ARNOLD U. "A *Barnaby Rudge* Source." *Dickensian* 54
(May 1958):80-82.

2299 GRAHAM, W. H. "Notes on *Barnaby Rudge." Contemporary Review*
194 (Aug. 1958):90-92.

2300 FOLLAND, HAROLD F. "The Doer and the Deed: Theme and
Pattern in *Barnaby Rudge." PMLA* 74 (Sept. 1959):406-17.

2301 GIBSON, FRANK A. "A Note on George Gordon." *Dickensian* 57
(May 1961):81-85.

2302 GOTTSHALL, JAMES K. "Devils Abroad: The Unity and Significance
of *Barnaby Rudge." Nineteenth Century Fiction* 16 (Sept. 1961):
133-46.

2303 LINDSAY, JACK. *"Barnaby Rudge." Dickens and the Twentieth
Century,* ed. J. Gross and G. Pearson, 91-106. London: Routledge
and K. Paul, 1962.

2304 HOLLINGSWORTH, KEITH. "The Newgate Theme of *Barnaby
Rudge." The Newgate Novel 1830-1847,* 177-82. Detroit: Wayne
State Univ. Press, 1963.

2305 MONOD, SYLVÈRE. "Rebel with a Cause: Hugh of the Maypole."
Dickens Studies 1 (Jan. 1965):4-26.

2306 LaRUE, RALPH W. "Dickens Reference." *Country Life* 140
(Dec. 1966):1587. [The hanging of dogs in Chap. 76.]

2307 STEVENS, JOAN. "'Woodcuts Dropped into the Text': The Illustrations in *The Old Curiosity Shop* and *Barnaby Rudge." Studies in Bibliography: Papers of the Bibliographical Society of the University of
Virginia* 20 (Jan. 1967):113-34.

2308 DYSON, A. E. *"Barnaby Rudge*: The Genesis of Violence." *Critical
Quarterly* 9 (Summer 1967):142-60.

2309 BRANTLINGER, PATRICK. "The Case Against Trade Unions in
Early Victorian Fiction." *Victorian Studies* 13 (Sept. 1969):37-52.

MARTIN CHUZZLEWIT

2310 CHORLEY, HENRY F. *"Martin Chuzzlewit." Athenaeum*
(July 1844):665-66.

2311 SHORE, WILLIAM T. "On Re-reading *Martin Chuzzlewit.*"
Dickensian 1 (May 1905):115-18.

2312 OSBORNE, CHARLES C. "Mr Pecksniff and His Prototype."
Independent Review 10 (Dec. 1906):107-20.

2313 ROMAYNE, LEICESTER. "The Chuzzlewit Family." *Dickensian* 6
(Sept. 1910):233-35.

2314 BENSON, ARTHUR C. "Fiction and Romance." *Contemporary Review*
100 (Dec. 1911):792-805; *The Living Age* 272 (Jan. 1912):76-85.

2315 PEMBERTON, MAX. "Introduction." *Martin Chuzzlewit.* Waverley
edition. London: Waverley Book Co., 1913-15.

2316 *"Martin Chuzzlewit,* An American Contemporary Review." *Dickensian*
10 (Apr. 1914):97-99. [Reprinted from *Brother Jonathan,* July 29, 1843.]

2317 CROSS, A. E. BROOKES. *"Martin Chuzzlewit*: A Few Random
Remarks." *Dickensian* 12 (Mar. 1916):64-66.

2318 KEANE, C. "Mark Tapley: Charles Dickens's Richest Legacy to
Humanity." *Dickensian* 14 (July 1918):175-77.

2319 HANDLEY, GEORGE M. *Notes on Dickens'* Martin Chuzzlewit.
London: Normal Press, 1921.

2320 ELLIS, M. A. *"Martin Chuzzlewit.* Elijah Pogram." *Notes and Queries*
8 (May 1921):389.

2321 McNULTY, J. H. "If *Martin Chuzzlewit* Appeared Today." *Dickensian*
17 (Oct. 1921):178-81; *The Living Age* 311 (Nov. 1921):402-5.

2322 WILLIAMS, ORLO. *"Martin Chuzzlewit." Some Great English Novels,*
36-52. London: Macmillan, 1926.

2323 OSBORNE, CHARLES C. "The Genesis of Mrs Gamp." *Dickensian*
23 (Dec. 1926):27-30.

2324 PIERCE, T. M. "The Names in *Martin Chuzzlewit." New Mexico
Quarterly* 1 (Feb. 1931):51-55.

2325 LAYTON, E. J. "These Failures." *Dickensian* 28 (Spring 1932):130-32.

2326 CHOVIL, A. S. "Tom Pinch A Failure?" *Dickensian* 28
(Summer 1932):202-4.

2327 WALTERS, J. CUMING. "The Gospel of *Martin Chuzzlewit.*"
Dickensian 29 (Summer 1933):221-26.

2328 OLDER, MARGARET A. "The Mysterious Mrs Harris." *Dickensian*
29 (Autumn 1933):310-12.

2329 OLIVE, H. T. "Sarah Gamp – Was She A Sober Nurse?" *Dickensian*
30 (Spring 1934):131-33.

2330 WEBLING, PEGGY. "The Truth About Mrs Harris." *Dickensian* 34 (Autumn 1938):251-52.

2331 BRADBY, M. K. "'In Jonadge's belly'." *Dickensian* 36 (June 1940): 175-77.

2332 McNULTY, J. H. "An Omitted Chapter." *Dickensian* 36 (June 1940): 147-49.

2333 McNULTY, J. H. "The Two Spirits of Fun and Beauty." *Dickensian* 38 (June 1942):143-46. [*Martin Chuzzlewit* and *A Christmas Carol.*]

2334 "A Bygone Quarrel." *Times Literary Supplement* (Jan. 9, 1943):19. [A "monument of misunderstanding between two peoples."]

2335 "Dickens in America: *Martin Chuzzlewit* Centenary." *Times Literary Supplement* (Jan. 9, 1943):20.

2336 CLAYTON, J. K. "*Martin Chuzzlewit* – The First Monthly Number." *Dickensian* 39 (Sept. 1943):166-68.

2337 McNULTY, J. H. "A Double Centenary." *Dickensian* 39 (Sept. 1943): 163-65. [*Martin Chuzzlewit* and *Christmas Carol* both published in 1843.

2338 HILL, THOMAS W. "Notes on *Martin Chuzzlewit.*" *Dickensian* 42 (June 1946):14-48; 42 (Sept. 1946):196-203; 43 (Dec. 1946):28-35.

2339 Pound, Louise. "The American Dialect of Charles Dickens." *American Speech* 22 (Apr. 1947):124-30.

2340 NISBET, ADA B. "The Mystery of *Martin Chuzzlewit.*" *Essays Critical and Historical Dedicated to Lily B. Campbell by Members of the Departments of English, University of California,* 201-16. Berkeley and Los Angeles, Calif.: Univ. of California Press, 1950.

2341 RUSSELL, GEOFFREY. "Introduction." *Martin Chuzzlewit.* New Oxford Illustrated Dickens. London: Oxford Univ. Press, 1951.

2342 MORLEY, MALCOLM. *Martin Chuzzlewit* in the Theatre." *Dickensian* 47 (Mar. 1951):98-102.

2343 NICHOLAS, H. G. *Martin Chuzzlewit* and the America of 1842." *History Today* 1 (Mar. 1951):58-61.

2344 BLIGH, SIR EDWARD. "A Defense of Mrs Gamp." *Dickensian* 48 (Dec. 1951):40-42.

2345 HAYENS, KENNETH. "Introduction." *Martin Chuzzlewit.* London: Collins, 1953. [Edition date.]

2346 FIELDING, KENNETH J. "*Martin Chuzzlewit* and *The Liberator.*" *Notes and Queries* 198 (June 1953):254-56.

2347 BENJAMIN, EDWIN B. "The Structure of *Martin Chuzzlewit.*" *Philological Quarterly* 34 (Jan. 1955):39-47.

2348 STONE, HARRY. "Dickens' Use of His American Experiences in *Martin Chuzzlewit.*" *PMLA* 72 (June 1957):464-78.

2349 STUART, DOROTHY M. "Sarah Gamp." *Contemporary Review* 192 (Oct. 1957):205-8.

2350 BAETZHOLD, HOWARD G. "What Place was the Model for Martin Chuzzlewit's 'Eden'? A Last Word on the 'Cairo Legend'." *Dickensian* 55 (Sept. 1959):169-75.

2351 BAUER, HARRY C. "Collector's Items." *Seasoned to Taste*, 52-55. Seattle: Univ. of Washington Press, 1961. [Bibliographical.]

2352 BUTT, JOHN E. "Dickens's Instructions for *Martin Chuzzlewit*, Plate XVIII." *Review of English Literature* 2 (July 1961):49-50.

2353 HARDY, BARBARA. *"Martin Chuzzlewit."* Dickens and the Twentieth Century, ed. J. Gross and G. Pearson, 107-20. London: Routledge and K. Paul, 1962.

2354 BROGUNIER, JOSEPH. "The Dreams of Montague Tigg and Jonas Chuzzlewit." *Dickensian* 58 (Autumn 1962):165-70.

2355 JOHNSON, EDGAR. "Introduction." *Martin Chuzzlewit*. New York: Dell, 1965.

2356 MUDRICK, MARVIN. "Afterword." *Martin Chuzzlewit*. New York: New American Library, 1965.

2357 WHITLEY, JOHN S. "The Two Hells of *Martin Chuzzlewit*." *Papers of the Michigan Academy of Science, Arts and Letters* 50 (1965): 585-97.

2358 DYSON, A. E. *"Martin Chuzzlewit*: Howls the Sublime." *Critical Quarterly* 9 (Autumn 1967):234-53.

2359 FURBANK, P. N. "Introduction." *The Life and Adventures of Martin Chuzzlewit*. Harmondsworth: Penguin, 1968.

2360 BUTT, JOHN E. "The Serial Publication of Dickens's Novels: *Martin Chuzzlewit* and *Little Dorrit*." *Pope, Dickens, and Others*, 149-64. Edinburgh: University Press, 1969.

2361 STEIG, MICHAEL. "Martin Chuzzlewit: Pinch and Pecksniff." *Studies in the Novel* 1 (Summer 1969):181-88.

A CHRISTMAS CAROL

2362 HAWEIS, REV. HUGH R. "Introduction." *A Christmas Carol*, and *The Chimes*. London: George Routledge, 1886.

2363 MORLEY, HENRY. "Introduction." *A Christmas Carol*, and *The Chimes*. London: Cassell, 1886.

2364 KITTON, FREDERICK G. "Introduction." *A Christmas Carol*. London: E. Stock, 1890.

2365 CAINE, HALL. "Introduction." *A Christmas Carol*. London: William Heinemann, 1906.

2366 BROWNE, E. GORDON. "Introduction." *A Christmas Carol*. London: Longmans, Green, 1907.

2367 TRELOAR, SIR WILLIAM P. "Introduction." *A Christmas Carol.*
London: Chapman and Hall, 1907.

2368 WHITCOME, CHARLES and C. A. VINCE. "*A Christmas Carol* and
Free Trade." *Dickensian* 5 (Apr. 1909):98-101. [Two opinions: that
of a Free Trader and that of a Tariff Reformer.]

2369 JOHNS, W. "The Death of Scrooge." *Dickensian* 9 (Dec. 1913):313-14.

2370 CHESTERTON, GILBERT K. "Introduction." *A Christmas Carol.*
Waverley edition. London: Waverley Book Co., 1913-15.

2371 JAQUES, EDWARD T. *Charles Dickens in Chancery: His Proceedings
in Respect of the* Christmas Carol. London: Longmans, Green, 1914.

2372 NEWTON, A. E. "The Greatest Little Book in the World." *Atlantic
Monthly* 132 (Dec. 1923):732-38.

2373 MARTIN-HARVEY, SIR JOHN. "Foreword." *A Christmas Carol.*
London: Odhams Press, 1930.

2374 AITCH, N. HOWARD. "Notes." [Introduction] *A Christmas Carol.*
Chicago: Hall and McCreary, 1931.

2375 OSBORNE, ERIC A. "Variants of *The Christmas Carol.*" *Bookman*
81 (Dec. 1941):192-94.

2376 SADLEIR, MICHAEL. "*A Christmas Carol.*" *Times Literary
Supplement* (Jan. 28, 1932):60.

2377 MEAD, EDWIN D. "About the *Christmas Carol* and Dickens in
Boston." *Unity* 110 (Dec. 1932):234-35.

2378 MAJOR, GWEN. "Scrooge's Chambers." *Dickensian* 29 (Winter 1932):
11-15.

2379 LEACOCK, STEPHEN. "Introduction." *A Christmas Carol.* Boston:
Printed for the members of the Limited Editions Club at the
Merrymount Press, 1934.

2380 LLOYD-BLOOD, J. K. "*A Christmas Carol.*" *Times Literary
Supplement* (Dec. 12, 1936):1040.

2381 OSBORNE, ERIC A. *The Facts About* A Christmas Carol. London:
Limited, private edition, 1937.

2382 OSBORNE, ERIC A. "*A Christmas Carol.*" *Times Literary
Supplement* (Oct. 30, 1937):808.

2383 McNULTY, J. H. "Our Carol." *Dickensian* 34 (Dec. 1937):15-19.

2384 BERROW, NORMAN. "Some Candid Opinions on 'A Christmas
Carol'." *Dickensian* 34 (Winter 1937-38):20-24.

2385 RUST, S. J. "At the Dickens House – Legal Documents Relating to
the Piracy of *A Christmas Carol.*" *Dickensian* 34 (Winter 1937-38):
41-44.

2386 BARRYMORE, LIONEL. "Introduction." *A Christmas Carol.*
Philadelphia: Winston, 1938.

2387 McNULTY, J. H. "The Two Spirits of Fun and Beauty." *Dickensian* 38 (June 1942):143-46. [*Martin Chuzzlewit* and *A Christmas Carol.*]

2388 McNULTY, J. H. "A Double Centenary." *Dickensian* 39 (Sept. 1943): 163-65. [*Martin Chuzzlewit* and *Christmas Carol* published in 1843.]

2389 BROWN, JOHN MASON. "Ghouls and Holly." *Seeing More Things,* 161-67. New York: McGraw-Hill, 1948.

2390 HEWITSON, THEODORE and CAROLINE. *A Chronicle of Dickens'* Christmas Carol. Los Angeles: Dawson's Book Shop, 1951.

2391 MORLEY, MALCOLM. "Curtain Up on *A Christmas Carol.*" *Dickensian* 47 (June 1951):159-64.

2392 JOHNSON, EDGAR. "The *Christmas Carol* and the Economic Man." *American Scholar* 21 (Winter 1952):91-98. Reprinted in *The Dickens Critics,* ed. G. H. Ford and L. Lane, Jr., 1961 q.v.

2393 BUTT, JOHN E. "*A Christmas Carol*: Its Origin and Design." *Dickensian* 51 (Dec. 1954):15-18.

2394 JOHNSON, EDGAR. "Introduction." *A Christmas Carol.* New York: Columbia Univ. Press, 1956.

2395 GIMBEL, RICHARD. "The Earliest State of the First Edition of Charles Dickens' *A Christmas Carol.*" *Princeton Univ. Library Chronicle* 19 (Winter 1958):82-86. [Dickens' contracts with facsimile of "Entry of Proprietorship" form for *A Christmas Carol.*]

2396 BRERETON, D. N. "Introduction." *Christmas Books.* London: Collins, 1959. [Edition date.]

2397 TODD, WILLIAM B. "Dickens's *Christmas Carol.*" *Book Collector* 10 (Winter 1961):449-54.

2398 STONE, HARRY. "Dickens' Artistry and *The Haunted Man.*" *South Atlantic Quarterly* 41 (Autumn 1962):492-505.

2399 FADIMAN, CLIFTON. "Afterword." *A Christmas Carol.* New York: Macmillan, 1963.

2400 ALLEN, WALTER. "Introduction." *A Christmas Carol* and *The Chimes.* New York: Harper and Row, 1965.

2401 MORRIS, WILLIAM E. "The Conversion of Scrooge: A Defense of That Good Man's Motivation." *Studies in Short Fiction* 3 (Fall 1965): 46-55.

2402 DICKENS, CEDRIC C. "A Reading Edition of the 'Carol'." *Bookseller* (Oct. 30, 1965):2016-17.

2403 TOMKINS, A. R. "Introduction." *A Christmas Carol.* London: Blackie and Son, 1966.

2404 JOHNSON, EDGAR. "Introduction and a Bibliographical Note." *A Christmas Carol.* Ann Arbor, Mich.: Univ. Microfilms Library

Services, 1967. [Illus. John Leech, facsimile of 1st edition, 1843.]
Reprinted as *"A Christmas Carol." Saturday Review* 50 (Dec. 30,
1967):13, 42.

DOMBEY AND SON

2405 *"Dealings With the Firm of Dombey and Son." Economist* 4
      (Oct. 10, 1846):1324-25.

2406 *"Dombey and Son." Athenaeum* (Oct. 31, 1846):1113-15.

2407 *"Dealings With the Firm of Dombey and Son." Economist* 4
      (Dec. 12, 1846):1622-23.

2408 *"Dombey and Son." Westminster and Foreign Quarterly Review* 5
      (Apr. 1847):1-11.

2409 "French Criticism of Dickens." *People's Journal* 5 (1848):228-31.

2410 *"Dombey and Son." Examiner* (Oct. 28, 1848):692-93.

2411 "Sentimentalism." *Saturday Review* 6 (Dec. 25, 1858):643-44.

2412 DOWDEN, EDWARD. "Introduction." *Dombey and Son.* 3 vols.
      Autograph edition. London: George G. Harrap, 1908.

2413 ALLEMANDY, VICTOR H. *Notes on Dickens'* Dombey and Son.
      London: Normal Press, 1910.

2414 MALET, LUCAS. "Introduction." *Dombey and Son.* Waverley
      edition. London: Waverley Book Co., 1913-15.

2415 MATCHETT, WILLOUGHBY. "A Chat About *Dombey." Dickensian*
      11 (May 1915):122-25.

2416 R., V. "Dickens, Mrs Blimber and Colley Cibber." *Notes and Queries*
      8 (Feb. 1921):149-50.

2417 HARTENSTEIN, JOHANNES. "Studien zu Dickens' Arbeitsweise
      auf Grund der Heftausgabe von *Dombey and Son.*" Leipzig, 1922.
      [Dissertation.]

2418 BILLINGTON, J. D. "Mr Dombey Travels by Rail." *Dickensian* 28
      (Summer 1932):205-8.

2419 WILLIAMS-MOORE, ELEANOR. "Dough and Granite: A Study of
      the Two Wives of Paul Dombey." *Dickensian* 28 (Summer 1932):
      209-13.

2420 HOLT, ALFRED H. "Captain Cuttle's Quotations." *Dickensian* 28
      (Autumn 1932):303-8.

2421 EDGAR, PELHAM. "A Group of Dickens's Novels." *The Art of the
      Novel from 1700 to the Present Time,* 117-24. New York: Macmillan,
      1933.

2422 DEXTER, WALTER. *"Dickensian* Peeps into *Punch* V." *Dickensian*
      32 (Autumn 1936):245-48.

2423 DEXTER, WALTER. "About *Dombey.*" *Dickensian* 38 (June 1942): 187.

2424 HILL, THOMAS W. (T. Kent Brumleigh, pseud.). "Notes on *Dombey and Son.*" *Dickensian* 38 (Sept. 1942):211-17; 39 (Dec. 1942):31-39.

2425 HILL, THOMAS W. (Kentley Bromhill, pseud.). "Phiz's Illustrations to *Dombey and Son.*" *Dickensian* 38 (Sept. 1942):219-21; 39 (Dec. 1942):48-51; (Mar. 1943):57-60.

2426 BRADBY, M. K. "Dombey, Cuttle, and Chesterton." *Dickensian* 39 (Mar. 1943):65-69.

2427 SACKVILLE-WEST, EDWARD (Lionel Cranfield, pseud.). "Books in General." *New Statesman and Nation* 30 (Nov. 1945): 301-2. Reprinted as part of "Dickens and the World of Childhood." *Inclinations.* London: Secker and Warburg, 1949.

2428 COURNOS, JOHN. "Introduction." *Dombey and Son.* New York: Dodd, Mead, 1950.

2429 GARROD, H. W. "Introduction." *Dealings with the Firm of Dombey and Son.* New Oxford Illustrated Dickens. London: Oxford Univ. Press, 1950.

2430 BUTT, JOHN E. and KATHLEEN TILLOTSON. "Dickens at Work on *Dombey and Son.*" *Essays and Studies* 4 (1951):70-93.

2431 TILLOTSON, KATHLEEN. "A Lost Sentence in *Dombey and Son.*" *Dickensian* 47 (Mar. 1951):81-82.

2432 MORLEY, MALCOLM. "Enter *Dombey and Son.*" *Dickensian* 48 (June 1952):128-33.

2433 STAPLES, LESLIE C. "Shavings From Dickens's Workshop. Unpublished Fragments from the Novels." Pt. 2, *Dombey and Son.* *Dickensian* 49 (Dec. 1952):37-43; (Mar. 1953):65-68. [Cancelled passages from the proofs.]

2434 TILLOTSON, KATHLEEN. *"Dombey and Son." Novels of the Eighteen-Forties,* 157-201. Oxford: Clarendon Press, 1954. Reprinted in *Dickens: A Collection of Critical Essays,* ed. M. Price, 1967 q.v.; *Dickens: Modern Judgements,* ed. A. E. Dyson, 1968 q.v.

2435 WHYTE, MARK. "Introduction." *Dombey and Son.* London: Collins, 1954. [Edition date.]

2436 BLAND, D. S. "The 'Lost' Sentence in *Dombey and Son* Once More." *Dickensian* 52 (Summer 1956):142-43.

2437 WINTERICH, JOHN T. "Introduction." *Dealings With the Firm of Dombey and Son, Wholesale, Retail and for Exportation.* New York: Limited Editions Club, 1957.

2438 STAPLES, LESLIE C. "The Dickens Fellowship Players in *Dombey and Son.*" *Dickensian* 56 (Sept. 1960):187. [A review.]

2439 EDMINSON, MARY. "Charles Dickens and *The Man in the Moon.*" *Dickensian* 56 (Winter 1960):50-59.

2440 MOYNAHAN, JULIAN. *"Dealings with the Firm of Dombey and Son:* Firmness *versus* Wetness." *Dickens and the Twentieth Century,* ed. J. Gross and G. Pearson, 121-31. London: Routledge and K. Paul, 1962.

2441 LEAVIS, F. R. *"Dombey and Son." Sewanee Review* 70 (Jan.-Mar. 1962):177-201.

2442 JOHNSON, EDGAR. "Introduction." *Dombey and Son.* New York: Dell, 1963.

2443 AXTON, WILLIAM F. "Tonal Unity in *Dombey and Son.*" *PMLA* 78 (Sept. 1963):341-48.

2444 STONE, HARRY. "Dickens and Leitmotif: Music-Staircase Imagery in *Dombey and Son.*" *College English* 25 (Dec. 1963):217-20.

2445 AXTON, WILLIAM F. *"Dombey and Son*: From Stereotype to Archetype." *ELH* 31 (Sept. 1964):301-17.

2446 MacDONALD, ROBERT H. "The Dog Diogenes." *Notes and Queries* 12 (Feb. 1965):59.

2447 LUCAS, JOHN. "Dickens and *Dombey and Son*: Past and Present Imperfect." *Tradition and Tolerance in Nineteenth-Century Fiction: Critical Essays on Some English and American Novels,* ed. David Howard, John Good, and John Lucas, 99-140. London: Routledge and K. Paul, 1966.

2448 STONE, HARRY. "The Novel as Fairy Tale: Dickens' *Dombey and Son.*" *English Studies* 47 (Feb. 1966):1-27.

2449 MAJOR, GWEN. "Miss Tox's Dwelling Place." *Dickensian* 62 (May 1966):122-24.

2450 COLLINS, PHILIP A. W. *"Dombey and Son* – Then and Now." *Dickensian* 63 (May 1967):82-94.

2451 TILLOTSON, KATHLEEN. "New Readings in *Dombey and Son.*" *Imagined Worlds: Essays on Some English Novels and Novelists in Honour of John Butt,* ed. Maynard Mack and Ian Gregory, 173-82. London: Methuen, 1968.

2452 CARLTON, WILLIAM J. "A Note on Captain Cuttle." *Dickensian* 64 (Sept. 1968):152-56.

DAVID COPPERFIELD

2453 "Charles Dickens and *David Copperfield.*" *Fraser's Magazine* 42 (Dec. 1850):698.

2454 *"David Copperfield* and *Pendennis." Prospective Review* 7 (1851): 157-91.

2455 MASSON, DAVID. *"Pendennis* and *Copperfield*: Thackeray and Dickens." *North British Review* 15 (May 1851):57-89.

2456 PHILLIPS, SAMUEL. *"David Copperfield* and *Pendennis." Times* (June 11, 1851):8.

2457 *"David Copperfield* and Charles Dickens." *Spectator* 44 (Dec. 9, 1861):1490-91.

2458 WHIPPLE, EDWIN P. "Introduction." *David Copperfield.* New York: Hurd and Houghton, 1877; Boston: Houghton Mifflin, 1879.

2459 BLUHM, GUSTAV R. *Autobiographisches in* David Copperfield. Reichenbach: Druck von Haun, 1891.

2460 KITTON, FREDERIC G. *"David Copperfield The Younger." Library Review* 2 (Mar. 1893):17-21. [Review article of Works ed. by Charles Dickens the Younger.]

2461 LEASK, WILLIAM K. "Introduction." *The Personal History of David Copperfield.* London: Gresham Publishing Company, 1900.

2462 JEROME, JEROME K. "My Favourite Novelist and his Best Book." *Munsey's Magazine* 23 (Apr. 1900):60-64.

2463 BARTER, A. A. "Introduction." *The Personal History and Experience of David Copperfield the Younger.* London: Adam and Charles Black, 1903. [Revised reprint of volume published in the Soho Edition of Dickens' works, 1903-4.]

2464 GISSING, GEORGE. "Introduction." *David Copperfield.* 3 vols. Autograph edition. London: George G. Harrap, 1903.

2465 STOCKWELL, NINA. *Notes on Dickens'* David Copperfield. London: Normal Press, 1904.

2466 BATELY, JOHN. "From Blunderstone to Yarmouth." *Dickensian* 5 (Sept. 1909):232-39.

2467 NORRIS, E. ASHBY. "Mr Peggotty, Gentleman." *Dickensian* 5 (Sept. 1909):241-44.

2468 BUCK, PHILO M. "Introduction." *The Personal History and Experience of David Copperfield the Younger.* Boston: Ginn, 1910.

2469 FAIRLEY, EDWIN. "Introduction." *The Personal History and Experience of David Copperfield, the Younger.* New York: The Macmillan Company, 1911.

2470 CAINE, HALL. "Introduction." *David Copperfield.* Waverley edition. London: Waverley Book Co., 1913-15.

2471 CRUSE, AMY. *English Literature Through the Ages, Beowulf to Stevenson,* 479-89. New York: Frederick A. Stokes, 1914; London: G. G. Harrap, 1922.

2472 NICOLL, SIR WILLIAM R. "The True Story of Dora Copperfield." *The Bookman Extra Number* (1914):26-82.

2473 ROE, FRANK G. "Some Remarks Upon the *Copperfield* Controversy." *Dickensian* 10 (June 1914):145-47.

2474 KIBBLEWHITE, E. "Introduction." *The Personal History of David Copperfield.* Oxford: Clarendon Press, 1916. [Revised reprint of the volume in the Oxford India Paper Edition of Dickens' Works, 1901-2.]

2475 *"David Copperfield* in Welsh." *Notes and Queries* 9 (Dec. 1921):445.

2476 KITCHEN, PAUL C. "Dickens, *David Copperfield* and Thomas Holcroft." *Schelling Anniversary Papers by his Former Students,* ed. A. H. Quinn, 181-88. New York: Century, 1923. [Felix E. Schelling (1858-1945).]

2477 G., St. J. O. B. "Literary Allusions in Dickens: *David Copperfield."* *Notes and Queries* 12 (Feb. 1923):155-56.

2478 MARSHALL, ARCHIBALD. *"David Copperfield."* *International Book Review* 2 (Mar. 1924):288-89.

2479 WOOLF, VIRGINIA. *"David Copperfield."* *Nation and Athenaeum* 37 (Aug. 1925):620-21. Reprinted in *The Moment and Other Essays.* London: Hogarth Press, 1947; *Collected Essays,* vol. 1. London: Hogarth, 1966.

2480 NEVINS, ALLAN. "Introduction." *David Copperfield.* New York: Macmillan, 1928.

2481 ROE, FRANK G. "The Original of Uriah Heep's Face at Wickfield House, Canterbury." *Connoisseur* 87 (Feb. 1931):102-3.

2482 DEXTER, WALTER. "The London of *David Copperfield."* *Dickensian* 27 (Spring 1931):113-19.

2483 GREEN, O. M. "Cost of Living in David Copperfield's Day." *Bookman* 80 (Apr. 1931):6-7.

2484 WULCKO, C. TYNDALL. "Life's Greatest Problem." *Dickensian* 26 (Summer 1931):189-90.

2485 McNULTY, J. H. "The Position and Influence of *David Copperfield."* *Dickensian* 27 (Autumn 1931):273-78.

2486 GRAVES, ROBERT. *The Real David Copperfield.* London: A. Barker, 1933.

2487 RUST, S. J. "The Education of David Copperfield." *Dickensian* 31 (Winter 1935):46-50.

2488 CHURCH, HOWARD W. "Otto Babendiek and *David Copperfield."* *Germanic Review* 11 (Jan. 1936):40-49.

2489 ALLEN, EDWARD H. "Phrase: 'To be Jorkins'd': *David Copperfield. Notes and Queries* 175 (Nov. 1937):350.

2490 MURDOCH, WALTER L. "Book and the Island." Collected Essays, 311-15. London: Angus and Robertson, 1938.

2491 WHITE, L. R. B. "Gormed." *Dickensian* 35 (June 1939):209.

2492 MARKS, ARTHUR W. "'Gormed'." *Notes and Queries* 177
(Aug. 1939):118.

2493 SAVAGE, OLIVER D. "Cheer Up, Old Mawther!" *Dickensian* 37
(Dec. 1940):37-38.

2494 DAVIS, EARLE R. *Creation of Dickens's David Copperfield:
A Study in Narrative Craft.* Wichita, Kans.: Municipal Univ. of
Wichita, 1941. [Same as *Municipal Univ. of Wichita Bulletin* 16
(Apr. 1941).]

2495 BECKER, MAY L. "Introduction." *David Copperfield.* New York:
Dodd, Mead, 1943.

2496 HILL, THOMAS W. "Notes to *David Copperfield.*" *Dickensian* 39
(Mar. 1943):79-88; (June 1943):123-31; (Sept. 1943):197-201; 40
(Dec. 1944):11-14.

2497 HILL, THOMAS W. (Kentley Bromhill, pseud.). "Phiz's Illustrations
to *David Copperfield.*" *Dickensian* 40 (Dec. 1943):47-50; (Mar. 1944):
83-86.

2498 MAJOR, GWEN. "Into The Shadowy World." *Dickensian* 40
(Dec. 1943):15-18.

2499 DEXTER, WALTER and THOMAS W. HILL (Kentley Bromhill,
pseud.). "The *David Copperfield Advertiser.*" *Dickensian* 41
(Dec. 1944):21-25.

2500 CAMERON, WILLIAM R. *David Copperfield in Copperplate:
46 Illustrations for the Famous Dickens Novel.* Augmented by inter-
pretative short passages taken from the original text. Los Angeles:
W. L. McNaughton, 1947.

2501 EASTWOOD, WILFRED. *Charles Dickens: David Copperfield.* (Notes
on Chosen English Texts.) London: J. Brodie, 1947.

2502 MASON, LEO. "*Jane Eyre* and *David Copperfield.*" *Dickensian* 43
(Sept. 1947):172-79.

2503 MALDEN, R. H. "Introduction." *David Copperfield.* New Oxford
Illustrated Dickens. London: Oxford Univ. Press, 1948.

2504 BROWN, E. K. "*David Copperfield.*" *Yale Review* 37 (June 1948):
651-66. Reprinted as "Introduction." *David Copperfield.* New York:
Modern Library, 1949.

2505 MAUGHAM, W. SOMERSET. "Charles Dickens." *Atlantic Monthly*
182 (July 1948):50-56. Reprinted as preface to *David Copperfield,*
London: J. C. Winston, 1948, and as "Charles Dickens and *David
Copperfield,*" in *Ten Novels and Their Authors,* London: Heinemann,
1954. Published in US with title *The Art of Fiction,* Garden City, NY:
Doubleday, 1954.

2506 FIELDING, KENNETH J. *"David Copperfield* and Dialect." *Times Literary Supplement* (Apr. 30, 1949):288.

2507 KATKOV, GEORGE. "Steerforth and Stavrogin. On the Sources of *The Possessed." Slavonic Review* 27 (May 1949):469-88.

2508 BUTT, JOHN E. "Dickens's Notes for His Serial Parts." *Dickensian* 45 (June 1949):129-38.

2509 CARLTON, WILLIAM J. "An Echo of the Copperfield Days." *Dickensian* 45 (June 1949):149-52.

2510 DARWIN, BERNARD. "'In Defence of Dora'." *Dickensian* 45 (June 1949):139-40.

2511 GIBSON, FRANK A. "Was Dickens Tired? or the Poem of Memory." *Dickensian* 45 (June 1949):157-59.

2512 HAMILTON, ROBERT. "Dickens's Favourite Child." *Dickensian* 45 (June 1949):141-43.

2513 HILL, THOMAS W. "David's Confidences." *Dickensian* 45 (June 1949):145-48.

2514 HILL, THOMAS W. (Kentley Bromhill, pseud.). "The 'Originals'." *Dickensian* 45 (June 1949):161-62.

2515 McNULTY, J. H. *"Copperfield,* Fact or Fiction." *Dickensian* 45 (June 1949):153-55.

2516 SHAW, GEORGE BERNARD. "George Bernard Shaw on *David Copperfield." Dickensian* 45 (June 1949):118.

2517 SHUCKBURGH, SIR JOHN. "Wilkins Micawber." *Dickensian* 45 (June 1949):125-28.

2518 THIRKELL, ANGELA. *"David Copperfield* Reconsidered." *Dickensian* 45 (June 1949):119-22.

2519 VACHELL, HORACE A. "Dickens as a Forty-Niner." *Dickensian* 45 (June 1949):123-24.

2520 PEARSON, HESKETH. "Most Popular Masterpiece of Fiction." *Listener* (June 16, 1949):1030-31. [On the Centenary of *David Copperfield.*]

2521 LEONHARDT, RUDOLF W. *"Soll und Haben* und *David Copperfield* – ein Vergleich ihres Aufbaus als Beitrag zur Formfrage des Romans. Bonn, 1950. [Dissertation.]

2522 BUTT, JOHN E. "The Composition of *David Copperfield." Dickensian* 46 (Mar. 1950):90-94; (June 1950):128-35; (Sept. 1950): 176-80; 47 (Dec. 1950):33-38.

2523 STRONG, LEONARD A. *"David Copperfield*: A Lecture Delivered to the Dickens Fellowship in London on October 4th, 1949." *Dickensian* 46 (Mar. 1950):65-75. Reprinted in *Personal Remarks.* New York: Liveright, 1953.

2524 BUTT, JOHN E. *"David Copperfield*: From Manuscript to Print." *Review of English Studies* N.S. 1 (July 1950):247-51.

2525 ADRIAN, ARTHUR A. *"David Copperfield*: A Century of Critical and Popular Acclaim." *Modern Language Quarterly* 11 (Sept. 1950): 325-31.

2526 WINTERICH, JOHN T. "Dickens: Young Man River." *Saturday Review of Literature* 33 (Nov. 11, 1950):30, 81.

2527 CARY, JOYCE. "Introducing Mr Micawber." *New York Times Book Review* (Apr. 15, 1951):4, 21.

2528 FIELDING, KENNETH J. "The Making of *David Copperfield*." *Listener* 46 (July 1951):93-95.

2529 COLLINS, NORMAN. "Introduction." *David Copperfield*. London: Collins, 1952. [Edition date.]

2530 MANHEIM, LEONARD F. *"The Personal History of David Copperfield."* *American Imago* 9 (Spring 1952):21-43.

2531 CARLTON, WILLIAM J. " 'The Deed' in *David Copperfield*." *Dickensian* 48 (June 1952):101-6.

2532 CRAMP, K. R. "Dr Strong of Canterbury." *Dickensian* 48 (June 1952):117-19.

2533 STAPLES, LESLIE C. "Shavings from Dickens's Workshop. Unpublished Fragments from the Novels." Pt. 1, *David Copperfield*. *Dickensian* 48 (Sept. 1952):158-61. [Cancelled passages from the proofs.]

2534 MORLEY, MALCOLM. "Stage Appearances of *Copperfield*." *Dickensian* 49 (Mar. 1953):77-85.

2535 NEEDHAM, GWENDOLYN B. "The Undisciplined Heart of David Copperfield." *Nineteenth Century Fiction* 9 (Sept. 1954):81-107.

2536 MUIR, P. H. "Note No. 53. The Tauchnitz *David Copperfield*, 1849." *Book Collector* 4 (Autumn 1955):253-54.

2537 TEDLOCK, E. W., Jr. "Kafka's Imitation of *David Copperfield*." *Comparative Literature* 7 (Winter 1955):52-62.

2538 MONOD, SYLVÈRE. "Introduction." *David Copperfield*. Paris: Garnier, 1956. [French translation.]

2539 SHARROCK, ROGER. "A Reminiscence of 'In Memoriam' in *David Copperfield*." *Notes and Queries* 201 (Nov. 1956):502.

2540 FORD, GEORGE H. "Introduction." *David Copperfield*. Riverside Edn. Boston: Houghton, Mifflin, 1958. Reprinted in *The Dickens Critics,* ed. G. H. Ford and L. Lane, Jr., 1961 q.v.

2541 HILLEGASS, CLIFTON K. *David Copperfield*. Notes, including scene by scene synopsis, character sketches, selected examination questions and answers. Lincoln, Neb.: Cliff, 1958.

2542 MERSAND, JOSEPH. "Introduction." *David Copperfield.* New York: Pocket Books, 1958.

2543 SPILKA, MARK. "*David Copperfield* as Psychological Fiction." *Critical Quarterly* 1 (Winter 1959):292-301. Reprinted in *Dickens: Modern Judgements*, ed. A. E. Dyson, 1968 q.v.

2544 SPILKA, MARK. "Kafka and Dickens: The Country Sweetheart." *American Imago* 16 (Winter 1959):367-78. [Parallel themes: *David Copperfield* and *Amerika.*]

2545 MARSHALL, WILLIAM H. "The Image of Steerforth and the Structure of *David Copperfield.*" *Tennessee Studies in Literature* 5 (1960): 57-65.

2546 CARDWELL, MARGARET. "Rosa Dartle and Mrs Brown." *Dickensian* 56 (Jan. 1960):29-33.

2547 MORLEY, MALCOLM. "Peggotty's Boat: Fact and Fiction." *Dickensian* 56 (May 1960):117-19.

2548 COLLINS, PHILIP A. W. "The Middlesex Magistrate in *David Copperfield.*" *Notes and Queries* 8 (Mar. 1961):86-91.

2549 KETTLE, ARNOLD. "Thoughts on *David Copperfield.*" *Review of English Literature* 2 (July 1961):64-74.

2550 KELTY, JEAN M. "The Modern Tone of Charles Dickens." *Dickensian* 57 (Sept. 1961):160-65.

2551 JONES, JOHN. "*David Copperfield.*" *Dickens and the Twentieth Century*, ed. John Gross and Gabriel Pearson, 133-43. London: Routledge and K. Paul, 1962.

2552 VANN, J. DON. "The Death of Dora Spenlow in *David Copperfield.*" *Victorian Newsletter* 22 (Fall 1962):19-20.

2553 BEEBE, MAURICE. "Art as Experience: The Sacred Fount Tradition." *Ivory Towers and Sacred Founts,* 65-113. New York: New York Univ. Press, 1964.

2554 STONE, HARRY. "Fairy Tales and Ogres: Dickens' Imagination and *David Copperfield.*" *Criticism* 6 (Fall 1964):324-30.

2555 DAICHES, DAVID. "Introduction." *David Copperfield; The Early Years.* Boston: Houghton, Mifflin, 1965. [Chapters 1-14 of *David Copperfield.*]

2556 SCHILLING, BERNARD N. "Mr Micawber's Difficulties." *The Comic Spirit; Boccacio to Thomas Mann,* 98-123. Detroit: Wayne State Univ. Press, 1965.

2557 SCHILLING, BERNARD N. "Mr Micawber's Abilities." *The Comic Spirit; Boccacio to Thomas Mann,* 124-44. Detroit: Wayne State Univ. Press, 1965.

2558 COLLINS, PHILIP A. W. "*David Copperfield* and East Anglia." *Dickensian* 61 (Jan. 1965):46-51.

2559 KINCAID, JAMES R. "The Darkness of *David Copperfield*." *Dickens Studies* 1 (May 1965):65-75.

2560 GARD, ROGER. *"David Copperfield." Essays in Criticism* 15 (July 1965):313-25.

2561 DUNN, RICHARD J. *"David Copperfield*: All Dickens is There." *English Journal* 54 (Dec. 1965):789-94.

2562 KINCAID, JAMES R. "A Critical Study of *David Copperfield*." *DA* 27 (1966):478A (Western Reserve 1965). [Dissertation.]

2563 KRAUS, W. KEITH. *Charles Dickens: David Copperfield*. New York: Barnes and Noble, 1966.

2564 KINCAID, JAMES R. "The Structure of *David Copperfield*." *Dickens Studies* 2 (May 1966):74-95.

2565 CALDER-MARSHALL, ARTHUR. "Introduction." *David Copperfield*. London: Pan, 1967.

2566 VANN, J. DON. *"David Copperfield* and the Reviewers." *DA* 28 (1967):3159A-60A (Texas Technological College). [Dissertation.]

2567 SCHWEITZER, JOAN. *"David Copperfield* and *Ernest Pontifex*." *Dickensian* 63 (Jan. 1967):42-45.

2568 ODDIE, WILLIAM. "Mr Micawber and the Redefinition of Experience." *Dickensian* 63 (May 1967):100-10.

2569 MILLER, J. HILLIS. "Three Problems of Fictional Form: First-Person Narration in *David Copperfield* and *Huckleberry Finn*." *Experience in the Novel*, ed. Roy H. Pearce, 21-48. New York: Columbia Univ. Press, 1968.

2570 MIYAZAKI, KOICHI. *Opposing Elements in David Copperfield*. (Seijo English Monographs no. 2.) Tokyo: Seijo, 1968.

2571 D'AVANZO, MARIO L. "Mr Creakle and His Prison: A Note on Craft and Meaning." *Dickensian* 64 (Jan. 1968):50-52.

2572 HARRIS, WENDELL V. "Of Time and the Novel." *Bucknell Review* 16 (Mar. 1968):114-29. [On *David Copperfield, Nostromo, The Sound and the Fury*.]

2573 KINCAID, JAMES R. "Dickens's Subversive Humor: *David Copperfield*." *Nineteenth Century Fiction* 22 (Mar. 1968):313-29.

2574 BELL, VEREEN M. "The Emotional Matrix of *David Copperfield*." *Studies in English Literature* 8 (Autumn 1968):633-49.

2575 HORNBACK, BERT C. "Frustration and Resolution in *David Copperfield*." *Studies in English Literature* 8 (Autumn 1968): 651-57.

2576 SKOTTOWE, P. F. "Thomas Talfourd and *David Copperfield*." *Dickensian* 65 (Jan. 1969):25-31. [Mr Justice Talfourd and Tommy Traddles.]

2577 KINCAID, JAMES R. "Symbol and Subversion in *David Copperfield.*" *Studies in the Novel* 1 (Summer 1969):196-206.

BLEAK HOUSE

2578 "Organic Reform." *Westminster Review* 55 (July 1851):472-504.

2579 DENMAN, THOMAS. "Bleak House." *The Standard* (Sept. 13, 1852) Reprinted in Uncle Tom's Cabin, Bleak House, Slavery and Slave Trade. London: Longmans, 1853.

2580 "A Gossip about New Books." *Bentley's Miscellany* 34 (1853): 372-74.

2581 "Harold Skimpole." *Bentley's Miscellany* 34 (1853):48-56.

2582 CHORLEY, HENRY F. *"Bleak House." Athenaeum* (Sept. 1853): 1087-88.

2583 *"Bleak House." Illustrated London News* 23 (Sept. 24, 1853):247.

2584 BRIMLEY, GEORGE. "Dickens's *Bleak House.*" *The Spectator* (Sept. 24, 1853):923-25. Reprinted in *The Essays of George Brimley,* ed. William G. Clark. London: Macmillan, 1858.

2585 SARGENT, W. *"Bleak House." North American Review* (Oct. 1853): 409-39.

2586 *"Bleak House." Examiner* (Oct. 8, 1853):643-45.

2587 *"Bleak House." Eclectic Review* 6 (Dec. 1853):665-79.

2588 KAYE, J. W. "Outrages on Women." *North British Review* 25 (May 1856):233-56.

2589 HERROLD, WALTER. "Introduction." *Bleak House.* 3 vols. Temple edition. London: Dent, 1899.

2590 WARD, H. SNOWDEN. "Topography of *Bleak House.*" *Dickensian* 1 (Aug. 1905):200-03.

2591 ROMAYNE, LEICESTER. "Turveydrop and Deportment." *Dickensian* 1 (Nov. 1905):285-86.

2592 HANDLEY, GEORGE M. *Notes on Dickens'* Bleak House. London: Normal Press, 1910.

2593 SUDDABY, JOHN. "The Crossing Sweeper in *Bleak House*: Dickens and the Original Jo." *Dickensian* 8 (Sept. 1912):246-50.

2594 WEAVER, FRANK. "My Favourite Dickens Novel." *Dickensian* 8 (Dec. 1912):313-15.

2595 GALSWORTHY, JOHN. "Introduction." *Bleak House.* Waverley edition. London: Waverley Book Co., 1913-15.

2596 FITZGERALD, PERCY H. "A Dickens Perplexity." *Dickensian* 12 (Feb. 1916):42-46 [Pt. 1, "Lady Dedlock's Flight"]. (Mar. 1916): 72-73 [Pt. 2, "Little Nell's Travels"].

2597 VALENTINE, B. B. "The Original of Hortense and the Trial of
      Marcia Manning for Murder." *Dickensian* 19 (Jan. 1923):21-22.

2598 GOULD, GERALD. "*Bleak House* Revisited." *Saturday Review* 141
      (June 1926):739-40.

2599 HOLDSWORTH, WILLIAM S. "*Bleak House* and the Procedure of
      the Court of Chancery." *Charles Dickens as a Legal Historian,*
      79-115. New Haven: Yale Univ. Press, 1928.

2600 RIDDELL, WILLIAM R. "'Dreary and Incoherent': A Study of
      Bleak House." *Dickensian* 26 (Winter 1929-30):29-36.

2601 BREWER, LUTHER A. *Leigh Hunt and Charles Dickens: The
      Skimpole Caricature.* Cedar Rapids, Ia.: Torch Press, 1930.

2602 GADD, W. LAURENCE. "The Topography of *Bleak House.*"
      Dickensian 26 (Summer 1930):207-12.

2603 PENDERED, MARY L. "Richard Carstone." *Dickensian* 26
      (Summer 1930):183-88.

2604 DEXTER, WALTER. "London Places in *Bleak House.*" *Dickensian*
      26 (Autumn 1930):300-3; 27 (Winter 1930-31):61-65.

2605 ASKEW, H. "Leigh Hunt and 'Harold Skimpole." *Notes and Queries*
      165 (Sept. 1933):213.

2606 R., V. "Leigh Hunt and Harold Skimpole." *Notes and Queries* 165
      (Oct. 1933):265.

2607 MITCHELL, E. J. "Jarndyce v. Jarndyce ... Bardell v. Pickwick:
      A Comparison." *Dickensian* 34 (Spring 1938):85-95.

2608 ROMM, A. S. "Dickens' *Bleak House.*" *Transactions of the Leningrad
      State University, Philology Series* 64 (Aug. 1941):292-307.

2609 BRADBY, M. K. "Social Wrongs in *Bleak House* and Today."
      Dickensian 38 (Sept. 1942):228-30.

2610 HILL, THOMAS W. "Notes on *Bleak House.*" *Dickensian* 40
      (Dec. 1943):39-44; (Mar. 1944):65-70; (June 1944):133-41.

2611 CHARTIER, EMILE. "Rambling About *Bleak House* With A French-
      speaking Canadian." *Dickensian* 40 (June 1944):121-25, 207-10.

2612 HILL, THOMAS W. (Kentley Bromhill, pseud.). "Phiz's Illustrations
      to *Bleak House.*" *Dickensian* 40 (June 1944):146-50; (Sept. 1944):
      192-95.

2613 "An Australian Reader: Mrs Jellyby and Caroline Chisholm." *Times
      Literary Supplement* (July 19, 1944):367.

2614 McNULTY, J. H. "*Bleak House* and Macbeth." *Dickensian* 40
      (Sept. 1944):188-91.

2615 WOOLLIAMS, W. P. "Of and Concerning 'Jarndyce vs. Jarndyce'."
      Dickensian 41 (Dec. 1944):26-29.

2616 STAPLES, LESLIE C. "On Chesney Wold." *Dickensian* 41 (Mar. 1945):80-81.

2617 STAPLES, LESLIE C. "*Bleak House* and the Critics." *Dickensian* 41 (June 1945):135-37.

2618 HILL, THOMAS W. "Hunt – Skimpole." *Dickensian* 41 (Sept. 1945): 180-84.

2619 STEVENSON, LIONEL. "Who Was Mr Turveydrop?" *Dickensian* 44 (Dec. 1947):39-41.

2620 SITWELL, SIR OSBERT. "Introduction." *Bleak House.* (New Oxford Illustrated Dickens.) London: Oxford Univ. Press, 1948.

2621 COTTERELL, T. STURGE. "The Real Boythorn – Walter Savage Landor." *Dickensian* 44 (Sept. 1948):209-16.

2622 COURNOS, JOHN. "Introduction." *Bleak House.* New York: Dodd, Mead, 1951.

2623 CARLTON, WILLIAM J. "Miss Fray and Miss Flite." *Notes and Queries* 196 (Nov. 1951):521-22.

2624 FOGLE, STEPHEN F. "Skimpole Once More." *Nineteenth Century Fiction* 7 (June 1952):1-18.

2625 JOHNSON, EDGAR. "*Bleak House*: The Anatomy of Society." *Nineteenth Century Fiction* 7 (Sept. 1952):73-89.

2626 FRIEDE, DONALD. "Introduction." *Bleak House.* Centennial edition. Garden City, NY: Doubleday, 1953.

2627 JOHNSON, R. BRIMLEY. "Introduction." *Bleak House.* London: Collins, 1953. [Edition date.]

2628 MORLEY, MALCOLM. "*Bleak House* Scene." *Dickensian* 49 (Sept. 1953):175-82.

2629 STAPLES, LESLIE C. "Shavings From Dickens's Workshop. Unpublished Fragments from the Novels." Pt. 5, *Bleak House. Dickensian* 50 (Sept. 1954):188-91. [Cancelled passages from the proofs.]

2630 FIELDING, KENNETH J. "Skimpole and Leigh Hunt Again." *Notes and Queries* N.S. 2 (Apr. 1955):174-75.

2631 MILLER, J. HILLIS. "The World View of *Bleak House.*" *Victorian Newsletter* 7 (Apr. 1955):10.

2632 BUTT, JOHN E. "*Bleak House* in the Context of 1851." *Nineteenth Century Fiction* 10 (June 1955):1-21.

2633 HAIGHT, GORDON S. "Dickens and Lewes on Spontaneous Combustion." *Nineteenth Century Fiction* 10 (June 1955):53-63.

2634 CRAIG, G. ARMOUR. "The Unpoetic Compromise: On the Relation Between Private Vision and Social Order in Nineteenth Century English Fiction." *Society and the Self in the Novel,* ed. Mark Schorer,

26-50. (English Institute Essays 1955.) New York: Columbia Univ. Press, 1956. [*Jane Eyre* and *Bleak House.*]

2635 GARIS, ROBERT E. "Moral Attitudes and the Theatrical Mode: A Study of Characterization in *Bleak House.*" Harvard, 1956. [Dissertation.]

2636 ZABEL, MORTON D. "Introduction." *Bleak House.* Riverside edition. Boston: Houghton, Mifflin, 1956. Reprinted as "Dickens: The Undivided Imagination," in *Craft and Character in Modern Fiction.* New York: Viking, 1957; *The Dickens Critics,* ed. G. H. Ford and L. Lane, Jr., 1961 q.v.

2637 GRENANDER, M. E. "The Mystery and the Moral: Point of View in Dickens's *Bleak House.*" *Nineteenth Century Fiction* 10 (Mar. 1956): 301-5.

2638 WHITLEY, ALVIN. "Two Hints for *Bleak House.*" *Dickensian* 52 (Sept. 1956):183-84.

2639 BUTT, JOHN E. and KATHLEEN TILLOTSON. "The Topicality of *Bleak House.*" *Dickens at Work,* 177-200. London: Methuen, 1957. Reprinted in *Discussions of Charles Dickens,* ed. W. R. Clark, 1961, q.v.

2640 FRIEDMAN, NORMAN. "The Shadow and the Sun: Notes Toward a Reading of *Bleak House.*" *Boston University Studies in English* 3 (Autumn 1957):147-66.

2641 FORD, GEORGE H. "Self-Help and the Helpless in *Bleak House.*" *From Jane Austen to Joseph Conrad,* ed. Robert C. Rathburn and Martin Steinmann, Jr., 92-105. Minneapolis: Univ. of Minnesota Press, 1958.

2642 CROMPTON, LOUIS. "Satire and Symbolism in *Bleak House.*" *Nineteenth Century Fiction* 12 (Mar. 1958):284-303.

2643 BRODERICK, JAMES H. and JOHN E. GRANT. "The Identity of Esther Summerson." *Modern Philology* 55 (May 1958):252-58.

2644 SØRENSON, KNUD. "Subjective Narration in *Bleak House.*" *English Studies* 40 (Dec. 1959):431-39.

2645 BUTT, JOHN E. "*Bleak House* Once More." *Critical Quarterly* 1 (Winter 1959):302-7.

2646 KRIEGER, MURRAY. "The World of Law as Pasteboard Mask." *The Tragic Vision,* 114-53. New York: Holt, Rinehart and Winston, 1960. [Pp. 138-40 only are a footnote on Dickens.]

2647 COLLINS, PHILIP A. W. "*Bleak House* and Dickens's *Household Narrative.*" *Nineteenth Century Fiction* 14 (Mar. 1960):345-49.

2648 COX, C. B. "A Dickens Landscape." *Critical Quarterly* 2 (Spring 1960):58-60. Reprinted in *Victorian Literature,* ed. Robert O. Preyer. New York: Harper and Row, 1967.

2649 COOPERMAN, STANLEY. "Dickens and the Secular Blasphemy: Social Criticism in *Hard Times, Little Dorrit* and *Bleak House.*" *College English* 22 (Dec. 1960):156-600.

2650 WORTH, GEORGE J. "The Genesis of Jo the Crossing-Sweeper." *Journal of English and Germanic Philology* 60 (Jan. 1961):44-47.

2651 DEEN, LEONARD W. "Style and Unity in *Bleak House.*" *Criticism* 3 (Summer 1961):206-18.

2652 HARVEY, W. J. "Chance and Design in *Bleak House.*" *Dickens and the Twentieth Century,* ed. J. Gross and G. Pearson, 145-57. London: Routledge and K. Paul, 1962. Reprinted in *Dickens: A Collection of Critical Essays,* ed. M. Price, 1967 q.v.

2653 COLLINS, PHILIP A. W. "Mr Pardiggle in *Bleak House.*" *Notes and Queries* N.S. 9 (Apr. 1962):150-51.

2654 WILEY, ELIZABETH. "Four Strange Cases." *Dickensian* 58 (May 1962):120-25. [Spontaneous combustion.]

2655 DONOVAN, ROBERT A. "Structure and Idea in *Bleak House.*" *ELH* 29 (June 1962):175-201. Reprinted in *The Shaping Vision: Imagination in the English Novel from Defoe to Dickens.* Ithaca, NY: Cornell Univ. Press, 1966.

2656 BLOUNT, TREVOR. "A Revised Image of the Opening Chapter of Dickens's *Bleak House.*" *Notes and Queries* 9 (Aug. 1962):303-04.

2657 [BROADSTAIRS]. *Charles Dickens and His* Bleak House. A story and a guide. 3rd ed. rev. Broadstairs, Kent: C. Eade, 1963.

2658 PRINS, ALBERT J. "The Fabulous Art: Myth, Metaphor and Moral Vision in Dickens' *Bleak House. DA* 25 (1964):1896 (Michigan 1963) [Dissertation.]

2659 LOVETT, ROBERT W. "Mr Spectator in *Bleak House.*" *Dickensian* 59 (May 1963):124-29.

2660 DETTELBACH, CYNTHIA. "Bird Imagery in *Bleak House.*" *Dickensian* 59 (Sept. 1963):177-81.

2661 BLOUNT, TREVOR. "The Graveyard Satire of *Bleak House* in the Context of 1850." *Review of English Studies* 14 (Nov. 1963): 370-78.

2662 TILLOTSON, GEOFFREY. "Afterword." *Bleak House.* New York: New American Library, 1964.

2663 PERKINS, GEORGE. "Death by Spontaneous Combustion in Marryat, Melville, Dickens, Zola and Others." *Dickensian* 60 (Jan. 1964):57-63.

2664 COLLINS, PHILIP A. W. "Inspector Bucket Visits the Princess Puffer." *Dickensian* 60 (Spring 1964):88-90.

2665 ROULET, ANN. "A Comparative Study of *Nicholas Nickleby* and *Bleak House*." *Dickensian* 60 (Spring 1964):117-24.

2666 BLOUNT, TREVOR. "The Chadbands and Dickens' View of Dissenters." *Modern Language Quarterly* 25 (Sept. 1964):295-307.

2667 PEDERSON, WINNIFRED J. "Jo in *Bleak House*." *Dickensian* 60 (Sept. 1964):162-67.

2668 HARVEY, W. J. "Freedom and Causality." *Character and the Novel*, 130-49. Ithaca, NY: Cornell Univ. Press; London: Chatto and Windus, 1965. Reprinted as *"Bleak House,"* in *Dickens: Modern Judgements*, ed. A. E. Dyson, 1968 q.v.; and as *"Bleak House*: The Double Narrative," in *Dickens: Bleak House*, ed. A. E. Dyson, 1969 q.v.

2669 JOHNSON, EDGAR. "Introduction." *Bleak House*. New York: Dell, 1965.

2670 STEIG, MICHAEL. "The Whitewashing of Inspector Bucket: Origins and Parallels." *Papers of the Michigan Academy of Science, Arts, and Letters* 50 (1965):575-84.

2671 SUCKSMITH, H. P. "Dickens at Work on *Bleak House*: A Critical Examination of His Memoranda and Number Plans." *Renaissance and Modern Studies* 9 (1965):47-85.

2672 BROGUNIER, JOSEPH. "The Funeral Pyre and Human Decency: the Fate of Chancery in *Bleak House*." *Dickensian* 61 (Jan. 1965): 57-62.

2673 PASSERINI, EDWARD M. "'Jo's Will,' Chapter XLVII of *Bleak House*." *Dickens Studies* 1 (Jan. 1965):27-33.

2674 BLOUNT, TREVOR. "Poor Jo, Education, and the Problem of Juvenile Delinquency in Dickens' *Bleak House*." *Modern Philology* 62 (May 1965):325-39.

2675 MOTH, SUSAN. "The Light/Darkness/Sight Imagery in *Bleak House*." *Dickens Studies* 1 (May 1965):76-85.

2676 BLOUNT, TREVOR. "Dickens's Slum Satire in *Bleak House*." *Modern Language Review* 60 (July 1965):340-51.

2677 BLOUNT, TREVOR. "Chancery as Evil and Challenge in *Bleak House*." *Dickens Studies* 1 (Sept. 1965):112-20.

2678 BLOUNT, TREVOR. "The Importance of Place in *Bleak House*." *Dickensian* 61 (Sept. 1965):140-49.

2679 DUNN, RICHARD J. "Skimpole and Harthouse: The Dickens Character in Transition." *Dickens Studies* 1 (Sept. 1965):121-28.

2680 BLOUNT, TREVOR. "The Ironmaster and the New Acquisitiveness: Dickens's Views on the Rising Industrial Classes as Exemplified in *Bleak House*." *Essays in Criticism* 15 (Oct. 1965):414-27.

2681 BOO, SISTER MARY R. "Jo's Journey Toward the Light in *Bleak House*." *Cithara* 5 (Nov. 1965):15-22.

2682 AXTON, WILLIAM F. "The Trouble with Esther." *Modern Language Quarterly* 26 (Dec. 1965):545-57.

2683 BLOUNT, TREVOR. "The Documentary Symbolism of Chancery in *Bleak House*." *Dickensian* 62 (Jan. 1966):47-52; (May 1966):106-11; (Sept. 1966):167-74.

2684 FRADIN, JOSEPH I. "Will and Society in *Bleak House*." *PMLA* 81 (Mar. 1966):95-109.

2685 DUNN, RICHARD J. "Esther's Role in *Bleak House*." *Dickensian* 62 (May 1966):163-66.

2686 AXTON, WILLIAM F. "Esther's Nicknames: A Study in Relevance." *Dickensian* 62 (Sept. 1966):158-63.

2687 BLOUNT, TREVOR. "Sir Leicester Dedlock and 'Deportment' Turveydrop: Some Aspects of Dickens's Use of Parallelism." *Nineteenth Century Fiction* 21 (Sept. 1966):149-65.

2688 ERICKSEN, DONALD H. "Dickens and the Critics of *Bleak House*, 1851-1965: A Study in Depth." *DA* 28 (1967):5050A-51A (Illinois). [Dissertation.]

2689 BLOUNT, TREVOR. "*Bleak House* and the Sloane Scandal of 1850 Again." *Dickens Studies* 3 (Mar. 1967):63-67.

2690 WILKINSON, ANN Y. "*Bleak House*: From Faraday to Judgment Day." *ELH* 34 (June 1967):225-47.

2691 GILL, STEPHEN C. "Allusion in *Bleak House*: A Narrative Device." *Nineteenth Century Fiction* 22 (Sept. 1967):145-54.

2692 McCOY, CONSTANCE. "Another Interpretation of Esther's Dream." *Dickensian* 63 (Sept. 1967):181-82. [Letter to Editor re R. J. Dunn's article on Esther: *Dickensian* 62 (Sept. 1966):163-66.]

2693 KORG, JACOB, ed. *Twentieth Century Interpretations of* Bleak House. Englewood Cliffs, NJ: Prentice-Hall, 1968.

2694 FIELDING, KENNETH J. "Leigh Hunt and Skimpole: Another Remonstrance." *Dickensian* 64 (Jan. 1968):5-9.

2695 GALVIN, THOMAS J. "Mr Vholes of Symond's Inn." *Dickensian* 64 (Jan. 1968):22-27.

2696 HARRIS, WENDELL V. "Jo at the Inquest and the Reports of Parliamentary Commissions." *Dickensian* 64 (Jan. 1968):48-49.

2697 AXTON, WILLIAM F. "Religious and Scientific Imagery in *Bleak House*." *Nineteenth Century Fiction* 22 (Mar. 1968):349-59.

2698 STEIG, MICHAEL. "The Iconography of the Hidden Face in *Bleak House*." *Dickens Studies* 4 (Mar. 1968):19-22.

2699 WEINSTEIN, PHILIP M. "Structure and Collapse, A Study of *Bleak House.*" *Dickens Studies* 4 (Mar. 1968):4-18.

2700 DELESPIHASSE, DORIS S. "The Significance of Dual Point of View in *Bleak House.*" *Nineteenth Century Fiction* 23 (Dec. 1968): 253-64.

2701 DYSON, A. E. "*Bleak House*: Esther Better Not Born?" *Dickens:* Bleak House, 244-73. London: Macmillan, 1969.

2702 DYSON, A. E., ed. *Dickens:* Bleak House. London: Macmillan, 1969.

2703 DYSON, A. E. "Introduction." *Dickens*: Bleak House, 11-19. London: Macmillan, 1969.

2704 FORD, GEORGE H. "The Titles for *Bleak House.*" *Dickensian* 65 (May 1969):84-89.

2705 ROSSO, MARTHA. "Dickens and Esther." *Dickensian* 65 (May 1969):90-94.

2706 EIGNER, EDWIN M. and JOSEPH I. FRADIN. "Bulwer-Lytton and Dickens' Jo." *Nineteenth Century Fiction* 24 (June 1969):98-102.

2707 NADELHAFT, JANICE. "The English Malady, Corrupted Humors, and Krook's Death." *Studies in the Novel* 1 (Summer 1969):230-39.

HARD TIMES

2708 *"Hard Times."* Gentleman's Magazine 42 (Sept. 1854):276-78.

2709 *"Hard Times."* Examiner (Sept. 9, 1854):568-69.

2710 "Belles Lettres." *Westminster Review* 62 (Oct. 1854):602-22.

2711 *"Hard Times."* British Quarterly Review 20 (Oct. 1854):581-82.

2712 RUSKIN, JOHN. "Footnote on *Hard Times.*" *Cornhill Magazine* 2 (Aug. 1860):1594+. Reprinted as "The Roots of Honour," in *"Unto This Last."* London: Smith, Elder, 1862; as "A Note on *Hard Times,*" in *The Dickens Critics,* ed. G. H. Ford and L. Lane, Jr., 1961 q.v. *Hard Times,* ed. G. H. Ford and S. Monod, 1966 q.v.

2713 WHIPPLE, EDWIN P. "*Hard Times.*" *Atlantic Monthly* 39 (Mar. 1877):353-58.

2714 STUMPF, WILLY. "Der Dickenssche Roman *Hard Times*: seine Entstehung und seine Tendenzen." Greifswald, 1911. [Dissertation.]

2715 HEARN, ARTHUR S. "Dickens and Schools." *Dickensian* 8 (Apr. 1912):98-100.

2716 SHAW, GEORGE BERNARD. "Introduction." *Hard Times.* Waverley edition. London: Waverley Book Co., 1913-15. Reprinted in *Hard Times,* ed. G. H. Ford and S. Monod, 1966 q.v.

2717 McCORMICK, I. C. "A Defense for *Hard Times.*" *Dickensian* 12 (July 1916):189-91.

2718 DORAN, W. J. "*Hard Times* and These Times." *Dickensian* 15 (Oct. 1919):199-200.

2719 KENT, W. "*Hard Times* From a Socialist Standpoint." *Dickensian* 24 (Sept. 1928):293-96.

2720 LEY, J. W. T. "[A Study of *Hard Times*]." *Dickensian* 24 (Sept. 1928):257-61. [Duplicates 2721.]

2721 LEY, J. W. T. "The Case of *Hard Times*." *Dickensian* 24 (Autumn 1928):257-61. [Duplicates 2720.]

2722 FAVORSKY, V. "Three Woodcuts for *Hard Times* by Charles Dickens." *London Mercury* 26 (July 1932):197-99.

2723 HARRISON, LEWIS. "Dickens's Shadow Show." *Dickensian* 39 (Sept. 1943):187-91.

2724 LEAVIS, F. R. "The Novel as Dramatic Poem (I): *Hard Times*." *Scrutiny* 14 (Spring 1947):185-203. Reprinted as "*Hard Times*: An Analytic Note" in *The Great Tradition*. London: Chatto and Windus, 1948; *Hard Times*, ed. G. H. Ford and S. Monod, 1966 q.v.

2725 WALDOCK, A. J. A. "The Status of *Hard Times*." *Southerly* 9 (1948):33-39.

2726 HILL, THOMAS W. "Notes on *Hard Times*." *Dickensian* 48 (June 1952):134-41; (Sept. 1952):177-85.

2727 FIELDING, KENNETH J. "Charles Dickens and the Department of Practical Art." *Modern Language Review* 48 (July 1953):270-77.

2728 RICHARDSON, JOANNA. "Dickens and *Hard Times*." [Afternote to] *Hard Times*. London: Dent, 1954.

2729 BOULTON, J. T. "Charles Knight and Charles Dickens: *Knowledge is Power* and *Hard Times*." *Dickensian* 50 (Mar. 1954):57-63.

2730 GERBER, HELMUT E. "*Hard Times*: an Experience in Teaching." *College English* 15 (Mar. 1954):351-53.

2731 MORLEY, MALCOLM. "*Hard Times* on the Stage." *Dickensian* 50 (Mar. 1954):69-73.

2732 FIELDING, KENNETH J. "The Battle for Preston." *Dickensian* 50 (Sept. 1954):159-62.

2733 FOOT, DINGLE. "Introduction." *Hard Times for These Times*. New Oxford Illustrated Dickens. London: Oxford Univ. Press, 1955.

2734 FIELDING, KENNETH J. "Mill and Gradgrind." *Nineteenth Century Fiction* 11 (Sept. 1956):148-51.

2735 HUMPHREY, HAROLD E. "The Background of *Hard Times*." *DA* 19 (1958):318 (Columbia). [Dissertation.]

2736 WATT, WILLIAM W. "Introduction." *Hard Times for These Times*. New York: Rinehart, 1958.

2737 WILLIAMS, RAYMOND. "*Hard Times*." *Culture and Society 1780-1950*, 92-97. London: Chatto and Windus, 1958.

2738 BRERETON, FREDERICK. "Introduction." *Hard Times*. London: Collins, 1959. [Edition date.]

2739 MIDDENDORF, JOHN H. "Introduction." *Hard Times*. New York: Harper, 1960.

2740 COOPERMAN, STANLEY. "Dickens and the Secular Blasphemy: Social Criticism in *Hard Times, Little Dorrit* and *Bleak House*." *College English* 22 (Dec. 1960):156-600.

2741 SHAPIRO, CHARLES. "Afterword." *Hard Times for These Times*. New York: New American Library, 1961.

2742 HOLLOWAY, JOHN. "*Hard Times*: A History and a Criticism." *Dickens and the Twentieth Century*, ed. J. Gross and G. Pearson, 159-74. London: Routledge and K. Paul, 1962. Reprinted in *Hard Times*, ed. G. H. Ford and S. Monod, 1966 q.v.

2743 CROCKETT, JUDITH. "Theme and Metaphor in *Hard Times*." *Spectrum* 6 (Fall 1962):80-81.

2744 ATKINSON, F. G. "*Hard Times*: Themes and Motifs." *Use of English* 14 (Spring 1963):165-69.

2745 SPECTOR, ROBERT D. "Introduction." *Hard Times*. New York: Bantam, 1964.

2746 WOODINGS, R. B. "A Cancelled Passage in *Hard Times*." *Dickensian* 60 (Jan. 1964):42-43.

2747 CARNALL, GEOFFREY. "Dickens, Mrs Gaskell and the Preston Strike." *Victorian Studies* 8 (Sept. 1964):31-48.

2748 DENEAU, DANIEL P. "The Brother-Sister Relationship in *Hard Times*." *Dickensian* 60 (Autumn 1964):173-77. Reprinted in *Hard Times*, ed. G. H. Ford and S. Monod, 1966 q.v.

2749 VOSS, A. E. "A Note on Theme and Structure in *Hard Times*." *Theoria* 23 (Oct. 1964):35-42.

2750 HIRSCH, DAVID M. "*Hard Times* and F. R. Leavis." *Criticism* 6 (Winter 1964):1-16. Reprinted in *Hard Times*, ed. G. H. Ford and S. Monod, 1966 q.v.

2751 GIBSON, JOHN W. "*Hard Times*, A Further Note." *Dickens Studies* 1 (May 1965):90-101.

2752 DUNN, RICHARD J. "Skimpole and Harthouse: The Dickens Character in Transition." *Dickens Studies* 1 (Sept. 1965):121-28.

2753 FORD, GEORGE H. and SYLVÈRE MONOD, eds. Hard Times: *An Authoritative Text; Backgrounds, Sources and Contemporary Reactions; Criticism*. New York: Norton, 1966.

2754 LODGE, DAVID. "The Rhetoric of *Hard Times*." *Language of Fiction*, 145-63. New York: Columbia Univ. Press; London: Routledge and K. Paul, 1966. Reprinted in *Twentieth Century Interpretations of* Hard Times, ed. P. E. Gray, 1969 q.v.

2755 WINTERICH, JOHN T. "Introduction." *Hard Times for These Times.*
New York: Limited Editions Club, 1966.

2756 GILMOUR, ROBIN. "Manchester Men and Their Books." *Dickensian*
63 (Jan. 1967):21-24.

2757 FIELDING, KENNETH J. "*Hard Times* for the Present." *Dickensian*
63 (Sept. 1967):149-52.

2758 BERMAN, RONALD. "Human Scale: A Note on *Hard Times.*"
Nineteenth Century Fiction 22 (Dec. 1967):288-93.

2759 GILMOUR, ROBIN. "The Gradgrind School: Political Economy in
the Classroom." *Victorian Studies* 11 (Dec. 1967):207-24.

2760 FIELDING, KENNETH J. "*Hard Times* and Common Things."
*Imagined Worlds: Essays on Some English Novels and Novelists in
Honour of John Butt,* ed. Maynard Mack and Ian Gregory, 183-204.
London: Methuen, 1968.

2761 JONES, FLORENCE. "Dickens and Langland in Adjudication upon
Meed." *Victorian Newsletter* 33 (Spring 1968):53-56.

2762 MONOD, SYLVÈRE. "Dickens at Work on the Text of *Hard Times.*"
Dickensian 64 (May 1968):86-99.

2763 SZIROTNY, J. S. "A Classical Reference in *Hard Times* and in
Middlemarch." *Notes and Queries* 15 (Nov. 1968):421-22.

2764 CRAIG, DAVID. "Introduction." *Hard Times for These Times.*
Harmondsworth: Penguin, 1969.

2765 GRAY, PAUL E., ed. *Twentieth Century Interpretations of* Hard Times.
Englewood Cliffs, NJ: Prentice-Hall, 1969.

2766 LINCKS, J. F. "Close Reading of *Hard Times.*" *English Journal* 58
(Feb. 1969):212-18.

2767 DYSON, A. E. "*Hard Times*: The Robber Fancy." *Dickensian* 65
(May 1969):67-79.

2768 SONSTROEM, DAVID. "Fettered Fancy in *Hard Times.*" *PMLA* 84
(May 1969):520-29.

2769 ALEXANDER, EDWARD. "Disinterested Virtue: Dickens and Mill
in Agreement." *Dickensian* 65 (Sept. 1969):163-70.

2770 BRANTLINGER, PATRICK. "The Case Against Trade Unions in
Early Victorian Fiction." *Victorian Studies* 13 (Sept. 1969):37-52.

LITTLE DORRIT

2771 "*Little Dorrit,* No. 1." *Athenaeum* (Dec. 1, 1855):1393-94.

2772 "Circumlocution vs. Circumvention." *Saturday Review* 2
(Nov. 22, 1856):649-50.

2773 "*Little Dorrit.*" *Athenaeum* (June 6, 1857):722-24.

2774 *"Little Dorrit."* Examiner (June 13, 1857):372-73.

2775 STEPHEN, JAMES FITZJAMES. *"Little Dorrit."* Saturday Review 4 (July 1857):15-16.

2776 TROLLOPE, ANTHONY. "The Civil Service as a Profession." *Cornhill Magazine* 3 (Feb. 1861):214-28.

2777 FRASER, W. A. *"Little Dorrit."* Dickensian 3 (Apr. 1907):99-101.

2778 SHAW, GEORGE BERNARD. "Charles Dickens and *Little Dorrit.*" *Dickensian* 4 (Dec. 1908):323.

2779 "Compagnon de la Marjolaine." *Dickensian* 5 (Feb. 1909):44-45.

2780 MATCHETT, WILLOUGHBY. "The Neglected Book." *Dickensian* 6 (Apr. 1910):98-102.

2781 ORCZY, BARONESS EMMUSKA. "Introduction." *Little Dorrit.* Waverley edition. London: Waverley Book Co., 1913-15.

2782 KENT, W. *"Little Dorrit* and *The Edinburgh Review."* Dickensian 15 (Apr. 1919):64-68.

2783 SISSONS, NELLIE R. *The Key to the Story of Charles Dickens'* Little Dorrit. London: Barrie, 1922.

2784 KENT, W. "The Marshalsea Prison." *Dickensian* 23 (Sept. 1927): 260-64.

2785 R., W. J. "Concerning *Little Dorrit.*" *Dickensian* 24 (Winter 1927-28): 54.

2786 FISHER, W. J. "Circumlocution." *Dickensian* 24 (Mar. 1928): 123-25.

2787 McNULTY, J. H. "Wisdom of Mr F.'s Aunt." *Dickensian* 24 (June 1928):187-90.

2788 STEVENS, JAMES S. "Dickens' Use of Quotations in *Little Dorrit.*" *Dickensian* 24 (June 1928):200-1.

2789 WOODFIELD, KATE. "Child of the Marshalsea." *Dickensian* 24 (June 1928):203-6.

2790 YOUNG, GEORGE F. "The Marshalsea Revisited." *Dickensian* 28 (Summer 1932):219-27.

2791 JOHNSON, R. BRIMLEY. *"Little Dorrit,* An Unpopular Classic." *Dickensian* 28 (Autumn 1932):283-86.

2792 YOUNG, GEORGE F. "Round and About Little Dorrit's Church." *Dickensian* 35 (Dec. 1939):58-60.

2793 HILL, THOMAS W. "Notes on *Little Dorrit.*" *Dickensian* 41 (Sept. 1945):196-203; 42 (Dec. 1945):38-44; (Mar. 1946):82-91.

2794 STUART-BUNNING, G. H. "The Circumlocution Office." *Dickensian* 42 (Dec. 1945):35-38.

2795 MAJOR, GWEN. "Some Damage Has Been Reported ..." *Dickensian* 42 (Mar. 1946):92-97, 124-29.

2796 BURN, WILLIAM LAWRENCE. "The Neo-Barnacles." *Nineteenth Century* 143 (Feb. 1948):98-103.

2797 BOOTH, BRADFORD A. "Trollope and *Little Dorrit.*" *Trollopian* 2 (Mar. 1948):237-40.

2798 McNULTY, J. H. "On the Alleged Gloominess of *Little Dorrit.*" *Dickensian* 45 (Dec. 1948):36-38.

2799 COURNOS, JOHN. "Introduction." *Little Dorrit.* New York: Dodd, Mead, 1951.

2800 STAPLES, LESLIE C. "Shavings From Dickens's Workshop. Unpublished Fragments from the Novels." Pt. 3, *Little Dorrit. Dickensian* 49 (Sept. 1953):169-74. [Cancelled passages from the proofs.]

2801 TRILLING, LIONEL. *"Little Dorrit." Kenyon Review* 15 (Autumn 1953):577-90. Reprinted as "Introduction" to *Little Dorrit.* New Oxford Illustrated Dickens. London: Oxford Univ. Press, 1953; and as *"Little Dorrit,"* in *The Opposing Self: Nine Essays in Criticism.* New York: Viking, 1955; *Dickens: A Collection of Critical Essays,* ed. M. Price, 1967 q.v.; *Dickens: Modern Judgements,* ed. A. E. Dyson 1968 q.v.; *Discussions of Charles Dickens,* ed. W. R. Clark, 1961 q.v.; *The Dickens Critics,* ed. G. H. Ford and L. Lane, Jr., 1961 q.v.

2802 MORLEY, MALCOLM. *"Little Dorrit,* On and Off." *Dickensian* 50 (June 1954):136-40.

2803 BERGLER, EDMUND. *"Little Dorrit* and Dickens' Intuitive Knowledge of Psychic Masochism." *American Imago* 14 (Winter 1957): 371-88.

2804 WHYTE, MARK. "Introduction." *Little Dorrit.* London: Collins, 1959. [Edition date.]

2805 BUTT, JOHN E. "The Topicality of *Little Dorrit.*" *University of Toronto Quarterly* 29 (Oct. 1959):1-10.

2806 SHERIF, NUR. "The Victorian Sunday in *Little Dorrit* and *Thyrza.*" *Cairo Studies in English* (1960):155-65.

2807 COOPERMAN, STANLEY. "Dickens and the Secular Blasphemy: Social Criticism in *Hard Times, Little Dorrit* and *Bleak House.*" *College English* 22 (Dec. 1960):156-600.

2808 McMASTER, ROWLAND D. *"Little Dorrit:* Experience and Design." *Queen's Quarterly* 67 (Winter 1960-61):530-38. Reprinted with annotations in *Thought, From the Learned Societies of Canada, 1960.* Toronto: Gage, 1961.

2809 SANTANIELLO, ANTHONY E. "Charles Dickens' *Little Dorrit:* A Study of the Heroine as Victim and Savior." Harvard, 1961. [Dissertation.]

2810 WAIN, JOHN. *"Little Dorrit." Dickens and the Twentieth Century*, ed. J. Gross and G. Pearson, 175-86. London: Routledge and K. Paul, 1962. Reprinted in *Essays on Literature and Ideas*. London: Macmillan, 1963.

2811 MAHER, JAMES. "Irish Bank Inspired Dickens." *Irish Digest* 77 (Mar. 1963):63-64. [A note – *L. D.* was inspired by the history of the Tipparary Joint Stock Bank.]

2812 JUMP, JOHN D. "Clennam at the Circumlocution Office: An Analysis." *Critical Survey* 1 (Spring 1963):103-6.

2813 NETHERCOT, ARTHUR H. "Prunes and Miss Prism." *Modern Drama* 6 (May 1963):112-16.

2814 HERRING, PAUL D. "The Background of Charles Dickens' *Little Dorrit.*" Chicago, 1964. [Dissertation.]

2815 WILDE, ALAN. "Mr F.'s Aunt and the Analogical Structure of *Little Dorrit.*" *Nineteenth Century Fiction* 19 (June 1964):33-44.

2816 BELL, VEREEN M. "Mrs General as Victorian England: Dickens' Image of his Times." *Nineteenth Century Fiction* 20 (Sept. 1965): 177-84.

2817 BRENNAN, M. "The Symbolic Organization of *Little Dorrit.*" *Australian Teacher* 42 (June 1966):27-31.

2818 HERRING, PAUL D. "Dickens' Monthly Number Plans for *Little Dorrit.*" *Modern Philology* 64 (Aug. 1966):22-63.

2819 REID, JOHN C. *Charles Dickens:* Little Dorrit. London: E. Arnold, 1967.

2820 MECKIER, JEROME. "Dickens's *Little Dorrit*: Sundry Curious Variations on the Same Tune." *Dickens Studies* 3 (Mar. 1967):51-62.

2821 KAPLAN, FRED. "Dickens's Flora Finching and Joyce's Molly Bloom." *Nineteenth Century Fiction* 23 (Dec. 1968):343-46.

2822 BUTT, JOHN E. "The Serial Publication of Dickens's Novels: *Martin Chuzzlewit* and *Little Dorrit.*" *Pope, Dickens, and Others*, 149-64. Edinburgh: University Press, 1969.

2823 McMASTER, ROWLAND D. "Introduction." *Little Dorrit.* (College Classics in English.) Toronto: Macmillan, 1969.

A TALE OF TWO CITIES

2824 STEPHEN, JAMES FITZJAMES. *"A Tale of Two Cities." Saturday Review* 8 (Dec. 17, 1859):741-43. Reprinted in *The Dickens Critics*, ed. G. H. Ford and L. Lane, Jr., 1961 q.v.

2825 MOORE, HAMILTON B. "Introduction." *A Tale of Two Cities.* Boston: D. C. Heath, 1901.

2826 BARTER, A. A. "Introduction." *A Tale of Two Cities.* London: Adam and Charles Black, 1905.

2827 BUEHLER, HUBER G. and LAWRENCE MASON. "Introduction and Notes." *A Tale of Two Cities.* London: Macmillan, 1906.

2828 JERROLD, WALTER. "Introduction." *A Tale of Two Cities.* Everyman's Library. London: J. M. Dent; New York: E. P. Dutton and Company, 1906-21.

2829 HANDLEY, GEORGE M. *Notes on Dickens'* Tale of Two Cities. London: Normal Press, 1907.

2830 ABERNATHY, JULIAN W. "Introduction." *A Tale of Two Cities.* New York: C. E. Merrill, 1908.

2831 ROE, FREDERICK W. "Introduction." *Charles Dickens' A Tale of Two Cities.* New York: Longmans, Green, 1910.

2832 MAGENNIS, WILLIAM. "Introduction." *A Tale of Two Cities.* London and Dublin: Blackie and Son, 1911.

2833 HUNTER, R. W. G. "*A Tale of Two Cities* and the French Revolution." *Dickensian* 8 (Aug. 1912):210-12.

2834 BÖTTGER, CURT. "Charles Dickens' historischer Roman *A Tale of Two Cities* und seine Quellen." Königsberg, 1913. [Dissertation.]

2835 POLACK, ERNEST E. "Mr Jarvis Lorry." *Dickensian* 9 (June 1913): 154-56.

2836 SHARP, CHARLES. "The Crunchers." *Dickensian* 10 (Oct. 1914): 263-69.

2837 BENNETT, ANNIE. "Sidney Carton." *Dickensian* 11 (Aug. 1915): 209-13.

2838 JACKSON, MARK H. *Helps to the Study of* A Tale of Two Cities. London: Arnold, 1916.

2839 FALCONER, J. A. "The Sources of *A Tale of Two Cities.*" *Modern Language Notes* 36 (Jan. 1921):1-10.

2840 LAW, FREDERICK H. "Government and the Governed and *A Tale of Two Cities.*" *The Independent* 108 (Mar. 1922):316-17.

2841 RASCOE, BURTON. "Mr Dickens's *A Tale of Two Cities.*" *Bookman* 58 (Jan. 1924):541-44.

2842 ERWIN, EDWARD. "Introduction." *A Tale of Two Cities.* Lincoln, Neb.: University Publishing Company, 1925.

2843 PHILLIPS, WALTER C. "Introduction." *A Tale of Two Cities.* New York: Macmillan, 1926.

2844 WAUGH, ARTHUR. "Introduction to *A Tale of Two Cities.*" *Dickensian* 23 (Dec. 1926):13-16.

2845 EPSTEIN, SAMUEL. *A Commentary and Questionnaire on* A Tale of Two Cities. London: Pitman, 1927.

2846 TYRRELL, T. W. "The Play Which Suggested *A Tale of Two Cities.*" *Notes and Queries* 152 (Jan. 1927):12. ["The Frozen Deep."]

2847 DRINKWATER, JOHN. "The Grand Manner: Thoughts Upon *A Tale of Two Cities." Essays of the Year (1929-30)*, 3-14. London: Argonaut, 1930.

2848 WARNER, PAULINE. "Introduction." *Dickens' A Tale of Two Cities.* Philadelphia: J. B. Lippincott, 1930.

2849 BOAS, MRS F. S. "Introduction." *A Tale of Two Cities.* London: Oxford Univ. Press, 1934.

2850 KINCHELOE, ISABEL. "Introduction." *A Tale of Two Cities.* Chicago: Lyons and Carnahan, 1934.

2851 POMERANZ, HERMAN. *Medicine in the Shakespearean Plays, and Dickens' Doctors.* New York: Powell, 1936.

2852 BOAS, J. H. "'The Period' in *A Tale of Two Cities." Dickensian* 33 (Winter 1936-37):33-34.

2853 EARL, HERBERT L. "Treatment of the French Revolution by Dickens in *A Tale of Two Cities." Lectures Given at the Torquay Natural History Museum.* Torquay: Devonshire Press, 1939.

2854 MILLEY, HENRY J. "Wilkie Collins and *A Tale of Two Cities." Modern Language Review* 34 (Oct. 1939):525-34.

2855 LUCAS, JOHN P. Jr. "To John Landseer, Esquire: A Note From Charles Dickens." *South Atlantic Quarterly* 39 (Oct. 1940):448-53.

2856 BECKER, MAY L. "Introductory Sketch." *A Tale of Two Cities.* New York: Dodd, Mead, 1942.

2857 HILL, THOMAS W. "Notes on *A Tale of Two Cities." Dickensian* 41 (Mar. 1945):68-74; (June 1945):129-35.

2858 SMITH, THOMAS W. *Charles Dickens: A Tale of Two Cities.* (Notes on Chosen English Texts.) London: J. Brodie, 1946.

2859 SHUCKBURGH, SIR JOHN. "Introduction." *A Tale of Two Cities.* (New Oxford Illustrated Dickens.) London: Oxford Univ. Press, 1949.

2860 LINDSAY, JACK. *"A Tale of Two Cities." Life and Letters* 62 (Sept. 1949):191-204.

2861 WAGENKNECHT, EDWARD. "Introduction." *A Tale of Two Cities.* New York: Modern Library, 1950.

2862 YOUNGHEM, EDITH C. "Introduction." *A Tale of Two Cities.* New York: Harcourt, Brace, 1950.

2863 MARKS, ARTHUR W. "Dickens and the Horn Tavern, Fleet Street." *Notes and Queries* 196 (Feb. 1951):81. [Source for a tavern in Bk. 2 Chap. 4.]

2864 DARK, SIDNEY. "Introduction." *A Tale of Two Cities.* London: Collins, 1954. [Edition date.]

2865 MORLEY, MALCOLM. "The Stage Story of *A Tale of Two Cities." Dickensian* 51 (Dec. 1954):34-40.

2866 JOHNSON, EDGAR. "Introduction." *A Tale of Two Cities.* New York: Washington Square Press, 1957, 1962.

2867 OSBOURN, BARBARA. "Critical Commentary." [Introduction.] *A Tale of Two Cities.* London: Univ. of London Press, 1957.

2868 ZABEL, MORTON D. "Dickens: The Revolutionary Fate." *Craft and Character in Modern Fiction,* 49-69. New York: Viking, 1957.

2869 BLAIR, WALTER. "The French Revolution and *Huckleberry Finn.*" *Modern Philology* 55 (Aug. 1957):21-35.

2870 STANGE, G. ROBERT. "Dickens and the Fiery Past: *A Tale of Two Cities* Reconsidered." *English Journal* 46 (Oct. 1957):381-90.

2871 ZABEL, MORTON D. "Introduction." *A Tale of Two Cities.* New York: Harper, 1958.

2872 TODD, WILLIAM B. "Note 94: Dickens, *A Tale of Two Cities,* 1859." *Book Collector* 7 (Spring 1958):80. [Bibliographical; on initial publications of *Tale of Two Cities.*]

2873 STAPLES, LESLIE C. "The New Film Version of *A Tale of Two Cities.*" *Dickensian* 54 (May 1958):119-20.

2874 MANHEIM, LEONARD F. "*A Tale of Two Cities* (1859): A Study in Psychoanalytic Criticism." *English Review* (New York City Association of Teachers of English) (Spring 1959):13-28.

2875 DOLMETSCH, CARL R. "Dickens and *The Dead Heart.*" *Dickensian* 55 (Sept. 1959):179-87. [On similarities between Watts Phillip's play *The Dead Heart,* produced in Nov. 1859, and *A Tale of Two Cities.*]

2876 MERSAND, JOSEPH. "Afterword." *A Tale of Two Cities.* New York: New American Library, 1960.

2877 McCELVEY, GEORGE. "*A Tale of Two Cities* and Gin-Drinking." *Notes and Queries* 8 (Mar. 1961):96-97.

2878 MARSHALL, WILLIAM H. "The Method of *A Tale of Two Cities.*" *Dickensian* 57 (Sept. 1961):183-89.

2879 FADIMAN, CLIFTON. "Afterword." *A Tale of Two Cities.* (Macmillan Classics.) New York: Macmillan, 1962.

2880 GROSS, JOHN. "*A Tale of Two Cities.*" *Dickens and the Twentieth Century,* ed. J. Gross and G. Pearson, 187-97. London: Routledge and K. Paul, 1962. Reprinted in *Dickens: Modern Judgements,* ed. A. E. Dyson, 1968 q.v.

2881 MARCUS, STEVEN. "Introduction." *A Tale of Two Cities.* New York: Collier Books, 1962.

2882 PICKREL, PAUL. "Revolution and Redemption in *A Tale of Two Cities.*" [Introduction.] *A Tale of Two Cities.* Boston: Houghton Mifflin, 1962.

2883 MELLON, JOHN C. "Introduction." *A Tale of Two Cities.* Evanston,
      Ill.: Harper and Row, 1963.

2884 REFFOLD, A. E. "Dr Manette in Soho: Some New Notes and
      Suggestions." *Dickensian* 59 (Autumn 1963):172-74.

2885 GIBSON, FRANK A. "The Saddest Book." *Dickensian* 60
      (Jan. 1964):30-32.

2886 WAGENKNECHT, EDWARD. *"A Tale of Two Cities." Dickens and
      the Scandal-Mongers,* 121-31. Norman: Univ. of Oklahoma Press,
      1965.

2887 GREGORY, MICHAEL. "Old Bailey Speech in *A Tale of Two Cities.*"
      Review of English Literature 6 (Apr. 1965):42-55.

2888 ELLIOT, RALPH W. *A Critical Commentary on Dickens'* A Tale of
      Two Cities. London: Macmillan, 1966.

2889 RYAN, J. S. *"A Tale of Two Cities*: London and Wellington."
      Dickens Studies 2 (Sept. 1966):147-51.

2890 TROMLY, FREDERICK B. "Introduction." *A Tale of Two Cities.*
      Bronxville, NY: Cambridge Book Company, 1968.

2891 ADRIAN, ARTHUR A. "Critical and Biographical Profile of
      Charles Dickens." [Introduction.] *A Tale of Two Cities.* New York:
      F. Watts, 1969.

GREAT EXPECTATIONS

2892 A., J. *"Great Expectations." The Ladies' Companion and Monthly
      Magazine* 20 (1861):218-20.

2893 *"Great Expectations." Athenaeum* (July 13, 1861):43-45.

2894 *"Great Expectations." Examiner* (July 20, 1861):452-53.

2895 *"Great Expectations." Saturday Review* 12 (July 20, 1861):69-70.

2896 *"Great Expectations." Atlantic Monthly* 8 (Sept. 1861):380-82.
      Reprinted in *Assessing* Great Expectations, ed. R. Lettis and W. E.
      Morris, 1960 q.v.

2897 *"Great Expectations." Eclectic Review* 114 (Oct. 1861):458-77.

2898 "Belles Lettres." *Westminster Review* 77 (Jan. 1862):286-302.

2899 "The Collected Works of Charles Dickens." *British Quarterly Review*
      35 (Jan. 1862):154.

2900 *"Great Expectations." The Rambler* (Jan. 1862):274-76.

2901 OLIPHANT, MARGARET. "Sensation Novels." *Blackwood's
      Edinburgh Magazine* 91 (May 1862):564-84.

2902 WHIPPLE, EDWIN P. "Dickens's *Great Expectations.*" *Atlantic
      Monthly* 40 (Sept. 1877):327-33. Reprinted in *Assessing* Great
      Expectations, ed. R. Lettis and W. E. Morris, 1960 q.v.

2903 WAUGH, ARTHUR. "Introduction." *Great Expectations*. London: Chapman and Hall, 1899.

2904 GADD, W. LAURENCE. "The Lonely Church on the Marshes." *Dickensian* 5 (Mar. 1909):68-69. [Cooling Church.]

2905 PHILIP, ALEX J. "With Pip in Kent." *United Methodist Magazine* (Mar. 1909):118-20.

2906 ROMAYNE, LEICESTER. "The Genius of Wemmick." *Dickensian* 5 (Sept. 1909):229-31.

2907 MATCHETT, WILLOUGHBY. "The Strange Case of Great Expectations." *Dickensian* 9 (Feb. 1913):33-36.

2908 DUNKERLEY, WILLIAM A. (John Oxenham, pseud.). "Introduction *Great Expectations*. Waverley edition. London: Waverley Book Co., 1913-15.

2909 SHARP, HELENA. "Herbert Pocket, Gentleman." *Dickensian* 11 (Sept. 1915):236-38.

2910 DICKENS, SIR HENRY F. "Cooling v. Higham." *Dickensian* 21 (Jan. 1925):13. [Letter re. the scene of the opening part of *Great Expectations* re. Colonel Gadd. See *Dickensian* 21 (Jan. 1925): 100-1, for Gadd's reply.]

2911 GADD, W. LAURENCE. *The* Great Expectations *Country*. London: Palmer, 1929.

2912 CLARK, EVERT M. "Introduction." *Great Expectations*. New York: Macmillan, 1931.

2913 BOLL, ERNEST M. *"Great Expectations." Times Literary Supplemer* (Aug. 15, 1935):513.

2914 MACY, GEORGE, GEORGE BERNARD SHAW, and WILLIAM MAXWELL. *The Mystery of the Unhappy Ending*. A correspondence between George Macy, Bernard Shaw, and William Maxwell referring to the "honest ending" printed in *Great Expectations*, ed. George Bernard Shaw. [See 2915.] New York: NY Public Library, Berg Collection [N.D.].

2915 SHAW, GEORGE BERNARD. "Introduction" and "Postscript." *Great Expectations*. New York: Limited Editions Club; Edinburgh: R. and R. Clark, 1937. Reprinted in *Book of Prefaces,* Van Wyck et al. New York: Limited Editions Club, 1941; "Introduction," *Great Expectations*. London: Hamish Hamilton, 1947; "Charles Dickens and *Great Expectations." Majority, 1931-32*. London: Hamish Hamilton, 1952.

2916 WASHBURN, CAROLYN. "The History, From 1832 to 1860, of British Criticism of Narrative Prose Fiction." Illinois, 1937. [pp. 281-87. Dissertation.]

2917 GADD, W. LAURENCE. "The House with the Bow-Window." *Dickensian* 33 (Mar. 1937):117-21. [Sources for places in *G.E.*]

2918 BECKER, MAY L. "Introduction." *Great Expectations*. New York: Dodd, Mead, 1943.

2919 ARNOLD, RALPH. *"Great Expectations." Nineteenth Century* 140 (Oct. 1946):197-203.

2920 DAVIS, EARLE R. "Introduction." *Great Expectations*. New York: Rinehart, 1948.

2921 SMITH, THOMAS W. *Charles Dickens*: Great Expectations. (Notes on Chosen English Texts.) London: J. Brodie, 1948.

2922 HOUSE, HUMPHRY. "G. B. S. on *Great Expectations*." *Dickensian* 44 (Mar. 1948):63-70; (Sept. 1948):183-86. Reprinted in *All In Due Time*. London: Hart-Davis, 1955. [Re. Shaw's introduction to *Great Expectations*.]

2923 VACHELL, HORACE A. "Mr Vachell On Pip." *Dickensian* 44 (June 1948):162.

2924 CARTER, JOHN A. "[A Note on the First Edition of *Great Expectations*] ." *New Colophon* 2 (Jan. 1949):84.

2925 RANDALL, DAVID A. *"Great Expectations*: Its Scarcity." *New Colophon* 2 (Jan. 1949):84-85.

2926 BUTT, JOHN E. "Dickens's Plan for the Conclusion of *Great Expectations*." *Dickensian* 45 (Mar. 1949):78-80.

2927 THOMPSON, BLANCHE J. "Introduction." *Great Expectations*. New York: Harcourt, Brace, 1950.

2928 LIVENSPARGER, CLARK C. "Introduction." *Great Expectations*. Cleveland: Fine Editions Press, 1952.

2929 HAYENS, KENNETH. "Introduction." *Great Expectations*. London and Glasgow: Collins, 1953. [Edition date.]

2930 PAGE, FREDERICK. "Introduction." *Great Expectations*. New Oxford Illustrated Dickens. London: Oxford Univ. Press, 1953.

2931 VAN GHENT, DOROTHY. "On *Great Expectations*." *The English Novel: Form and Function,* 125-38. New York: Rinehart, 1953. Reprinted in *Assessing* Great Expectations, ed. R. Lettis and W. E. Morris, 1960 q.v.; *Dickens: Modern Judgements,* ed. A. E. Dyson, 1968 q.v.

2932 HAGAN, JOHN H., Jr. "Structural Patterns in Dickens's *Great Expectations*." *Journal of English Literary History* 21 (Mar. 1954): 54-66.

2933 FRIEDMAN, NORMAN. "Versions of Form in Fiction – *Great Expectations* and *The Great Gatsby*." *Accent* 14 (Autumn 1954): 246-64.

2934 JONES, HOWARD M. "On Rereading *Great Expectations*." *Southwest Review* 39 (Autumn 1954):328-35.

2935 STANGE, G. ROBERT. "Expectations Well Lost: Dickens' Fable for His Time." *College English* 16 (Oct. 1954):9-17. Reprinted in *Discussions of Charles Dickens,* ed. W. R. Clark, 1961 q.v.; *The Dickens Critics,* ed. G. H. Ford and L. Lane, Jr., 1961 q.v.; *Assessing* Great Expectations, ed. R. Lettis and W. E. Morris, 1963 q.v.

2936 HAGAN, JOHN H., Jr. "The Poor Labyrinth: The Theme of Social Injustice in Dickens's Great Expectations." *Nineteenth Century Fiction* 9 (Dec. 1954):169-78. Reprinted in *Assessing* Great Expectations, ed. R. Lettis and W. E. Morris, 1963 q.v.

2937 CONNOLLY, THOMAS E. "Technique in *Great Expectations.*" *Philological Quarterly* 34 (Jan. 1955):48-55. Reprinted in *Assessing* Great Expectations, ed. Lettis, 1963 q.v.

2938 FRASER, RUSSELL. "A Charles Dickens Original." *Nineteenth Century Fiction* 9 (Mar. 1955):301-7. [On the original source of the story of Miss Havisham's unhappy love affair.]

2939 MORLEY, MALCOLM. "Stages of *Great Expectations.*" *Dickensian* 51 (Mar. 1955):79-83.

2940 STONE, HARRY. "An Added Note on Dickens and Miss Havisham." *Nineteenth Century Fiction* 10 (June 1955):85-86.

2941 FIELDING, KENNETH J. "The Piracy of *Great Expectations.*" *Notes and Queries* N.S. 2 (Nov. 1955):495-96.

2942 WAGENKNECHT, EDWARD. "Introduction." *Great Expectations.* New York: Pocket Books, 1956.

2943 DREW, ARNOLD P. "Structure in *Great Expectations.*" *Dickensian* 52 (June 1956):123-27.

2944 WAGENKNECHT, EDWARD. "*Great Expectations* and Ellen Glasgow." *Boston University Studies in English* 3 (Spring 1957): 57-60.

2945 HILL, THOMAS W. "Notes on *Great Expectations.*" *Dickensian* 53 (May 1957):119-26; (Sept. 1957):184-86; 54 (Jan. 1958):53-60; (May 1958):123-25; (Sept. 1958):185; 55 (Jan. 1959):57-59; 56 (May 1960):121-26.

2946 EDMINSON, MARY. "The Date of the Action in *Great Expectations.*" *Nineteenth Century Fiction* 13 (June 1958):22-35.

2947 STEWART, JAMES T. "Miss Havisham and Miss Grierson." *Furman Studies* 6 (Fall 1958):21-23. [Faulkner's Miss Emily Grierson in "A Rose for Emily."]

2948 MONOD, SYLVÈRE. "Introduction." *Great Expectations.* Paris: Garnier, 1959. [French translation.]

2949 REED, JAMES. "The Fulfillment of Pip's Expectations." *Dickensian* 55 (Jan. 1959):12-18.

2950 NISBET, ADA B. "The Autobiographical Matrix of *Great
Expectations*." *Victorian Newsletter* 15 (Spring 1959):10-13.

2951 PICKREL, PAUL. "Teaching the Novel: *Great Expectations*."
*Essays in the Teaching of English: Reports of the Yale Conferences
on the Teaching of English*, ed. Edward J. Gordon and Edward S.
Noyes, 216-29. New York: Appleton-Century-Crofts, 1960. Partially
reprinted as "*Great Expectations*," in *Dickens: A Collection of
Critical Essays*, ed. M. Price, 1967 q.v.

2952 SPILKA, MARK. "Dickens' *Great Expectations*: A Kafkan Reading."
Twelve Original Essays on Great English Novelists, ed. Charles
Shapiro, 103-24. Detroit, Mich.: Wayne State Univ. Press, 1960.

2953 MOYNAHAN, JULIAN. "The Hero's Guilt: The Case of *Great
Expectations*." *Essays in Criticism* 10 (Jan. 1960):60-79. Reprinted
in *Discussions of Charles Dickens*, ed. W. R. Clark, 1961 q.v.;
Assessing Great Expectations, ed. R. Lettis and W. E. Morris, 1963
q.v.; *Victorian Literature*, ed. R. O. Preyer. New York: Harper and
Row, 1967.

2954 CARLTON, WILLIAM J. "The Strange Story of Thomas Mitton."
Dickensian 56 (Sept. 1960):141-52.

2955 MONOD, SYLVÈRE. "*Great Expectations*: A Hundred Years After."
Dickensian 56 (Sept. 1960):133-40.

2956 LANE, LAURIAT, Jr. "On *Great Expectations*." *Great Expectations*,
601-23. New York: Harper, 1961.

2957 VANDE KIEFT, RUTH M. "Patterns of Communication in *Great
Expectations*." *Nineteenth Century Fiction* 15 (Mar. 1961):325-34.
Reprinted in *Assessing* Great Expectations, ed. R. Lettis and W. E.
Morris, 1963 q.v.

2958 FORKER, CHARLES R. "The Language of Hands in *Great
Expectations*." *Texas Studies in Literature and Language* 3
(Summer 1961):280-93.

2959 FIELDING, KENNETH J. "The Critical Autonomy of *Great
Expectations*." *Review of English Literature* 2 (July 1961):75-88.

2960 CLINTON-BADDELEY, V. C. "Wopsle." *Dickensian* 57 (Sept. 1961):
150-59.

2961 COOLIDGE, ARCHIBALD C., Jr. "*Great Expectations*: the
Culmination of a Developing Art." *Mississippi Quarterly* 14
(Fall 1961):190-96.

2962 LINDBERG, JOHN. "Individual Conscience and Social Injustice in
Great Expectations." *College English* 23 (Nov. 1961):118-22.
Reprinted in *Assessing* Great Expectations, ed. R. Lettis and W. E.
Morris, 1963 q.v.

2963 PARTLOW, ROBERT B., Jr. "The Moving I: A Study of the Point of View in *Great Expectations.*" *College English* 23 (Nov. 1961): 122-31. Reprinted in *Assessing* Great Expectations, ed. R. Lettis and W. E. Morris, 1963 q.v.

2964 CHAPMAN, FRANK. "Introduction." *Great Expectations.* New York: Collier Books, 1962.

2965 ENGEL, MONROE. "Introduction." *Great Expectations.* (Riverside edition.) Boston: Houghton Mifflin, 1962.

2966 RICKS, CHRISTOPHER. *"Great Expectations." Dickens and the Twentieth Century,* ed. J. Gross and G. Pearson, 199-211. London: Routledge and K. Paul, 1962.

2967 GOLDFARB, RUSSELL M. "The Menu of *Great Expectations.*" *Victorian Newsletter* 21 (Spring 1962):18-19.

2968 STONE, HARRY. "Fire, Hand, and Gate: Dickens' *Great Expectations.*" *Kenyon Review* 24 (Autumn 1962):662-91.

2969 PARISH, CHARLES. "A Boy Brought Up 'By Hand'." *Nineteenth Century Fiction* 17 (Dec. 1962):286-88.

2970 DREW, ELIZABETH A. "Charles Dickens 1812-1870: *Great Expectations.*" *The Novel,* 191-207. New York: Norton, 1963.

2971 LETTIS, RICHARD and WILLIAM E. MORRIS, eds. *Assessing* Great Expectations: Materials for Analysis. San Francisco: Chandler, [1963].

2972 McKEE, CATHERINE. "Introduction." *Great Expectations.* Evanston, Ill.: Harper and Row, 1963.

2973 ROLL-HANSEN, DIDERIK. "Characters and Contrasts in *Great Expectations.*" *The Hidden Sense, and Other Essays,* ed. Maren-Sofie Røstvig, et al., 197-226. (Norwegian Studies in English 9.) Oslo: Universitesforlaget; New York: Humanities Press, 1963.

2974 WILSON, ANGUS. "Afterword." *Great Expectations.* New York: New American Library, 1963.

2975 WATERS, EDGAR. "A Possible Australian Source For Miss Havisham." *Australian Literary Studies* 1 (June 1963):134-36.

2976 MARSHALL, WILLIAM H. "The Conclusion of *Great Expectations* as the Fulfilment of Myth." *Personalist* 44 (July 1963):337-47.

2977 HYNES, JOSEPH A. "Image and Symbol in *Great Expectations.*" *Journal of English Literary History* 30 (Sept. 1963):258-92.

2978 LEVINE, GEORGE. "Communication in *Great Expectations.*" *Nineteenth Century Fiction* 18 (Sept. 1963):175-81.

2979 HARDY, BARBARA. "Work in Progress IV: Food and Ceremony in *Great Expectations.*" *Essays in Criticism* 13 (Oct. 1963):351-63.

2980 RYAN, J. S. "A Possible Australian Source for Miss Havisham." *Australian Literary Studies* 1 (Dec. 1963):134-36.

2981 CROMPTON, LOUIS. "Introduction." *Great Expectations*. Indianapolis: Bobbs-Merrill, 1964.

2982 ROSSER, G. C. "Critical Commentary." [Introduction.] *Great Expectations*. London: Univ. of London Press, 1964.

2983 THOMAS, R. GEORGE. *Charles Dickens*: Great Expectations. London: E. Arnold, 1964.

2984 DENEAU, DANIEL P. "Pip's Age and Other Notes on *Great Expectations*." *Dickensian* 60 (Jan. 1964):27-29.

2985 MARCUS, MORDECAI. "The Pattern of Self-Alienation in *Great Expectations*." *Victorian Newsletter* 26 (Spring 1964):9-12.

2986 VASTA, EDWARD. "*Great Expectations* and *The Great Gatsby*." *Dickensian* 60 (Sept. 1964):167-72.

2987 CALDER, ANGUS. "Introduction." *Great Expectations*. Harmondsworth, Eng.: Penguin, 1965.

2988 GILLIE, CHRISTOPHER. "Pip of *Great Expectations*." *Character in English Literature*, 156-63. New York: Barnes and Noble, 1965.

2989 McMASTER, ROWLAND D. "Introduction." *Great Expectations*. Toronto: Macmillan, 1965.

2990 WAGENKNECHT, EDWARD. "*Great Expectations*." *Dickens and the Scandal-Mongers*, 132-36. Norman: Univ. of Oklahoma Press, 1965.

2991 JACOBSON, DAN. "Out of Empire." *New Statesman* 69 (Jan. 1965):153-54.

2992 MOORE, JACK B. "Hearts and Hands in *Great Expectations*." *Dickensian* 61 (Jan. 1965):52-56.

2993 PEYROUTON, NOEL C. "John Wemmick: Enigma?" *Dickens Studies* 1 (Jan. 1965):39-47.

2994 BELL, VEREEN M. "Parents and Children in *Great Expectations*." *Victorian Newsletter* 27 (Spring 1965):21-24.

2995 MEISEL, MARTIN. "The Ending of *Great Expectations*." *Essays in Criticism* 15 (July 1965):326-31.

2996 LEVINE, M. H. "Hand and Hearts in *Great Expectations*." *Ball State University Forum* 6 (Autumn 1965):22-24.

2997 KENNEDY, RICHARD S. "*Great Expectations* in the Classroom." *College Languages Association Journal* 9 (Dec. 1965):165-70.

2998 RIDLAND, J. M. "Huck, Pip and Plot." *Nineteenth Century Fiction* 20 (Dec. 1965):286-90.

2999 BARNES, RICHARD J. *A Critical Commentary on Dickens'* Great Expectations. London: Macmillan, 1966.

3000 RODRIGUES, EUSEBIO L. "The Dickens of *Great Expectations*." *Literary Criterion* 7 (1966):41-53.

3001 HALLAM, CLIFFORD B. "The Structure of *Great Expectations* in Respect to Style and Artistry." *Dickens Studies* 2 (Jan. 1966):26-32.

3002 FINKEL, ROBERT J. "Another Boy Brought Up 'By Hand'." *Nineteenth Century Fiction* 20 (Mar. 1966):389-90.

3003 BORT, BARRY D. "Trabb's Boy and Orlick." *Victorian Newsletter* 29 (Spring 1966):27-28.

3004 MARCUS, PHILLIP L. "Theme and Suspense in the Plot of *Great Expectations*." *Dickens Studies* 2 (May 1966):57-73.

3005 MEISEL, MARTIN. "Miss Havisham Brought to Book." *PMLA* 81 (June 1966):278-85.

3006 REEVES, BRUCE. "Pipes and Pipe-Smoking in *Great Expectations*." *Dickensian* 62 (Sept. 1966):174-78.

3007 WENTERSDORF, KARL P. "Mirror-Images in *Great Expectations*." *Nineteenth Century Fiction* 21 (Dec. 1966):203-24.

3008 DUNN, RICHARD J. "Drummle and Startop: Doubling in *Great Expectations*." *Dickensian* 63 (Jan. 1967):125-27.

3009 ENDICOTT, ANNABEL. "Pip, Philip and Astrophil: Dickens's Debt to Sidney?" *Dickensian* 63 (Sept. 1967):158-62.

3010 NEW, WILLIAM H. "The Four Elements in *Great Expectations*." *Dickens Studies* 3 (Oct. 1967):111-21.

3011 CROUCH, W. GEORGE. *Critical Study Guide to Dickens'* Great Expectations. Totowa, NJ: Littlefield, Adams, 1968.

3012 BARRY, JAMES D. "Wopsle Once More." *Dickensian* 64 (Jan. 1968): 43-47.

3013 SWEENEY, PATRICIA R. "Mr House, Mr Thackeray and Mr Pirrip: The Question of Snobbery in *Great Expectations*." *Dickensian* 64 (Jan. 1968):55-63.

3014 STONE, HARRY. "Dickens' Woman in White." *Victorian Newsletter* 33 (Spring 1968):5-8.

3015 STONE, HARRY. "The Genesis of a Novel: *Great Expectations*." *Charles Dickens 1812-1870,* ed. E. W. F. Tomlin, 109-31. London: Weidenfeld and Nicolson, 1969.

3016 GORDON, ANDREW. "Jaggers and the Moral Scheme of *Great Expectations*." *Dickensian* 65 (Jan. 1969):3-11.

3017 SIMMONS, S. "Pip: A Love Affair." *English Journal* 58 (Mar. 1969):416-17.

OUR MUTUAL FRIEND

3018 CHORLEY, HENRY F. *"Our Mutual Friend." Athenaeum* (Oct. 28, 1865):569-70. Reprinted in *Dickensian* 4 (Jan. 1908): 5-8.

3019 *"Our Mutual Friend." Examiner* (Oct. 28, 1865):681-82.

3020 "Mr Dickens's Romance of a Dust Heap." *Eclectic Review* 9 (Nov. 1865):455-76.

3021 *"Our Mutual Friend." Saturday Review* 20 (Nov. 11, 1865):612-13.

3022 JAMES, HENRY. *"Our Mutual Friend." Nation* 1 (Dec. 1865): 786-87. Reprinted as "The Limitations of Dickens," *Views and Reviews.* Boston: Ball, 1908; *The Dickens Critics,* ed. G. H. Ford and L. Lane, Jr., 1961 q.v.

3023 "Belles Lettres." *Westminster Review* 85 (Apr. 1866):582-98.

3024 FIELD, KATE. *"Our Mutual Friend* in Manuscript." *Scribner's Monthly Magazine* 8 (Aug. 1874):472-75.

3025 PHILIPSON, DAVID. *The Jew in English Fiction.* Cincinnati: R. Clarke, 1889.

3026 STOCKTON, FRANK R. "My Favorite Novelist and His Best Book." *Munsey's Magazine* 17 (1897).

3027 MINIKEN, EMILIE M. "Betty Higden." *Dickensian* 4 (Sept. 1908): 229-33.

3028 CALISCH, RABBI EDWARD N. *The Jew in English Literature, as Author and as Subject.* Richmond, Va.: Bell Book and Stationery, 1909.

3029 De MORGAN, WILLIAM F. "Introduction." *Our Mutual Friend.* Waverley edition. London: Waverley Book Co., 1913-15. Reprinted as "Dickens' Best Story" in *The Bookman Extra Number* (1914).

3030 "Fagin and Riah." *Dickensian* 17 (July 1921):144-52.

3031 MIDGLEY, MARION. *"Our Mutual Friend* – Why It Is My Favorite Book." *Dickensian* 17 (Oct. 1921):200-6.

3032 CAMPBELL, EVA M. "On the Title, *Our Mutual Friend." Modern Language Notes* 38 (Apr. 1923):250-51.

3033 PENDERED, MARY L. "Twemlow, Knight of the Simple Heart." *Dickensian* 24 (Dec. 1927):16-22.

3034 DAVIS, HELEN I. "When Charles Dickens Atoned: the Story of his Sinister Character Fagin Which he Offset with the Benign Figure of Riah." *American Hebrew* 122 (May 1928):980, 1008, 1024-25.

3035 DAVIS, SAMUEL. "Chesterton and *Our Mutual Friend." Dickensian* 33 (Winter 1936-37):41-46.

3036 EVANS, MABEL. "The Tragedy of Gaffer Hexam." *Dickensian* 34 (Summer 1938):171-74.

3037 NEWMAN, V. M. "The Most Human Heroine." *Dickensian* 38 (June 1942):181-82. [Bella Wilfer.]

3038 BOLL, ERNEST M. "The Plotting of *Our Mutual Friend." Modern Philology* 42 (Nov. 1944):96-101.

3039 R., V. "Dickens and a Classical Reference." *Notes and Queries* 188
      (June 1945):232-33.

3040 WELPLY, W. H. "Railway Signals." *Notes and Queries* 190
      (June 1946):260.

3041 FELLOWS, REGINALD B. "Railway Signals." *Notes and Queries*
      191 (July 1946):21; (Oct. 1946):152; (Nov. 1946):218.

3042 WULCKO, LAWRANCE M. "Railway Signals." *Notes and Queries*
      191 (Aug. 1946):64-65.

3043 MABBOTT, THOMAS O. "Railway Signals." *Notes and Queries* 191
      (Sept. 1946):129.

3044 HILL, THOMAS W. "Betty." *Dickensian* 43 (Dec. 1946):41-42.
      [Betty Higden.]

3045 YOUNG, GEORGE F. "Noddy Boffin's Misers." *Dickensian* 43
      (Dec. 1946):14-17.

3046 HILL, THOMAS W. "Notes to *Our Mutual Friend*." *Dickensian* 43
      (Mar. 1947):85-90.

3047 MORSE, ROBERT. *"Our Mutual Friend."* *Partisan Review* 16
      (Mar. 1949):277-89. Reprinted in *The Dickens Critics*, ed. G. H.
      Ford and L. Lane, Jr., 1961 q.v.; *Dickens: Modern Judgements*, ed.
      A. E. Dyson, 1968 q.v.

3048 KLOTS, ALLEN, Jr. "Introduction." *Our Mutual Friend*. New York:
      Dodd, Mead, 1951.

3049 DAVIES, E. SALTER. "Introduction." *Our Mutual Friend*. New
      Oxford Illustrated Dickens. London: Oxford Univ. Press, 1952.

3050 QUENNELL, PETER C. *"Our Mutual Friend."* *The Singular
      Preference*, 152-58. London: Collins, 1952.

3051 MORLEY, MALCOLM. "Enter *Our Mutual Friend*." *Dickensian* 52
      (Dec. 1955):39-43.

3052 PRIESTLEY, J. B. "Introduction." *Our Mutual Friend*. London:
      Macdonald, 1957.

3053 WEINTRAUB, STANLEY. "Ibsen's 'Dolls' House' Metaphor Fore-
      shadowed in Victorian Fiction." *Nineteenth Century Fiction* 13
      (June 1958):67-69.

3054 JEROME, JEROME K. "Introduction." *Our Mutual Friend*. London:
      Collins, 1959. [Edition date.]

3055 STONE, HARRY. "Dickens and the Jews." *Victorian Studies* 2
      (Mar. 1959):223-53; 3 (June 1960):459-60.

3056 ENGEL, MONROE. "Introduction." *Our Mutual Friend*. New York:
      Modern Library, 1960.

3057 McMASTER, ROWLAND D. "Birds of Prey: A Study of *Our Mutual
      Friend*." *Dalhousie Review* 40 (Autumn 1960):372-81.

3058 STONE, HARRY. "From Fagin to Riah: Jews and the Victorian Novel." *Midstream* 6 (Winter 1960):21-37.

3059 SHEA, Fr. FRANCIS X., S. J. "The Text of *Our Mutual Friend*: A Study of the Variations Between the Copy Text and the First Printed Edition." *DA* 22 (1961):2007 (Minnesota). [Dissertation.]

3060 SHARP, SISTER M. CORONA. "The Archetypal Feminine: *Our Mutual Friend.*" *Univ. of Kansas City Review* 27 (Summer 1961): 307-11.

3061 BARNARD, ROBERT. "The Choral Symphony: *Our Mutual Friend.*" *Review of English Literature* 2 (July 1961):89-99.

3062 SHARP, SISTER M. CORONA. "A Study of the Archetypal Feminine: *Our Mutual Friend.*" *Univ. of Kansas City Review* 28 (Autumn 1961):74-80.

3063 KETTLE, ARNOLD. *"Our Mutual Friend." Dickens and the Twentieth Century*, ed. J. Gross and G. Pearson, 213-25. London: Routledge and K. Paul, 1962.

3064 HOBSBAUM, PHILIP. "The Critics and *Our Mutual Friend.*" *Essays in Criticism* 13 (July 1963):231-40.

3065 LANHAM, RICHARD A. *"Our Mutual Friend:* The Birds of Prey." *Victorian Newsletter* 24 (Fall 1963):6-12.

3066 LE VOT, A. E. *"Our Mutual Friend* and *The Great Gatsby.*" *Fitzgerald Newsletter* 20 (Winter 1963):1-4.

3067 MILLER, J. HILLIS. "Afterword." *Our Mutual Friend.* New York: New American Library, 1964. Reprinted as *"Our Mutual Friend,"* in *Dickens: A Collection of Critical Essays*, ed. M. Price, 1967 q.v.

3068 THOMPSON, LESLIE M. "The Masks of Pride in *Our Mutual Friend.*" *Dickensian* 60 (May 1964):124-28.

3069 MIYOSHI, MASAO. "Resolution of Identity in *Our Mutual Friend.*" *Victorian Newsletter* 26 (Fall 1964):5-9.

3070 O'LEARY, SISTER JEANINE. "The Function of City as Setting in Dickens's *Our Mutual Friend*, Trollope's *The Way we Live Now*, James's *The Princess Casamassima*, and Conrad's *The Secret Agent.*" *DA* 26 (1965):6048-49 (Notre Dame). [Dissertation.]

3071 WRIGHT, AUSTIN. *"Our Mutual Friend* a Century Later." *Carnegie Magazine* 39 (Jan. 1965):29-31.

3072 NELSON, HARLAND S. "Dickens's *Our Mutual Friend* and Henry Mayhew's *London Labour and the London Poor.*" *Nineteenth Century Fiction* 20 (Dec. 1965):207-22.

3073 MUIR, KENNETH. "Image and Structure in *Our Mutual Friend.*" *Essays and Studies* 19 (1966):92-105.

3074 GIBSON, FRANK A. "The 'Impossible' Riah." *Dickensian* 62 (May 1966):118-19.

3075 WINTERS, WARRINGTON. "Charles Dickens: *Our Mutual Friend.*"
     North Dakota Quarterly 34 (Autumn 1966):96-99.

3076 SHEA, Fr. FRANCIS X., S. J. "No Change of Intention in *Our Mutual
     Friend.*" *Dickensian* 63 (Jan. 1967):37-40.

3077 SHEA, Fr. FRANCIS X., S. J. "Mr Venus Observed: the Plot Change
     in *Our Mutual Friend.*" *Papers on Language and Literature* 4
     (Spring 1968):170-81.

3078 GARDNER, JOSEPH H. "Gaffer Hexam and Pap Finn." *Modern
     Philology* 66 (Nov. 1968):155-56.

3079 COLLINS, THOMAS J. "Some Mutual Sets of Friends: Moral
     Monitors in *Emma* and *Our Mutual Friend.*" *Dickensian* 65
     (Jan. 1969):32-34.

3080 PAGE, NORMAN. "'A language fit for heroes': Speech in *Oliver
     Twist* and *Our Mutual Friend.*" *Dickensian* 65 (May 1969):100-7.

EDWIN DROOD

3081 LAWRENNY, H. *"Edwin Drood." Academy* (Oct. 22, 1870):1-3.

3082 JAMES, THOMAS P. "Medium's Preface." *The Mystery of Edwin
     Drood.* Brattleboro, Vt.: T. P. James, 1873. [By the spirit-pen of
     Charles Dickens, through a medium.]

3083 MEYNELL, ALICE. "How *Edwin Drood* was Illustrated." *Century
     Magazine* 27 (Feb. 1884):522-28.

3084 PROCTOR, RICHARD A. *Watched by the Dead: A Loving Study of
     Dickens' Half-told Tale.* London: W. H. Allen, 1887.

3085 LANG, ANDREW. *The Puzzle of Dickens's Last Plot.* London:
     Chapman and Hall, 1905.

3086 WALTERS, J. CUMING. *Clues to Dickens's* Mystery of Edwin Drood
     London: Chapman and Hall, 1905.

3087 MATZ, BERTRAM W. "Solving *The Mystery of Edwin Drood.*"
     Dickensian 1 (July 1905):184-85.

3088 GADD, GEORGE F. "The History of a Mystery: A Review of the
     Solutions to *Edwin Drood.*" *Dickensian* 1 (Sept. 1905):240-43;
     (Oct. 1905):270-73; (Nov. 1905):293-96; (Dec. 1905):320-23.

3089 FILDES, LUKE. "The Mysteries of *Edwin Drood.*" *Times* (Nov. 3,
     1905):373. Replies by A. Lang and J. W. T. Ley, *Times* (Nov. 10,
     1905, Nov. 21, 1905).

3090 GADD, GEORGE F. "'Datchery, the Enigma.' The Case for Tartar."
     Dickensian 2 (Jan. 1906):13-16.

3091 PERUGINI, KATE DICKENS. *"Edwin Drood* and the Last Days of
     Charles Dickens." *Pall Mall Magazine* 37 (June 1906):643-52.

3092 CHARLES, EDWIN. *Keys to the* Drood *Mystery.* London: Collins,
     1908, 1915.

3093 MATCHETT, WILLOUGHBY. "Mr Datchery." *Dickensian* 4
      (Jan. 1908):17-21.

3094 MATZ, BERTRAM W. "*The Mystery of Edwin Drood*: Dickens'
      Half-told Tale." *Bookman* 33 (Mar. 1908):229-40.

3095 WALTERS, J. CUMING. "Desultory Thoughts on *Drood*."
      Dickensian 4 (Mar. 1908):65-68.

3096 JACKSON, HENRY. *About* Edwin Drood. Cambridge, Eng.: The
      University Press, 1911.

3097 WALTERS, J. CUMING. "*Drood* and Datchery." *Dickensian* 7
      (Mar. 1911):61-63.

3098 MATZ, BERTRAM W. "*The Mystery of Edwin Drood*: a Bibliography."
      Dickensian 7 (May 1911):130-33.

3099 NICOLL, SIR WILLIAM R. *The Problem of* Edwin Drood. London:
      Hodder and Stoughton, 1912.

3100 WALTERS, J. CUMING. *The Complete Mystery of* Edwin Drood ...
      The History, Continuations, and Solutions (1870-1912). London:
      Chapman and Hall, 1912.

3101 WALTERS, J. CUMING. "Andrew Lang and Dickens's Puzzles."
      Dickensian 8 (Sept. 1912):229-32.

3102 FENNELL, CHARLES A. *"The Opium-Woman" and "Datchery"*
      in The Mystery of Edwin Drood. London: Simpkin, Marshall;
      Cambridge, Eng.: E. Johnson, 1913.

3103 KING, PETER. "The Secret of the *Drood* Mystery." *Dickensian* 9
      (May 1913):121-24.

3104 VACHELL, HORACE A. "Introduction." *Edwin Drood.* Waverley
      edition. London: Waverley Book Co., 1913-15.

3105 LEY, J. W. T. *Trial of John Jasper* [Lay Precentor of Cloisterham
      Cathedral ... for the Murder of Edwin Drood, Engineer.] London:
      Chapman and Hall, 1914.

3106 SAUNDERS, MONTAGU. *The Mystery in the* Drood *Family.*
      Cambridge, Eng.: Cambridge Univ. Press, 1914.

3107 MATCHETT, WILLOUGHBY. "A Talk Round *Drood*." *Dickensian*
      10 (Jan. 1914):11-14; (Feb. 1914):45-48; (Mar. 1914):61-66.

3108 WALTERS, J. CUMING. "The *Drood* Trial Reviewed." *British
      Weekly* (Jan. 15, 1914). Reprinted in *Dickensian* 10 (Feb. 1914):
      42-44.

3109 WALTERS, J. CUMING. "*Edwin Drood* Continued." *Dickensian* 10
      (Sept. 1914):238-41.

3110 WALTERS, J. CUMING. "The 'Devotion' of John Jasper." *Dickensian*
      11 (Feb. 1915):37-41.

3111 SAUNDERS, MONTAGU. "The Mystery in the *Drood* Family."
       Dickensian 11 (Mar. 1915):65-67.

3112 SUDDABY, JOHN. "A Night Amongst the *Drood* Opium Dens."
       Dickensian 12 (Aug. 1916):210-14.

3113 KAVANAGH, MARY (M. M. Spain, pseud.). *A New Solution of*
       The Mystery of Edwin Drood. London: J. Lang, 1919, 1922. [With
       Dickens' text.]

3114 THE DICKENSIAN. Edwin Drood *Number.* 15 (Mar. 1919).

3115 CARDEN, PERCY T. "Datchery: The Case for Tartar Restated."
       Dickensian 15 (Oct. 1919):189-94.

3116 SAUNDERS, MONTAGU. "Dickens, *Drood* and Datchery."
       Dickensian 15 (Oct. 1919):182-88.

3117 SQUIRE, JOHN C. "The *Drood* Mystery Insoluble." *Dickensian* 15
       (Oct. 1919):195-96.

3118 WALTERS, J. CUMING. "*Drood* and Datchery." *Dickensian* 15
       (Oct. 1919):177-81.

3119 CARDEN, PERCY T. *The Murder of Edwin Drood.* Recounted by
       John Jasper; being an attempted solution of the mystery based on
       Dickens' manuscript and memoranda. With an introd. by B. W. Matz.
       New York: Putnam's, 1920.

3120 SQUIRE, JOHN C. "The Great Unfinished." *Life and Letters,* 173-79
       London: Hodder and Stoughton, 1920.

3121 ELLIS, M. A. "Predecessors of *Edwin Drood.*" *Notes and Queries*
       8 (Apr. 1921):349.

3122 BOYD, AUBREY. "A New Angle on the *Drood* Mystery." *Washington*
       University Studies: Humanistic Series 9 (Oct. 1921):35-85.

3123 MATZ, BERTRAM W. "The Murder of *Edwin Drood.*" *Times*
       Literary Supplement (Nov. 15, 1923):770.

3124 SMITH, HARRY B. "Sherlock Holmes Solves *The Mystery of Edwin*
       Drood." *Munsey's Magazine* 83 (Dec. 1924):385-400. Reprinted as
       How Sherlock Holmes Solved The Mystery of Edwin Drood. Glenrock
       Pa.: W. Klinefelter, 1934.

3125 LEAVER, HAROLD R. *The Mystery of John Jasper.* Edmonton,
       Alta.: the Author, 1925.

3126 BECKER, MAY L. "The Reader's Guide." *Saturday Review of*
       Literature 1 (Apr. 4, 1925):653. [Survey and review of continuations
       and scholarly studies of *Edwin Drood.*]

3127 CONWAY, EUSTACE. "*The Mystery of Edwin Drood.*" *Anthony*
       Munday and Other Essays, 79-99. New York: Privately printed, 1927.

3128 AYLMER, FELIX. "The Sapsea Tomb." *Dickensian* 23 (June 1927):
       177-79.

3129 GADD, W. LAURENCE. "Modern Writers of Mystery Stories and *Edwin Drood.*" *Dickensian* 24 (June 1928):223-24.

3130 MATZ, WINIFRED, comp. "A Bibliography of *Edwin Drood.*" *Dickensian* 24 (Summer 1928):236; (Autumn 1928):301-2; 25 (Winter 1928-29):42-44; (Spring 1929):185-87. [Continued from bibliography in Nicoll, *The Problem of Edwin Drood*, 1912 q.v.]

3131 JAMIESON, H. W. and F. M. B. ROSENTHAL. "*Mystery of Edwin Drood*: New Keys That Fit." *Dickensian* 25 (Dec. 1928):28-36.

3132 CHESTERTON, GILBERT K. "On *Edwin Drood.*" *Generally Speaking*, 261-67. New York: Dodd, Mead, 1929.

3133 EVERETT, EDWARD S. "The Cloisterham Murder Case." *Fred Newton Scott Anniversary Papers*, 157-74. Chicago: Univ. of Chicago Press, 1929.

3134 DEXTER, WALTER. "New Light on *Edwin Drood* (the Illustrations)." *Sphere* (Feb. 9, 1929).

3135 LEHMANN-HAUPT, C. F. "New Facts Concerning *Edwin Drood.*" *Dickensian* 25 (Summer 1929):165-75.

3136 DUFFIELD, HOWARD. "John Jasper – Strangler." *American Bookman* 70 (Feb. 1930):581-88.

3137 CARDEN, PERCY T. "Dickens's 'Number Plans' for *The Mystery of Edwin Drood.*" *Dickensian* 27 (Summer 1931):183-85; (Autumn 1931):266-69, 284-85, 300-1.

3138 RINES, EDWARD F. "The Technique of *Edwin Drood.*" *Dickensian* 28 (Spring 1932):105-10; (Autumn 1932):287-89.

3139 HOPKINS, ALBERT A. "A Notable *Drood* Collection." *Dickensian* 28 (Summer 1932):231-34.

3140 SANDERS, E. L. "The Technique of *Edwin Drood*: a Rejoinder." *Dickensian* 28 (Summer 1932):190-92.

3141 ALEXANDER, R. VANES. "Mr Sapsea The Murderer Of Edwin Drood." *Dickensian* 29 (Summer 1933):217-19.

3142 DUFFIELD, HOWARD. "*Edwin Drood.*" *Times Literary Supplement* (May 31, 1934):392.

3143 CARDEN, PERCY T. "*Edwin Drood.*" *Times Literary Supplement* (June 14, 1934):424.

3144 DUFFIELD, HOWARD. "The Macbeth Motif in *Edwin Drood.*" *Dickensian* 30 (Sept. 1934):263-71.

3145 THOMPSON, CHARLES W. "The Track of Edwin Drood." *Catholic World* 140 (Oct. 1934):51-58. [The mystery is not the murder, but events "long anterior to it."]

3146 LEHMANN-HAUPT, C. F. "Studies on *Edwin Drood.*" *Dickensian* 31 (Autumn 1935):299-305; 32 (Winter 1935-36):29-34;

Spring 1936):135-37; (Summer 1936):219-20; (Autumn 1936): 301-6; 33 (Winter 1936-37):57-62.

3147 CLARK, W. A. "*Edwin Drood* Again." *Dickensian* 33 (June 1937): 191-95.

3148 RUBOW, PAUL V. *"The Mystery of Edwin Drood."* Nationaltidende (Oct. 24, 1937):13.

3149 ROE, FRANK G. "The *Edwin Drood* Mystery: An American Gift to London." *Connoisseur* 104 (Nov. 1939):227-31.

3150 WILSON, EDMUND. *"The Mystery of Edwin Drood." New Republic* 102 (Apr. 1940):463-67.

3151 STARRETT, VINCENT. "Introduction." *Edwin Drood.* New York: Heritage, 1941.

3152 PRITCHETT, V. S. *"Edwin Drood." New Statesman* 27 (Feb. 1944): 143. Reprinted in *The Living Novel.* New York: Random House, 1964. [Rev. ed.]

3153 C., D. "A Mystery of *Edwin Drood.*" *Notes and Queries* 186 (Mar. 1944):131-33; 186 (Apr. 1944):184.

3154 HILL, THOMAS W. "*Drood* Time in Cloisterham." *Dickensian* 40 (June 1944):113-17.

3155 HILL, THOMAS W. "Notes on *The Mystery of Edwin Drood.*" *Dickensian* 40 (Sept. 1944):198-204; 41 (Dec. 1944):30-37.

3156 MILLS, WALTER W. *Historical and Critical Notes on Charles Dickens' Unfinished Novel,* The Mystery of Edwin Drood. Together with a synopsis for the continuation and completion of the story. London, 1947. [Typewritten, ff. 17.]

3157 BAKER, RICHARD M. "Who was Dick Datchery? A Study for Droodians." *Nineteenth Century Fiction* 2 (Mar. 1948):201-22; 3 (June 1948):35-53. Reprinted in *The Drood Murder Case,* 1951 q.v.

3158 BAKER, RICHARD M. "John Jasper – Murderer." *Trollopian* 3 (Sept. 1948):99-118; (Dec. 1948):177-99. Reprinted in *The Drood Murder Case,* 1951 q.v.

3159 WINTERS, WARRINGTON. "Dickens and the Psychology of Dreams." *PMLA* 63 (Sept. 1948):984-1006.

3160 BAKER, RICHARD M. "The Genesis of *Edwin Drood.*" *Nineteenth Century Fiction* 3 (Mar. 1949):281-95; 4 (June 1949):37-50. Reprinted in *The Drood Murder Case,* 1951 q.v.

3161 BAKER, RICHARD M. "The Datchery Assumption: Reply." *Nineteenth Century Fiction* 4 (June 1949):77-81.

3162 MacVICAR, H. M. "The Datchery Assumption: Expostulation." *Nineteenth Century Fiction* 4 (June 1949):75-77.

3163 BAKER, RICHARD M. "Was Edwin Drood Murdered?" *Nineteenth Century Fiction* 4 (Sept. 1949):111-28; (Dec. 1949):221-36. Reprinted in *The Drood Murder Case,* 1951 q.v.

3164 STEWART, JOHN INNES M. (Michael Innes, pseud.). "Introduction." *The Mystery of Edwin Drood.* London: John Lehmann, 1950.

3165 BAKER, RICHARD M. "What Might Have Been: A Study for Droodians." *Nineteenth Century Fiction* 4 (Mar. 1950):275-97; 5 (June 1950):47-65. Reprinted in *The Drood Murder Case,* 1951 q.v.

3166 WINSTEDT, E. O. "Helena Landless." *Note and Queries* 195 (July 1950):325.

3167 BAKER, RICHARD M. *The Drood Murder Case.* Five Studies in Dickens's *Edwin Drood.* Berkeley; Los Angeles: Univ. of California Press; London: Cambridge Univ. Press; Toronto: Oxford Univ. Press, 1951.

3168 AYLMER, FELIX. "First-Aid for the 'Drood' Audience." *Dickensian* 47 (June 1951):133-39. [Aylmer's "probable development of the plot" of *The Mystery of Edwin Drood.*]

3169 THIRKELL, ANGELA. "*Edwin Drood* on the Stage." *Dickensian* 47 (June 1951):130-32.

3170 FIELDING, KENNETH J. "*Edwin Drood* and Governor Eyre." *Listener* 48 (Dec. 1952):1083-84.

3171 FORD, GEORGE H. "Dickens's Notebook and *Edwin Drood.*" *Nineteenth Century Fiction* 6 (Dec. 1952):275-80.

3172 FIELDING, KENNETH J. "The Dramatization of *Edwin Drood.*" *Theatre Notebook* 7 (Apr.-June 1953):52-58. Reply: Eric Jones-Evans 8 (Oct.-Dec. 1954):24.

3173 BLEIFUSS, WILLIAM W. "A Re-examination of *Edwin Drood.*" *Dickensian* 50 (June 1954):110-15; 50 (Sept. 1954):176-86; (Dec. 1954):24-29.

3174 BENGIS, NATHAN L. "Sherlock Holmes and The *Edwin Drood* Mystery." *Baker Street Journal* 5 (Jan. 1955):5-12.

3175 BREND, GAVIN. "A Re-examination of *Edwin Drood.*" *Dickensian* 51 (Mar. 1955):87-88.

3176 PAKENHAM, PANSY. "The Memorandum Book, Forster and *Edwin Drood.*" *Dickensian* 51 (June 1955):117-21.

3177 BLAKENEY, T. S. "Problems of *Edwin Drood.*" *Dickensian* 51 (Sept. 1955):182-85.

3178 BREND, GAVIN. "*Edwin Drood* and the Four Witnesses." *Dickensian* 52 (Dec. 1955):20-24.

3179 LEWIS, CECIL DAY. "Introduction." *The Mystery of Edwin Drood.* London: Collins, 1956. [Edition date.]

3180 ROBERTS, S. C. "Introduction." *The Mystery of Edwin Drood.*
New Oxford Illustrated Dickens. London: Oxford Univ. Press, 1956.

3181 MORLEY, MALCOLM. "Stage Solutions to *The Mystery of Edwin
Drood.*" *Dickensian* 53 (Jan. 1957):46-48; (May 1957):93-97;
(Sept. 1957):180-84.

3182 GREENHALGH, MOLLIE. "*Edwin Drood:* The Twilight of a God."
Dickensian 55 (May 1959):68-75.

3183 WRIGHT, JAMES. "Afterword." *The Mystery of Edwin Drood.*
New York: Doubleday, 1961. Reprinted as *"The Mystery of Edwin
Drood."* in *Dickens: Modern Judgements,* ed. A. E. Dyson, 1968 q.v.

3184 COCKSHUT, A. O. J. *"Edwin Drood:* Early and Late Dickens
Reconciled." *Dickens and the Twentieth Century,* ed. J. Gross and
G. Pearson, 227-38. London: Routledge and K. Paul, 1962.

3185 COX, ARTHUR J. "The Morals of *Edwin Drood.*" *Dickensian* 58
(Jan. 1962):32-42.

3186 AYLMER, FELIX. *The* Drood *Case.* London: R. Hart-Davis, 1964;
New York: Barnes and Noble, 1965.

3187 WILLIAMS, CHARLES. "Supplementary Note." [Introduction.]
The Mystery of Edwin Drood. London: Oxford Univ. Press, 1964.

3188 COLLINS, PHILIP A. W. "Inspector Bucket Visits the Princess
Puffer." *Dickensian* 60 (Spring 1964):88-90.

3189 COX, ARTHUR J. "The *Drood* Remains." *Dickens Studies* 2
(Jan. 1966):33-44.

3190 MITCHELL, CHARLES. "*The Mystery of Edwin Drood:* The Interior
and Exterior of Self." *ELH* 33 (June 1966):228-46.

3191 BILHAM, D. M. "*Edwin Drood* – To Resolve a Mystery." *Dickensian*
62 (Sept. 1966):181-83.

3192 COX, ARTHUR J. "'If I hide my watch – '." *Dickens Studies* 3
(Mar. 1967):22-37.

3193 COHEN, JANE R. "Dickens's Artists and Artistry in *The Mystery
of Edwin Drood.*" *Dickens Studies* 3 (Oct. 1967):126-45.

3194 HAYTER, ALETHEA. "Some Writers Who Took Opium Occasionally
Opium and the Romantic Imagination, 295-96, 305. Berkeley; Los
Angeles: Univ. of California Press; London: Faber, 1968.

LETTERS

3195 "The Height of Impudence." *Brother Jonathan* 1 (Feb. 1842):239.
[Dickens sends note saying he cannot attend ball at Park Theatre,
attaches a letter from his physician.]

3196 "History of *Pickwick.*" *Athenaeum* (Mar. 31, 1866):430. Correction
to "History of *Pickwick*": (Apr. 7, 1866):464. [On the Seymour
claims.]

3197 HOGARTH, GEORGINA and MAMIE DICKENS, eds. *The Letters of Charles Dickens*. 2 vols. New York: Scribner's, 1879.

3198 HEAPHY, THOMAS. *A Wonderful Ghost Story*. With unpublished letters from Charles Dickens respecting it. London: Griffith and Farran, 1882. [Reprinted from *All Year Round*.]

3199 HUTTON, LAURENCE, ed. *Letters of Charles Dickens to Wilkie Collins, 1851-1870*. London: J. R. Osgood; New York: Harper, 1892.

3200 ANDREWS, WILLIAM L., ed. *A Stray Leaf From the Correspondence of Washington Irving and Charles Dickens*. New York: DeVinne Press, 1894.

3201 WILKINS, W. GLYDE, ed. *Some Letters of Charles Dickens*. Pittsburgh: Privately printed, 1907.

3202 *Charles Dickens and Maria Beadnell Private Correspondence*. Boston: Bibliophile Society, 1908.

3203 SUDDABY, JOHN. "The Death of Dickens's Little Dora: A Memorable Letter and Prayer." *Dickensian* 5 (Mar. 1909):61-65. [On the death of Dora Annie in 1851, with a letter and prayer by Dickens.]

3204 "Dickens and Jonathan Chapman." *Dickensian* 5 (Aug. 1909): 217-18. [Transcript of a letter from Dickens to Chapman, Mayor of Boston, dated Oct. 15, 1842.]

3205 *The Earliest Letters of Charles Dickens (Written to his Friend Henry Kolle)*. Cambridge, Mass.: The University Press, 1910.

3206 SMITH, HARRY B., ed. *The Dickens-Kolle Letters*. Boston: Bibliophile Society, 1910.

3207 "Dickens and Jonathan Chapman." *Dickensian* 6 (Aug. 1910): 212-14. [Three letters from Dickens to Chapman.]

3208 "Extracts from the Letters of Charles Dickens on American Slavery." *Americana* 5 (Sept.-Oct. 1910):979-80.

3209 LEHMANN, R. C., ed. *Charles Dickens as Editor, Being Letters Written by Him to William Henry Wills, His Sub-Editor*. London: Smith, Elder; New York: Sturgis and Walton, 1912.

3210 OTTO, K., ed. *Der Verlag Bernhard Tauchnitz 1837-1912*. Leipzig, 1912. [Letters to Dickens' German publisher.]

3211 ORR, LYNDON. "Charles Dickens as a Husband." *Bookman* (NY) 34 (Feb. 1912):627-30.

3212 "Charles Dickens to Leigh Hunt: An Interesting Letter." *Dickensian* 12 (Feb. 1916):40-41.

3213 WISE, T. J., ed. *Letters to Mark Lemon*. London: Privately printed, 1917.

3214 "A Letter From Dickens to C. Felton." *North American Review* 205
      (June 1917):955-58.

3215 CLARK, CUMBERLAND. *The Story of a Great Friendship: Dickens
      and Clarkson Stanfield.* With seven unpublished letters. London:
      Chiswick Press, 1918.

3216 WILLIAMS, STANLEY T. "The Letters of Charles Dickens. Part 2
      of The Founding of Main St." *North American Review* 216
      (July 1922):121-28.

3217 ELLIS, CHRISTOPHER H. "A Dickens Letter." *Times Literary
      Supplement* (Oct. 19, 1922):666. [A letter from Dickens to Lady
      Blessington, 1845.]

3218 DEXTER, WALTER, ed. *The Unpublished Letters of Charles Dickens
      to Mark Lemon.* London: Halton and T. Smith, 1927.

3219 WHITING, MARY B. "Mrs Trollope and an Unpublished Letter from
      Charles Dickens." *Bookman* 73 (Nov. 1927):104-6. [On Mrs
      Trollope's novels alongside those of Dickens, with letters from
      Dickens.]

3220 GILSON, J. P. "Letter 'to George Eliot'." *British Museum Quarterly*
      2, no. 4 (1928):69 facs.

3221 GODDEN, G. M. "Two Unpublished Letters of Elizabeth Barrett
      Browning and Charles Dickens." *Country Life* (May 12, 1928):703.

3222 YEATS-BROWN, F. "Dickens in Genoa." *Spectator* 141 (Sept. 1928,
      358. [Includes letters from Dickens to Angus Fletcher and Timothy
      Yeats-Brown.]

3223 *Dickens to His First Publisher, John Macrone.* Some Hitherto Un-
      published Letters. London: Privately printed for Walter Dexter, 1931

3224 MEYNELL, WILFRID, ed. *A Dickens Friendship Told in His Own
      Letters.* London: Privately printed, 1931.

3225 OSBORNE, CHARLES C., ed. "Letters of Charles Dickens to the
      Baroness Burdett-Coutts." *Cornhill Magazine* 70 (June 1931):641-57
      71 (July 1931):1-15; (Aug. 1931):129-41; (Sept. 1931):257-70;
      (Oct. 1931):385-401. Published as *Letters of Charles Dickens to the
      Baroness Burdett-Coutts.* London: J. Murray, 1931.

3226 DARWIN, BERNARD, ed. "Charles Dickens and His Oldest Friend."
      American Bookman 74 (Oct. 1931):146-56; (Nov. 1931):271-80;
      (Dec. 1931):429-39; (Jan.-Feb. 1932):526-36. [A series of "recently
      discovered Dickens letters.]

3227 DEXTER, WALTER, ed. *Dickens to His Oldest Friend: the Letters
      of a Lifetime from Charles Dickens to Thomas Beard.* London:
      Putnam, 1932.

3228 DEXTER, WALTER. "Dickens' Earliest Literary Friendship: Some Unpublished Letters to Harrison Ainsworth." *Dickensian* 28 (Summer 1932):173-79.

3229 *An American Friend of Dickens.* New York: T. F. Madigan, 1933. [Letters to Dr Elisha Bartlett.]

3230 LIVINGSTON, FLORA V., ed. *Charles Dickens's Letters to Charles Lever.* Cambridge, Mass.: Harvard Univ. Press; London: Milford, 1933.

3231 "A Further American Note: An Unpublished Letter of Dickens to Maclise." *Dickensian* 29 (Spring 1933):115-17.

3232 "Dickens's Correspondence with John Hullah. [Some New Light on His Early Dramatic Work.]" *Dickensian* 29 (Sept. 1933):257-65; 30 (Dec. 1933):17-22.

3233 MABBOTT, THOMAS O. "Correspondence of John Tomlin: Letters from Dickens." *Notes and Queries* 166 (Jan. 1934):6-7.

3234 DEXTER, WALTER, ed. "Dickens's First Publisher. More Correspondence with John Macrone Hitherto Unpublished." *Dickensian* 30 (Mar. 1934):135-43; (June 1934):163-72.

3235 SUZANNET, ALAIN de. "The Letters of Dickens to F. D. Finlay. With Notes by A. de Suzannet." *Dickensian* 30 (Sept. 1934):273-82.

3236 DEXTER, WALTER. "Dickens and *The Morning Chronicle:* Unpublished Letters." *Fortnightly Review* 142 (Nov. 1934):591-98.

3237 DEXTER, WALTER, ed. *Mr and Mrs Charles Dickens: His Letters to Her.* London: Constable, 1935.

3238 DEXTER, WALTER, ed. *The Love Romance of Charles Dickens, Told in His Letters to Maria Beadnell (Mrs Winter).* London: Argonaut, 1936.

3239 "Some Dickens Letters About *Pickwick.*" *Dickensian* 32 (Spring 1936):118-25.

3240 "An Amusing Letter to Georgina Hogarth." *Dickensian* 33 (Mar. 1937):101-2. [A letter from Tavistock House dated Mon., May 5, 1856.]

3241 "An Amusing Letter from Italy. [Dickens to Georgina Hogarth.]" *Dickensian* 33 (Sept. 1937):243-44. [A letter from Hotel de la Ville, Milan dated Tues., Oct. 25, 1853.]

3242 "Dickens Letters at Hodgson's." *Times Literary Supplement* (Nov. 27, 1937):916.

3243 "A Dickens Letter on 'Drink'." *Listener* 18 (Dec. 1937):1326.

3244 "Letters to John Leech." *Dickensian* 34 (Dec. 1937):3-13.

3245 "The Suppressed Letter respecting 'Grimaldi'." *Dickensian* 34 (Dec. 1937):65-66.

3246 DEXTER, WALTER, ed. *The Letters of Charles Dickens.* 3 vols. London: Nonesuch Press, 1938. [Includes 65 speeches.]

3247 ROLFE, FRANKLIN P. "The Dickens Letters in the Huntington Library." *Huntington Library Quarterly* 1 (Apr. 1938):335-63.

3248 LEY, J. W. T. "Dickens's Letters." *Dickensian* 35 (Winter 1938-39): 29-31.

3249 "Unpublished Letters to Lady Holland." *Dickensian* 36 (Dec. 1939): 33-41.

3250 "Dickens's Earliest Known Letter." *Dickensian* 36 (Mar. 1940):103-4.

3251 "A New Dickens Letter About his Amateur Theatricals." *Dickensian* 36 (Mar. 1940):75-77.

3252 "A Letter for P. Toots Esquire." *Dickensian* 37 (Dec. 1940):36.

3253 UDY, D. HUBBLE, ed. "The Balloon Club: Some Unpublished Documents." *Dickensian* 37 (Mar. 1941):85-88. [Letters of Dickens to Forster and papers relating to the Balloon Club "for the Encouragement of Science and the Consumption of Spirits," a chiefly imaginary club invented in 1838.]

3254 ROLFE, FRANKLIN P. "Additions to the Nonesuch Edition of Dickens' Letters." *Huntington Library Quarterly* 5 (Oct. 1941): 115-40.

3255 ROLFE, FRANKLIN P. "More Letters to the Watsons." *Dickensian* 38 (Mar. 1942):113-23; (June 1942):161-66; (Sept. 1942):189-95.

3256 DEXTER, WALTER. "Adventures Among Dickens Letters." *Dickensian* 39 (June 1943):133-40; (Sept. 1943):177-82.

3257 STAPLES, LESLIE C. "Dickens and a Baronetcy." *Notes and Queries* 189 (Dec. 1945):284.

3258 WOODMAN, R. E. G. "Dickens and His Publishers." *Times Literary Supplement* (Jan. 25, 1947):51. [A short letter by Woodman introducing a letter by Dickens, printed here, which deals with his problems with publishers.]

3259 MILLER, C. WILLIAM. "Letters From Thomas White of Virginia to Scott and Dickens." *English Studies in Honor of James Southall Wilson,* ed. Fredson Bowers, 67-71. (Univ. of Virginia Studies 4.) Charlottesville, Va.: Univ. of Virginia Press, 1951.

3260 FIELDING, KENNETH J. "Dickens to Miss Burdett-Coutts." *Times Literary Supplement* (Mar. 2, 1951):140; Pt. 2 (Mar. 9, 1951):156.

3261 WHITLEY, ALVIN. "Hood and Dickens: Some New Letters." *Huntington Library Quarterly* 14 (Aug. 1951):385-413.

3262 FIELDING, KENNETH J. "Dickens, Thackeray and W. A. Chatto." *Dickensian* 48 (Dec. 1951):15-16.

3263 JOHNSON, EDGAR, ed. *The Heart of Charles Dickens: As Revealed in his Letters to Angel Burdett-Coutts.* From the collection in the Pierpont Morgan Library, with a critical and biographical introduction. Boston: Little, Brown; Toronto: McClelland; New York: Duell, Sloan and Pierce, 1952.

3264 WEBER, CARL J. "An Unusual Dickens Autograph." *Colby Library Quarterly* 3 (Nov. 1954):257-60. [On a letter printed in Nonesuch Edition of *Letters of Charles Dickens,* Vol. 1, pp. 180-81 and the actual letter at the Colby Library. The text differs from the Nonesuch.]

3265 GRUBB, GERALD G., ed. "Some Unpublished Correspondence of Dickens and Chapman and Hall." *Boston University Studies in English* 1 (Spring 1955):98-127.

3266 GRIFFITH, BEN W. "Two Misdated Dickens Letters." *Notes and Queries* N.S. 3 (Mar. 1956):122-23.

3267 RUST, JAMES D. "Dickens and the Americans: An Unnoticed Letter." *Nineteenth Century Fiction* 11 (June 1956):70-72.

3268 FIELDING, KENNETH J. and GERALD G. GRUBB. "New Letters from Charles Dickens to John Forster: Pt. 1, How the letters were found; Pt. 2, The significance of the letters; Pt. 3, The letters themselves." *Boston University Studies in English* 2 (Autumn 1956): 140-93.

3269 SHAFFER, ELLEN. "The Rare Book Department of the Free Library of Philadelphia." *College and Research Library* 18 (July 1957): 284-89. [Brief descriptions of the "Charles Dickens Collection" and the "D. Jacques Benoliel Collection of Dickens Letters" in the Free Library of Philadelphia.]

3270 GRIFFITH, BEN W. "Dickens the Philanthropist: An Unpublished Letter." *Nineteenth Century Fiction* 12 (Sept. 1957):160-63.

3271 DUPEE, F. W., ed. *The Selected Letters of Charles Dickens.* New York: Farrar, Straus and Cudahy, 1960.

3272 CARLTON, WILLIAM J. "Mr and Mrs Dickens: The Thomson-Stark Letter." *Notes and Queries* 7 (Apr. 1960):145-47.

3273 PEYROUTON, NOEL C. "When the Wine Merchant Wrote to Dickens: The Dickens-Ellis Correspondence." *Dickensian* 57 (May 1961):105-11.

3274 TILLOTSON, KATHLEEN. "A Letter from Mary Hogarth." *Times Literary Supplement* (Dec. 23, 1960):833; *Dickensian* 57 (Sept. 1961):133-37.

3275 HOUSE, MADELINE and GRAHAM STOREY, eds. *The Letters of Charles Dickens.* Vol. 1, 1820-1839. Pilgrim edition. Oxford: Clarendon Press, 1965.

R3276 [HOUSE, MADELINE and GRAHAM STOREY, eds. *The Letters of Charles Dickens,* Vol. 1, 1965 q.v.] BUTT, JOHN E. "Reviews." *Review of English Studies* 17 (1st quarter 1966):99-103.

R3277 [HOUSE, MADELINE and GRAHAM STOREY, eds. *The Letters of Charles Dickens,* Vol. 1, 1965 q.v.] GROSS, JOHN. "Yours in Haste." *New Statesman* 69 (Mar. 1965):444-46.

R3278 [HOUSE, MADELINE and GRAHAM STOREY, eds. *The Letters of Charles Dickens,* Vol. 1, 1965 q.v.] McMASTER, ROWLAND D. "The Letters of Charles Dickens." *University of Toronto Quarterly* 35 (Apr. 1966):313-14.

R3279 [HOUSE, MADELINE and GRAHAM STOREY, eds. *The Letters of Charles Dickens,* Vol. 1, 1965 q.v.] TILLOTSON, GEOFFREY. "The English Scholars Get Their Teeth into Dickens." *Sewanee Review* 75 (Apr.-June 1967):325-37.

3280 STAPLES, LESLIE C. "Ellen Ternan: Some Letters." *Dickensian* 61 (Jan. 1965):30-35.

3281 TILLOTSON, KATHLEEN. "A Letter from Dickens on Capital Punishment." *Times Literary Supplement* 64 (Aug. 12, 1965):704.

3282 CHANING, WALTER. "The Dexter Bust of Dickens." *Dickensian* 62 (May 1966):120-21. [Letter to Henry Dexter, dated Mar. 26, 1842, sculptor of bust given to Dickens in Boston, 1842.]

3283 HOUSE, MADELINE and GRAHAM STOREY, eds. *The Letters of Charles Dickens.* Vol. 2, 1840-1841. Pilgrim edition. Oxford: Clarendon Press, 1969.

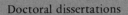Doctoral dissertations

George Cruikshank.

"The dancing booth where boisterous young men with cigars in their mouths, bulbous cardboard noses and false spectacles danced with excited girls."
From *Sketches by Boz,* drawn by George Cruikshank

3284 BLUHM, GUSTAV R. "Autobiographisches in *David Copperfield.*" Leipzig, 1891.

3285 BENIGNUS, SIEGFRIED. "Studien über die Anfänge von Dickens." Strasbourg, 1895.

3286 WILSON, FRANK W. "Dickens in seinen Beziehungen zu den Humoristen Fielding und Smollet." Leipzig, 1899.

3287 WINTER, ALBERT. "Joseph Addison als Humorist in seinem Einfluss auf Dickens Jugendwerke." Leipzig, 1899.

3288 SCHMIDT, THEODOR. "Frauengestalten bei Dickens." Halle, 1907.

3289 BERNDT, ARNOLD. "Entstehungsgeschichte der *Pickwick Papers.*" Greifswald, 1908.

3290 MUNRO, WILLIAM A. "Charles Dickens et Alphonse Daudet, Romanciers de l'Enfant et des Humbles." Toulouse, 1908.

3291 SCHIEBOLD, WILHELM. "Kindergestalten bei Dickens." Halle, 1908.

3292 FRIESER, WALTER. "Die Schulen bei Dickens, auf ihre geschichtliche Wahrheit geprüft: ein Beitrag zur Geschichte der Erziehung in England." Leipzig, 1909.

3293 LIPPOLT, KURT. "Das Gerichtswesen in Dickens' Romanen." Halle, 1909.

3294 NIERTH, HORST. "Die Weihnachtserzählung in der englischen Literatur (mit besonderer Berücksichtigung von Charles Dickens)." Leipzig, 1909.

3295 SCHULZE, FERDINAND. "Charles Dickens als Schilderer der Londoner Armen- und Verbrecherwelt." Halle, 1909.

3296 BOOTH, MEYRICK. "Charles Dickens und seine Werke in pädagogischer Beleuchtung." Jena, 1910.

3297 LÜDER, FRITZ. "Die epischen Werke Otto Ludwigs und ihr Verhältnis zu Charles Dickens." Greifswald, 1910.

3298 STUMPF, WILLY. "Der Dickenssche Roman *Hard Times*: seine Entstehung und seine Tendenzen." Greifswald, 1911.

3299 FIEDLER, FRITZ. "Entstehungsgeschichte von Charles Dickens' *Oliver Twist.*" Halle, 1912.

3300 GEISSENDOERFER, JOHN T. "Dickens' Einfluss auf Ungern-Sternberg, Hesslein, Stolle, Raabe, und Ebner-Eschenbach." Pennsylvania, 1912.

3301 JÜGLER, RICHARD. "Uber die Technik der Charakterisierung in den Jugendwerken von Charles Dickens (*Sketches, Pickwick Papers, Oliver Twist, Nicholas Nickleby*)." Halle, 1912.

3302 BÖTTGER, CURT. "Charles Dickens' historicher Roman *A Tale of Two Cities* und seine Quellen." Königsberg, 1913.

3303 GEIST, HUGO. "Fritz Reuters literarische Beziehungen zu Charles Dickens." Halle, 1913.

3304 GRUENEWALD, KARL. "Die Verwendung der Mundart in den Romanen von Dickens, Thackeray, Eliot, und Kingsley." Giessen, 1914.

3305 EDELMANN, ERNST. "Die Charakterzeichnung in den Romanen von Dickens." Giessen, 1915.

3306 JOHANNPETER, WILHELM. "Handlungs-, Charakter- und Situations– Kontrast in den Jugendwerken von Charles Dickens (*Sketches, Pickwick Papers, Oliver Twist, Nicholas Nickleby*)." Halle, 1915.

3307 MUELLER, ELMA. "Das subjective Hervortreten des Dichters im neueren englischen Roman, Dickens, Thackeray, Eliot." Giessen, 1916.

3308 PHILLIPS, WALTER C. "Dickens, Reade and Collins, Sensation Novelists: A Study in the Conditions and Theories of Novel Writing in Victorian England." Columbia, 1919.

3309 SCHWEIZER, FRIEDRICH. "Die Ausländer in den Romanen von Dickens." Giessen, 1920.

3310 HARTENSTEIN, JOHANNES. "Studien zu Dickens' Arbeitsweise auf Grund der Heftausgabe von *Dombey and Son*." Leipzig, 1922.

3311 REHFELD, WALTER. "Der Vergleich bei Charles Dickens." Greifswald, 1923.

3312 WESTENDORPF, KARL. "Das Prinzip der Verwendung des Slang bei Dickens." Greifswald, 1923.

3313 GUTERMUTH, ELSE. "Das Kind im englischen Roman von Richardson bis Dickens." Giessen, 1924.

3314 THURN, GEORG. "Der Einfluss Dickens' auf Samuel Warren." Erlangen, 1925.

3315 AMERONGEN, JUDA B. van. "The Actor in Dickens." Amsterdam, 1926.

3316 HUDSON, VIRGINIA O. "Charles Dickens and the American Theatre." Chicago, 1926.

3317 GIESSEL, CHRISTEL. "Dickens und das Kunstprinzip des Realismus" Vienna, 1927.

3318 HEUER, HERMANN. "Romaneske Elemente im Realismus von Charles Dickens." Marburg, 1927.

3319 WIERSTRA, FRANK D. "Smollett and Dickens." Amsterdam, 1928.

3320 SWANN, GEORGE R. "Philosophical Parallelisms in Six English Novelists: The Conception of Good, Evil, and Human Nature." Pennsylvania, 1929.

3321 HOUTCHENS, LAWRENCE H. "Carlyle's Influence on Dickens."
      Cornell, 1931.

3322 ULRICH, ALFRED. "Studien zu Dickens' Roman *Barnaby Rudge*."
      Jena, 1931.

3323 HILLIER, RICHARD L. "Traces of Dickens's Caricatures in the
      Early Novels of George Meredith." Colorado, 1932.

3324 WAGENKNECHT, EDWARD. "Personality as a Subject for
      Scientific Investigation: An Addendum to *The Man Charles Dickens,
      A Victorian Portrait*." Univ. of Washington, 1932.

3325 WICKARDT, WOLFGANG. "Die Formen der Perspektive in
      Charles Dickens' Romanen, ihr sprachlicher Ausdruck und ihre
      strukturelle Bedeutung." Göttingen, 1933.

3326 RATH, JOSEPH. "Die Personenbeschreibung der humoristichen
      Charaktere in der erzaehlenden Literatur von Addison bis Dickens."
      Münster, 1934.

3327 DAVIS, EARLE R. "Literary Influences Upon the Early Art of
      Charles Dickens." *DA* 28 (1967):3666A (Princeton 1935).

3328 SENNEWALD, CHARLOTTE (geb. Köckeritz). "Die Namengebung
      bei Dickens; eine Studie über Lautsymbolic." Berlin, 1936.

3329 WASHBURN, CAROLYN. "The History, From 1832 to 1860, of
      British Criticism of Narrative Prose Fiction." Illinois, 1937.

3330 BAMBERGER, RICHARD. "Die erste Aufnahme von Charles
      Dickens in der deutschen Literatur." Vienna, 1938.

3331 CANNELL, LEWIS D. "Charles Dickens' Attitude Toward Economic
      Theories." Univ. of Washington, 1939.

3332 RAND, FRANK H. "Les Adaptations Théatrales des Romans de
      Dickens en Angleterre (1837-1870)." Paris, 1939.

3333 GRUBB, GERALD G. "Charles Dickens: Journalist." North
      Carolina, 1940.

3334 MALY-SCHLATTER, FLORENCE. "The Puritan Element in
      Victorian Fiction with Special Reference to the Works of George
      Eliot, Dickens, Thackeray." Zürich, 1940.

3335 GOGEISSL, L. "Das Bürgertum in England, dargestellt nach
      Romanen von Thackeray, Dickens und Galsworthy. Nürnburg, 1941.

3336 MILLEY, HENRY J. "The Achievement of Wilkie Collins and
      His Influence on Dickens and Trollope." *DA* 28 (1967):4182A
      (Yale 1941).

3337 WINTERS, WARRINGTON. "Unusual Mental Phenomena in the
      Life and Works of Charles Dickens." Minnesota, 1942.

3338 KORSTER, CÄCILIE. "Ausdrucksformen des Humors in Dickens'
      Charakteren." Bonn, 1943.

3339 BÖHM, CHARLOTTE. "Charles Dickens' *Household Words* und ihr Beitrag zur Meinungsbildung über Deutschland und Österreich um 1859 in Grossbritannien." Vienna, 1944.

3340 JÜDT, LYDIA. "Die Gestalt des Biedermeiers in den Jugendwerken von Charles Dickens." Marburg, 1944.

3341 MÜLLER, HERBERT. "Die englische Aristokratie im Spiegel von Dickens' Romanen." Leipzig, 1944.

3342 OEHLBAUM, ISAAK. "Das pathologische Element bei Charles Dickens." Zürich, 1944.

3343 ADRIAN, ARTHUR A. "Charles Dickens: *The Life and Adventures of Nicholas Nickleby.*" Western Reserve, 1946.

3344 YOWELL, PHYLLIS K. "The Techniques of Characterization in the Novels of Charles Dickens." Univ. of Washington, 1946.

3345 MATICS, JOHANNA. "Dialektgebrauch und individuelle Sprechweise als Kuntsmittel in Werken von Scott, Dickens, Shaw, Sayers, Priestley Vienna, 1947.

3346 SCHÜTZE, JOHANNES. "Dickens' Frauenideal und das Biedermeier. Erlangen, 1947.

3347 KALLSEN, ANNI-MARTHA. "Disraeli, Dickens, und Thackeray in ihrer Stellung zur englisch-aristokratschen Gesellschaftsschicht." Hamburg, 1949.

3348 VIVIAN, CHARLES H. "Samuel Laman Blanchard, A Member of the Dickens Circle." Harvard, 1949.

3349 WOLTER, PIUS. "Das Drollige bei Dickens." Erlangen, 1949.

3350 COWDEN, DAVID. "The Structure of Dickens's Novels." Harvard, 1950.

3351 DONNELLY, MABEL W. "Convention and Invention From Dickens to Gissing." Radcliffe, 1950.

3352 KATARSKIJ, I. M. "Pozdnee Tvorčestvo Dikkensa. (Romany Poslednego Perioda)." Avtoreferat dissertacii na soiskanie učenoj stepeni kandidata filologičeskix nauk. Moscow: Moskovskij gorodskoj pedagogičeskij institut im. V. P. Potemkina, 1950. ["Dickens' Later Work. (Novels of the Last Period)."]

3353 LEONHARDT, RUDOLF W. "*Soll und Haben* und *David Copperfield*: – ein Vergleich ihres Aufbaus als Beitrag zur Formfrage des Romans." Bonn, 1950.

3354 MANHEIM, LEONARD F. "The Dickens Pattern: A Study in Psychoanalytic Criticism." Columbia, 1950.

3355 YAMAMOTO, TADAO. "Growth and System of the Language of Dickens." Tokyo, 1950.

3356 BENDER, HENRIETTE. "Charles Dickens und die Zeit des buergerlichen Realismus in Holland." Bonn, 1951.

3357 BLEIFUSS, WILLIAM W. "Charles Dickens and the Law." Minnesota, 1951.

3358 HAHN, CHARLOTTE (geb. WEISS). "Archaisches in Wortgebrauch und Syntax in den Werken von Charles Dickens." Jena, 1952.

3359 IVASEVA, V. V. "Tvorčeskoe Nasledie Dikkensa." Avtoreferat dissertacii na soiskanie učenoj stepeni doktora filologičeskix nauk. Leningrad: Leningradskij gosudarstvennyj universitet, 1952.

3360 MILLER, J. HILLIS. "Dickens's Symbolic Imagery: A Study of Six Novels." Harvard, 1952.

3361 MONOD, SYLVÈRE. "Dickens Romancier: Étude sur la Création Littéraire dans son Roman." Paris, 1952.

3362 OFFENHÄUSER, AGNES. "Die Tierseele bei Charles Dickens." Erlangen, 1952.

3363 PIRA, GISELA. "Der Todesgedanke im Roman der Dickenszeit." Göttingen, 1952.

3364 ADAMS, DONALD K. "Studies in Allegory in the Works of Charles Dickens." Northwestern, 1953.

3365 ADAMS, RUTH R. "A Study of Dickens' Imagery." Maryland, 1953.

3366 ATHERTON, JOHN W. "The Critical Reception of Dickens's Novels in England: 1836-1850." Chicago, 1953.

3367 LANE, LAURIAT, Jr. "Dickens and the Archetypal Villain." Harvard, 1953.

3368 RICE, THERESA A. "The Religious and Moral Ideas in the Novels of Charles Dickens." Wisconsin, 1953.

3369 BEL'SKIJ, A. "Satira v Social'nyx Romanax Č. Dikkensa. 1849-1857 gg." Avtoreferat dissertacii na soiskanie učenoj stepeni kandidata filologičeskix nauk. Moscow: Moskovskij Gosudarstvennyj Universitet, 1954. ["Satire in the Social Novels of Charles Dickens, 1849-1857."]

3370 ENGEL, MONROE. "The Novel of Reality: An Illustrative Study of the Genesis, Method and Intent of *Our Mutual Friend*." DA 15 (1955):1612-13 (Princeton 1954).

3371 FIELDING, KENNETH J. "Studies in the Biography of Dickens." Oxford, 1954.

3372 KOGAN, BERNARD R. "Narrative Techniques in the Later Novels of Charles Dickens." Chicago, 1954.

3373 WALLER, JOHN O. "The American Civil War and Some English Men of Letters: Carlyle, Mill, Ruskin, Arnold, Kingsley, Hughes, Trollope, Thackeray, and Dickens." Southern California, 1954.

3374 FUTRELL, MICHAEL H. "Dickens and Three Russian Novelists: Gogol', Dostoyevsky, Tolstoy." London, 1955.

3375 STONE, HARRY. "Dickens's Reading." University of California, Los Angeles, 1955.

3376 CARTER, JOHN A., Jr. "Dickens and Education: The Novelist as Reformer." *DA* 17 (1957):628-29 (Princeton 1956).

3377 COBURN, LLOYD P. "Charles Dickens: Parent-Child Relationships." Western Reserve, 1956.

3378 COOLIDGE, ARCHIBALD C., Jr. "Serialization in the Novels of Charles Dickens." *DA* 16 (1956):2455-56 (Brown).

3379 GARIS, ROBERT E. "Moral Attitudes and the Theatrical Mode: A Study of Characterization in *Bleak House*." Harvard, 1956.

3380 LOW, DONALD R. "The Speeches, Lectures, and Readings of Charles Dickens and William M. Thackeray in the United States, 1842-1868." *DA* 16 (1956):2555-56 (Northwestern).

3381 SPILKA, MARK. "Dickens and Kafka: A Mutual Interpretation." *DA* 16 (1956):2462-63 (Indiana).

3382 THALMANN, LISELOTTE. "Charles Dickens in seinen Beziehungen zum Ausland." Zurich, 1956.

3383 MILLER, MELVIN H. "The Collected Speeches of Charles Dickens with Introduction and Notes." *DA* 17 (1957):3124-25 (Wisconsin).

3384 RATHBURN, ROBERT C. "Dickens' Periodical Essays and Their Relationships to the Novels." *DA* 17 (1957):2002 (Minnesota).

3385 SHARPLES, SISTER MARIAN. "Dickens' Use of Imagery: A Study of Narrative Technique in Four Novels." Southern California, 1957.

3386 GOTTSHALL, JAMES K. "Dickens' Rhythmic Imagery: Its Development from *Sketches by Boz* Through *Bleak House*." *DA* 19 (1958): 797-98 (Cincinnati).

3387 HEAD, WALTER D. "An Analysis of the Methods Used by Dickens in Presenting His Characters." *DA* 19 (1959):3304-5 (Vanderbilt 1958).

3388 HUMPHREY, HAROLD E. "The Background of *Hard Times*." *DA* 19 (1958):318 (Columbia).

3389 PERRY, JOHN O. "The Dickens Melodrama. Structure and Morality in Dickens's Novels." California, Berkeley, 1958.

3390 SMITH, GEORGE W., Jr. "Dickens and Periodical Publication." Harvard, 1958.

3391 McMASTER, ROWLAND D. "Charles Dickens, a Study of the Imagery and Structure of his Novels." Toronto, 1959.

3392 MORITZ, HAROLD K. "Visual Organization in Dickens." *DA* 20 (1959):1026-27 (Univ. of Washington).

3393 NELSON, HARLAND S. "Evangelicalism in the Novels of Charles Dickens." *DA* 20 (1959):2295-96 (Minnesota).

3394 SEEHASE, GEORG. "Zur Oddity als realistischem Gestaltungsprinzip in den Romanen von Charles Dickens." Leipzig, 1959.

3395 WRIGHT, JAMES A. "The Comic Imagination of the Young Dickens." *DA* 20 (1959):294 (Univ. of Washington).

3396 BORT, BARRY D. "A Study in Dickens' Heroes from Oliver Twist to John Jasper." *DA* 23 (1962):1696-97 (Brown 1960).

3397 DE LEEUW, MARGARET L. "The Significance of Humor in the Early Works of Charles Dickens." *DA* 21 (1960):872-73 (Columbia).

3398 HOLLINGSWORTH, JOSEPH K. "The Newgate Novel, 1830-1847: Bulwer, Ainsworth, Dickens and Thackeray." *DA* 21 (1960):1948 (Columbia).

3399 STOEHR, TAYLOR. "The Dickens Formula, a Study of Narrative Structure in the Later Novels." California, Berkeley, 1960.

3400 AXTON, WILLIAM F. "Dramatic Style in Dickens' Novels." *DA* 22 (1961):2788-89 (Princeton).

3401 BARRETT, EDWIN B. "Charles Dickens: The Essential Fable. Character, Idea, Form and Diction in Four Novels of His Maturity." *DA* 22 (1961):2789 (Columbia).

3402 GLENN, ROBERT B. "Linguistic Class-Indicators in the Speech of Dickens' Characters." *DA* 22 (1961):569 (Michigan).

3403 IRWIN, EDWARD E. "Dickens and Thackeray: The Reciprocal Influences." *DA* 22 (1961):247 (Florida).

3404 MARCUS, STEVEN. "Dickens From *Pickwick* to *Dombey*." *DA* 25 (1964):1195 (Columbia 1961).

3405 METWALLI, A. K. "Charles Dickens as a Social Critic." Manchester, 1961.

3406 SANTANIELLO, ANTHONY E. "Charles Dickens' *Little Dorrit*: A Study of the Heroine as Victim and Savior." Harvard, 1961.

3407 SHEA, Fr. FRANCIS X., S. J. "The Text of *Our Mutual Friend*: A Study of the Variations Between the Copy Text and the First Printed Edition." *DA* 22 (1961):2007 (Minnesota).

3408 TARTELLA, VINCENT P. "Charles Dickens's *Oliver Twist*: Moral Realism and the Uses of Style." *DA* 22 (1961):1616-17 (Notre Dame).

3409 WHEELER, BURTON M. "Charles Dickens: In Service of Two Masters, a Study of the Novel of Social Protest." Harvard, 1961.

3410 AITKEN, DAVID J. "The Victorian Idea of Realism: A Study of the Aims and Methods of the English Novel Between 1860 and 1875." *DA* 23 (1962):2910 (Princeton). [Chap. II.]

3411 CHAUDHRY,GHULAM ALI. "Symbolism in Dickens." Edinburgh, 19

3412 FANGER, DONALD L. "Dostoevsky and Romantic Realism – Balzac
Dickens, Gogol." Harvard, 1962.

3413 LAZENBY, WALTER S., Jr. "Stage Versions of Dickens's Novels in
America to 1900." *DA* 23 (1962):2250 (Indiana).

3414 MADZIGON, M. V. "Realizm Rannego Tvorčestva Dikkensa."
Avtoreferat dissertacii na soiskanie učenoj stepeni kandidata
filologičeskix nauk. Tbilisi: Tbilisskij Gosudarstvennyj Universitet,
1962. ["The Realism of Dickens' Early Works."]

3415 YANKO, ANN E. "Technique and Vision in *Bleak House, Little
Dorrit* and *Our Mutual Friend.*" *DA* 23 (1962):2143 (Wisconsin).

3416 BLOOM, LYNN M. "How Literary Biographers Use Their Subjects'
Work: A Study of Biographical Method, 1865-1962." *DA* 24 (1963):
2458 (Michigan). [Chapter 4 on Dickens.]

3417 CLIPPER, LAWRENCE J. "Crime and Criminals in the Novels of
Charles Dickens." *DA* 24 (1963):2474-75 (North Carolina).

3418 EDMINSON, M. "The Development of Dickens' Novels as Occasioned
by Serial Publication." Durham, 1963.

3419 PRINS, ALBERT J. "The Fabulous Art: Myth, Metaphor and Moral
Vision in Dickens' *Bleak House. DA* 25 (1964):1896 (Michigan
1963).

3420 SHERWIN, RICHARD E. "The Use of Character in Dickens: A Study
of Dickens' Later Novels." *DA* 28 (1967):3685A-86A (Yale 1963).

3421 STEIG, MICHAEL. "Erotic Themes in Dickens' Novels." *DA* 24
(1963):4704-5 (Washington).

3422 DABNEY, ROSS H. "Love and Property in the Novels of Dickens."
Harvard, 1964.

3423 DeVRIES, DUANE K. "Dickens's *Sketches by Boz,* Exercises in the
Craft of Fiction." *DA* 25 (1964):5273-74 (Michigan State).

3424 DUNN, RICHARD J. "Aspects of a Novelist's Development: Dickens
Mastery of Horror and Terror." Western Reserve, 1964.

3425 FLEISSNER, ROBERT F. "Shakespeare and Dickens: Some
Characteristic Uses of the Playwright by the Novelist." *DA* 25
(1964):4686 (New York Univ.).

3426 HARRIS, STEPHEN L. "The Mask of Morality: A Study of the
Unconscious Hypocrite in Representative Novels of Jane Austen,
Charles Dickens, and George Eliot." *DA* 25 (1964):4699 (Cornell).

3427 HERRING, PAUL D. "The Background of Charles Dickens' *Little
Dorrit.*" Chicago, 1964.

3428 MILTON, EDITH C. "Dickens on Growth and Time: A Study of Six
of His Novels." *DA* 28 (1967):2214A-15A (Yale 1964).

3429 BRANNAN, ROBERT L. "*The Frozen Deep*: Under the Management of Mr Charles Dickens." *DA* 26 (1965):5429 (Cornell).

3430 HANEY, CHARLES W. "The Garden and The Child: A Study of Pastoral Transformation." *DA* 26 (1965):2212 (Yale).

3431 KINCAID, JAMES R. "A Critical Study of *David Copperfield*." *DA* 27 (1966):478A (Western Reserve 1965).

3432 LEVY, HERMAN M., Jr. "Dickens and the Novel in Parts." *DA* 26 (1965):6024 (Florida).

3433 McLEAN, ROBERT S. "Charles Dickens' Villainous Characters: A Study in Ethical Values and Esthetic Control." *DA* 27 (1966): 183A-84A (New York University 1965).

3434 O'LEARY, SISTER JEANINE. "The Function of City as Setting in Dickens's *Our Mutual Friend*, Trollope's *The Way we Live Now*, James's *The Princess Casamassima*, and Conrad's *The Secret Agent*." *DA* 26 (1965):6048-49 (Notre Dame).

3435 PATTEN, ROBERT L. "Plot in Charles Dickens' Early Novels." *DA* 26 (1965):4670 (Princeton).

3436 SLATER, M. D. "*The Chimes*: Its Materials, Making, and Public Reception; with an Assessment of its Importance as a Turning-point in the Work of Dickens." Oxford, 1965.

3437 BOO, SISTER MARY R. "The Concept of Society in Dickens' Later Novels." *DA* 27 (1966):4216A (Illinois).

3438 BRACHER, PETER S. "Dickens and His American Readers, 1834-1870: A Study of the American Reception, Reputation and Popularity of Charles Dickens and His Novels During His Lifetime." *DA* 27 (1966):1332A-33A (Pennsylvania).

3439 BURKE, ALAN R. "Dickens's Image of the City." *DA* 27 (1966): 2130A (Indiana).

3440 GASSER, ELIZABETH. "Love as Goal and Symbol in Three of the Novels of Charles Dickens." *DA* 27 (1966):202A-3A (Yale).

3441 GOLDBERG, MICHAEL K. "Dr Pessimist Anticant and Mr Popular Sentiment: The Influence of Carlyle on Dickens." *DA* 28 (1967): 195A (Cornell 1966).

3442 HARVEY, WILLIAM R. "Four Character Types in the Novels of Charles Dickens." *DA* 27 (1966):1056A (Florida State).

3443 JARMUTH, SYLVIA L. "Dickens' Use of Women in his Novels." *DA* 29 (1968):568A-69A (New York University 1966).

3444 KAPLAN, FRED. "The Development of Dickens' Style." *DA* 27 (1966):747A-48A (Columbia).

3445 MILLS, NICOLAUS C. "Romance and Society: A Re-Examination of Nineteenth Century American and British Fiction." *DA* 28

(1967):687-A (Brown 1966). [*Adam Bede, Hard Times, Jude the Obscure, Heart of Darkness, Great Expectations.*]

3446 PAYNE, CLYDE L. Jr. "Dickens and Mammon: Character Corruption in the Novels." *DA* 27 (1966):2134A (Stanford).

3447 SAINT VICTOR, CAROL H. de "The Unplanned Novels of Charles Dickens: A Portrait of the Artist." *DA* 27 (1966):2149A-50A (Indiana).

3448 TICK, STANLEY. "Forms of the Novel in the Nineteenth Century: Studies in Dickens, Melville, and George Eliot." *DA* 27 (1966): 1349A-50A (California, San Diego).

3449 ANDERSEN, SALLY S. "Dickens and the Problem of Maturity: *Dombey and Son, David Copperfield, Bleak House, Great Expectations* and *Our Mutual Friend.*" *DA* 28 (1967):3135A (Illinois).

3450 BROWN, ARTHUR W. "Dickens' Props: An Analysis of Their Sexual Significance with a Chapter of Death." *DA* 28 (1967):2236A-37A (Columbia).

3451 CHEEK, EDWIN R. "Dickens's Views of Women." *DA* 28 (1967): 3633A-34A (North Carolina).

3452 CLARK, HAROLD F. Jr. "Dickensian Journalism: A Study of *Household Words. DA* 28 (1967):1390A-91A (Columbia).

3453 ERICKSEN, DONALD H. "Dickens and the Critics of *Bleak House,* 1851-1965: A Study in Depth." *DA* 28 (1967):5050A-51A (Illinois).

3454 HARRIS, JACK T. "The Factory Hand in the English Novel, 1840-1855." *DA* 28 (1967):4176A (Texas). [Chapter 4 about *Hard Times.*]

3455 HEINEMAN, HELEN K. "Three Victorians in the New World: Interpretations of America in the Works of Frances Trollope, Charles Dickens, and Anthony Trollope." *DA* 28 (1967):196A-97A (Cornell).

3456 HOLLINGTON, MICHAEL A. "Dickens and the Double." *DA* 28 (1967):5018A (Illinois).

3457 HURSEY, RICHARD C. "The Elusive Angel: The Development of the Orphan Theme in the Early Novels of Charles Dickens." *DA* 28 (1967):3144A (Ohio).

3458 NEWCOMB, MILDRED E. "Imagistic Patterns in Charles Dickens." *DA* 28 (1967):3645A-46A (Ohio State).

3459 NEWELL, KENNETH B. "Structure in H. G. Wells's Dickensian Novels." *DA* 28 (1967):239A (Pennsylvania).

3460 ROGERS, PHILIP E. "Dickens and the Image of Time." *DA* 28 (1967):5068A-69A (Illinois).

3461 SEIDEN, MARK A. "Dickens' London: The City as Comic Apocalypse." *DA* 28 (1967):1086A-87A (Cornell).

3462 SWEENEY, PATRICIA R. "The Dangerous Journey: The Initiation Theme in Eight Victorian Novels." *DA* 28 (1967):1451A (California, Berkeley).

3463 VANN, J. DON. "*David Copperfield* and the Reviewers." *DA* 28 (1967):3159A-60A (Texas Technological College).

3464 WESTBURG, BARRY R. "Studies in Personal History: *Oliver Twist, David Copperfield,* and *Great Expectations.*" *DA* 28 (1967): 2269A-70A (Cornell).

3465 AUGBURN, GERALD R. "The Function of Death in the Novels of Charles Dickens." *DA* 29 (1969):266A (Columbia 1968).

3466 BANK, SYLVIA PEARL. "Dickens as Satirist." *DA* 29 (1968):559A (Yale).

3467 BROGAN, JAMES E. "The Character of Society in the Panoramic Novels of Thackeray and Dickens." *DA* 29 (1968):592A (Yale).

3468 BROWN, JAMES W. "Charles Dickens in Norway: 1839-1912." *DA* 30 (1969):273A (Michigan 1968).

3469 FOURNIER, LUCIEN F. "Charles Dickens and the Middle-Class Gentleman: A Study in the Correlation of Grotesque Satire and Sentimental Idealism." *DA* 29 (1969):3134A-35A (Notre Dame 1968).

3470 FRANK, LAWRENCE D. "The Enigmatic Hero: Atonement and the Urban Man in the Later Novels of Charles Dickens." *DA* 29 (1969): 2259A (Minnesota 1968).

3471 GRAYSON, NANCY J. "The Mentor Figure in Selected Novels by Thackeray, Dickens, and Meredith." *DA* 29 (1968):1511A (Austin; Univ. of Texas).

3472 KOTZIN, MICHAEL C. "Dickens and the Fairy Tale." *DA* 30 (1969):328A (Minnesota 1968).

3473 LAUN, EDWARD C. "The Self-Made Gentleman as a Hero in Victorian Fiction." *DA* 29 (1969):4496A (Wisconsin 1968).

3474 MACDOUGALL, JAMES K. "Dickens' Comedy: A Study of Plot and Character." *DA* 29 (1969):4497A (Case Western Reserve 1968).

3475 MULVEY, CHRISTOPHER E. "Dickens and His People: Character Organization in *David Copperfield, Bleak House,* and *Little Dorrit.*" *DA* 29 (1968):1875A (Columbia).

3476 PAROISSIEN, DAVID H. "A Critical Edition of Charles Dickens's *Pictures from Italy.*" *DA* 29 (1968):1876A-77A (California, Los Angeles).

3477 SHEREIKIS, RICHARD J. "From Pickwick to Pecksniff: An Analysis of *Martin Chuzzlewit* and its Significance in Dickens' Career." *DA* 29 (1969):3588A (Colorado 1968).

3478 SKURATOVSKAJA, L. I. "Social'nyj Roman Dikkensa 1830-x –
      Načala 1840-x gg." Avtoreferat dissertacii na soiskanie učenoj stepeni
      kandidata filologičeskix nauk. L'vov: L'vovskij Gosudarstvennyj
      Universitet imeni I. Franko, 1968. ["Dickens' Social Novel of the
      1830s and Early 1840s."]

3479 TARR, RODGER L. "Carlyle's Influence Upon the Mid-Victorian
      Social Novels of Gaskell, Kingsley, and Dickens." *DA* 29 (1969):
      2285A (South Carolina 1968).

3480 TERRY, LEE C. "Fictional Melodrama in the Early Novels of
      Charles Dickens." *DA* 29 (1968):1907A-8A (Texas).

3481 HEAMAN, ROBERT J. "Love, Adversity, and Achievement of
      Identity: A Study of the Young Men in the Novels of Charles
      Dickens." *DA* 30 (1969):2024A (Univ. of Michigan).

3482 LANSBURY, CORAL. "Australia in English Literature in the 19th
      Century." Auckland, 1969. [The influence of Dickens' novels on
      Australia's attitudes, and Dickens' own attitude to Australia.]

3483 LARSON, GEORGE S. "Religion in the Novels of Charles Dickens."
      DA 30 (1969):328A-29A (Massachusetts).

3484 THEIMER, ROBERT H. "Fairy Tale and the Triumph of the Ideal
      in Three Novels by Charles Dickens." *DA* 30 (1969):1185A (Stanford

Books, essays and articles
with significant mention of
Dickens or with special relevance
to the study of Dickens

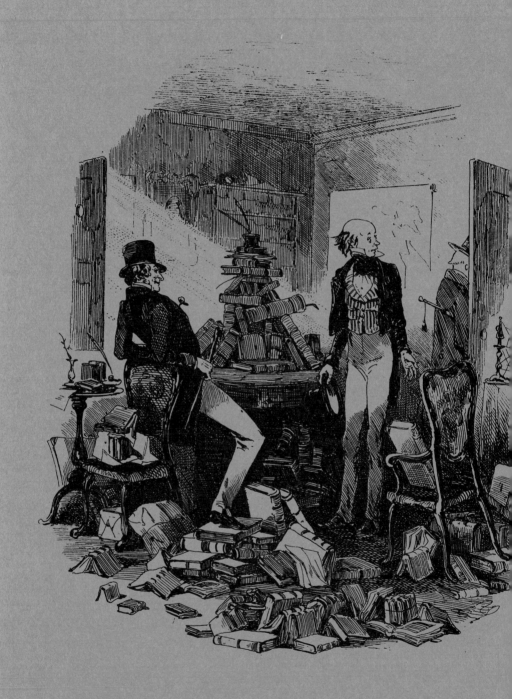

Mysterious Installation of Mr Pinch. *Martin Chuzzlewit*, drawn by Phiz

3485 HOLCROFT, THOMAS. *A Plain and Succinct Narrative of the Late Riots and Disturbances in the Cities of London and Westminster, and Borough of Southwark* ... With an account of the commitment of Lord George Gordon to the Tower, and anecdotes of his life. 2nd ed. London: Fielding and Walker, 1780.

3486 MASSON, DAVID. *British Novelists and Their Styles: Being a Critical Sketch of the History of British Prose Fiction.* Cambridge, Eng.: Macmillan; Boston: Gould and Lincoln, 1859.

3487 DEPRET, LOUIS. *Chez les Anglais.* Paris: Hachette, 1879.

3488 FIELDS, JAMES T. *Biographical Notes and Personal Sketches.* Boston: Houghton, Mifflin, 1881.

3489 KITTON, FREDERIC G. *'Phiz' (Hablot Knight Browne): A Memoir.* London: G. Redway, 1882.

3490 TROLLOPE, ANTHONY. *An Autobiography.* London: Oxford Univ. Press, 1883.

3491 HONE, PHILIP. *The Diary of Philip Hone.* Ed. Bayard Tuckerman. 2 vols. New York: Dodd, Mead, 1889.

3492 HOWELLS, WILLIAM DEAN. *Criticism and Fiction.* New York: Harper; London: Osgood, 1891. Reprinted in *Criticism and Fiction and Other Essays by W. D. Howells,* ed. Clara M. and Rudolph Kirk. New York: New York Univ. Press, 1959.

3493 WELSH, ALFRED H. *Development of English Literature and Language.* Chicago: S. C. Griggs, 1891.

3494 FITZGERALD, PERCY H. *Memoirs of an Author.* London: R. Bentley, 1894.

3495 CROWE, JOSEPH. *Reminiscences of Thirty-Five Years of My Life.* London: J. Murray; New York: Dodd, Mead, 1895. [On the *Daily News.*]

3496 MOULTON, RICHARD G., ed. *Four Years of Novel Reading: an Account of an Experiment in Popularizing the Study of Fiction.* Boston: Heath, 1895.

3497 SAINTSBURY, GEORGE. *A History of Nineteenth Century Literature 1780-1895.* New York: Macmillan, 1896.

3498 OLIPHANT, JAMES. *Victorian Novelists.* London: Blackie, 1899.

3499 CAZAMIAN, LOUIS F. *Le Roman Social en Angleterre: (1830-1850), Dickens, Disraeli, Mrs Gaskell, Kingsley.* 2 vols. Paris: Société Nouvelle de Librairie et d'Edition, 1904. Nouvelle éd. Paris: H. Didier, éditeur, 1934.

3500 ROBINSON, SIR JOHN R. *Fifty Years of Fleet Street.* London: Macmillan, 1904.

3501 DAWSON, WILLIAM J. *The Makers of English Fiction.* Toronto: F. H. Revell, 1905.

3502 RICKETT, ARTHUR. *Personal Forces in Modern Literature.* London: Dent, 1906.

3503 BURTON, RICHARD. *Masters of the English Novel: a Study of Principles and Personalities.* New York: Henry Holt, 1909.

3504 DIBELIUS, WILHELM. *Englische Romankunst.* Die technik des englischen Romans im achtzehnten und zu Anfang des neunzehnten Jahrhunderts. Berlin: Mayer und Müller, 1910.

3505 CAZAMIAN, LOUIS F. *L'Angleterre Moderne. Son Évolution.* Paris: Flammarion, 1911.

3506 WILLIAMS, HAROLD. *Two Centuries of the English Novel.* London: Smith, Elder, 1911.

3507 CHESTERTON, GILBERT K. *The Victorian Age in Literature.* London: Williams and Norgate, 1913; London: Oxford Univ. Press, 1966.

3508 DELATTRE, FLORIS. *De Byron à Francis Thompson.* Paris: Payot, 1913.

3509 SAINTSBURY, GEORGE. *The English Novel.* London: Dent, 1913.

3510 PHELPS, WILLIAM L. *Essays on Books.* New York: Macmillan, 1914.

3511 WHITEFORD, ROBERT N. *Motives in English Fiction.* New York: Putnam, 1918.

3512 CAZAMIAN, LOUIS F. *L'Evolution Psychologique et la Littérature en Angleterre (1600-1914).* Paris: F. Allan, 1920.

3513 RUSSELL, FRANCES T. *Satire in the Victorian Novel.* New York: Macmillan, 1920.

3514 LUBBOCK, PERCY. *The Craft of Fiction.* London: J. Cape, 1921.

3515 SANTAYANA, GEORGE. *Soliloquies in England and Later Soliloquies.* New York: Scribner, 1922. With new introd. by Ralph Ross, Ann Arbor: Univ. of Michigan Press, 1967.

3516 LEGOUIS, ÉMILE H. and LOUIS F. CAZAMIAN. *Histoire de la Littérature Anglaise.* Paris: Hachette, 1924. 1st. English ed.: *A History of English Literature.* 2 vols. London: Dent; New York: Macmillan, 1926-27. Vol. 2, *Modern Times* trans. by Louis Cazamian and W. D. MacInnes.

3517 WEYGANDT, CORNELIUS. *A Century of the English Novel.* New York: The Century Co., 1925.

3518 DeCASTRO, JOHN P. *The Gordon Riots.* London: Oxford Univ. Press, 1926.

3519 WILLIAMS, ORLO. *Some Great English Novels: Studies in the Art of Fiction.* London: Macmillan, 1926.

3520 FORSTER, E. M. *Aspects of the Novel.* London: E. Arnold, 1927; Harmondsworth: Penguin, 1964.

3521 MAUROIS, ANDRÉ. *Études Anglaises – Dickens, Walpole, Ruskin and Wilde: La Jeune Littérature.* Paris: Grasset, 1927.

3522 PRIESTLEY, J. B. *The English Novel.* London: Nelson, 1927.

3523 VOOYS, SIJNA de. *The Psychological Element in the English Sociological Novel of the Nineteenth Century.* Amsterdam: H. J. Paris, 1927.

3524 MUIR, EDWIN. *The Structure of the Novel.* London: L. and V. Woolf, 1928; New York: Harcourt, Brace, 1929; London: Hogarth Press, 1967.

3525 DEVONSHIRE, MARIAN G. *The English Novel in France, 1830-1870.* London: Univ. of London Press, 1929.

3526 FORD, FORD MADOX (HUEFFER). *The English Novel: From the Earliest Days to the Death of Joseph Conrad.* London: Lippincott, 1929.

3527 PHELPS, WILLIAM L. *The Advance of the English Novel.* New York: Dodd, Mead, 1929.

3528 PRIESTLEY, J. B. *English Humour.* London: Longmans, Green, 1929.

3529 WAUGH, ARTHUR. *A Hundred Years of Publishing.* Being the Story of Chapman and Hall, Ltd. London: Chapman and Hall, 1930.

3530 LEAVIS, Q. D. *Fiction and the Reading Public.* London: Chatto and Windus, 1932.

3531 LOVETT, R. M. and H. S. HUGHES. *The History of the Novel in England.* Boston: Houghton Mifflin, 1932.

3532 EDGAR, PELHAM. *The Art of the Novel: From 1700 to the Present Time.* New York: Macmillan, 1933.

3533 CECIL, LORD DAVID. *Early Victorian Novelists.* London: Constable, 1934.

3534 *Early Victorian England, 1830-1865.* London: Oxford Univ. Press, 1934.

3535 JAMES, HENRY. *The Art of the Novel: Critical Prefaces.* Introd. Richard P. Blackmur. New York: Scribners, 1934.

3536 SMITH, WARREN H. *Architecture in English Fiction.* London: Oxford Univ. Press, New Haven, Conn.: Yale Univ. Press, 1934.

3537 CAZAMIAN, MADELEINE L. *Le Roman et les Idées en Angleterre.* Paris: Société D'Édition: Les Belles Lettres, 1935.

3538 BAKER, ERNEST A. *The History of the English Novel.* 10 vols. London: H. F. and G. Witherby, 1936.

3539 POMERANZ, HERMAN. *Medicine in the Shakespearean Plays, and Dickens' Doctors.* New York: Powell Publishing Co., 1936.

3540 SANTAYANA, GEORGE. *Interpretations of Poetry and Religion.*
New York: Scribners, 1936.

3541 YOUNG, GEORGE M. *Victorian England: Portrait of an Age.* London:
Oxford Univ. Press, 1936.

3542 FOX, RALPH. *The Novel and the People.* London: Lawrence and
Wishart, 1937; New York: International, 1945.

3543 BATHO, EDITH and BONAMY DOBRÉE. *The Victorians and After,
1830-1914.* New York: R. M. McBride, 1938. [Chapter on Economic
Background by Guy Chapman.]

3544 MATTHEWS, WILLIAM. *Cockney Past and Present.* London:
G. Routledge; New York: Dutton, 1938.

3545 ROBINSON, HENRY CRABB. *Henry Crabb Robinson On Books
and Their Authors*, ed. Edith J. Morley. 3 vols. London: Dent, 1938.
[Many references to Dickens 1837-64.]

3546 DAICHES, DAVID. *The Novel and the Modern World.* Chicago:
Univ. of Chicago Press, 1939.

3547 EVANS, B. IFOR. *A Short History of English Literature.*
Harmondsworth: Penguin, 1940.

3548 MALY-SCHLATTER, FLORENCE. *The Puritan Element in
Victorian Fiction, with Special Reference to the Works of G. Eliot,
Dickens and Thackeray.* Zurich: Leemann, 1940.

3549 BURKE, KENNETH. *The Philosophy of Literary Form.* Baton
Rouge: Louisiana State Univ. Press, 1941.

3550 GEROULD, GORDON H. *The Patterns of English and American
Fiction: a History.* Boston: Little, Brown, 1942.

3551 WAGENKNECHT, EDWARD. *Cavalcade of the English Novel.*
New York: Holt, Rinehart and Winston, 1943.

3552 BENTLEY, PHYLLIS. *Some Observations on the Art of Narrative.*
London: Home and Van Thal, 1946.

3553 CRUIKSHANK, ROBERT J. *The Roaring Century, 1846-1946.*
London: Hamish Hamilton, 1946.

3554 LAIRD, JOHN *Philosophical Incursions into English Literature.*
New York: Russell and Russell, 1946.

3555 LIDDELL, ROBERT. *A Treatise on the Novel.* London: J. Cape,
1947.

3556 GLAUSER, LISA. *Die Erlebte Rede im Englischen Roman des 19
Jahrhunderts.* Bern: A. Francke, 1948.

3557 LEAVIS, F. R. *The Great Tradition.* London: Chatto and Windus,
1948.

3558 SIMON, IRÈNE. *Formes du Roman Anglais de Dickens à Joyce.*
Liège: Publications de la Faculté de Philosophie et Lettres, 1949.

3559 WILLEY, BASIL. *Nineteenth Century Studies*. London: Chatto and Windus, 1949.

3560 BAKER, JOSEPH E., ed. *The Reinterpretation of Victorian Literature*. Princeton, NJ: Princeton Univ. Press, 1950.

3561 LUKACS, GYÖRGY. *Studies in European Realism*. Trans. Edith Bone. London: Hillway, 1950.

3562 ROLAND HOLST, HENRIETTE (van der Schalk). *Romankunst als Levensschool: Tolstoi, Balzac en Dickens*. (Gastmed der eeuwen; taferelen mit de cultuurgeschudenis van Europa 7.) Arnhem: Van Loghum Slaterus, 1950.

3563 BUCKLEY, JEROME H. *The Victorian Temper: a Study in Literary Culture*. Cambridge, Mass.: Harvard Univ. Press, 1951.

3564 CHURCH, RICHARD. *The Growth of the English Novel*. London: Methuen; New York: Barnes and Noble, 1951.

3565 KETTLE, ARNOLD. *An Introduction to the English Novel*. 2 vols. London: Hutchinson House, 1951-53.

3566 MAUROIS, ANDRÉ. *L'Angleterre Romantique*. Paris: Gallimard, 1953.

3567 ALLEN, WALTER. *The English Novel: A Short Critical History*. London: Phoenix House; New York: Dutton, 1954; Harmondsworth: Penguin, 1958.

3568 BRIGGS, ASA. *Victorian People: Some Reassessments of People, Institutions, Ideas and Events, 1851-1867*. London: Odhams Press, 1954.

3569 LIDDELL, ROBERT. *Some Principles of Fiction*. Bloomington: Indiana Univ. Press, 1954.

3570 ALLEN, WALTER. *Six Great Novelists: Defoe, Fielding, Scott, Dickens, Stevenson, Conrad*. London: Hamish Hamilton, 1955.

3571 DAVIS, NUEL P. *The Life of Wilkie Collins*. Urbana: Univ of Illinois Press, 1956.

3572 THOMSON, PATRICIA. *The Victorian Heroine: a Changing Ideal, 1837-1873*. London: Oxford Univ. Press, 1956.

3573 ALTICK, RICHARD D. *English Common Reader: A Social History of the Mass Reading Public 1800-1900*. Chicago: Univ. of Chicago Press, 1957.

3574 BORINSKI, LUDWIG. *Die Utopie in der modernen Englischen Literatur*. (Die neueren Sprachen [n.f.] Beiheft 2.) Frankfurt am Main: M. Diesterweg, n.d. [1957?]

3575 COVENEY, PETER. *Poor Monkey: the Child in Literature*. London: Rockliffe, 1957. Published as *The Image of Childhood*. Baltimore: Peregrine Books, 1967. Introd. F. R. Leavis.

3576 DALZIEL, MARGARET. *Popular Fiction 100 Years Ago; an Unexplored Tract of Literary History.* London: Cohen and West, 1957.

3577 FRYE, NORTHROP. *The Anatomy of Criticism.* Princeton, NJ: Princeton Univ. Press, 1957.

3578 HOUGHTON, W. E. *The Victorian Frame of Mind 1830-70.* New Haven: Yale Univ. Press, 1957.

3579 WEST, REBECCA. *The Court and the Castle; Some Treatments of a Recurrent Theme.* New Haven: Yale Univ. Press, 1957.

3580 ZABEL, MORTON D. *Craft and Character in Modern Fiction.* New York: Viking, 1957.

3581 RAY, GORDON N. *Thackeray: The Age of Wisdom (1847-1863).* New York: McGraw-Hill, 1958.

3582 SUTHERLAND, JAMES R. *English Satire.* Cambridge, Eng.: Cambridge Univ. Press, 1958.

3583 WILLIAMS, RAYMOND. *Culture and Society. 1780-1950.* London: Chatto and Windus, 1958.

3584 STANG, RICHARD. *The Theory of the Novel in England: 1850-1870* New York: Columbia Univ. Press; London: Routledge and K. Paul, 1959.

3585 WALSH, WILLIAM. *The Use of Imagination.* London: Chatto and Windus, 1959.

3586 WEST, PAUL. *The Growth of the Novel.* Eight Radio Talks as heard on CBC University of the Air. Toronto: Canadian Broadcasting Corporation, 1959.

3587 BLYTH, R. W. *Zen in English Literature.* New York: Dutton, 1960.

3588 CLARK, AUBERT J. *The Movement for International Copyright in Nineteenth Century America.* Washington: Catholic Univ. of America Press, 1960.

3589 KORG, JACOB, ed. *London in Dickens' Day.* Englewood Cliffs, NJ: Prentice-Hall, 1960.

3590 MODDER, MONTAGU F. *The Jew in the Literature of England.* New York: Meridian; Philadelphia: Jewish Publication Society of America, 1960.

3591 ROSENBERG, EDGAR. *From Shylock to Svengali: Jewish Stereotypes in English Fiction.* Stanford, Calif.: Stanford Univ. Press, 1960.

3592 STEVENSON, LIONEL. *The English Novel: A Panorama.* Boston: Houghton Mifflin; London: Constable, 1960.

3593 BOOTH, WAYNE C. *The Rhetoric of Fiction.* (Phoenix Books.) Chicago: Univ. of Chicago Press, 1961.

3594 SCHOLES, ROBERT, ed. *Approaches to the Novel.* San Francisco: Chandler Publishing Co., 1961.

3595 STONE, A. E. *The Innocent Eye: Childhood in Mark Twain's Imagination.* New Haven: Yale Univ. Press, 1961. [Compares Dickens.]

3596 LUKACS, GYÖRGY. *The Historical Novel.* Trans. Hannah and Stanley Mitchell. London: Merlin, 1962. [Translation of *Der historische Roman.* Berlin: Aufbau-Verlag, 1955.]

3597 WAGENKNECHT, EDWARD. *The Movies in the Age of Innocence.* Norman: Univ. of Oklahoma Press, 1962.

3598 YOUNG, GEORGE M. *Victorian Essays.* London: Oxford Univ. Press, 1962.

3599 BORINSKI, LUDWIG. *Meister des modernen englischen Romans: Dickens, Galsworthy, H. G. Wells, Joseph Conrad, Virginia Woolf, Aldous Huxley, Graham Greene [und] George Orwell.* Heidelberg: Quelle and Meyer, 1963.

3600 KILLY, WALTHER. *Wirklichkeit und Kunst Charakter: neun Romane des 19 Jahrhunderts.* München: Beck, 1963. [Poe, Goethe, Dickens, Stendhal, etc.]

3601 PRIESTLEY, J. B. *The English Comic Characters.* London: Bodley Head, 1963.

3602 COOPER, F. RENAD. *Nothing Extenuate: The Life of Frederick Fox Cooper.* London: Barrie and Rockliff, 1964.

3603 MARCUS, STEVEN. *The Other Victorians.* New York: Basic Books, 1964.

3604 UZZELL, THOMAS H. *The Technique of the Novel.* New York: Citadel Press, 1964.

3605 WALSH, WILLIAM. *A Human Idiom: Literature and Humanity.* London: Chatto and Windus, 1964.

3606 CLAYBOROUGH, ARTHUR. *The Grotesque in English Literature.* Oxford: Clarendon, 1965.

3607 EASTMAN, RICHARD M. *A Guide to the Novel.* San Francisco: Chandler Publishing Co., 1965.

3608 FREUND, PHILIP. *The Art of Reading the Novel.* New York: Collier Books, 1965.

3609 HARVEY, W. J. *Character and the Novel.* Ithaca, NY: Cornell Univ. Press, 1965.

3610 KARL, FREDERICK R. *A Reader's Guide to The Nineteenth Century British Novel.* New York: Noonday Press of Farrar, Straus and Giroux, 1965.

3611 THOMPSON, E. P. *The Making of the English Working Class.* London: Gollancz, 1965.

3612 TILLOTSON, GEOFFREY and KATHLEEN. *Mid-Victorian Studies.* London: The Athlone Press, 1965.

3613 ADRIAN, ARTHUR A. *Mark Lemon, First Editor of* Punch. London: Oxford Univ. Press, 1966.

3614 ARUNDEL, DENNIS. *The Story of Sadler's Wells.* London: Hamish Hamilton, 1966.

3615 WALCUTT, CHARLES C. *Man's Changing Mask; Modes and Methods of Characterization in Fiction.* Minneapolis: Univ. of Minnesota Press, 1966.

3616 MARSHALL, WILLIAM H. *The World of the Victorian Novel.* New York: A. S. Barnes; London: Thomas Yoseloff, 1967.

3617 MAYHEW, HENRY. *Mayhew's Characters.* Ed. with a note on the English character by Peter Quennell. Selected from *London Labour and the London Poor,* first published 1851. London: Spring Books, 1967.

3618 CHAPMAN, RAYMOND. *The Victorian Debate: English Literature and Society 1832-1901.* London: Weidenfeld and Nicolson; New York: Basic Books, 1968.

3619 FINDLATER, RICHARD, ed. *Memoirs of Joseph Grimaldi.* London: Stein and Day, 1968.

3620 HIMMELFARB, GERTRUDE. *Victorian Minds.* New York: Knopf, 1968.

3621 HOLLAND, NORMAN N. *The Dynamics of Literary Response.* New York: Oxford Univ. Press, 1968.

3622 LEVINE, GEORGE and WILLIAM MADDEN, eds. *The Art of Victorian Prose.* New York: Oxford Univ. Press, 1968.

3623 MILLER, J. HILLIS. *The Form of Victorian Fiction: Thackeray, Dickens, Trollope, George Eliot, Meredith, and Hardy.* Notre Dame, Ind.: Univ. of Notre Dame Press, 1968.

3624 MIYOSHI, MASAO. *The Divided Self: A Perspective on the Literature of the Victorians.* New York: New York Univ. Press, 1969.

3625 MIYAZAKI, KOICHI. *A Treatise on the English Novel.* Tokyo: Kaitaku, n.d.

Index

This is primarily an index of authors and editors. It includes, however, all of Dickens' major works. The prefix R signifies that the item is a review.

A., J. 2892
Abernathy, Julian W. 2830
Adams, Donald K. 3364
Adams, Ruth R. 3365
Addison, William 1279
Adrian, Arthur A. 1224, 1239, 1309, 1316, 1343, 1353, 1493, 1511, 2192, 2197, 2525, 2891, 3343, 3613
Ainger, A. 67
Aitch, N. Howard 2374
Aitken, D. F. 852
Aitken, David J. 3410
"Alain" (pseud.). See Chartier, Emile
Alderson, B. R. 2207
Aldington, Richard 1102
Alexander, Edward 2769
Alexander, R. Vanes 3141
Allbut, Robert 383, 1961; with "F" and Roade, C. T. 2219
Allemandy, Victor H. 532, 2413
Allen, Edward H. 2489
Allen, M. L. 1775
Allen, Walter 1144, 1280, R1882, 2400, 3567, 3570
Altick, Richard D. 1134, 3573
AMERICAN NOTES 4, 6, 313, 330, 374, 477, 505, 552, 599, 633, 856, 908, 969, 970, 973, 986, 995, 1134, 1178, 1224, 1365, 1388, 1532, 1640, 1707, 1896, 1912, 3438
Amerongen, Juda B. van 602, 3315

Amis, Kingsley R1283
Andersen, Hans Christian 63, 69, 828, 1103
Andersen, Sally S. 3449
Anderson, David D. 1514
Anderson, Kate 361
André, Robert 1861
Andrews, William L. 3200
Annenskaja, A. N. 131
Apostolov, Nikolay 603
Archer, Thomas 139
Arnold, Beth R. 1844
Arnold, Ralph 2919
Arundel, Dennis 3614
Ashby-Norris, E. E. 265
Ashforth, A. 2072
Ashley, Robert P. 1145, 1240
Askew, H. 2081, 2187, 2605
Atherton, John W. 3366
Atkins, Stewart 1098
Atkinson, F. G. 2744
Atthill, Robin 1540
Auberon, Francis 2294
Auden, W. H. 2068, 2135
Augburn, Gerald R. 3465
Austin, James C. 1232
Axon, William E. A. 132
Axton, William F. 1776, 1870, 2076, 2443, 2445, 2682, 2686, 2697, 3400
Aydelotte, William O. 1104
Aylmer, Felix 1276, 1431, 3128, 3168, 3186

Goodheart, Eugene 1410
Gordan, John D. 989
Gordon, Andrew 3016
Gordon, Elizabeth H. 465
Gottshall, James K. 2302, 3386
Gould, Gerald 2598
Graham, Eleanor 1258
Graham, Richard D. 160
Graham, W. H. 2195, 2299
Gran, Gerhard Von Der Lippe 594
Grant, Douglas 1553
Grant, James 73
Grant, John E. See Broderick,
 James H.
Graves, Robert 2486
Gray, Paul E. 2765
Gray, W. Forbes 621, 799, 2280
Grayson, Nancy J. 3471
GREAT EXPECTATIONS 2892-
 3017
Greaves, John 1029, 1749, 1795,
 1816, 1855, 1856, 1932, 2070,
 2077
Grech, Wyndham L. 307
Green, Frank 743, 1171
Green, Martin R1718
Green, O. M. 2483
Green, Roger L. 1030, 1549
Greene, Graham 2128
Greenhalgh, Mollie 3182
Grego, Joseph 1957
Gregory, Michael 2887
Gregory, S. E. 1177
Grenander, M. E. 2637
Griffith, Ben W. 3266, 3270
Griffin, Montagu 158
Grigg, John 1851
Grob, Shirley 1710
Gross, John R1578, 1583, 2880,
 R3277; with Pearson, Gabriel
 1584
Grove, J. S. P. 542
Grubb, Gerald G. 947, 982, 994,
 1010, 1018, 1054, 1140, 1152,

1178, 1199, R1214, 1225, 1247,
 1268, 1294, 1330, 1340, 2121,
 2249, 3265, 3333
Gruenewald, Karl 3304
Grylls, R. Glynn 1694
Gummer, Ellis N. 874
Gurian, O. 918
Gusev, N. 736
Gutermuth, Else 3313

H., A. 1158
H., S. S. 895
Hagan, John H., Jr. 2932, 2936
Hagberg, Knut 1991
Hahn, Charlotte (geb. Weiss) 3358
Haight, Anne L. 888
Haight, Gordon S. 1331, 2633
Haight, Sherman P. 673
Hale, Osborne R1829
Hallam, Clifford B. 3001
Halton, Laurence 159
Ham, James P. (The Elder) 44
Hamblen, Abigail A. 1711
Hamilton, Louis 1164
Hamilton, Robert 948, 1096, 1263,
 1266, R1832, 1890, 2512
Hamilton, Walter J. 501
Hamley, E. B. 24
Hammerton, Sir John A. 289, 290
Hammond, R. A. 2216
Hampshire, Stuart R922
Hanaford, Phebe A. (Coffin) 64
Handley, George M. 2319, 2592,
 2829
Haney, Charles W. 3430
Hannam-Clark, Frederic 401
Hanson, John L. 2107
HARD TIMES 2708-70
Harder, Kelsie B. 1460
Hardwick, Michael, with Hardwick,
 Mollie 1722
Hardwick, Mollie 1807, 1878; see
 also Hardwick, Michael
Hardy, Barbara 1565, R1736, 1879,
 2353, 2979

Charles Dickens at 56. Photographed in America, engraved by J. C. Armytage

This book

was designed by

ELLEN HUTCHISON

under the direction of

ALLAN FLEMING

University of

Toronto

Press